The Future of the International Economic Order: An Agenda for Research

C. Fred Bergsten
Brookings Institution

Contributions by

John A. Mathieson   Joseph S. Nye
Assar Lindbeck   Samuel Schurr
Robert M. Stern   James W. Howe
Raymond Vernon   Franklyn D. Holzman
Robert O. Keohane   Ingo Walter

Lexington Books
D.C. Heath and Company
Lexington, Massachusetts
Toronto   London

Library of Congress Cataloging in Publication Data

Bergsten, C. Fred, 1941-
    The future of the international economic order.

    1. International economic relations. 2. International economic rela-
tions—Research. I. Mathieson, John A. II. Title.
HF1007.B3947   382.1   73-9592
ISBN 0-669-90225-x

Published simultaneously in Canada.

Printed in the United States of America.

International Standard Book Number: 0-669-90225-x

Library of Congress Catalog Card Number: 73-9592

Contents

List of Figures

List of Tables

Foreword

In March of 1972 the Board of Trustees of the Ford Foundation decided that the importance and complexities of international economic issues justified a special inquiry into the possible need for new efforts to understand them. C. Fred Bergsten of the Brookings Institution directed the inquiry, which took place from July 1972 through March 1973 and which encompassed meetings and discussions with a wide range of public officials and scholars throughout the world, as well as the research efforts of those involved directly in it. This volume presents the results of the study in the belief that they will be of interest to an audience beyond the Foundation.

The core report by Dr. Bergsten draws some important conclusions. It states that the new era which has been entered in international economic relations requires new policies and new intellectual understanding as the basis for such policies. Failure to resolve these issues, it goes on, could confront the world with the breakdown of a generation of economic peace.

Dr. Bergsten's report identifies twelve major issues whose importance and difficulty call for new research efforts. It recommends in particular that greater attention be given to interdisciplinary methods, intensified empirical investigation, and wide-ranging consideration of new concepts, policy institutions, and strategies. Not every reader will agree with all of Dr. Bergsten's recommendations or to the priorities of his agenda for research, but few will dispute the sense of urgency which he conveys. Backing up the core report are a collection of essays on some of the key topics by a distinguished group of social scientists.

In the immediate future the Ford Foundation expects to increase its own attention to the vital questions raised in this book. We hope that others will join in our concern.

McGeorge Bundy
President
The Ford Foundation

The Future of the International Economic Order: An Agenda for Research

1 The Future of the International Economic Order: An Agenda for Research

C. Fred Bergsten in association
with John A. Mathieson
Brookings Institution

Introduction

The objective of this study is the development of a program of research that will provide a foundation for meeting the chief international economic problems of the next decade. Its stress is on policy issues, defined broadly to include the problems of the private sector as well as those confronting national governments and international organizations. We focus on the advances in knowledge needed to provide a basis for more informed policy in the future—including advances in theory, empirical understanding, and direct consideration of policy alternatives and their implementation. Our perspective is international, rather than the policy of any particular country.

Such a program of research must first identify the questions which require study, and then formulate strategies for pursuing answers to them. This book presents an agenda for research. It makes no effort to submit a set of solutions to the problems which lie ahead.

Throughout the course of this study, we have focused on three questions:

1. What are likely to be the dominant international economic issues of the next decade, and how important are they likely to be in economic and political terms?
2. Is the present state of knowledge adequate for society to cope with these issues? On those issues where present knowledge is not sufficient, what new work is needed—at the theoretical, empirical, police-formulating, and policy-implementing levels?
3. What resources are available to seek the needed advances in knowledge? What research strategies can best mobilize the available resources to do so?

In seeking to answer these questions, we first solicited the views of hundreds of leading experts around the world. We queried government officials, international economists, domestically-oriented economists, political scientists, businessmen, bankers, and labor union officials from more than twenty countries, including developing and Communist countries. Our correspondents ranged from

1

pure theorists to practitioners of policy. Over 80 percent of those contacted replied, and over 60 percent contributed substantively to our thinking. A number of U.S. experts met with us at several stages during the course of the project.

We also commissioned leading experts to prepare papers on eight of the most important individual issues facing the international economic order. Each paper addresses the same three sets of questions noted above to the specific topic which it considered, to provide both inputs for our core report and elaborated research agendas for each specific topic. The papers make up Chapters 2-9 of this volume.

Finally, we surveyed the state of existing research and institutional activity throughout the world as thoroughly as our time and resources permitted, including extensive interviewing in the United States and Western Europe. These formal efforts, along with innumerable informal conversations and our own research, have provided us with a wide variety of specific ideas and proposals on both substance and research strategies. A major part of our task is thus to assess priorities, to analyze the interrelationships among the plethora of specific issues, and to predict how importantly they will affect the broad stream of human history into the relevant future.

The international economic order encompasses much of the activity of mankind, and has implications for most of that activity. Surveying the entire field is thus an enormous job, particularly in the limited time available to us from July 1972 through March 1973. Nevertheless, we are confident that our results provide a solid start toward judging whether, where, and how to proceed with research on international economics in the 1970s.

The Salience of the Issue

International economic issues have always been important to the domestic economies of most countries, and have figured heavily in the formulation of overall foreign policies. However, the breadth and depth of international economic interpenetration which has now developed virtually all countries, and the reactions to it in virtually all countries as well, are accelerating so rapidly that international economic relations among nations have moved onto a qualitatively new plane of both economic and political importance. In addition, international economic issues have until quite recently been relatively unimportant in economic terms to the two superpowers, the United States and the Soviet Union, ever since they became the largest economies and political powers in the world. And the effect of international economics on international politics had until recently been overshadowed by the protracted security crisis which extended for more than half a century from Sarajevo through Vietnam.

This new importance of international economics, in both economic and political terms, is likely to grow continuously into the foreseeable future. And the political-economic trends which are likely to affect the world economy differ appreciably from those encountered in the 1950s and even most of the 1960s: the deep and accelerating interpenetration of domestic economies, the tensions which have resulted between groups which benefit from these trends and groups which bear their costs, major shifts in economic power among the national actors in the international economic system, the emergence of new national and transnational actors, and the reduction in the relative concern over security interests.

As a result of all these developments, the monetary and trading systems which governed international economic relations during the first postwar generation have collapsed. The international monetary system is no longer, in practice, based on fixed exchange rates and gold. The international trading system is no longer, in practice, based on steady reductions in barriers to trade, nondiscrimination, and tariffs. International economic relations have reached a crossroads, and we cannot now tell whether in the immediate future the world will resume the postwar path toward greater freedom for international economic transactions, replicate the proliferation of restrictions of the interwar years, or find some new middle course. We do know that the Bretton Woods and GATT systems provided the foundations for a generation of economic peace, but could hardly be expected to govern a world economy so radically different from the one for which they were constructed. Any new system must be built on very new underlying circumstances.

First, the interpenetration of national economics is increasing dramatically, and all signs indicate that this trend will continue to accelerate unless it is consciously checked by national policies. The magnitudes have become enormous: annual sales of perhaps $400 billion by the foreign subsidiaries of multinational firms; energy import needs of perhaps an additional $50 billion in the industrialized countries alone by 1980; a U.S. balance of payments deficit of $30 billion in a single year; reserve gains of almost $3 billion by a single central bank in a single day.

Between 1950 and 1971, world exports increased over fivefold in value and now exceed $300 billion; over the past decade, trade has grown at an average annual rate of 10 percent—much faster than world income. The flow of international services, such as tourism, has increased even faster. Still more impressive has been the growth of international capital flows, ranging from direct investment through portfolio movements to shifts of liquid balances— despite the proliferating panoply of controls designed to check them. The production process has become nearly as mobile among nations as trade in the goods which are produced. Technology and management expertise are frequently "exported," rapidly diffusing acquired knowledge. Even labor has become internationally mobile in some regions (especially Europe and the Mediterranean) and some sectors (especially management and skilled professions). Virtually all sectors of virtually all economies now rely heavily on external transactions.

The United States remains the least reliant of all market economies on international transactions, but its engagement in the world economy has grown dramatically. Exports have become essential to U.S. agriculture and to many sectors of U.S. industry, and hence responsible for millions of American jobs. Imports have become critical to the United States, in two senses: in some sectors, especially oil and meat, the United States has sought increases to help fight inflation (and it may soon depend on imports to meet much of its energy and other raw material needs), while in other major sectors, such as textiles and steel, it has limited the rise of imports because of their impact on domestic jobs and profits. An important share of U.S. corporate profits now derives from the foreign sector, and foreign investment by U.S. firms may have wide-ranging effects on domestic employment and other key economic variables. The international role of the dollar has become so large that it can significantly affect U.S. monetary policy, and liabilities to foreigners have become a sizable part of the U.S. national debt. The dollar has been devalued twice, after almost forty years of a fixed parity, with important consequences for U.S. jobs and prices. So the United States has at last joined the rest of the world in depending on the world economy for an important share of its own national wealth and prosperity.

Second, the sharp increase in international transactions, both in absolute magnitudes and as a share of total economic activity, has coincided with a steady proliferation of the economic and social policy objectives sought by most nation-states through their governments. Societies now demand more equitable distribution of income and increases in a vast array of social services as well as stable growth. Achievement of these objectives calls for increasingly effective control by nation-states of their own destinies.

But such control may frequently be undermined by external influences of precisely the type which are increasing so rapidly. The integration of the world economy causes both secular and cyclical fluctuations to be transmitted between countries more quickly, and to a much higher degree, diminishing the effectiveness of domestic policy instruments. Foreign ownership of capital may erode national economic control, and is widely perceived as doing so. This confluence of international interpenetration with proliferating national policy objectives is what differentiates the present from the pre-1914 period; that other great era of international economic exchange certainly had the former, but it was virtually devoid of the latter and hence conflict between international and national goals seldom arose.

Thus the contemporary world economy confronts centrifugal as well as centripetal forces, both of unprecedented scale and rising pace. One result has been deep tension within individual countries between the benefits of economic interpenetration to some sectors and its costs to others. Indeed, effective national sovereignty often seems far more threatened by economic interdependence at this stage of history than by losses of territory to hostile invaders. International integration often seems to threaten national disintegration.

Third, because nations and sectors within nations are now more affected by international economic relations than ever before, national and sectoral views on these issues have become increasingly politicized. Because some nations and some sectors gain from economic interpenetration while others lose, or gain less, these political views are in turn increasingly polarized. Groups (including countries and groups of countries) who feel they are paying for the benefits derived by others from international transactions seek to reject economic interdependence. Conflicts between nations as they pursue competing internal goals thus become ever more likely. The most extreme manifestation of this trend is the ardent support of some elements of organized labor in the United States for the erection of a virtually impenetrable wall around the U.S. economy, shutting out imports of goods and people and shutting in exports of capital and technology. But the pressures exist elsewhere, and are rising rapidly. There is a risk, of sufficient possibility to merit attention, that governments could lose control of events—as they did politically in 1914 and economically in 1929-1932—with unpredictable and possibly disastrous results for the world economy and international politics.

Fourth, foreign policies around the world must therefore focus increasingly on economics if only because of their increased economic importance and the internal politicization and polarization of views which have resulted. In fact, key economic issues have already in recent years risen at least temporarily to the top of bilateral and multilateral political agendas (e.g., British entry into the European Communities, textile trade and overall economic relations between the United States and Japan, military offset between the United States and Germany, the systemic crisis of August-December 1971 among the major trading countries).

But this conclusion is buttressed further by several key trends in international politics. The intensity of the Cold War has clearly receded, and perceptions of its intensity have receded even further. With external threats reduced, if by no means eliminated, security concerns will decreasingly determine overall relations among political allies within the East and especially the West, and between East and West. Coalition leaders will be less able to use their security leverage to maintain economic cooperation from their allies, and many of those allies will be less restrained in surfacing their economic disagreement with coalition leaders. In the case of the West, the resurgence of Japan and Western Europe as major economic powers, and potential political powers as well, reinforces this likelihood. The nudging aside of the security blanket has exposed intra-alliance economic discord, and adds to the thrust of economic issues toward the top of international political agendas. Indeed, we shall later see that the complex relationship between security and economic concerns in this new milieu is one of the issues which most needs new research.

Fifth, these problems are further complicated by the emerging importance of new actors of two types—additional countries, and nonnational entities. The Communist countries are just now beginning to enter the world economy, and their inclusion raises a whole set of new issues which will be discussed in detail later as a prime focus for new research. A number of Third World countries are commencing a major role in the world economy, for a variety of reasons: they may possess a strategic resource (e.g., the oil countries, but many others as well), or they may be rapidly bridging the gap between developed and less developed and becoming important in world trade and investment patterns (e.g., Brazil and Korea). Transnational actors, including multinational corporations and the network of banks which make up the Eurodollar market, must now be considered independently along with the national states within whose jurisdictions they reside. All of these changes add to the complexity of the international economic order, and complicate both its economic interactions and the power relationships which affect its politics.

Finally, due to all these economic and political changes, the United States will no longer hold an economic umbrella over the other non-Communist countries (and questions are raised as to how long it will continue to hold a nuclear umbrella over their security as well). For most of the postwar period, sizable U.S. payments deficits and trade concessions served both U.S. and global interests. Now they serve neither, and willingness to continue them has been abandoned by both the United States and most other major countries. Foreign policy begins at home; thus the United States—like Britain in the late 1920s—can no longer sacrifice at home, e.g., by accepting the unemployment consequences of an overvalued exchange rate, to stabilize abroad even if its leadership wanted to do so.

But this reduction in the role of the United States has produced a leadership vacuum in the world economy. The international economic power—a concept which itself needs much research, as will be noted later—of the expanded European Community and Japan has been growing rapidly. Both are approaching the United States in their ability to achieve their international economic objectives, and both outstrip the United States on some key measures of international economic power. The global economy is thus dominated by three major actors, one of whose relative power is probably still greatest but waning, with the other two gaining rapidly.

However, neither Europe nor Japan has yet demonstrated a political capacity to utilize its economic power constructively. This is party because each is engaged in an internal evolution of historic dimensions—the broadening and deepening of regional integration in Europe, the turn from quantity to quality in the economic orientation of Japan. They are able to block change, but have yet to lead. At the same time, the United States is uncertain about the role it should play in a world it can no longer dominate but in which it continues to have enormous economic and political stakes.

The results so far are twofold. The old international institutional framework—a monetary system based on fixed exchange rates and the dollar, a trading system led by a United States devoted to the principles of free trade and nondiscrimination—has broken down. Indeed, that framework will have been turned upside down if the United States now actively joins the mercantilist race for trade and payments surpluses, as seems quite possible. Second, there is stalemate in the efforts to achieve a new and stable system to replace the old, and even to settle immediate specific issues, be they citrus trade or the creation of Special Drawing Rights. Such a stalemate—unlike nuclear stalemate, which is stabilizing—may be very dangerous. The potential for either constructive cooperation based on true equality, or destructive competition in an environment of mutual hostility, is greater than ever before.

The world has never before encountered such a dilemma. The economic systems which provided relative stability in the past were based on the hegemony of a single country (the United States in the postwar period), a confluence of goals among at least the major countries (the decade or so preceding World War I), or both (the "gold standard" dominated by the United Kingdom in the nineteenth century). When the hierarchy has been uncertain (the whole interwar period), and/or when goals were in conflict (the 1930s, due of course in large part to the failures of internal economic policies), the systems have failed. The present configuration of relatively equal major powers pursuing goals which often conflict, which is already central to the collapse of the postwar system, is perhaps the most difficult from which to create a durable and stable international economic order. It is uncomfortably reminiscent of the U.S. failure to seize its opportunity to succeed Britain as world economic leader after World War I. However, it is far more difficult even than that closest historical analogue—both conceptually and politically—because there are now two new powers instead of one and because Europe and Japan now almost match the economic power of the United States, whereas the United States clearly surpassed Britain's material capacity in the 1920s and its failure was "only" one of resolve.

But a major effort must be made to construct a new order, for the alternative could be severe economic loss and serious political disharmony. Indeed, we have already stood close to that brink. Confidence in the entire fabric of international economic cooperation nearly collapsed in late 1971, when it took four months to resolve the crisis triggered by the United States actions of August 15. Throughout the world, investment plans and economic projections plummeted. The British prime minister refused to meet the American president at the summit to discuss high politics until the United States took steps toward ending the economic suspense. The crisis was overcome with little time to spare, and partly due to fortuitous circumstances. But the monetary and trading systems which had provided the structure of the international economic order—and which had been dying at least since 1967—were finally buried in the process, and we do not know what will take their place.

To be sure, even the worst breakdown in economic relations now conceivable would be far short of total disaster. Governments now know how to prevent depressions, so a repetition of the 1930s is virtually impossible (though we can be less confident that governments know how to avoid a "great inflation"). Each country has such stakes in the world economy that major trade wars seem politically unreal. Breakdown has been averted despite all the pressures cited, and efforts to achieve basic reform are at least haltingly underway. Even the deterioration now observable is of fairly short duration, and may prove to be merely a temporary aberrant. Indeed, it is clear that international economic exchange has continued to grow rapidly despite all the crises, new controls, and cries of alarm—and we shall see later that there is need to test the hypothesis that any "system" at all is really required to manage the world economy. It is thus possible to be far too gloomy.

A sober outlook for the future does suggest continued tensions, however, and the possibility of accelerating and more serious crises if countries continue to pursue the "new mercantilism" in support of a proliferating host of conflicting "internal" objectives. This in turn conjures up images of the national efforts of the 1930s to export unemployment (or inflation and other problems) to one's neighbors—with consequent threats to world peace and prosperity. The absence of functioning monetary and trade systems would seem to increase the probability that countries will act in such a way, by obviating any effective constraint on their behavior from international law and functioning institutions, and stimulate equally dangerous responses from others. The apocalypse here is not nuclear war, but it could be exceedingly costly in both human and material terms. The biggest losers, in relative terms, would probably be the developing countries, much of whose future development depends on an open world economy in which they can avoid wasteful policies such as protectionist trade measures, undervalued exchange rates, and industrialization strategies based on import substitution. So the importance of the subject seems assured for the relevant future, and we turn now to its component parts.

Three Underlying Problems

Three major problems must be mentioned briefly before we turn in detail to the specific issues.

The first is that the study of international economics, because it fuses "domestic" economics, international and domestic politics, and often social psychology and other social sciences, suffers from gaps in our understanding of these underlying topics as well as from problems unique to the narrower field itself. For example, economists have neither an adequate theory of inflation nor a satisfactory policy answer to the increasingly prevalent problem of stagflation (high inflation coupled with high unemployment); until they do, it is difficult to suggest what kind of foreign economic policy can best contribute to the solution of such problems. The shortcomings of economic models to capture dynamic effects make it impossible to assess accurately the costs and benefits of trade restrictions or of different modes of balance-of-payments adjustment. The rudimentary state of knowledge on how to devise and carry out effective manpower programs, which require sociological and psychological advances as well as economic incentives and political skills, badly hampers all efforts to devise improved policies to smooth internal adjustment to external disturbances. Political scientists have not produced an accepted model of the present multipolar world polity to supplement the balance of power and tight bipolar models of the past. The list goes on and on.

We can make no effort in this report to deal with the numerous gaps in these underlying fields. We do suggest that the international economic implications of some "domestic economic" (e.g., controlling U.S. inflation) and "international political" (e.g., continued Arab-Israeli hostility, which could have a major impact on world energy flows) issues add to the need to devote efforts to them in the years ahead. Similarly, progress on international economic issues can, as in the past, help in the development of solutions to internal economic problems.

A second major problem is the gaping void in interdisciplinary approaches. Every issue of international economics has at least an economic dimension and a political one, which in turn comprises both national and international politics. Development problems, which almost always encompass sociological and cultural considerations as well, are a particularly acute case in point. These issues should therefore be addressed by people with expertise in the several relevant areas.

One problem is that most of the relatively few economists who consider international issues at all (especially in the United States) view them from the standpoint of global welfare. That view is essential. But the world is not a decision-making unit, and welfare is not the only relevant consideration. Yet we have no systematic basis for analyzing why national policies—the foundation of international economic relations—on given issues differ. Policy-relevant analysis must consider international economic issues from the standpoint of individual countries, of interest groups within countries, and of transnational interest groups which cut across geographical borders. This requires political as well as economic analysis, treating power as well as welfare. Few non-Marxist economists or political scientists are even attempting to achieve such syntheses, and even fewer are qualified to do so.

Many issues require the additional talents of sociologists, historians, psychologists, scientists, etc. Solutions to the crucial problem of internal adjustment to external economic disturbances, for example, must draw on all these fields; they cannot simply assume a set of reactions from business, labor, foreign countries, and other relevant parties. Virtually every policymaker and private expert we approached stressed the need for interdisciplinary study, and agreed that there exist no more than a tiny handful of people pursuing it at present. (It is also useful for the cross-fertilization of ideas to mesh people who view the international economy from all three of the key functional vantage points:

academia, responsible government positions, and the private sector.) The need to handle most of the specific issues in ways which require new intellectual approaches must be kept in mind as each is discussed, and we will then recommend new research strategies to do so.

A third problem is the lack of systematic ways to share the experience and knowledge which have already developed and are constantly developing. This problem has both geographic and functional dimensions. The industrialized countries have a great deal to learn from each other on such issues as adjustment assistance and incomes policies, which are primarily "domestic" in nature. The developing countries have a great deal to learn from each other on such issues as export promotion. The industrialized and developing countries have a great deal to learn from each other; for example, there have been no major efforts to compare and contrast domestic welfare programs and foreign aid programs, which deal with similar problems and have often been run by the same people but occur within a wide variety of sociocultural contexts.

At the same time, there is inadequate exchange of information among government, the private sector, and the academic world—even within individual countries, let alone internationally. The "Bellagio" and "Burgenstock" series of meetings in the monetary field demonstrated clearly that academics could provide much greater help to government and private-sector policymakers if they knew what issues were of primary policy concern, and that policymakers could act with more responsibility and confidence if they were abreast of the latest research results. But the world is not even beginning to maximize its use of the knowledge which already exists, and new steps for doing so must form an important part of any new policy-oriented research strategy in international economics.

The Economic Core

Scores of important issues have been suggested to us during the course of this study, and there is of course a tendency to want to know everything. But choices must obviously be made. In this and the following two sections we discuss those issues whose importance over the next decade or so seem at present to make them the leading candidates for new research.

Two criteria dominated our choice of issues: their policy importance, and the adequacy with which they are now being addressed by researchers around the world. Even the most crucial issue would not rank high on our list if it were already the object of sufficient effort. There is of course a large body of existing knowledge on most of the issues we discuss; neither our focus on the gaps in present knowledge, nor our decision to wholly avoid the decisions involved in citing some existing work while ignoring other, should obscure that fact.

We will suggest both positive and normative research. In most cases, more knowledge is needed of existing relationships and attitudes. In other cases, we advocate work to assess the interests of different groups as well—including sectors within countries, countries, regions, and the world. The nature of the different issues will produce recommendations for different types of research, by different types of people, which will be pulled together in the concluding section on research strategies. We could not hope to provide in this chapter a comprehensive list of questions for research, of course, and have tried only to illustrate each broad area with the few questions within each which seem to us of greatest importance. The succeeding chapters present more detailed research agendas for each component topic of international economics.

Two specific issues were affected by the overall framework of our effort. The sponsor of the project, the Ford Foundation, is already engaged in extensive research and action programs addressed to the problems of population and Third World development. In addition, the Foundation simultaneously undertook a separate study to discover what additional efforts were needed to deal with the problem of unemployment and underemployment in the developing countries, which of course embraces most aspects of the development issue. Our study therefore includes the Third World primarily with regard to its role in the overall international economic order. Our discussions of development problems per se, and of population, are thus intended to be less comprehensive than our discussions of the other issues treated herein.

The Theory of International Economics

For at least 150 years, international economic policies have rested on the fundamental concept that the objective of all such policies is to maximize the level and growth of international economic transactions by relying on market forces and minimizing barriers to them, because this maximizes economic welfare and minimizes political conflict. The concept was applied, with varying degrees of confidence, to all types of international transactions: merchandise trade, flows of services, the movement of people and ideas, and capital transfers. Even when policy deviated from the prescriptions of the reigning conventional wisdom, as during the Great Depression, there was little lasting impact on that wisdom itself. Modern theory does envisage circumstances in which "optimal tariffs" or "optimal capital controls" will maximize the welfare of a single country, but still views such approaches clearly as "second bests" which, in light of the limited circumstances in which they might be applied, represent at most a minor deviation from the policy implications of traditional thought. So the basic concept underlying international economic policies has remained intact for an impressive period of time.

That basic concept is now under serious attack on different levels and from several quarters. One assault comes from those espousing the general case against growth. Purely within the framework of international economics, however, serious doubts have arisen as to whether policy can be based on the conventional model, which assumes, among other things, free competition among atomistic actors. The real world may be dominated instead by oligopolists. There are market oligopolists, such as multinational corporations and state enterprises. And there are bargaining oligopolists, of which the extreme example is the centrally planned economies but which many view as including "Japan, Inc." and the governments of other nominally market economies, and even some large firms in their negotiations with small countries. (There is of course some overlap between the two categories, strengthening doubts about the applicability of the conventional model.)

The market may thus no longer be the primary allocator, in which case the conclusions of traditional theory would certainly fall; many argue that "the invisible hand is nowhere to be seen." In addition, some of the assumptions of traditional theory, such as the presumed international immobility of capital and even labor are proving to be at variance with observed reality. Harry Johnson has put it most succinctly: "The scientific issue is whether observed deviations of fact from assumptions are empirically significant enough to destroy the validity of the conclusions of the theory."[1] No one has comprehensively addressed this central empirical issue.

Another key problem is that the static approach of most theory, which has always been its major shortcoming, seems even more unrealistic in the face of the rapid pace of change in the modern world economy. Dynamic models, to incorporate such key features of modern economic life as economies of scale and monopoly effects, are needed more than ever. Still another problem is that few economic models have even tried to encompass expectational effects, despite the obvious fact that market operators and policymakers alike are largely motivated by expectations concerning future interest rates, exchange-rate relationships, etc., rather than events already recorded. And economic theory has said very little about the time paths over which disequilibria cumulate and adjustment can be expected to take place, despite the critical political importance of, e.g., whether a devaluation can be expected to restore payments balance in six months or five years.

Nor has anyone tried to develop a comprehensive new international economic policy, or even a comprehensive policy for individual countries, to take into account the fundamental changes in the world economy already discussed. Are restrictions now more costly than ever in economic and/or political terms because of the degree of interdependence already achieved? Are they more costly because of structural changes in underlying economic conditions, such as the inflationary impact of national oligopolies which face real competition *only* from external competitors? Are they less likely to be effective, even if tried, because of the increasingly close interrelationships between flows of goods, people, and money?

On the other hand, does this very increase in interdependence mean that the marginal gains from further expansion of international exchange are very small? Does the widespread advent of affluence in the industrialized world make barriers more acceptable because inefficiencies can easily be tolerated in (at least the industrialized portion of) a world of high incomes where there is increasing demand for leisure, job stability, and "quality of life" relative to achieving the maximum quantity of GNP? Should some resources, such as the atmosphere and the oceans, be regarded as the common property of mankind whose allocation *should* no longer be left to the market? Or can *all* of these questions be answered affirmatively, with the traditional model to continue to apply in particular sectors but with derogations accepted in other sectors or for particular reasons?

There is much agreement that the world must now aim for "socially optimal" rather than "maximum" growth, but little consensus on what this means and how policy should pursue it. Many governments have recently been deviating increasingly from the policy prescriptions of the traditional model, revealing a preference for reduced—rather than greater—freedom of trade and factor movements. We do not know if this trend will continue, but its existence suggests either that governments no longer believe the guidelines of the past or that they cannot hold back the forces which oppose those guidelines in trying to adapt to the rapid changes which confront them. Governments and private sectors alike are clearly groping, because nothing has been developed to replace the traditional leitmotiv—the challenge to which may have played an important role in the collapse of the postwar monetary and trading systems. If nothing does replace it, policy will be determined ad hoc—and tend to be dominated by whatever special interest can muster the most political clout at the proper strategic moment. Indeed, this discussion highlights the general need for more analysis of why governments act as they do in this area, which should be a fertile field for political scientists but could also employ the theories of public choice now being developed by several economists.

The problems go far beyond economic theory. Even if the traditional concepts still hold, the rapid accerlation of the pace of international change, which brings benefits to many, may require new policy prescriptions to prevent overloads on social and domestic political systems. As Assar Lindbeck points out, in Chapter 2, the increased rate of change in comparative advantage among countries speeds the need for structural change within countries. ("Purely domestic" change is also accelerating and causing adjustment problems, but it is a universal political fact that change induced from abroad is regarded as "different" and it is possible that international patterns may be changing even faster than "purely domestic" patterns anyway.) This in turn raises structural and frictional unemployment, and the cost and/or disutilities of adjustment. Yet social concerns (e.g., better income distribution, income and locational stability, "equity" participation in high-technology industries) rank higher relative to efficiency and GNP than ever before, in virtually all countries, and breed increased resistance to change at the very time that change is accelerating. So a fundamental question arises: Should the world continue to rely largely on comparative advantage as the basis for international trade flows?

As already noted, answers to that question require measurement of the effects of different trade policies on individual countries, and individual sectors within countries. For example, some developing countries are increasingly eager to rely on comparative advantage, as their positions have strengthened, while some industrialized countries increasingly resist it due to their allegiance to the new policy objectives which accompany affluence. Many large U.S. firms and their allies in other countries want to retain the approach of the past, from which they derive great profit, while many groups of U.S. workers oppose the destabilizing effect of rapid change and a variety of groups in other countries reject "dictation" of their welfare and "undermining" of their political sovereignty by external forces. Only with national and sectoral analyses of such phenomena can governments formulate judgments about the costs and benefits of alternative policies in terms of their broad ranges of objectives. Most international economic analysis has been limited to macroeconomic welfare and efficiency effects,[2] however, and thus takes only the first step toward answering crucial policy questions. Indeed, it may turn out that few conceptual postulates or policy prescriptions can be widely generalized in a modern world economy comprised of such a diversity of countries, commodities, and interest groups.

One more complication in the application of traditional theory to present events is the emergence of new international economic actors. As already noted, many governments are playing an increasingly direct role. Regional groupings of states, of which the European Community is by far the most important but by no means the sole example, are also an increasing force. Even more dramatic is the acceleration of the importance of transnational actors, most notably multinational corporations and banks (including their creation of the Eurocurrency markets), which both reduce the power of sovereign states and draw them into more active intervention to preserve their jurisdictions. Transnational elites, including officials from national governments who may work more closely with each other than they do with other parts of their own governments, are developing rapidly in various functional areas. These elites may often interact through international organizations, whose own staffs are also playing an important role in some areas. Any new international economic theory, and set of policy prescriptions, must therefore encompass a new range of institutional components.

On the international political side, it is not clear that harmonious inter-country relations are now promoted by reducing international economic barriers. Indeed, new liberalization could even intensify political frictions, especially between countries which have had very little economic interchange (such as the United States and the Soviet Union or China). New barriers could even reduce political frictions in some cases, and have done so in recent years.

Analysis is needed of the impact of different international economic policies on international politics under present economic and political conditions, which as already indicated present both marked similarities with, and real differences from, any historical periods which we have experienced in the past.

Another fundamental political issue is whether international economic relations should in the future be governed by unconditional most-favored-nation treatment, as remains true in principle, or by regional and bilateral arrangements, as has become increasingly true in practice. Are blocs inherently bad? Should developing countries be exempted from MFN requirements? Liberal trade and multilateralism have often gone together in the past, but there have been notable periods (including recent ones) where discrimination fostered liberalization and served broadly agreed political purposes. The several combinations between them must therefore be considered.

The fundamental issue of how economic transactions and policies affect different countries and groups, and hence what they want from the world economy, must be addressed at all levels. New theory may be needed, whether or not it wholly replaces traditional theory, to explain better the new phenomena which increasingly dominate the world economy. Different conceptual approaches, such as oligopoly and bargaining theory, should be applied to international issues. Empirical work is needed to test existing theories, and new candidates to modify them. Political scientists should address normatively the interests of different groups, and positively the question of how policies in this area are decided—e.g., do relatively unrepresentative but politically strong interest groups wield a disproportionate share of power? New policies (e.g., to promote effective internal adjustment to external disturbances) may be needed, and old policies may need to be viewed differently (e.g., it might be a virtue of more flexible exchange rates if they actually dampen the rate of growth of international trade and capital movements, as many of their *critics* charge).

As already noted, a basic issue is the extent to which any generalizations can be expected to apply to the diversity of countries, commodities, and interest groups which make up the modern world economy. At the same time, all aspects of international economic relations—including trade, money, and investment—must now be viewed much more closely together than in the past. We turn next to an appraisal of the research needs which are specific to each of these component fields.

Trade

Many of the conceptual and empirical issues just discussed, such as the impact of market imperfections and new value judgments on the validity of traditional policy conclusions, relate directly to international trade. In addition, there are a number of specific gaps in present understanding in this area.

Several relatively new explanations of the determinants of world trade in its present economic and political environment have been offered. Some relate to relative income levels among countries, some to the size of different countries, some to modified versions of the traditional focus on labor costs and factor endowments (including skill levels of labor and access to modern technology), some to differing national production functions and factor prices. All require further empirical testing, and further elaboration to cover the variety of types of trade which now take place. In addition, it is now extremely important to try to synthesize the various approaches to see if a comprehensive explanation can be achieved, or whether different models need to be applied to trade in different commodity categories and/or to different countries.

Measurement issues are particularly important in the trade area. For example, there exists no present basis for readily assessing the impact on trade flows of changes in trade policy. Government officials have very little intellectual basis on which to decide such key policy issues as whether reciprocity has been achieved in an international trade negotiation, or how to determine an equitable degree of compensation or retaliation when new trade barriers are imposed. Quantification of the trade effects of tariffs and changes in tariffs would be a good start, but the very difficult task of quantifying the effects of nontariff barriers (including the growing effect of national industrial, regional, and other "purely internal" policies on trade) should now be pursued as well. The ultimate objective should be a widely agreed set of "tariff" and "NTB" elasticities, disaggregated as much as possible among industry groups or commodities and individual countries.

Beyond trade effects, quantification of the impact of barriers on the welfare of individual countries and groups within countries is needed to permit cost/benefit assessments of existing trade policies and possible changes in them. To complete that equation, quantification is also needed of the costs to some sectors of adjusting to present barriers (and to any increases in them) and the costs to other sectors of adjusting to their reduction or elimination. Work on such topics would help answer questions about the impact of the structure of existing trade barriers on the developing countries, or on countries not members of customs unions or free trade areas, or on consumers, or on organized labor. Case studies of past events, such as the net effect on trade flows of the Kennedy Round (including the reduction in the rate of growth of trade in cotton textiles which made it politically possible) and the adjustment of the Common Market to free trade, could be extremely instructive in answering these questions.

One specific component of the international trade issue which deserves special attention is agricultural trade, since it is especially important both for relations among the industrialized countries (as the United States seeks to build on its comparative advantage to sell more to Europe and Japan) and for the development prospects of many countries in the Third World—and since some observers see the possibility that industrial policies in many countries will over the next decade or so tend to emulate the trend of agricultural policies in the past. A great deal of work has been done on the issue and there is widespread agreement that a major expansion of farm trade can occur only through basic changes in domestic support systems. However, more is needed on the locus of comparative advantage in several of the key agricultural products, on the costs of the present systems in the various major countries, and how they could be modified in light of existing social and political problems. Since pressure groups play such a major role in agricultural issues it would be a particularly fruitful area for political analysis.

Finally, a new and perhaps dominating issue of trade policy has been raised by the possibility that, for the first time in at least forty years, inflation has replaced unemployment as the central structural economic problem in most industrialized countries. The primacy of unemployment among economic problems has led to the primacy of import controls among trade problems (and of competitive depreciation, or at least competitive non-appreciation, among international monetary problems). But the trade policy problem may have already begun to undergo a fundamental change. Numerous major countries, including the United States, have been unilaterally cutting their barriers to a wide range of imports, and/or revaluing their currencies, to fight inflation. Hence the problem of import controls has been reduced, at least temporarily. At the same time, however, the pendulum in some of those same countries has swung so far that they have begun to apply *export* controls, and/or resisting the depreciation of their currencies, with effects as disruptive to other countries as the import controls of the past.

Numerous questions arise for trade policy. *Is* inflation likely to replace unemployment permanently as the central structural problem of economic policy? If so, should countries be enjoined from efforts to export inflation to each other? How could they be stopped? If they are not, will the appeal of self-sufficiency in the production of economic necessities (such as food and raw materials) rise throughout the world, intensifying the traditional problem of trade protectionism? Are new international rules needed? How would such a shift affect power relationships between exporters, especially of primary commodities and foodstuffs, and importers? In one sense, these issues are simply the symmetrically obverse side of the problems of recent years. However, they may raise fundamentally new issues, in both economic and political terms. This appears to be a basically new area, of possibly critical importance, for both conceptual and policy research.

International Investment

A second and related issue is the desirability of international investment and the proper policy response of governments to it. Foreign direct investment touches every concern of international economic policy: trade flows and trade policy, the functioning of the monetary system, LDC development, energy supply and demand, and the most sensitive political concerns which exist—the capacity of national governments to meet the goals of their constituents, national sovereignty and security, "equity" considerations surrounding the location of high-technology production, and fundamental ideological issues such as the proper role for private enterprise and *"dependencia."* Unquestionably, it has important effects on jobs, price levels, growth, and national self-perception in all countries it touches. (Portfolio and short-term capital flows will be discussed later, in the section on "International Money.")

Policy views toward foreign direct investment are becoming increasingly polarized, at least in the United States. On the one hand, some view multinational firms as breaking down market imperfections and increasing the validity of traditional economic theory. On the other, some view these same firms as ignoring the pricing mechanism and hence both cartelizing the world economy and fouling the adjustment processes of the monetary system. Some claim that foreign investment creates jobs in both capital-exporting and capital-importing countries, and boosts home-country as well as host-country growth. Others believe that it exports jobs and undermines the economy of its home country, while still others believe that it bleeds the host country to the benefit of the home country. There are numerous such conflicts of view about the effects of foreign investment on host countries, especially in the Third World. There is even dispute over the outlook for these firms: some see them "taking over the world" and supplanting nation-states as effective decision-making units, while others foresee a process of "dinosaurization" through which their size both dulls their dynamism and compels governments to assert their own authority by bringing the firms firmly under their control.

Of course, each of these different viewpoints might be correct in particular cases. But there is no agreed welfare theory of international investment against which to judge such views, at the global let alone national or sectoral levels, in the way that proposals for trade restrictions have always been tested against basic free trade doctrine. There remains considerable dispute over the motivations for foreign direct investment, with some analysts clinging to the traditional portfolio model and others focusing on risk aversion by far-flung corporate systems. We have no firm understanding of the impact of foreign direct investment on international trade. Any new theory would clearly have to rest, at least in part, on oligopoly rather than free market models and on concepts of industrial organization as well as traditional approaches to international capital movements.

More empirical studies of different countries and different industries are badly needed, since there may be no general answer to the questions raised. But our empirical knowledge of the phenomenon remains limited, and the raw data remain grossly inadequate. No good data are widely available on foreign production by multinationals, the internal prices at which they transact business, their profits (indeed, what is meant by "profits" in this context), the cost factors which determine their locational choices, how they respond to national policies such as exchange-rate changes (and thus how they affect the balance-of-payments adjustment process), the degree to which head offices or host governments actually control foreign subsidiaries, or numerous other key aspects of their behavior.

Finally, the only satisfactory methodology for analyzing the economic effects of foreign investment is one which compares actual events with the most likely alternative scenarios, at both the macroeconomic and microeconomic levels. This suggests the use of simulation and game-theoretic techniques in a dynamic setting, but such work has barely begun. Raymond Vernon discusses a number of the issues which need basic study in Chapter 4.

There is particular need on investment issues for research which goes beyond economic data and analysis. We know that national perceptions of foreign investment differ widely, even among countries which might normally be classified together (as capital exporters or importers, as industrialized or developing countries, as relatively open or closed economies). We know that ideological concerns may loom large enough to override even sophisticated economic cost/benefit analyses in the determination of policy in many countries. Yet there is little systematic information on these perceptions, as evidenced by national actions as well as rhetoric; even less understanding as to why they differ; and virtually no understanding of how they are affected by the behavior of the firms themselves. The uncertain "nationality" of multinational firms differentiates the issue, psychologically and therefore politically, from other types of capital flows (even other types of direct investment) in many minds. The international mobility of multinational firms and their executives, relative to most of their own workers, heightens political tensions—indeed, such tensions may run higher over this issue than any other on our agenda—whose form and implications are not yet understood. Political analysis must therefore complement economic analysis before comprehensive understanding of this relatively new phenomenon can begin to emerge.

No basis thus exists on which national governments can formulate coherent policies on foreign investment at present. The United States has no such policy. There is not even the beginning of an international regime on international investment, like the GATT on trade and the IMF on international money, despite the fact that investment flows now rival trade flows in their international importance and have a major impact on the functioning of the monetary system. We know little about the effectiveness of the ad hoc measures already adopted by numerous host countries in their efforts to maximize their national returns from foreign investment, the extent to which those measures are internationally compatible, or the effects of such measures on home-country and firm attitudes. There have been few systematic efforts to develop policy proposals which would distribute the costs and benefits of international investment on any given set of criteria (global, national, or sectoral). In addition, the issue of direct investment poses unique three-way bargaining situations among the firm and the parent and host countries (which may become a four-way affair when, in addition, a large part of the output is marketed in neither the home or host country, as in oil and other raw materials). Analysis is needed of the varying strategies open to each party and how they would interact. This is one of the clearest cases where economic and political analysis must fuse, because of the varying impact of international investment on different countries and different groups within each.

Labor and the International Economy

By comparison with the vast (but largely redundant and irrelevant) amount of work already launched on foreign investment, virtually no attention has been given to the interrelationships between the international economy and the other key factor of production—labor, which is of course a heterogeneous grouping ranging from top management (whose interests are usually associated with capital) to blue-collar workers at a wide variety of skill levels (who are the focus of this section). Perhaps the neglect reflects the assumption of full employment in most economic models, and the lack of interest of most economists in dealing with the "transitional problems of frictional employment" which are permitted by such models—despite their social and political significance. Substantively, the neglect comes in two directions: economists have seldom addressed either the effects of the international economy on labor, or the effects of labor (except as a "factor cost") on the international economy. Functionally, it comes from both labor economists and specialists on the international economy.

Such neglect is particularly surprising in view of the political importance of labor in all countries, and the increasing interest which it is taking in international issues—often in directions which run directly counter to established orthodoxy. Jobs and labor's share of national income are increasingly affected by international flows, as are workers in their role as consumers. This is true both in the United States, the least open of the market economies, and in developing countries suffering from widespread unemployment and underemployment (The Ford Foundation is carrying out a separate study of unemployment in the developing countries, as already noted, so this crucial issue is not dealt with extensively here.) In the modern world, pursuit of an optimal international division of labor determined soley by market forces might well produce a steady transfer of manufacturing jobs to LDCs from the industrialized world, which would in turn devote an increasing share of its output to services. In both sets of countries, this would raise fundamental structural questions which could have national security as well as purely economic implications.

Yet virtually no work has been done on the most basic issues:

1. What are the costs and benefits to workers in particular countries, both in absolute terms and relative to capital, of freer trade? of foreign investment? of changes in exchange rates? For example, will labor in a capital-exporting country gain enough in absolute terms from foreign investment by firms based in that country to offset the decline which will result in its future share of national

income? Does labor resist trade liberalization because its share of income is raised by the incidence of present trade barriers? How do the costs of job displacement affect the national welfare effects of trade and foreign investment? How can labor itself trade off the job and price effects of international flows?

2. Do international flows create greater instability for workers than comparable changes emanating from solely domestic sources, or are they "different" only in the sense that they are more susceptible to resistance because they are "foreign"? How do these relative levels of instability differ between "open" and "closed" economies? How important is this instability in the perceptions of workers, relative to the standard components of their income (wages, fringe benefits, seniority, etc.), and relative to the reduced productivity which could be expected to result from increasing their job stability by limiting imports?

3. What are the welfare implications for individual nations, and international society as a whole, of the bargaining confrontation between internationally mobile capital and relatively immobile labor? Does this dichotomy of mobility eliminate the main countervailing power to oligopolistic corporations, or does it represent management's countervailing power to union monopolies at the national level? Is the importance of the dichotomy increasing, or is it declining as capital becomes increasingly subjected to national restraints and labor becomes increasingly mobile and finds countervailing strategies even without sizable emigration?

4. Does unionization within individual countries signficantly change any of these calculations?

5. How is the overall foreign policy of individual countries affected by the views of their labor forces on international economic relations?

Without the benefit of much analysis along these lines, labor unions at both the national and international levels have already begun to develop policy responses to their problems as they perceive them. Their basic objectives appear to be both economic and political: the preservation of jobs and maximum wages, and the enhancement of their own mobility relative to capital. The responses range across an entire spectrum. One approach, supported by the AFL-CIO in the United States, is to build impenetrable walls around national economies, restricting imports of goods and people and exports of capital and technology to such an extent that the international mobility of products and factors of production other than labor will be rolled back. A less extreme policy is the effort to reduce the economic distinctions between labor in different countries through "international fair labor standards."

An opposite approach, embodied by the efforts of the International Metal-workers Federation (including the United Auto Workers in the United States) and some others, is international cooperation among national trade unions to bargain on more equal terms with multinational business within a context of liberal trade and investment policies. In Europe, and now globally as well, labor groups are accelerating their efforts to consolidate national unions for individual multinational firms. This approach raises potentially critical issues for economic policy: Would multinational unions be a constructive countervailing force to multinational firms, or would the two join forces in disregard of the broader public interest as they have in numerous national industries?

A different route to international integration is labor migration, a major tool of international adjustment in past periods and an important tool in Europe at present for fighting both unemployment in less developed countries and regions and inflation in economies which generate higher levels of demand than can be satisfied by domestic workers. Still another route to the same objective is the effort of many European (especially German) unions to participate directly in management. At least two other approaches are conceivable: global antitrust policies, to prevent excessive concentration of power in individual firms and/or multinational industry unions, and income redistribution policies within individual countries to obviate any net shift of national income to capital which resulted from free flows of international trade and investment.

Each of these strategies would have very different effects on different countries, including labor in different countries. For example, unemployment in the Third World would be further increased as a result of a successful protectionist strategy by workers in the industrialized countries. Migration of workers and trade, which may frequently be policy alternatives, might have very different effects on both the countries which would expect net emigration and net immigration. None of these policy issues, with the exception of migration in a different historical context, has been subjected to rigorous analysis. In fact, we do not really know why different groups of national and industry workers have adopted such differing strategies; is it related, for example, to the structural differences in meeting worker needs in Japan (where the firm, backed up by the government, guarantees lifetime employment), in Europe (where governments provide generous social security, national health insurance and other "fringe benefits," and unemployment compensation), and in the United States (where neither most firms nor the government accept such responsibility)?

Our ability to deal with the problems of labor in the international economy suffers even more than other issues from gaps in overall economic theory, data, and policy. For example, there is no adequate conceptual framework for trading off unemployment against inflation; the choice is usually left to the interplay of political pressures within individual countries. We have no basis for choosing an optimal point on the world Phillips curve, even if we could construct such a curve; indeed, that choice is proving to be quite difficult even for the European Community, the most tightly integrated regional grouping. The results of many manpower programs are disappointing so far, making it more difficult to smooth the internal adjustment of workers to external disturbances. Resistance to standardized work is growing, at least in the United States, and raises basic questions as to whether management can create job functions which combine high productivity and worker satisfaction. Conversely, can one envisage labor contracts which would guarantee workers their jobs in return for worker agreement to alter their specific tasks in order to boost productivity, along the lines practiced in Japan, or to accept lower wages? The answers to these questions will have profound international implications, ranging all the way from the basic competitiveness of individual countries to the possible deliberate exporting of boring jobs. Additional examples of such problems are described by Assar Lindbeck in Chapter 2.

The international problems of labor are an area where sharing of national experiences could be particularly fruitful. Cooperation among union officials from different countries is growing, but is still infrequent as contrasted with the active interchanges among executives of multinational firms. Cooperation among outside observers of labor developments is even less frequent. This is a field where interdisciplinary approaches are vital. It is also the most neglected issue of international economics today, relative to its substantive importance, and one which deserves particular attention from scholars from a variety of disciplines in the years ahead.

International Money

All international economic transactions must rest on an effective international monetary system, and it was the final breakdown of the Bretton Woods system which triggered the near-collapse of international economic cooperation in late 1971. In recognition of this importance, more recent research has been undertaken on international monetary issues than any other aspect of international economics. Yet major gaps remain on matters of central importance.

For example, a consensus began to emerge in the late 1960s, among government officials and the private sector as well as academic economists, that greater flexibility of exchange rates would dramatically improve the balance of payments adjustment process and increase monetary stability. That consensus was based primarily on theoretical considerations, however, and we have little firm evidence of the actual effects of exchange rate changes on individual countries.

Now there are again a growing number of "elasticity pessimists" who think that exchange rates changes can only provide limited help in restoring and maintaining world payments equilibrium. They take the view that much of international trade and investment is relatively insensitive to price changes, because multinational corporations are playing a growing role in those transactions and do not respond in the manner prescribed by conventional theory; because trade in goods such as foodstuffs and raw materials—including energy resources, whose share of world trade will probably climb sharply in the coming years—is not very sensitive to price changes; and because various national barriers to trade insulate large sectors from the full effects of price changes.

At the same time, the "elasticity optimists" believe that international flows have become so increasingly responsive to price changes that small exchange-rate changes will have massive effects. These two approaches, which appear to polarize the debate, may not be inconsistent: elasticity pessimism may be in order for some sectors and perhaps some countries, and elasticity optimism in order for others. Or the distinction may merely be one of timing: the structural changes cited may lengthen the response period of exchange-rate changes, e.g., because multinational firms respond to changed cost considerations only when constructing their next long-term capital budget and because supply elasticities are lower in the short run for energy sources than for manufactured goods. In the aggregate, however, as Paul Samuelson has recently observed: "The jury is still out on this empirical question."[3] And the jury cannot even begin to judge the impact of exchange-rate changes on international capital flows, because there has been virtually no work on this essential question.

Again, problems arise at all levels of knowledge. The price data currently available provide a notoriously weak base for any credible analysis of international trade, and compound the empirical problem of determining elasticities. Virtually every study so far has been forced to rely on unit values and on domestic price indexes (which include nontradeable goods), and the pioneering work on actual transactions prices by the National Bureau of Economic Research has not yet been systematized or generalized. Once we had better transactions prices, we could study the critical question of how responsive they are in practice to exchange-rate changes, i.e., what percentage of those changes is actually "passed through" to the market? There appear to be significant differences among countries regarding both income and price elasticities, but much more work is needed both to refine the size of the differences and to understand why they occur: do different economies react differently because of the difference in importance of their foreign sectors or its composition, or their stage of development, or the strength of their labor unions, or some other systematic variable?

Theoretically, how can we fuse the three leading explanations of the effect of exchange-rate changes—the elasticities, absorption, and monetarist approaches? There is still no widely agreed definition of an optimum currency area—that group of countries among whom rates should remain fixed but whose (joint) rate should fluctuate toward the rest of the world. And what time paths can we expect for the adjustment triggered by exchange-rate changes in different countries?

Historical analyses of past exchange-rate changes, and regimes with fluctuating rates, could shed new light on all these questions. They might also help answer two other key questions concerning the desirability of greater flexibility: whether it stabilizes or destabilizes capital flows, and the time paths through which its effects proceed. Political and institutional analysis could shed important light on the crucial question of the impact of exchange-rate changes on money wages (and other distributional issues), and hence its net effect on both external and internal economic developments in different settings. At the policy level, is it inevitable that *any* increase in flexibility induces "dirty" floating—and, if so, is this a serious problem in economic and/or political terms?

The adjustment problem goes well beyond exchange rates. Indeed, we have very little work on the welfare effects of payments imbalances themselves—again on the global, national, and sectoral levels. What are the costs and benefits to a country—economic and political—of running a balance-of-payments deficit or surplus, under differing sets of domestic economic conditions? The problem is complicated by the additional targets of external economic structure—especially trade surpluses—adopted by most countries. Such structural factors are often ignored in payments studies; as a result, their economic analysis may be misleading (e.g., because the capital account improves more than the current account deteriorates under conditions of excess domestic demand) and their policy relevance sharply reduced.

Assuming the desirability of eliminating disequilibria, however, adjustment can be sought through changes in internal policy and selective external measures as well as through exchange-rate changes. Systematic analysis is thus needed of the costs and benefits of alternative adjustment policies to different countries, and to sectors within countries. The option of greater coordination of national economic policies raises sufficiently important additional issues that it will be discussed separately below. Selective controls are increasing in frequency, but few case studies have attempted to determine their effectiveness in achieving adjustment and other objectives, and their various side effects. The selective measures apply mainly to trade and capital flows, so this analysis would dovetail with the needs already discussed for additional work on the effects of each on welfare and on levels of transactions.

Before such work can progress far on capital controls, however, a good deal of further work is needed to enhance our understanding of international capital flows (other than direct investment, which has already been discussed and which is relevant here as well). More conceptual work is needed on the determinants of such flows: differences in interest rates and changes therein, changes in exchange rates and expectations thereof, trade flows, changes in national economic conditions, and perhaps other variables as well. More empirical work is needed to test the different concepts, to follow up on the promising starts which have been made (at least at the macroeconomic level). Of particular importance is better understanding of the impact of international flows on national monetary policies, as well as more refined work on the impact of national monetary (and other) policies on international flows. A specific issue on which much work remains to be done, at both the conceptual and empirical levels, is the Eurocurrency market.

Less urgent, but still in need of further work, are several issues concerning the liquidity aspect of international monetary arrangements. Despite much effort, no comprehensive study of the optimum level and growth of world reserves—under different adjustment regimes, including the present regime of managed exchange-rate floats—has been successfully completed. We still need to know much more about the nature and motivation of the responses of individual countries to positive and negative changes in their reserves, following up Michael

Michaely's start for the National Bureau. Further work in this particular direction would better link the liquidity and adjustment issues, including optimum tradeoffs between them for individual countries, and provide a more solid base for comprehensive reform of the monetary system encompassing both. And there remains the fundamental issue of whether global liquidity arrangements should attempt to aggregate national liquidity needs or desires, or whether they should relate directly to global economic variables—and, if so, what global economic variables?

Part of the question is whether the responses of a given country differ as a result of different *compositions* of its reserve changes. Related to this point, and to the management issue to be discussed later, is the question of whether one or more key currencies, for official as well as private use, are a necessary (or even desirable) component of an effective monetary system. This question carries great current relevance, in view of the rapid ascendancy of the German mark to second place among world currencies and the increased international use of several other national monies as well. In this context, there is still wide disagreement as to what shares of the U.S. payments deficits (at least before 1971-72) were supply-determined and demand-determined, respectively, a question of political as well as economic importance. Still another liquidity issue is the optimal distribution of world reserves, and increments therein, which raises both economic and political considerations and relates to the desire of the developing countries to get a larger share of future allocations of Special Drawing Rights. Indeed, it may not be too early to start analyzing the effectiveness to date of SDRs and whether they are winning acceptance as the first truly international money in history. Data gaps underlie many of the liquidity problems, as they do many others already discussed.

The Political Implications

Management of the World Economy

Overarching all of these issues is the question of management of the new world economy, which we have already discussed at some length in the introductory section. Global management can take place only through some combination of three approaches. One option is to eschew conscious management altogether: "let the market do it," through flexible exchange rates and unilateral national decisions on trade, investment, and other microeconomic issues. A second option is hegemonial management by a single dominant power capable and willing to do so, as Britain in the nineteenth century and the United States in the early postwar period. The third option is multilateral management by a group of national actors sufficiently cooperative to pull it off.

In today's world, no country seems willing to leave matters wholly to the market. It is clear that no single country is able to dominate the world. So it seems that multilateral cooperation must play a central role. In its absence, a fourth option—disintegration of international economic relations—is quite possible.

To be sure, some issues require less management than others. One can envisage "management" limited to the broad systemic structures, with daily operations left largely to the market or unilateral action (e.g., a payments adjustment process based on flexible exchange rates with multilateral surveillance of the market intervention or by national authorities). Or, as in the past, there could be lots of "management" of some issues (e.g., money) and little or none of others (e.g., investment). Some issues can be handled on the regional rather than global level, as by the EC. Indeed, we need much more analysis of what is really meant by "management of the world economy," and the different forms it can take.

It seems clear, however, that any such management in the future must be far more complex than the past efforts to provide leadership in reducing trade barriers and supplying international finance. It must treat the wide and intense array of interplay which now exists among national economies, through such instruments as "internal" industrial (including agricultural) policies and manpower policies at the microeconomic level and exchange-rate relationships at the macroeconomic level. Indeed, it is this very complexity which induces some observers, including some governments, to seek to eschew overt management in favor of reliance on market forces. Unfortunately, there is serious risk that these "market" forces—including the oligopolists referred to at the outset—will tug and haul to carry the day, or that some countries which dislike the distributional effects produced by the market will seek to check them, in uncoordinated and perhaps dangerous ways, if at least a minimum degree of multilateral management cannot be achieved.

We noted above that U.S. hegemony is gone, that three relatively equal powers whose short-term goals often differ now dominate the scene, and that such a situation is unprecedented in modern history and laden with potential for inaction or even overt conflict. A host of politico-economic questions thus arise. Will the United States withdraw from economic leadership too rapidly, or even become a destructive force? Will Western Europe and Japan exercise responsibility consistent with their new economic power quickly enough to avoid a leadership vacuum? How serious would such a vacuum be; would it propel all three leading powers toward nationalist, bilateral, and increasingly mercantilist solutions? Can the three forge a cooperative new international economic order to govern relations among them, and their relations with others? Are new processes or new institutions needed to enable them to exercise leadership at the global, regional, national, and subnational levels? How can any "one-world" solution reconcile the European taste for regional priorities and the American taste for globalism, or the French-Japanese penchant for controls and the American-German preference for reliance on the market? What role can regional groupings play in constructing a new order? What kinds of blocs would be compatible with a stable world order, and what kind would destroy such an order?

There remain fundamental questions about the rest of the world even if the United States, Western Europe, and Japan manage to organize relations among themselves. How can any such management structure accommodate the many new actors that have appeared on the scene? What will be the role of the major Communist powers; should a place be made for them, especially the Soviet Union, in any new structures? What will be the role of poorer countries, especially those who are rich in strategic commodities (copper, bauxite, etc.), and how will their relations with the rich be managed? What about the oil countries, with their gigantic wealth? How can the system manage the transition of those "new Japans" which are rapidly growing richer (e.g., Brazil, Iran)? How will nation-states cope with the growing roles of transnational actors, whose domains of effective action often exceed the jurisdictions of those nation-states? Multinational corporations and banks are now the most powerful of such transnational actors, but others—e.g., multinational labor—may well add significantly to the picture in the future. The multiplicity of actors adds to the complexity of the "management" issue, and belies any notion that even the creation of stable new arrangements among the United States, Western Europe, and Japan—necessary and central as that would seem to be—would suffice to restore a relatively stable world economy.

What are the institutional implications of all these developments? Will new international institutions be required to provide effective management of those new issues (e.g., investment and energy) not now handled effectively by any existing organization? How can existing organizations adapt to a set of political and market relationships completely different from those on which their charters are still based, including both the underlying power structure among their members and the intimate interrelationships among the different economic issues? Can any of these institutions, perhaps in new form, meet some of the needs for leadership? Can they help develop national policies, or even to coordinate such policies? How can national governments organize effectively to deal coherently with this maze of issues and competing interests? What are the political effects on particular national groups of the different approaches to international management (e.g., does reliance on global institutions strengthen transnational elites relative to organized labor, whose political power is limited to the national level)? Can new techniques of political science (e.g., conflict resolution and the study of bureaucratic politics) and sociology (e.g., the study of national and transnational elites) provide new insights as to how it all might work? At a more mundane level, but highly important, is the need for internationally reliable sources of data, analysis, and projections of international economic trends, including data on the overall global economy as well as on its national and regional components, on which firms and others can plan their own activities.

Coordination of National Economic Policies

One aspect of managing the world economy is the coordination of national economic policies. This chapter has already stressed the potential for using international economic policies more effectively to help countries cope with their internal problems. Here we look to the possibility of relating domestic economic policies more effectively to the problems of the world economy and international economic relations.

The first section of this chapter concluded that one of the major underlying problems of the international economic order is the sizable and growing tension between (a) the large and multiplying number of targets of national economic policies and (b) the declining capability of national policy instruments to meet those targets unilaterally as a result of the rapid expansion of international economic interpenetration. Governments are thus prone to react defensively to block, or at least retard, the integration of the world economy. One way to ease the tension is through international coordination of national policy instruments, at both the macroeconomic (e.g., monetary policy) and microeconomic (e.g., agricultural policy) levels. Through such efforts, governments could, at a minimum, protect themselves against the effects of moves of other governments; at best, they could maximize the effectiveness of their own individual efforts.

The problem, however, is further complicated by the *international* incompatibility of national policy targets in many areas. For example, it is impossible for everyone to run a trade surplus. Even in the absence of new steps toward active coordination of national policies, there is an urgent need for better understanding of the interplay among national objectives and their implications for the ability of each nation to meet its own targets.

A related issue is the problem posed for all governments by transnational actors which often appear beyond their control. As Richard Cooper has put it so well,[4] the "domains" of these actors (multinational firms, the Eurodollar market, perhaps multinational labor in the future, etc.) exceed the policy jurisdictions of national governments, complicating or even frustrating the efforts of governments to meet their own goals (and often frustrating their psyches even more). Coordinated efforts in these areas may thus appear attractive to governments; the specific possibilities are described in the sections on the relevant issues.

In addition, we have seen above that better coordination of national policies is one way to improve the balance-of-payments adjustment process. Some major work has been done in this area, particularly concerning the conflict between internal and external balance and the ways in which national policies could be "mixed" to achieve optimal results. But several aspects of the issue require basic new work.

Empirical investigation is needed to determine which domestic policy instruments in various countries are most undermined by external events, and how much their effectiveness is diminished. At the same time, governments should know which of their national instruments of domestic policy most affect other countries and hence disrupt the internal efforts of others. (A good deal of work has already been done on aggregate monetary policy, in both respects, but industry studies are needed to provide a similar basis for considering microeconomic measures.) The results of this research could produce a far better guide than now exists for coordinating national policies to maximize their effectiveness in pursuit of their targeted objectives. Such analyses could also help disseminate the experiences of particular countries with particular policy instruments to the benefit of other countries facing similar policy problems, and the experiences of regional efforts (particularly in Europe) to the benefit of dealing with the same issues on a global basis. Both national and international forecasting could be improved as a result. Project LINK has already taken initial steps in these directions.

All these problems suffer from gaps in "purely domestic" economic understanding. Why do Phillips curves differ between countries? Why do different countries have different preferences along their Phillips curves? We need more knowledge of the effectiveness of policy instruments in purely internal terms before we can make sound judgments about their effects on other countries, and the effects on them of external events. We need to know more about the internal consistency of policy targets and instruments before we can go far in assessing their international consistency, and examining whether national instruments suffice in both quantity and quality to meet them.

In view of all these intellectual gaps, as well as the political tensions already cited, it is not surprising that governments and monetary authorities have done little to coordinate national macroeconomic or microeconomic policies. Yet such coordination could play a major role in dealing with domestic economic problems in all countries, the responses of governments to transnational actors, the adjustment process at both the aggregate and industry levels, and the development of new management techniques in world economic relations.

Indeed, the issue can be viewed as one of centralized versus decentralized decision-making on a global scale, much as many countries are currently debating that issue on a national scale. It is probably time to consider seriously the possibility for truly global economic policies, such as a world monetary policy and open-market operations by an expanded IMF. It is essential to include the global and regional levels in any stable new pattern of decision-making on economic policy, whether through coordination of national policies as discussed in this section or through some alternative devices. And it is necessary to assess the compatibility of greater global decision-making on some issues with the widely observable trend toward greater local autonomy, within individual countries, on many others.

International Economics and World Politics

This chapter has continually stressed the interaction between international economics and world politics. We have demonstrated that each specific issue has important political as well as economic content, on both the domestic and international levels. Such key "economic" issues as differences in national Phillips curve preferences are of course deeply rooted in internal politics, which are in turn based on sociological and even psychological factors as well as differing economic structures. And one cannot understand the role of the dollar in the postwar monetary system without considering the dependence of Germany and Japan on the United States for their national security.

In addition, however, there is a discrete issue of great importance which, along with the labor issue, may have been neglected more than any other relative to its substantive importance: the impact of the international economic order on global political relations. The close relationship between international politics and economics was elaborated in the introductory section. As international economic interpenetration increases and the number and complexity of domestic policy targets pursued by governments rise as well, international tensions are bound to increase. Hence domestic politics will be increasingly affected by international economics, which will in turn thus increasingly determine the foreign policy agendas of individual countries. The probability of this outcome is reinforced by the nudging aside of the security blanket, which until fairly recently precluded overt economic conflict among allied countries. It will be particularly acute while the basic structure of the international economic order is in flux, perhaps for the rest of this decade.

The implications of the changing international economic relationships for international politics run much deeper, however, than just their increased importance. A number of these implications are analyzed by Robert Keohane and Joseph Nye in Chapter 5. A major problem, for example, flows from the asymmetrical interdependencies among the major countries. Europe and Japan will continue to rely on the United States, if to a lesser degree than in the past, for their security. Yet both Europe and Japan, in some senses, possess international economic power superior to the United States (much larger reserves, a much larger trade level in the case of Europe, etc.). The United States may thus be tempted to employ the principle of comparative bargaining advantage by trying to use its security leverage to pursue its economic objectives; the United States might even seek to maintain (or expand) its politico-military role in the world for this purpose.

In response, Europe and Japan might refuse to play either because they thought that the United States was bluffing, given its own security interests, or because of their own perceptions of the relative importance of their economic targets vis-à-vis the real risks to their security. Or they might even try to use their economic leverage to pursue political objectives, as de Gaulle did. Some Third World countries might attempt to use their growing economic importance, particularly as suppliers of key raw materials and as custodians of large chunks of the environment, to extract concessions from the industrialized world on development or political issues of high priority to them—and the great powers might respond in the security field to avoid such economic costs. There have been a number of efforts in recent history to use economic leverage for political reasons, running from the League of Nations sanctions against Italy through the U.S. export embargoes toward Communist countries to the United Nations sanctions against Rhodesia, from which we should be able to learn much about such possibilities for the future.

The results of the politico-economic interplay in the years ahead could be profoundly destabilizing for both the world economy and the world political structure. Or, if managed effectively, they could contribute to a stable new order based on greater equality among all participants. Fundamental to this issue is the problem of defining "international economic power." Is it based on GNP? the level of trade? competitive position? the degree of openness of an economy? ownership of foreign investments? reserves? Bergsten has suggested elsewhere a distinction between negative power, based largely on the ability of a country to resist external pressure for changes in its own policies; veto power, through which a country can block efforts of others to achieve their own policy objectives, including systemic changes; and positive power, by which a country can compel others to change their own internal policies and accept its systemic objectives.[5] On this analysis, different attributes contribute to the different types of power. An even broader question concerns the role of economic power in aggregate national power, which some political scientists believe is increasing sharply relative to the traditional importance of military power. But these key issues have been barely touched, and need the attention of both political science and economic techniques. The question of leadership and management of world economic relations, which we have just discussed, is closely related but only one aspect of this broader issue.

Another central issue is the optimum level of international economic transactions from the international political standpoint. Excessive barriers to trade and factor movements could produce major political tensions. Complete freedom for such movements would eliminate the political problems which the barriers cause, but the resulting movements could themselves levy unbearable strains on interstate relations and raise pressures for new barriers. Indeed, we have seen recent examples of both types of problems, especially when individual countries perceive important asymmetries between their own behavior and the behavior of other countries. It is also important to identify those economic issues which should be routinely regulated by the system and those which should be overtly politicized, again from the standpoint of international political relations. Yet there has been virtually no effort to try to answer these questions.

There is potential conflict between the optimal level of international economic transactions on traditional economic criteria, which focus on maximizing global welfare, and on international political criteria, which focus both on an "equitable" distribution of world income among nations and encompass noneconomic considerations (e.g., prestige) as well. There are other sharp differences between the economic and political approaches to international relations. Many more actors (both countries and parties within countries) participate meaningfully in economic than security issues, so economic issues are much more politicized and hence less susceptible to control by governments. Transnational actors (e.g., multinational firms) and transnational elites play a far bigger role in economic than security issues, and influence governments in different ways. Nuclear stalemate is stabilizing, but policy stalemate on economic matters may be very destabilizing. So a whole host of new complications for both the analysis and practice of international relations is evolving from the increasing importance of international economics.

The Special Issues

Energy

Will there be an "energy crisis"? Our business and banking advisors were nearly unanimous that this is *the* most pressing problem of the world economy, and some U.S. government officials agree. Most academic economists, noting that we have heard these alarms before, believe that market forces will largely take care of any such "crisis."

Which view is right? Or are they compatible, with major changes in trade, payments, and income patterns in store even if "the market takes care of it" in the sense of avoiding actual shortages of energy inputs? If so, what will such changes mean? Will the oil countries be able to preserve an oligopoly price for their products as successfully as the oil companies have done in the past? Will the oil situation be replicated in other raw materials; if so, which ones and with what effects?

The amounts of money involved are huge. According to some estimates, the oil exporters alone will be earning more than $50 billion annually by 1985. On the other hand, it is possible that new sources of energy (nuclear, solar, hydrogen, geothermal, gasification of coal, oil shale, tar sands, etc.) and new discoveries of oil (North Sea, North American Arctic, etc.) will moderate the need for oil imports over the longer term. Whatever the outcome, the issue touches all aspects of the international economy and has far-ranging security implications as well, and could radically change present configurations of both economic and political power.

Will consuming countries join together to exercise their potential market power in resisting producer demands, or will they engage in "cannibalistic" competition? What would be the implications for overall U.S.-Europe-Japan relations of either course? How will the Soviet Union fit into the picture? Will the development efforts of individual developing countries not endowed with oil or other resources be shattered by their energy import needs? How will the oil countries (and any successful emulators) spend their vast fortunes—and how is the basic concept of money affected if some of its holders have no economic need for it at all? How will national security and environmental considerations affect the economics of energy trade? What will be the effects on international politics, e.g., U.S. support for Israel in the Middle East? What does history teach us about efforts to use commodity embargoes to pursue political ends?

A good deal of work has now been launched on the oil issue, although there is as yet no comprehensive analysis of the probable trade patterns that will emerge, their economic and political effects, and the costs of devising new energy sources. A recent government survey concludes that *all* present energy "models" are inadequate in their consideration of possible price changes and alternative sources. Sam Schurr, of Resources for the Future, describes in Chapter 6 the issues raised by oil alone.

Perhaps it is equally important, however, to apply the lessons of the emerging oil problem to similar issues. Will shortages develop in other key raw materials, with serious price effects and threats of rationing? Will the countries which supply these materials seek to emulate OPEC? If so, will they succeed in overcoming the political problems which often divide them and the economic possibilities of substitution? What changes in economic patterns and power positions would result if they did succeed? Are there policy opportunities to prevent such developments that were either missed in oil or not applicable to that situation? The "oil crisis" has seemed to emerge without much warning despite the existence of widespread industry forecasting; can we learn from this episode and do better for other commodities?

Schurr also focuses on the international political problems raised by energy trade, in two senses. Most of the energy exchange flows between developing and industrialized countries, and much of it is engineered by multinational firms based in industrialized countries. It thus figures importantly in some of the issues discussed elsewhere in this chapter, especially in the contexts of investment and North-South relations: "exploitation," "*dependencia*," sharing of profits, terms of trade, fluctuation in commodity prices, the trade impact of environmental policies. Some of these questions are not new, but the potential quantitative leap in the magnitude of energy flows seems likely to assign them a far greater role in world economic and political relations than they have played heretofore.

North-South Economic Relations

North-South relations cut across the whole spectrum of international economics.[a] They raise fundamental issues for the two-thirds of mankind which now lives in the poor countries but consumes a miniscule share of world output. Many of these issues have already been discussed in their functional context—the

---

[a] The term "North-South" is unsatisfactory, if only because some poorer countries lie in the North (e.g., Korea, Turkey) and some richer countries lie in the South (e.g., Australia, Kuwait, New Zealand, South Africa). The term also conceals the great heterogeneity within both "North" and "South," as does the equally misleading "Third World" synonym for "the developing countries." Nevertheless, both terms will be used because of their brevity and widespread acceptance.

impact of the pattern of present trade barriers on developing countries, the distribution of international liquidity, the many economic and political implications for development of foreign investment—because we believe that Third World problems should be addressed as integral components of all of these global problems. In addition, as noted in the introduction to this chapter, we consciously avoid detailed analysis of research needs on most of the internal aspects of development in view of the massive efforts already underway in this area (including by the Ford Foundation) and the separate study of the issue of unemployment in the LDCs undertaken simultaneously by Ford. This short section devoted specifically to the North-South relationship thus by no means contains the only comments on that relationship in this chapter—nor does it include our comprehensive views on the subject of development in its broadest sense.

Before turning to the role of North-South relations in the new international economic order, we must note that there is a good deal of uncertainty about the outlook for the Third World itself. On the one hand, aggregate LDC growth (of GNP, exports, and most other objective indicators—but also population) has been exceptionally high and a number of LDCs seem to have "made it." On the other hand, some of the fundamental goals of development (low rates of unemployment, improved income distribution, reduced economic and political dependence on the rich countries) have not been achieved and some countries have actually regressed in some of these regards. And the very success of some countries in achieving certain goals has intensified other problems, as in those countries where increased exports have promoted rapid growth of GNP but produced further imbalances in internal income distribution.

Much research continues to address the internal efforts of LDCs and how outside assistance can fill gaps in those efforts. Even within that context, however, key questions remain unanswered, partly (as we shall elaborate in the final section on research strategies) because of the dearth of interdisciplinary work in this area where it is most clearly needed. Do we need new theoretical models of development based on different priorities among the conventional policy targets, e.g., with reduction of unemployment or better income distribution instead of GNP growth viewed as primary objectives? Why have some countries "succeeded" while others, often better endowed with human or natural resources, have so far "failed"? Indeed, what are alternative ways of defining "success" and "failure" in this context? Why has foreign aid had such a mixed impact in different countries? Can these differences be explained by the different approaches of different donors? What level of resource transfers is needed from rich countries to poor; does the UN target of transferring 1 percent of the GNP of the industrialized countries annually make sense, economically or politically? What is the optimal composition of transfers, and through what mechanisms should they flow? Are whole new approaches needed, focused perhaps on new modes of technology transfer and migration of workers? How do the rapid structural changes now occurring in the industrialized countries affect the less developed? Does the emergence of "local leviathans" (Brazil, Mexico, Iran, perhaps Indonesia and India) threaten or enhance the outlook for their neighbors, economically and politically? There remains unanswered the classic question of how economic development affects political and social development, and vice-versa.

Of most direct concern, however, is the need to add a basically new dimension to the study of North-South relations and North-South policy in both hemispheres. The LDCs want to reduce their dependence on the North and are increasingly capable of acting independently in many respects; many of them are now reaching the point where they can compete actively in world trading and capital markets. On the other hand, many LDCs are becoming more dependent on external markets and sources of capital, at a time when interest in aid and other forms of direct support for development are lagging in the industrialized countries, particularly the United States. At the same time, many industrialized countries are becoming increasingly dependent on particular LDCs in a number of areas,[6] most notably for raw materials as noted above, and the LDCs are thus able to play an important role in the economic competition among the United States, Europe, and Japan.

All of these trends call for increasing integration of the developing countries into the world economy, to replace the donor-client relationship of the first postwar generation. A necessary step to this end is for the industrialized countries to reconcile among themselves the trade and monetary problems which we have already addressed. If the industrialized world turns protectionist, developing countries are almost certain to turn inward; if they face an open world trading system, they will be able to choose outward-oriented economic strategies. Indeed, the developing countries would probably be the greatest losers from a breakdown of the international economic order, which is one key reason why we have stressed the need to create a viable new structure. In addition, political reality suggests that the industrialized countries will not turn to the specific problems of the developing world until they have their own houses in order, unless major new pressures are exerted on them by the developing countries in the interim.

In addition, however, the integration of the developing world into the international economic order raises a host of issues specific to that process, most of which have received inadequate attention to date. Purely economic analysis here must be conditioned by political, and even ideological, considerations perhaps to an even greater degree than in our other areas of inquiry.

We indicated in the section on "The Theory of International Economics" that fundamental challenges have arisen, at a variety of points, to the basic concepts which have governed the main thrust of peacetime international economic policies for well over a century (with the notable exception of the 1930s). Most of the challenges noted so far come primarily from observers in the industrialized world. An additional set of challenges, however, emanates from the developing countries. Some are modern versions of Marxist doctrine, which view the present structure of international economic relations as based on exploitation of the poor countries by the rich through such modern manifestations as multinational corporations, effective tariffs skewed against LDC manufactured goods, and exchange-rate regimes and other deliberate policies which turn the terms of international trade increasingly against LDCs. Closely related are non-Marxist theories of imperialism, which are advocated both within the developing world and by a growing number of serious scholars in the developed countries, and which view with deep suspicion the motivation of all external "assistance." One policy result is a renewed attraction to Communist development models within the developing countries, or at least renewed efforts to combine centrally planned economics with non-Communist political systems to achieve "optimum development."

The basic underlying perception is of an inherent asymmetry in the world economy which favors the rich. This perception underlies a great deal of thinking about economic issues in the developing world, much of which centers on whether the South can achieve "independence within interdependence" or whether it will be forced to the unpleasant choice between extreme dependence and extreme independence. Serious research in both the developing countries themselves, and in the industrialized world at which these views are aimed, is needed on the accuracy of these perceptions, the depth with which they are held, and their consequences for policy. The results of such research, which of course requires the most sophisticated linkage between political ideas and economic policies, could have a pervasive effect: on general thinking about North-South relations, on whether policy should aim to "reduce the asymmetry" by overt intervention on behalf of the Third World, on the development models adopted by individual LDCs, and on all of the specific issues which are considered within this framework.

A wealth of those specific issues are detailed by James W. Howe et al. of the Overseas Development Council in Chapter 7. Many concern trade. What is the appropriate division of labor between North and South, in static but more especially in dynamic terms, in view of all the questions raised above about the theory of international economic relationships? What are the benefits to the North from increased imports from the South? What are the costs of adjusting to them? How can the South overcome its competitive weaknesses in such areas as export marketing and finance? What role can multinational firms play in that process? What forms of cooperation among developing countries can best help meet their trade problems, and increase their bargaining power? What can we learn from the experiences of different countries in both North and South on these issues so far?

A range of questions concerns capital flows, both private and public. How can countries of North and South satisfy their often-conflicting national interests about the conditions under which direct investment takes place, as each tries to maximize its own benefits? For example, can LDCs reconcile the technology normally provided by multinational firms with their own needs for labor-intensive investment to reduce unemployment? Are there packages of portfolio capital, leased technology, and hired management which can be developed to substitute for direct investment and ease the political tensions which often accompany it? What would be the effects on LDC debt burdens, and on their policies toward direct investment (including expropriation)? Should foreign aid continue? If so, should it take new forms in this new milieu? Who should receive it? How should it be channeled? Will new institutional arrangements be required to manage the North-South aspect of the new interdependence among nations?

Finally, broad political and institutional questions need to be addressed from the perspectives of the range of different countries involved in North-South relations. Do the LDCs maximize their bargaining position by creating new institutions (UNCTAD), or by working together to achieve a greater role in existing institutions (within the IMF via their "Group of 24"), or by "going outside the system" altogether, or by avoiding direct representation (e.g., might they lose if their demands for a SDR "link" torpedoed overall monetary reform)? Aside from institutional questions, do they maximize through confrontation tactics or conciliation? How can they manage their own diversity of viewpoints? How can they set up bargaining units of optimal size on specific issues, such as maximizing their returns from the sale of particular raw materials? And how do both the developing and industrialized countries manage the transition of individual nations from "poor" to "rich" status?

A particular need is for work on these LDC problems *in the LDCs by LDC nationals*, and an increase in LDC scholarly capacity to deal with these problems on a continuing basis. The LDCs are rightly concerned about their intellectual *dependencia*. The bulk of the research so far on the interaction between the LDCs and the international economic order has been done in the rich countries, and much of it has been extremely useful. Yet there is no substitute for work on particular problems by those most deeply engaged in them, and most affected by their outcomes, especially to incorporate the crucial political and other noneconomic factors which loom especially heavily in this area and where cultural differences are so important. LDC policymakers quite legitimately will place more trust in work done by their own citizens. Moreover, the perspective of an LDC scholar is quite likely to differ from the perspective of a DC scholar. We shall make recommendations on this particular problem in the discussion of research strategies.

East-West Economic Relations

Economic relations between the non-Communist and Communist countries have always raised major issues because of the difficulty of interaction between market and planned economies, and a good deal of work has pursued that theme. It has also been clear that East-West trade and investment are far below the level which would prevail if they were determined by market forces, so unexploited welfare gains probably exist.[b] The topic has, however, suffered from neglect in four major respects.

First, this is the most highly politicized area of international economic relations. Because of the political competition between East and West, countries in each camp have—to different degrees, to be sure—linked economic exchange closely to the state of political relations. Each side (and particularly the coalition leaders of each side) has tried to entice the other to cooperate politically by offering economic incentives, and has used economic denial policies or threats in an effort to weaken the other. Yet few economists have tried to factor these critical political considerations into their analyses, which have often been sterile as a result. More importantly, few political scientists, even specialists in East-West problems, have considered economic issues as an integral part of overall East-West relations. Past work on possible convergence between capital-ism and communism addressed the comparative economics of the two systems, not their direct interaction. The need for interdisciplinary work is particularly clear in this area, to provide material relevant for policy purposes. This is true both for policies of economic warfare laden with ideological considerations, as in the past, and for policies of economic cooperation as may evolve in the future.

Second, a whole new environment for East-West economic relations appears to be developing. Analysis of these relations has been framed by the network of controls from both sides and an absence of contacts in the most important international economic institutions (IMF, GATT, IBRD, etc.). In short, the Communist countries were outside the "world economic system" and hence were disregarded in most analyses.

Now, however, marked liberalization is taking place on both sides. Barring a resumption of frigid Cold War, this process could move very fast. In any event, a far higher level of economic transactions is likely to develop over time. Indeed, the United States may be in the process of a quick policy reversal: from restricting exports to the Communist countries, for security reasons, to eagerly promoting exports to them to help deal with its balance of payments problem. (This would be one clear indication, of course, of the growing ascendency of economic over security considerations in international politics.) The new environment offers major new opportunities for economic and political relations between East and West, and will raise new problems between them. Hence it calls for new research on how to capture the opportunities and cope with the problems, including innovative thinking on new ways to bridge the gulf between

[b]The term "East-West," like "North-South," is also unsatisfactory, if only because European Russia and other Communist areas in Europe are more "West" than "East," and because Japan is more "East" than "West," in a cultural sense. The term also implies monolithic unity within each area and implacable hostility between the two areas, neither of which even begins to accurately portray the situation at present. Nevertheless, the term will be used because of its brevity and widespread acceptance.

market and planned economies. For example, thought should be devoted to the implications of further Communist internal reforms for East-West trade and vice-versa, ways to deal with the inconvertibility of Communist currencies, and how to accommodate expanded East-West trade (e.g., the "market disruption" formula in the U.S.-Soviet Commercial Agreement of 1972) within the framework of the trading goals and practices of the non-Communist world.

Third, the bulk of the East-West economic analysis heretofore has focussed on trade. In the new environment, however, the potential scope is much broader. At least the European part of the "East" now appears to welcome some types of Western direct investment, licensing, management and perhaps other forms of involvement. Indeed, low-wage Eastern Europe (and Communist Asia!) with its peculiar kind of political stability may become a real magnet for U.S. investment. (On his visit to the United States in 1970, President Ceaucescu told American business leaders that they should invest in Rumania because they knew where they stood—there was no fear there of nationalization!) A few Communist countries are even joining the economic institutions of the West, and more such moves are likely. A special issue is possible economic linkages between Eastern and Western Europe.

Thus the systemic restructuring which must take place anyway should plan for the contingency that all or most of the Eastern countries will "join" the global economic community over the next decade or so, and research undertaken now on this issue could have an important impact as events unfold. Even the U.S.S.R. and Communist China could someday soon eye membership in the IMF—if only to get a share of new SDR allocations, since there seems to exist a perfect correlation between membership in the nuclear club and endemic balance of payments weakness. Another new area of interest is East-West cooperation vis-à-vis the Third World, where rudimentary steps have already taken place. A large number of the experts with whom we consulted, especially those in LDCs, Japan, and Communist countries, stressed the need for study of the future of economic relations between the developing countries and the East.

Fourth, excessive generalizations about "East" and "West" have continued to dominate much work in this field. Yet it has been clear for some time that there are sharp economic as well as political differences among Moscow, Peking, and their erstwhile "satellites." Why do the Soviets want foreign credits while the Chinese have so far rejected them? Should individual Communist countries be viewed in fundamentally different ways from the U.S.S.R. concerning economic objectives and tactics? Does the diminution of a security threat make obsolete the concept of "Western" solidarity in economic relations with the East? On the other hand, are there reasons to maintain a common Western "position" in economic bargaining with the Communist world, if only to avoid destabilizing new competition among the Western powers?

Reinvigorated study of East-West economic relations is important from both the political and economic standpoints. How will alternative paths of economic interaction affect the general development of East-West political relations over time, particularly between the United States and the U.S.S.R.? For example, would heavy U.S. dependence on Soviet natural gas improve U.S.-Soviet relations, or jeopardize them by tempting the Soviets to use their resulting leverage for political reasons and heightening U.S. anxiety in response? More generally, are U.S.-Soviet political relations *eased* by the absence of economic interpenetration, which has placed major strains on U.S.-European and U.S.-Japanese, Soviet-East European and, at an earlier stage, Sino-Soviet relations? Are specific political problems, such as arms control agreements, susceptible to economic verification? How will East-West economic trends affect the internal cohesion of the Communist world, and how would these trends be affected by internal economic reforms there?

Each of these issues, and a host of others outlined by Frank Holzman in Chapter 8, raises major problems which have seldom been addressed intellectually, let alone resolved. Indeed, government and business practitioners may be well ahead of academic researchers in this area. The assumption of possible hostility cannot be relaxed completely, of course, and so these issues must be differentiated politically, as well as economically, from conventional analysis.

There is also much interplay between East-West economic issues and other items on our international economics agenda. The study of Communist state trading could add to our understanding of certain "nontariff distortions" to trade, and students of the latter might shed new light on the former. The discrimination inherent in East-West economic relations, due to the Eastern practices and Western responses which produce bilateral arrangements, could have interesting implications for the future of the most-favored-nation clause in trade arrangements among market economies. Since the Eastern countries are in some senses economically similar to less developed countries, each might be able to learn from the experience of the other (e.g., participation in international trade and investment relationships despite currency inconvertibility and administered internal prices). What role will Eastern countries play in the settlement of world energy problems, both as consumers and producers?

Environmental Management

One need not accept the apocalyptic forecasts of the Club of Rome to recognize that new concerns about the environment may come to deeply affect international trade, foreign investment, the energy problem, development in the Third World, and perhaps other issues in the relatively near future. However, many of the economic aspects of the environmental issue are simply additional considerations to factor into the traditional areas of research and policy, rather than discrete new topics themselves: adverse environmental effects can be treated as external diseconomies in most conventional models, any new barriers to trade created by national environmental standards would be conceptually similar to existing nontariff barriers, and the effects of sharp differences among national standards on the balance-of-payments positions of individual countries would be similar to disequilibria caused by differences in rates of change of other costs (such as wages). In addition, some of the discrete environmental problems which do exist do not relate directly to the international economic order: the problems of climatic and oceanic change, for example, primarily need scientific and technological attention.

Yet we include environmental management on this list of priority issues for research because we are not confident that it can be fully handled within the conventional headings already discussed; we are less confident that it *will* be handled even if it logically could be, because some of the problems (e.g., the seabeds and outer space) seem too esoteric to generate research at this time yet are uniquely susceptible to scholarly attention *before* national policies become imbedded; and because no one really knows the magnitudes which will be involved—it could turn out to rival the energy problem, which we have highlighted because of dramatic change in orders of magnitude rather than the discovery of new conceptual problems. Environmental issues affect the world economy through the movement of polluted products in international trade, the differences in national rules governing (or ignoring) the pollution content of production processes, and activities of industrial countries which affect other countries through altering the environment itself. All three aspects could prove important to international economic relations.

Measurement efforts are particularly important here; we need to know the magnitude and nature of trade and investment distortions arising from environmental management. Conceptual issues relate to the distribution of the gains from economic exploitation of the "common properties of mankind," notably the seabeds and outer space. The spectre of a cannibalistic race among nations to hoard resources, or even the more immediate problem of transnational pollution, raise politically explosive possibilities. Ingo Walter spells out all of these issues in great detail in Chapter 9.

The related issue of population growth permeates most of our concerns about the international economic order. As noted at the outset, however, a great amount of energy is already being devoted to finding measures, economic and scientific, to deal with it. It is most important that these efforts continue. Indeed, we feel that the population issue is sufficiently important to be pursued separately, in its own right, and not as a subtopic of the international economic order.

Research Strategies

The first section of this study concluded that the field of international economics merits priority attention in the years ahead, and the second section discussed the specific issues of greatest importance. However, our analysis has also suggested that new approaches to the study of international economics are needed to equip the world to deal effectively with those issues at the policy level. This concluding section will outline some components of a possible strategy for research.

Diversity of Approaches

Any comprehensive strategy will have to operate at a variety of conceptual levels, in addition to covering the variety of functional issues already discussed.

We have pointed out that some issues require new theoretical foundations before quantitative and policy research can make much progress. Indeed, we have called for rethinking of the general theoretical framework which continues to underlie most research in international economics, because of the significant changes in the real world to which theory must now be applied and because of the increasing deviations of policy from the conclusions of the conventional model in recent years.

Beyond this general problem, we may also need new theoretical precepts to better explain some of the specific categories of transactions discussed in the last section. In the past, economists have generally attempted to apply one or a very few general theories to all international economic phenomena. We may now need not just *a* new theory, but *many* theories, each adapted to specific problem areas and perhaps even to explain different *kinds* of trade flows and the international economic responses of different countries.

Many experts have advised us that it is impossible to "program" theory in the manner suggested here. They may be right. But it has been done in some fields. And we have concluded that the need is urgent; that it might be accomplished if real problems are effectively delineated, as we have attempted to do here; and if interest is generated in the field and resources made available.[7]

Other issues primarily require empirical testing of existing theories on the global level, for individual countries, and for particular sectors within countries. Some of the quantitative work may have to be quite rudimentary, at least in the initial stages, and consist primarily of identifying and collecting new data. Existing data are adequate in other areas, but need more sophisticated econometric manipulation. Government officials have particularly stressed the need for better data and more empirical analysis. Special priority should be accorded this area, particularly in view of the challenges to conventional wisdom which we have stressed and the resultant need for inductive work to relate broad concepts to observable phenomena in the international economy. In fact, Harberger concluded " ... it appears that the time is ripe for a whole new stream of scientific work in international economics, based on a collection of mass data that was previously seriously incomplete, and promising major new insights into the structure and functioning of the world economy."[8]

Special support is also needed for the experimental application of new methodologies to these international economic problems. Several such possibilities have been cited. Bargaining theory could help shed light on the relations between multinational firms and labor, multinational firms and the several different governments with which they must interact, centrally planned governments (and economic entities) and free enterprise governments (and firms). Oligopoly and location theory need to be further applied to foreign investment and international trade. Cost/benefit analysis is needed in many areas. Policy simulation and game-playing could prove useful in studying operational questions. Models of bureaucratic politics, at both the national and international levels, could be applied to firms, unions, international organizations, and key national governments. Comparative history can provide important new insights, and the postwar period is now old enough to permit "historical" treatment of some fairly recent and highly relevant issues. Many other imaginative approaches are undoubtedly possible.

In some areas, both theory and data may. be sufficient to permit the rational consideration of policy alternatives. If the issues are sufficiently important, direct policy research should be pursued in such cases. Such applied research must mesh domestic and international political factors, as well as economic analysis and institutional problems, through interdisciplinary devices, to which we turn shortly.

Finally, there are some problems for which there exists a solid intellectual consensus on needed courses of action, but where no action is forthcoming due to inadequate dissemination of that consensus to policymakers and relevant political groups, or because of particular political rigidities. In such cases, support may be needed for educational or other political action programs.

Any comprehensive program for research in international economics will thus have several dimensions. A number of major topics need to be addressed: trade, investment, etc. Different topics will have to be viewed at different functional levels: theory, data, etc. They will have to be viewed at different levels of aggregation and disaggregation: the world, individual countries, etc. Some may require simultaneous work on more than one level. Table 1-1 presents a very rough breakdown of the functional division of the work which might be needed in each issue area, to illustrate one aspect of this complex. It will be noted that major gaps exist in most of the cells of this two-dimensional matrix.

The Broad Picture

Most present analyses of international economic issues focus narrowly on relatively finite topics. Such analysis is necessary and should be encouraged if the subjects are themselves significant for policy, such as those discussed here.

However, there are two risks in limiting research to this approach. One is that

Table 1-1

Rough Illustrative Estimates of the Functional Distribution of Research Needed on Key Issues of International Political Economics

	(Percentage*)			
Needed:	Basic Concepts	Empirical	Policy Formulation**	Policy Implementation***
Issue:				
Theory of international economics	50	50	–	–
International trade	30	30	20	20
International investment	40	30	30	–
Labor in the world economy	30	50	20	–
International monetary system	20	40	20	20
Systemic management	30	10	40	20
Coordination of national economic policies	30	30	30	10
Impact of international economics on world politics	50	20	20	10
Energy (excluding scientific aspects)	–	50	50	–
North-South issues	20	30	25	25
East-West economic relations	20	30	30	20
Environment	30	60	10	–

*Total work needed on *each issue* equals 100%. The entry of the same percentage in a given column on two different issues by no means implies that the two require an equal amount of work *in absolute terms.*

**The development of policy programs based on existing theoretical and empirical knowledge.

***The implementation of policy programs already developed.

the research takes inadequate account of broader but related economic issues, let alone of related issues from other disciplines, and thus itself suffers fatally from its partial equilibrium nature. The other is that inadequate attention will be paid to the broad issues which are of overwhelming importance in setting the intellectual and policy milieu for all of the specific issues, and have the most significant impact on human progress.

For example, among the research topics discussed in this book, we view as most critical of all the two with the broadest possible scope: the underlying theoretical foundation for international economic policy, and the management of the world economy. These issues raise the questions, respectively, of the goals of international economic policies and, once that is decided, how to go about meeting them. Both are enormously complex, and extremely difficult to tackle in their entireties. So are comprehensive analyses of the international monetary system, the energy problem, North-South relations, and even those topics less cosmic in scope, let alone an effort to fuse them together.

But these are also the most crucial issues, and their enormity must not be permitted to prevent new work on them. The policy responses to these problems, whether taken consciously and in full cognizance of their importance or ad hoc in response to particular issues as they arise, will determine the structure of world economic relations and define the parameters within which the daily policy and market processes will function. More subtly, they determine the intellectual and emotional milieu within which millions of decisionmakers, in governments and the private sectors, choose particular courses of action.

These broadest of issues thus deserve a place of extremely high priority in any research strategy. Indeed, substantial progress in the scientific study of economics has frequently come with the formulation of a major new theoretical approach, which in turn spawned a host of detailed tests and modifications. Alternatively, new inductive work might produce important new conclusions at the broad conceptual level. Whichever new route is tried, and both should be, it is extremely important for individuals to step back from day-to-day international transactions and policies to view the broad philosophical implications behind the theory and reality of market activity and governmental action. A major breakthrough on any of these major issues could generate new levels of knowledge and guidance for attacking related problems.

Breakthroughs at this level are most likely to come from persons with exceptionally deep and broad backgrounds, preferably both academic and operational. Yet the few people who meet these criteria are, precisely because of their unique backgrounds, in constant demand—and the present system of rewards places high priority on their quantity of output. One result is fragmentation of the most precious of all resources, the time of people with exceptional abilities. The big thinking which is needed requires inducements to potential big thinkers to spend considerable time thinking big.

Interdisciplinary Research

Every issue of international economic policy blends economics, internal politics, and international politics. Virtually every expert in every country consulted in the course of this study—government officials, business and labor leaders, scholars—called for interdisciplinary analysis of these phenomena.

Yet very few people now engaged in international economics reach outside their own disciplines, and fewer still have even participated in attempts at truly interdisciplinary scholarship. In addition, some of the people who could have the most to say about international economics, and contribute most meaningfully to the needed interdisciplinary work, never address the issues at all. Most economists, especially in the United States, still regard international issues as marginal to their primary concern with domestic issues. They acknowledge that there are international implications to domestic policies, and implications of international events for domestic policies, and then return to their essentially closed models. Most political scientists, even further behind, don't address international economic issues at all.

The continuing emphasis on subspecialization within the broad fields of economics, political science and other disciplines, both in academia and in the institutions of government, compounds the problem of obtaining integration among fields. Most noninternational economists are content to leave the study of international economics to the international economists, despite its far broader ramifications. Labor economists have barely devoted *any* attention to the issues, for example, despite their impact on workers and the advocacy of organized labor for fundamental policy changes; they could provide new insights on such key questions as the likely response of wages to exchange-rate changes, and the job effects of raising or lowering trade barriers. Most political scientists are content to leave any mention of international economics to the international relations scholars, despite the importance of many of these issues in domestic politics—even the comeback of protectionism as an important political issue in the U.S.

Major efforts are thus needed in two directions. First, the universe of researchers working on international economic issues needs to be broadened, to draw on new skills in an effort to provide new insights and whole new approaches. Scholars from disciplines such as sociology and history (in addition to Marxists and revisionists) should be drawn into the study of international economics. Scholars from subfields of economics and political science, as already noted, should be drawn in as well. One fruitful result should be methodological innovations adapted from one field to the others, as has frequently occurred in the physical sciences. It might turn out that economists have a comparative advantage in analyzing *how* things should be done, in politics and economics, while other social scientists have comparative advantages in analyzing *why* things are done or should be done, including in economics.

Second, *every* study of international economics should have an interdisciplinary component. This would not require that more than one person be involved in every project, since some individuals possess interdisciplinary capacity. And the degree of interdisciplinary input would differ sharply from project to project. Purely theoretical economic analyses, for instance, would need a political component only at the outset so that the right questions would be asked and the most realistic assumptions made in the construction of models. Frontier work, of both the theoretical and empirical types, could still be carried out primarily by economists working alone in the traditional manner.

But all relevant fields should be integrated in studies aimed directly at producing policy proposals. Such applied research of necessity permeates all serious policy work within governments, and should be systematized outside government as well. Yet it is frequently discouraged by the disdain attached to "policy studies," and by the prestige accorded by the economic and other social science professions to abstract models, even when such work is so divorced from policy relevance that the resources devoted to it are largely wasted from a social standpoint. Instead, studies which are relevant to policy need to be encouraged, and actively promoted.

Any new research strategy for international economics should thus focus on policy-relevant issues, broaden participation in the field to include experts from new specializations, and seek truly integrated efforts among the various fields from which expertise is required to deal effectively with particular topics. An additional desideratum would be to internationalize some of the needed research. There is already a good deal of joint international work by specialists within fields, such as the series of "trilateral" efforts among Americans, Western Europeans, and Japanese carried out under the aegis of the Brookings Institution, the European Community Institute for European Studies in Brussels, and the Japan Economic Research Center. And there is evidence that transnational experts in a given field can work together at least as effectively as national experts in different fields. Such efforts should be encouraged and expanded, since the relevance of studies done solely by nationals of a single country is often reduced by the ignorance or insensitivity of researchers in one country to the economic and political situation in other countries, which may differ substantially. Such problems show up most frequently in studies of developing countries carried out in industrialized countries, and there is a particular need for joint work by DC and LDC scholars in this area.

Internationalization of research cannot be pushed too far. We have stressed the need for national and sectoral emphasis, to modify the economist's usual penchant for global welfare and aggregate utility functions, and this work can often be done completely within the country at issue (though outside viewers may be able to provide more objective analyses on occasion). But a large and growing number of economic problems are not very susceptible to resolution by a single country—particularly in view of the importance of multinational actors and the multipolar power structure which now underlies the world economy. The countries which need to collaborate will vary according to the particular issue: most of the present systemic problems must be solved primarily by cooperation among the United States, Western Europe, and Japan, but different sets of countries (including a variety of developing countries) are needed to deal effectively with a growing number of key problems such as energy and environmental management. Internationalization of the needed interdisciplinary research would add a further new dimension to the study of international economics which would help move the world toward resolution of important policy issues.

These proposals are very ambitious. Interdisciplinary research has a spotty record, and is difficult even to launch. International interdisciplinary research has seldom been tried, and is presumably even harder to obtain. We turn next to an examination of the feasibility of the proposals.

The standard formula for meeting the widely agreed need for interdisciplinary research is to try to induce good economists to "think about politics" and good political scientists to address economic issues. To be sure, such efforts have produced some useful work, and multidisciplinary thinking by individual experts is a minimum requirement for expanding the relevance of research at all levels.

However, most experts trained in a specific discipline become trapped by the mental sets imposed by that discipline and find it extremely difficult to integrate other disciplines into their subsequent thinking. Existing academic systems generally promote such evolution, viewing with great skepticism any ventures outside the conventional boundaries of each discipline. Indeed, shifting fields—or even shifting subfields—is often regarded negatively by one's peers, and hence subtly discouraged. Good young talent seldom makes the effort. As one of the most experienced observers of this field put it, "A man who tries it (interdisciplinary work) before he has tenure runs the risk of cutting his throat."

At the other extreme, it is true that the absence of adequate training in *any* discipline, perhaps in the pursuit of an interdisciplinary capability, may produce dilettantes with no firm intellectual foundations at all. And efforts to link economists and political scientists (and perhaps others) in specific research projects may produce the lowest common denominators which each can accept.

There are thus two broad options for seeking interdisciplinary research. One is to promote interdisciplinary capabilities for individuals, in essence reviving the old "discipline" of political economy (here with an international focus). The other is to bring individual, different disciplines together in team efforts based on a common orientation toward particular problems. They are not exclusive options, of course, and there are many gradations between them.

Individual economists and political scientists have made sporadic attempts to do interdisciplinary international economic research in the postwar period. These efforts have increased in the past few years, in response to the increasingly perceived need for such studies, despite the general tendency for the disciplines to branch off in different directions. Some have been undertaken by political scientists, though a few economists have applied economic models to international relations and others have examined the political dimensions of international economics. The most continuous efforts of political-economic analysis have been the neo-Marxist critiques of international economic relations, which appear occasionally in the United States but moreso in Europe and in the developing countries.

There have been even fewer interdisciplinary team efforts. Some of the studies to date have been useful, but they have barely scratched the surface. Immense methodological problems are involved. It is probably necessary, at least at first, to focus on very specific issues.

The individual approach may be more suited to efforts to produce new intellectual breakthroughs, the team approach to synthesis of existing knowledge into policy proposals—although there may be notable cases where the opposite results can be envisaged. We make no effort here to resolve this debate but would only conclude that, in view of the shortages of human resources now available, both approaches will need support if any research program is to approach the needs outlined in this report. It seems clear, however, that the gestation period of new interdisciplinary training programs would be fairly long, and hence unlikely to provide many resources for the near future to actually deal with the research problems outlined in this chapter. (We regard such training as essential for the long term, and turn to it below.) For the short run, therefore, the real options are to induce individuals from one field to broaden the scope of their work or to create research teams. Three broad institutional approaches to do both can be envisaged:

1. Option One: creation of a new Institute of International Political Economics, along the lines of the Institute for International Strategic Studies or Resources for the Future.
2. Option Two: mobilization of talent already in residence at existing centers through research programs at those centers.
3. Option Three: fusion of talent from different locations through integrated research programs directed from one of those locations or from some outside point.

A new institute could dramatize the new importance of the subject, and the support which was available to study it. By providing a new home for people working in the field, it might also be the surest way to focus substantive attention on international economics and create an environment to pursue the new methodologies which are needed. Though basically relying on resident scholars, it could bring in outside experts from all relevant fields to avoid in-breeding. The institute could also play the much needed role of lubricant between scholars of different countries, and between the public and private sectors. It could be truly international in terms of personnel, funding, and subject matter, and thus escape the national limitations (both real and cosmetic) which to some extent pervade existing institutions.

However, there are major drawbacks to a new institute from both the substantive and procedural standpoints. We have stressed that international economics represents a fusion among economics, domestic politics and international politics, beneath which lie social psychology and other fields as well. Yet a new institute focused specifically on international economics could easily tend to treat the field as too discrete, rather than as an amalgamation of its component parts. By virtue of its singleminded purpose, which would represent much of its merit, it could lose the linkages to those components and hence become less useful. There might also be a tendency to look to any such institute as *the* center which could be relied upon to provide *all* the needed answers, at precisely the time when the need is for more work by more people from a far wider range of fields than could ever possibly be brought under one roof.

On the procedural side, any successful research institute must attain a certain "critical mass," particularly in terms of personnel and core financial support, to make a real impact. Yet it takes time to build such a mass, which has been achieved to date in only a few existing locations with far broader mandates. Start-up costs would be high, and important time would be lost in getting underway. Current resources are now spread thinly among existing institutes, which would suffer with a further diversion of funds and scholars. To operate effectively, an institute needs to command a reputation which cannot be achieved overnight. We therefore conclude that the creation of a new international institute does not represent the optimum solution at this time, but that the option should be kept constantly in mind (and perhaps studied in depth by those more expert than we on institutional questions) if the alternatives proposed below do not turn out to meet the needs.

The alternatives are to induce existing centers with adequate human resources to focus more attention on the study of international economics, or to create programs integrated in substance but comprising researchers from a variety of different institutions. Under either approach, foundations or others providing major financial support would need adequate in-house staff to determine what issues should be pursued, who should pursue them, and how to put the two together. (In addition to actively seeking such projects, foundations should of course also continue to respond positively to worthy proposals made by individual researchers or institutes.)

The alternative of looking to existing centers is only viable, of course, if such centers exist. In the United States, only two candidates with major capabilities for interdisciplinary research come readily to mind: Harvard University (with its Center for International Affairs, Department of Economics, John F. Kennedy School of Public Administration, Center for West European Studies, and Business School), perhaps jointly with MIT and the Fletcher School of Law and Diplomacy; and the Brookings Institution (with its programs of Economic Studies, Foreign Policy Studies, and Government Studies). There may of course be others, such as Princeton and the University of Chicago.

Even fewer candidates are readily apparent in the rest of the world. Europe houses a plethora of small institutes which, with a few exceptions such as the Institute for World Economics at the University of Kiel and the Stockholm School of Economics, possess limited capacity for major internal research on economics let alone interdisciplinary topics. There is little interdisciplinary work in Japan, although the Japan Economic Research Center does important economic analysis. The situation in the developing countries appears even less encouraging. There is thus a strong case for creating new institutes, perhaps on a regional basis, outside the United States.

This shortage of potent research institutions means that pursuit of Option Two would, at present, center a large share of the available support in a relatively few locations. For short-term payoff, such an approach might be desirable—indeed, it might be the only way to get relatively quick results. For the longer term, however, it would be unfortunate—and possibly risky—to put so many eggs in a few baskets. Even if the direct results met expectations, the variety of ideas and basic approaches which would more likely come from sponsoring a variety of institutional work, diversified geographically and ideologically, might be lost. And there is increasing evidence of outstanding work, if not yet of critical mass, in new centers. The optimum would be the development of a large number of institutes which would qualify under this criterion, which relates to the problem of training people for good work in this field, to which we turn shortly.

But it is clear that any major new research program in international economics will, in the short run, have to fuse existing talent from different locations in studies of individual issues such as those emphasized in this chapter. Each program could be directed by a single full-time expert in the field, who would assess research needs and develop and coordinate a network of projects relating to the major issue. The individual projects would be undertaken by a variety of university and research institutes, and individual scholars, perhaps in different countries. A model is the energy study now underway for Ford which includes inter alia economic model-building at Harvard and international political studies at Brookings. This third option would seek to influence scholars from different institutions and disciplines to work closely together, and to establish common methodologies and techniques. Such personal interchange among counterparts from several substantive fields would accelerate the development of interdisciplinary capabilities to deal with like issues in the future, as well as deal with the immediate project which brought them together. It would do so on a transnational basis if individual projects were internationalized.

Efforts to link people from different sites into coherent studies face important drawbacks, however. Geographical separation alone reduces the value of the interdisciplinary interchange, no matter how frequently the people get together, which is particularly important in such a new approach. (On the other hand, bringing people together from different parts of a single institution— especially a large university—is not always simple either.) Institutional ties will often continue to weigh heavily and divert participants from their joint endeavors. This approach is thus likely to be less efficient than Option Two, which maximizes neighborhood effects. On the other hand, it is of course susceptible to far wider use in view of the relative paucity of single centers with the requisite resources, and has the merit of opening the research program to broader participation. Of critical importance under either approach is the need for central direction of each project and interdisciplinary interchange at every relevant stage.

As part of the third option, or as a separate program to develop international interdisciplinary research capability in any event, one could create a coordinated placement program which would fund specialists to work on research projects in organizations which specialize in a different but related field and/or are located in another country. (For example, such a program could place economists at ISS or Chatham House, international and domestic scientists at GATT and OECD, and more foreign scholars at Brookings.) Under such a program, the scholars would not be permitted to work on a project in isolation but would have to fit into the overall program of the host institution. Two objectives would be sought: the strengthening and broadening of existing institutes and organizations, and the interdisciplinary and international education of the placed individuals.

Interdisciplinary Training

The second aspect of the interdisciplinary issue, training for the more distant future, adds to the case for relying on existing institutions. The major function of any new Institute of International Political Economics would be research. It would certainly not offer academic degrees and would probably not do any teaching (though it could provide valuable training through research assistantships). Yet we conclude that international economics will deserve priority attention over the longer term, and that increasing capability in the field will be needed from an increasing number of people to fill positions in national (and perhaps subnational) governments, international organizations, multinational (and "purely" national) firms and banks, other transnational groups, the press, and academia itself. Future research certainly needs larger numbers of people who are better trained than at present. So there is an institutional presumption in favor of existing settings which can provide facilities for both research and training.

It is difficult, however, to provide interdisciplinary training even in such settings. There is substantial debate over the time in an individual's career when he should become "interdisciplined." There are two schools of thought. The dominant view argues that a scholar should first firmly establish himself in one field. Then, at the postdoctorate level, he can learn another discipline by accretion. In the field of international political economics, this school feels that a doctorate in traditional economics is needed first. Any dilution of economic training at the early stages of one's education would force him into permanent dilettantism—like the much-abused Foreign Service Officer with no deep knowledge of any field. To support this contention, it is argued that the best interdisciplinary output to date has been produced by individuals firmly rooted in one discipline. Once a scholar establishes himself as an economist, political scientist, sociologist, etc., he can then apply his tools *qua* economist, *qua* political scientist, or *qua* sociologist to problems traditionally examined by other disciplines (e.g., the *economics* of security concerns, the *politics* of international monetary reform).

The opposing school of thought maintains that the near-absence of serious interdisciplinary research is the result of the absence of interdisciplinary training at *any* stage of present careers. The increasing compartmentalization of disciplines renders research more and more irrelevant to policy. The rigidity of university departments forces young scholars to work within the confined framework of their fields to achieve career success. Thus they become coopted exclusively into their limited fields and themselves come to disapprove of interdisciplinary efforts by other scholars—which may explain the predominance of the first school. "Politicizing" economists via bringing them into responsible governmental positions can certainly acquaint them with the political constraints precluding "optimal" economic solutions, but this approach is obviously limited to a relatively few people and, in any event, fails to introduce the techniques of political science analysis. This school concludes that teaching teams should introduce the interdisciplinary aspects of specific issues in undergraduate and graduate curricula, and that students should subsequently be required to apply economic, political, historical, etc., analyses to concrete problems. Many believe that the long-term benefits of such approaches will more than compensate for their initially higher costs.

There are few truly "interdisciplinary" programs today. Some universities and colleges have developed undergraduate interdisciplinary majors, most of which combine several natural sciences (bio-physics) or natural science with social science (environmental management). A few undergraduate "political economy" majors do exist. In these programs, the student typically chooses individual courses from the political science and economics departments. "Multidisciplinary" better describes them, since courses with a truly interdisciplinary flavor are extremely rare. The amount of material to be covered is enormous, so light treatment is given even to key areas. Rigorous study of specific issues is infrequent.

Interdisciplinary programs at the graduate level are administered either by joint departmental programs or by "public policy schools." The joint programs are primarily business-law, economics-law, urban management, and the like. To our knowledge, there exist no joint departmental programs in political economics.

Public policy schools relevant to training in international economics fit into one of two groups: schools of international relations (e.g., Columbia School for International Affairs, Fletcher School of Law and Diplomacy, Georgetown School of Foreign Service, the Graduate Institute of International Studies at Geneva, School for Advanced International Studies at Johns Hopkins) and schools with broader programs which include an international relations component (Kennedy School at Harvard, Maxwell School at Syracuse, Woodrow Wilson

School at Princeton, an undergraduate program at Duke). The purpose of most of these schools is to train students for careers in national governments or international organizations. The programs tend to be concurrent and not truly interdisciplinary in nature. The common complaint is that they fail to integrate, and provide too little of too much. Little attempt is made to train students for basic research, and the schools primarily prepare students to synthesize existing knowledge for policy purposes—an essential function, but one which seldom develops individuals adequately trained to do frontier thinking. All of these schools of course provide training for a variety of public policy fields, not just international economics.

It would seem possible to build on these existing foundations. Two changes are required: more intensive work in at least one of the underlying disciplines, and truly interdisciplinary work at least at the graduate level. Foundations could provide funds for additional professors, the development of new curricula, and doctoral and postdoctoral fellowships on relevant international political-economic research topics. These changes would probably require both additional time and more intensive study by graduate students, but would seem to be feasible—particularly since existing curricula could frequently be cut to make room for more relevant courses.

An alternative approach, which might be more likely to produce people capable of frontier thinking, is postgraduate work in a related discipline for those who have already mastered one discipline. At the extreme, a student could earn consecutive doctorates in two fields. Moving directly from one to another would avoid the onset of rigid mental sets conditioned by the first discipline. The Foreign Service Institute of the Department of State, for example, has turned several generalists (or political scientists) into reasonably good economists from scratch. Physicists and chemists have been responsible for most of the recent breakthroughs in biology, and it might often be especially fruitful to mix two quite different fields. This approach could be especially effective if additional time were then spent to integrate the first and second disciplines.

We conclude that the training question is quite important for the longer run, and that both of the basic approaches—interdisciplinary work from an early stage and consecutive training in more than one discipline—merit close attention. We therefore propose the establishment of a study group comprised of educators and people substantively involved in the various aspects of international economics to follow up these ideas in detail, to assess the best means to a successful interdisciplinary educational program to provide professional competence in international political economics—both for innovative research and for public policy analysis and implementation.

A final institutional issue is the proposal for a new Journal of International Political Economics. No journal today pursues the scholarly interdisciplinary approach which is recommended; some have set out to do so, but largely failed. None focuses on current issues of international economic policy in the same way as, for example, the Brookings Papers on Economic Activity focus on current issues of U.S. economic policy (occasionally including issues of U.S. foreign economic policy). There is no comprehensive vehicle to call the attention of policymakers and interested laymen to the findings of current research, nor to disseminate such findings among the several relevant academic communities. None brings serious work on international economics to the broader audience which now needs deeper understanding of the field. There is thus a case for such a journal, which could pursue any or all of several different courses, perhaps linked to one of the centers which provided a focal point for the new research and/or training effort discussed above. Whether or not a new journal were created, it is desirable to expand the interdisciplinary flow and policy relevance of articles in those which already exist.

Conclusion

The conclusions of this chapter are simple and straightforward. International economic issues have become extremely important for the economies and foreign policies of all countries, including the United States, and are likely to remain so indefinitely. They are especially urgent now, because the international economic order which provided a postwar generation of economic peace has collapsed and we do not know what will take its place. Indeed, the very intellectual foundation of the old order—not just its institutions and specific policies—is under serious attack. Fundamental questions must therefore be answered about the goals of international economic relations in the post-postwar period, and how to go about achieving them.

Twelve specific issues stand out as requiring high priority attention. Some are quite new—the role of labor in international economic relations, the impact of international economics on world politics, the magnitude of energy flows and of the effects of environmental management. Others must be looked at in new ways—the basic theoretical precepts underlying international economic policy, the role of the developing countries in the world economy, East-West economic relations in a world of détente rather than Cold War, the management of the international economic structure in a world of three major power centers. Some are not new, but remain central to the construction of a new economic order and still pose a variety of critical unanswered questions—international monetary relations, trade, investment, and the coordination of national economic policies.

All of these issues are profoundly political, at both the national and international levels, as well as economically complex. Most relate at least partly to each other, and one suspects that progress is needed on each to maximize progress on all. Some require new theoretical breakthroughs, most call for intensive empirical examination, all require new policy thinking. At the same time, resources of the highest quality must be devoted to looking at the broad overall picture within which each of the individual issues exists.

New research strategies are needed to answer these questions. Truly interdisciplinary work is crucial to their success. Researchers need to be induced to come together, both within existing institutions and from disparate locales, or perhaps a new institution should be created. New training programs need to be started to build greater capacity to deal with these problems over the longer haul.

The problems have three separate time dimensions. In the short run, new crises—far worse in their real impact than the monetary runs which have already occurred so often—could severely disrupt the world economy and international politics. They are particularly likely until a new system is constructed to replace the Bretton Woods and GATT regimes, which have collapsed. Such restructuring will take considerable time. In the meanwhile, individual problems will be approached ad hoc, within a framework of overall uncertainty. A new outburst of massive monetary speculation or a major step toward protectionism by a sizable country could trigger a spiral of new deterioration in economic relations among nations. Concerted, cooperative efforts will be needed to avoid breakdown while construction of a new order is taking place.

For the medium term, the task is to construct a new system. Reform of the world monetary system has begun, and commitments have been made to begin on trade in 1973. But neither process is assured of success. Indeed, there is real chance of failure. And countries have yet to even approach the negotiating table on other key issues. At best, the process seems likely to take most of this decade.

For the longer term, new and more intense forms of international economic cooperation will be needed. No new system is likely to provide the stability of the past orders, based on a quasi-automatic "gold standard" among countries with like aims, under the clear leadership of the United Kingdom for many years, or a Bretton Woods regime operating under the security and economic umbrella of the United States. The hierarchy among nations is now uncertain and the goals of the major (and many lesser) countries often conflict, at least in the short run. The internal problems which are now the focus of priority attention in each major country may persist far into the future. For both international and domestic reasons, it is likely that the preservation of any new economic order will thus require far more attention in the years ahead than it has received in the past, if somewhat less than is needed in the immediate future as the new order is being built.

This scenario has clear implications for a research program on the future of the international economic order. Perhaps the inauguration of a major new effort could marginally help to avert serious breakdown in the short run, by highlighting the importance of the issues and the need to learn more before some of them can be resolved with confidence. However, the world will have to rely essentially on the existing intellectual foundation as a basis for policy in the immediate future.

If the construction of the new order will take the rest of the decade, as argued above, then new work promptly begun could make an important contribution to that process. Indeed, new work is needed to provide direction for part of the new construction, especially in the monetary, trade, investment and systemic management (and perhaps energy) areas. In addition, much effort is needed on some of the central intellectual underpinnings and politically most important aspects of that construction, such as the basic theory of international economics (are free trade and free capital movements desirable today?) and the international role of labor. Some of the crucial gaps in present understanding, which often derive from failures to integrate domestic and international considerations, and political and economic factors, must be filled in this process.

The critical importance of constructing the new system suggests high potential payoff from a major research push launched promptly and lasting for the next three to five years. Realization of the potential would depend, however, on finding sufficient human and financial resources to undertake a research program with the new (especially interdisciplinary) specifications called for here, and translating the results quickly into policy, neither of which is a trivial task. Rapid payoff is of course more likely in those areas where the basic need is for direct policy research, and empirical investigation of existing concepts, rather than fundamentally new theory.

Any big push might not have to be maintained beyond a period of five years or so, although that possibility cannot be ruled out since the problems could deepen and systemic reconstruction take even longer. In any event, the outlook for ongoing difficulties, the full flowering of some issues we can now foresee— East-West economic relations, North-South relations, environmental factors—and the emergence of new issues will require a greater focus on international economic issues throughout the indefinite future than they have received heretofore. The long-term equilibrium level for research in this field is likely to call for an effort well above the present, if below the big-push level which is needed in the years immediately ahead, and training programs to supply that long-term need should start soon.

Research strategies over all three of these time horizons must be based on the fundamental changes in the world economy outlined in this chapter. A new era is clearly being entered, in terms of the scope and depth of international transactions and the international power structure on which they rest—and which they increasingly help construct. New policies are needed to govern these transactions, and new intellectual breakthroughs are needed in several areas to provide a basis for such policies. Both governments and private sectors through-out the world are groping for new approaches. The time appears ripe for a major effort, if the problems can be adequately defined and strategies devised for seeking answers to them.

It is widely hoped that the world now faces a generation of peace. At the same time, however, the world faces a grave risk of the breakdown of a generation of economic peace. That peace began eroding after 1967, when international economic cooperation reached its zenith with the completion of the Kennedy Round to liberalize world trade and the Rio agreement to create Special Drawing Rights to start the reform of the international monetary system. Within a few months of those historic achievements, the devaluation of sterling presaged the end of the fixed-rate system of Bretton Woods; the institution of the two-tier gold system effectively took gold out of the monetary system and put the world on a largely inconvertible dollar standard, which became a wholly inconvertible dollar standard in 1971; and protectionist pressures began their renewed ascent. The U.S. actions of August 1971 signalled the final collapse of the postwar systems.

The two trends—toward military peace and away from economic peace—are closely related. The removal of the security blanket from economic relations, as a result of the thawing of the Cold War, makes possible the emergence of real commercial conflicts within alliance structures both East and West. And military peace could prove elusive in the absence of a restoration of economic peace. The issues covered in this report thus touch far more than GNP. We urge early and active pursuit of its principal recommendations.

Notes

1. Harry G. Johnson, "Comparative Cost and Commercial Policy Theory for a Developing World Economy," Wicksell Lectures 1968 (Stockholm: Almquist and Wicksell, 1968), p. 10.

2. Arnold C. Harberger, "International Economics," in Nancy D. Ruggles (ed.), *Economics* (Englewood Cliffs, N.J.: Prentice-Hall, 1970), p. 163.

3. Paul Samuelson, "Heretical Doubts About the International Mechanisms," *Journal of International Economics* 2, 4 (September 1972), p. 450.

4. Richard N. Cooper, *The Economics of Interdependence* (New York: McGraw-Hill, Inc., for the Council on Foreign Relations, 1968), *passim.*

5. C. Fred Bergsten, *The International Roles of the Dollar and US International Monetary Policy* (New York: Praeger Publishers, for the Council on Foreign Relations, forthcoming 1973), Chapter 1.

6. For a myriad of examples see Lester R. Brown, *World Without Borders* (New York: Random House, 1972), esp. Chapter 10.

7. In his short survey of the field in 1970, Harberger, "International Economics," p. 169, concluded that "It is quite possible that a theory of international economic policy will emerge . . . "

8. Harberger, "International Economics," p. 170.

2

Research on Internal Adjustment
to External Disturbances:
A European View

Assar Lindbeck
Stockholm School of Economics

Introduction

The issue of "internal adjustments to external disturbances" is extremely broad. In general, it will be interpreted here as the behavior of the economy and the role of economic policy after exposure to disturbances emerging in other countries or on the world market. As to the choice of problems, the discussion will deal both with changes in the internal economy under a given domestic economic policy, and with changes in the policy itself for the purpose of dealing with disturbances emanating from abroad. From the point of view of methods of analysis we shall deal both with changes in the (hypothetical or factual) equilibrium position, as usually defined, and with the dynamic adjustments outside such an equilibrium situation—where most policy problems may exist.

Older literature in this field, especially prior to the mid-1930s, emphasized "automatic" adjustments, i.e., adjustments without (much) deliberate discretionary change in economic policy. This holds both for analyses of the adjustment mechanism of the balance of payments, as formulated by the theory of the gold standard, and for adjustments in domestic economic variables, as in older unemployment theory. In both cases, "automatic" (endogenous) fluctuations in prices and wages, and in the somewhat more recent literature also in output and employment, were then at the center of the analysis of adjustments. In reality, the adjustments were, of course, never completely "automatic." Some discretionary policies, such as tariff policy to protect the balance of payments, domestic production, employment and incomes of various groups and classes in society, took place in most countries. Interest rate policy was also developed quite early, in many countries at the end of the nineteenth century, to influence short-term capital for the purpose of limiting the necessity for rapid short-run adjustments in the real sectors of the domestic economy.

The adjustment problems have to a large extent changed character during the last decades, due to a number of new developments. It may be useful, as a general background, to try to pinpoint some of these developments. They will be classified under two headings: (1) increased importance of domestic policy targets, and (2) changes in types and importance of external disturbances.

Several of the traditional mechanisms of adjustment to external disturbances are now regarded as politically less feasible because they interfere with domestic policy objectives concerning employment, output, income distribution, and prices. This means that new policy tools have to be developed to reconcile equilibrium in the balance of payments with today's rather ambitious domestic policy targets. The development towards ambitious domestic policy targets has obviously been particularly rapid since the mid-thirties and early forties, in connection with the Keynesian revolution and the new political emphasis on full employment. Domestic policy targets (except possibly the price level target) during the last decade have become both more ambitious and more disaggregated. For instance, the target of full employment increasingly refers not only to the economy as a whole, but to specific regions, branches and subsets of the labor force such as married women, handicapped, ethnic minority groups, the young, the very old, etc. This means in fact an increase in the number of policy targets, which both makes it necessary to develop new instruments and increases the risk of conflicts of goals in economic policy. A first obvious research topic might therefore be:

Topic 1: To study empirically the changes during recent years (or decades) in domestic economic policy targets and instruments in various countries. The study should cover how sets of targets and instruments have changed, how priorities have shifted among them, and how values often are now attached also to some policy instruments, implying that some instruments have in fact become targets.

For instance, it seems to have been a tendency in many countries in recent years to pay ever increasing attention to the security of the individual, and to resist new income gaps between groups of income earners, e.g., people living in different regions. It might also be interesting to study how the targets of politicians are influenced by the performance of the economy, and by the achievements and failures of policy itself.

Another development that has influenced the general conditions of internal adjustments is the change in frequency, character, and size of external disturbances. If we compare the postwar period with the prewar period, to begin with, it is probably safe to argue that the size of short-term external disturbances, i.e., disturbances relevant for stabilization policy, has fallen dramatically due to the reduced amplitude of the international business cycle. This probably also means that short-term disturbances of the distribution of income and the domestic allocation of resources are much smaller today than they were before the Second World War.

However, there is evidence that international disturbances have tended to increase again during the very last decade, due to the continuously increased internationalization of national economies, and thereby produced increased interdependence between the economies of various countries. This process shows up both in the internationalization of markets—for commodities, factors, and credit—and in the increasingly international character of market-oriented institutions, such as production firms, credit institutes, travel agencies, marketing and consulting firms, etc.

Some of the driving forces behind this process are fairly well known: a fall in the costs of transportation and information over large distances due to technological developments; increased demand for heterogeneous products, which stimulates intrasector trade; increased returns to scale in some sectors, forcing small countries in particular to increase their specialization; trade liberalization; the emergence of competitive export sectors for manufacturing products in a number of LDCs and "semi-developed" countries; etc. However, additional research about these issues would no doubt be of great interest. This leads to a second research topic:

Topic 2: To study theoretically and empirically the substance and importance of the economic internationalization process of the national economies. How does the process manifest itself? How far has it gone in various fields and in different countries? What are the "causes," or driving forces and mechanism, behind the process?

However, at the same time as the domestic economies are becoming increasingly internationalized, economic policy continues to be conducted mainly on a national level: the geographic domain of firms coincides less and less with the geographical "preserve" of the national governments, resulting in obvious difficulties for any national economic policy. Many new tendencies in economic policy in recent years may fruitfully be seen in this perspective. It is probably too much to talk about a "death-struggle" of the national state, but we are no doubt entitled to look at some of the new tendencies in national economic policies, some of them to be mentioned below, as a "defense mechanism" against increased external dependence. This leads us directly to the policy problems related to adjustments to external disturbances.

It is very difficult to organize such a discussion in a systematic and nonrepetitive way. In this chapter the analysis will be organized around a traditional classification of economic policies into its three "branches": stabilization policy, allocation policy (including growth policy), and distribution policy. (Alternatively the analyses could, for instance, have been organized in terms of the policy instruments rather than broad policy targets.)

Stabilization Policy

Recent theoretical literature on stabilization policy for open economies seems to have dealt mainly with four related issues:

1. the possibilities of reaching internal policy targets in an internationalized domestic economic system;
2. the conflict between internal and external balance (with Robert Mundell as one of the pioneers);

3. the relative efficiency of monetary and fiscal policy in the context of different exchange rate systems (with Marcus Fleming as one of the pioneers); and

4. the interdependence between stabilization policy in different countries (with Harry Johnson and Richard Cooper as two of the pioneers).

More theoretical and empirical work along these and similar lines are not only worthwhile but crucial for economic policy. For instance:

Topic 3: Problems related to stock-flow adjustments are extremely important to clarify; they are still not very well worked out in the literature, in spite of important recent efforts. The issue includes relations between portfolio adjustments for various types of (domestic and foreign) assets and flows of capital, commodities, and factors of production.

It would also be important to have:

Topic 4: More empirical studies on the time-lags in the adjustment process of strategic variables, in particular the time-path of the effects of various policy instruments on the balance of payments and various domestic economic variables, such as output, employment, wages, and prices.

For a deeper understanding of adjustment problems in the field of stabilization policy, it is also important to specify and penetrate:

Topic 5: The various mechanisms by which economic fluctuations in the domestic economy—of volumes as well as prices—are related to developments on the world market by way of, for instance: (1) a "direct" price influence from abroad; (2) internationally generated fluctuations in export (and possibly import) volumes; (3) external disturbances transmitted by way of profits in exporting and import-competing firms; (4) influences on the domestic economy by way of monetary and financial markets; (5) international flows of labor in response to cyclical fluctuations in unemployment and wages.

Many of these mechanisms have been highlighted by recent work on macroeconomic models (for instance in connection with "Project LINK").

The size and importance of the first three mechanisms depends presumably not only on the share of foreign trade in total GNP, but also on the share of foreign trade in certain "strategic" sectors such as manufacturing. The importance of the fourth and fifth factors depends inter alia on the freedom and institutional organization of cross-country movements of capital and labor, and might be measured by variables such as the interest rate elasticity of capital movements and the sensitivity of international labor mobility to differences in wages and unemployment between countries. Some specific issues worth studying in this context are:

Topic 6: To what extent are the amplitude and timing of business fluctuations synchronized between countries and branches? For instance, do we find systematic lead and lag patterns between branches so that, for instance, fluctuations in raw materials lead to fluctuations in intermediary products and finished goods—with implications for the lead and lag pattern between countries as well?

Of even greater importance, from the point of view of the problem dealt with in the present chapter, is the implications of the various external disturbances for stabilization policy in various countries. It may be useful here to distinguish between two closely related aspects of the problem: (1) What are the possibilities for the national authorities in an individual country to choose targets independently of the outside world; and (2) How great is the national autonomy of various policy instruments? The answer to the first question depends, of course, to a large extent on the answer to the second. These questions lead naturally to a third question: (3) What can be gained by international cooperation and integration of stabilization policies?

The limitations on national autonomy for the targets of stabilization policy are perhaps most clearly seen in the case of inflation. Here it is, of course, necessary to distinguish between alternative exchange rate systems. It is obvious that price stability is, in general, impossible in an open economy with fixed exchange rates. This is most easily understood if international prices are rising. However, the difficulties exist even if world market prices for exported and imported commodities are constant, as long as the rate or productivity increase is more rapid in the commodity-producing sectors than in the service sector (as emphasized for instance by the Norwegian Aukrust model). If wage rates in the economy as a whole tend to follow the rate of productivity increase in the commodity-producing sectors (mainly manufacturing), production costs in the service sector will tend to rise continuously at the same time as prices in the commodity-producing sector follow the international price trend. Only continuous revaluations, implying falling domestic prices for commodities, could solve the problem of price stability in this case. However, then there is the obvious complication that the balance of payments situation may not call for revaluation. Domestic pressure groups may also successfully prevent revaluations for a long time, as suggested by the West German and Japanese experiences.

This type of "structural inflation" for open economies presupposes, of course, a certain type of domestic demand management policy, by monetary and fiscal tools, so that the aggregate demand curve (in money terms) shifts (to the right) *pari passu* with increased supply costs. In fact, full-employment guarantees will usually make such a "passive" (accommodating) monetary-fiscal policy quite likely. Moreover, balance-of-payments surpluses for countries with a tendency to a smaller rate of price increase than the outside world will tend to create financial and monetary situations that will not only "accommodate" cost impulses from abroad, but also create domestic excess demand in markets for securities, commodities, services, and labor—with tendencies to a rather classical form of domestic demand-inflation (the West German case).

As models of "structural inflation" and monetary models of inflation tend to live rather separate lives, an obvious and important research project is:

Topic 7: To combine "structuralist" and monetarist models of inflation for open economies by showing the interdependence between the markets for money, credit, commodities, services, and labor, considering the influence on domestic prices of international price changes and the different rates of productivity increase in various sectors.

As the international price trend is usually taken as given in analyses of national economies, it is also quite important:

Topic 8: To explain the price trend on the world market—"world inflation." How is inflation on international markets related to inflation within individual countries?

The fact that price stability is usually impossible to achieve at fixed exchange rates does not, of course, mean that other types of exchange rate systems are easy to reconcile with price stability. For instance, even if freely fluctuating exchange rates would help to reduce the inflationary tendencies in countries with a tendency (*ex ante*) to balance-of-payments surpluses (and hence market-induced revaluations) in booms, such a system will tend to accentuate the inflationary tendencies for countries with tendencies (*ex ante*) to balance-of-payments deficits (and hence market-induced depreciations) in boom periods. It would therefore be of interest to penetrate further:

Topic 9: During what conditions do freely fluctuating exchange rates, or frequent discretionary exchange rate changes, help to fight inflation and for which types of countries would these conditions be expected to hold? This is, of course, an application of stabilization policy to the problem of "optimum currency areas."

A very difficult problem in this context is how the behavior of politicians and leaders of important organizations are influenced by alternative exchange rate systems. Here "pure" economic theory does not provide any answers. This is unfortunate, as a rational choice among exchange rate systems can hardly be made without some assumptions about the behavior of these very groups of people. For instance, does a system of fixed exchange rates limit inflation-generating demands by union leaders and politicians because of fears of unemployment, balance-of-payments crises, and discretionary devaluations? Or are these groups of people more "disciplined" by automatic, market-induced depreciations of the exchange rate in systems with freely fluctuating exchange rates? Moreover, are there "ratchet effects" of fluctuating exchange rates, due to price inflexibility downwards in our present economies (as suggested by, for instance, Robert Triffin)?

Topic 10: In spite of the difficulties in answering these questions—or maybe because of these very difficulties—empirical research that sheds some light on the economic policy behavior of politicians and leaders of organizations in various countries is extremely important.

The difficulties of realizing domestic employment targets are partly of a different character. It is obvious that short-term economic fluctuations in output and employment in most developed countries are closely connected with fluctuations in international demand for their exports. The policies in various countries to counteract the disturbances created by these fluctuations take quite varied forms. For instance, they may be designed (1) to reduce directly the fluctuations in exports themselves (e.g., by way of taxes of subsidies on exports); (2) to reduce the output effects of fluctuations in exports (e.g., by methods such as tax subsidy policies that stimulate firms to accumulate, or decumulate, inventories of export products in the opposite direction to the fluctuations in export deliveries); (3) to limit the employment effects in the export sector caused by fluctuations in output (e.g., to stimulate "hoarding" of labor within firms, for instance by way of increased repair and maintenance work in the export firms). Or the policy might try (4) to "compensate" for the fluctuations in output and employment in the export sector by countercyclical fluctuations in the sectors that produce for the domestic markets (private or public consumption, and private or public investment).

If the authorities choose this last strategy, to "compensate" for the fluctuations in exports by countercyclical movements in demand, output, and employment in other sectors, there are some serious problems about the costs and disutilities connected with movements of factors of production from the export sector to other sectors and back again later on. Such a policy might concentrate on "demand management" or "supply management," including attempts to increase the mobility of factors of production. There will arise a number of important consequences for the allocation of resources in all these cases, in particular if the policy becomes very selective for regions, branches, and even by discriminating between individual firms. These allocation problems are both national (domestic) problems and problems about the international allocation of resources. The costs and disadvantages of using such tools for internal adjustment then have to be compared with the costs of alternative ways of bringing about adjustments in the balance of payments, for instance capital imports and domestic cutbacks in aggregate demand. For instance, in a country with a marginal propensity to import of 0.25, the reduction necessary in domestic aggregate demand to reduce imports by 1 percent of GNP is, schematically speaking, 4 percent of GNP, neglecting other types of adjustments. Several important research topics are suggested by these problems:

Topic 11: To analyze theoretically and empirically the effects of different policy instruments, including "new" instruments, designed to limit fluctuations in sales, output, and employment in the export sector caused by international fluctuations in export demand.

Topics 12: To study the effects of policy instruments designed to influence demand, output, and employment in *other* sectors of the economy for the purpose of compensating for fluctuations in the export sector. Such policies might be more or less general or selective (for branches, regions, and individual firms).

Topic 13: To analyze the effects of policy instruments designed to increase the mobility of factors of production such as retraining, compensations for costs connected with labor mobility, improved information on work and general improvement of the functioning of factor markets in general including problems related to factor price flexibility. Benefit-cost studies of the advantages and disadvantages of such policies—from the point of view of the individual, a nation, a large region of countries, etc.—would be desirable.

Topic 14: One important problem is to find methods other than exchange rates and tariffs which differentiate the effects between the domestic economy and the external markets. For instance, perhaps taxes could be used more systematically both to influence commodity flows and capital movements.

An example of tools which may be used during recessions to limit unemployment is the payment of temporary subsidies on the use of labor, or possibly on marginal use of labor, if governments want to avoid strong income redistribution in favor of profits. For instance, it is possible to pay high subsidies to the marginal labor force in firms, defined for instance as labor in excess of 95 percent of employment some (specified) time ago. Thus it is important to study the consequences of varying degrees of selectivity in stabilization policy.

Two increasingly important aspects of short-term stabilization policy are (1) to what extent certain instruments are no longer effective on a national level, and (2) to what extent different types of policies used by national states in stabilization policy disturb other countries. One type of "disturbance" occurs if a country does not pursue a deliberate stabilization policy, as business fluctuations in one country then tend to spread to other countries. A more complicated problem is that certain instruments disturb other countries considerably: tariffs, subsidies, interest rate changes, exchange rate variations, etc. It is a delicate issue to determine when the effects created by using specific instruments in stabilization policy is more or less "disturbing" for other countries than would be "undisturbed" business fluctuations. We can also see that many of the instruments that disturb other countries are not always very effective for domestic stabilization policy because of international interdependence. All this suggests a number of important research topics:

Topic 15: Analysis of the effects on other countries of changes in certain policy instruments by one country, and investigations of whether "new" policy instruments with smaller disturbances on other countries can be developed.

Topic 16: A related important issue is to study what might be gained in domestic stabilization policy by intercountry coordination of policy decisions. (Richard Cooper and others have already made interesting attempts to penetrate these issues.)

Topic 17: How great is the national autonomy of various policy targets and policy instruments? In a general sense this topic, as well as topics 15 and 16, is in fact an application to a rather general theory of optimum decision-making in interdependent systems, in particular to the theory of the possibilities and consequences of decentralization in interdependent systems.

We shall come back to these problems about intercountry disturbances in connection with the discussion of allocation and distribution policies. Finally:

Topic 18: One important problem is whether there are reasons to "prefer" public intervention on the capital accounts to intervention on the trade account. We can presumably only hope for some systematization of the pros and cons on this issue.

Allocation Policy

International disturbances of national economies also affect resources allocation and hence the rate and character of structural change. It is often alleged that the increased openness of domestic economies during the recent decade—partly the effects of trade liberalization and the increased competition from a number of LDCs—has increased the frequency and size of both short-term and long-term disturbances of the allocation of resources of national economies, and brought about important changes in trade patterns. This would then show up inter alia (1) as an acceleration in the rate of change in comparative advantage between countries; (2) in a tendency to a more rapid rate of structural change; (3) in more structural and frictional unemployment; and (4) hence also in higher total costs and/or disutilities of adjustments. It would therefore be of great importance to study inter alia the following problems:

Topic 19: Has there, in fact, been a tendency to more rapid changes in comparative advantage, structural change, structural and frictional unemployment, and higher costs and disutilities of adjustment? If so, to what extent are these developments connected with "international disturbances," and to what extent are they more directly connected with technological development and related changes in returns to scale and changed comparative advantages? Are there any methods to compare the costs and welfare losses connected with the dynamic adjustments and the static reallocation gains? If so, it would be interesting to apply such methods empirically to various countries.

As in the case of stabilization policy, it would also be of great interest to study methods to reduce the costs and disutilities connected with these adjustments: demand management, cost management, mobility policy, etc. This brings us to the fields of manpower policy, industrial policy, trade policy, and general problems of protectionism. Several important research problems are then raised, for instance:

Topic 20: Theoretical and empirical studies of factors changing the international allocation of production, and the likely consequences thereof in the future for trade patterns among nations, as well as the requirements for reallocation of resources within different countries induced by these international developments.

One possible policy strategy towards internationally generated disturbances in the domestic allocation of resources is (1) to facilitate the reallocations rather than trying (2) to stop them, or alternatively (3) to create new comparative advantages. By improving factor mobility and by reducing the costs and disutilities connected with reallocations, it is likely that protectionist policies can be limited. This strategy suggests the following research topic:

Topic 21: The possibilities of reducing the social costs and disutilities of domestic reallocations in response to changes in comparative advantages and trade patterns.

The costs and benefits from adjustment policies—such as retraining and other manpower policies—will most likely differ dramatically depending on circumstances. For instance, in certain cases, a newly trained person might simply be more efficient without many other effects on the economy. In other situations he might push somebody else out of employment. In some cases, retraining might remove bottlenecks with very strong secondary effects on the efficiency of the economy as a result. Empirical studies of these problems can draw on the experiences of a number of countries. There have also been a number of institutional reforms in this field in recent years such as the European Social Fund, the special adjustment assistance provisions in the U.S. Trade Expansion Act, and similar legislation in Japan. There is also a tendency to "three-party" councils—with capital, labor, and government represented—to deal with these issues.

A bridge to stabilization policy problems is provided by the possibility of concentrating retraining programs in periods of slack in the economy, when the macro-economic costs of retraining are particularly low. In the U.S., the government has in fact declared itself an advocate of a system where increases in appropriations for manpower training are automatically triggered when unemployment reaches a certain level. And in some countries, such as Sweden, retraining is sharply increased during recessions.

Another strategy would be to stop, or slow down, the reallocations—what might be called "defensive actions." These are basically designed to protect declining sectors against foreign competition and deteriorations of comparative advantages in general. The most far-reaching actions in actual policy are probably to be found in sectors such as agriculture, coal, and several labor-intensive sectors, such as textiles, where a number of LDCs are getting improved comparative advantages. The various techniques used are still not well documented or systematically analyzed. Thus, an important research topic might be:

Topic 22: The role of import regulations, tariffs, subsidies, credit priorities, "voluntary" agreements on import limitations, discriminatory public purchases, etc., in various countries for the purpose of avoiding or slowing down contractions of sectors with falling comparative advantages. The effects on world allocation of resources, and on the trade patterns of these "defensive" and often in fact protectionist actions, should be considered.

A third type of action might be called "offensive." It is often found in "new" research-heavy and "prestigious" sectors, such as the aircraft, space, atomic energy, data, electronic, and petrochemical industries. The arguments, and possibly also the motives, are usually of the infant-industry type. An important research topic might therefore be:

Topic 23: Studies of the use of "offensive actions" in industrial policies, such as subsidies of research and development, and various types of subsidies and credit priorities of the "infant industry" type.

It would also be interesting to have more research on the effects of both defensive and offensive actions as compared to conventional protectionism, i.e.:

Topic 24: Comparisons of, on the one hand, the antiprotectionist effects of the reduction in tariffs and, on the other hand, the new protectionist (or "mercantilist") policies which in recent years have replaced conventional protectionism: discriminatory government purchases, protectionist use of product standards, selective subsidies of exports and production, and various other types of nontariff barriers.

From the point of view of actual policy, it would also be interesting to discuss whether some common international rules of conduct—in the case of both defensive and offensive adjustment policies—could be established. For instance, should individual countries be allowed to establish their own targets irrespective of the outside world (for instance, a certain size of the agricultural or shipbuilding sector)? And if such national targets are formulated, should individual countries be allowed to use any instruments they may choose, or should certain types of internal policy instruments be ruled out in the same way as certain trade policy instruments—such as tariffs, import controls, and, to some extent, exchange-rate changes—have been (partly) ruled out by international agreements?

For instance, such rules of conduct might say that general subsidies of labor costs in underdeveloped regions, as well as fees (taxes) on activities disturbing the environment, are allowed, whereas measures such as discrimination against foreign enterprises in the case of government purchases, selective subsidies of investments in environmental protection, and strongly selective subsidies of specific firms and selective branches would be allowed only if certain well-defined conditions are fulfilled. The EEC has in fact in recent years shown an increasing interest and activity in this field. All this suggests an important research topic:

Topic 25: Studies of alternative rules of conduct in the field of domestic allocation policies, to limit the risks of severe disturbances to international competition and trade patterns by the emergence of a strong new protectionism.

Income Distribution Policy

Short-term and long-term changes in the distribution of income occur as a result of a great number of external disturbances: changes in international trade patterns, exchange-rate changes, short-term international business fluctuations, etc. It is therefore quite natural that many internal policy actions have been undertaken to counteract such effects. In fact, much so-called "adjustment assistance" in a number of countries has been implemented largely for distributional reasons since it is regarded as unfair to let special groups of individuals experience hardships for reasons these groups can never control themselves: cyclical fluctuations, changes in trade patterns, and general changes in comparative advantage because of external factors, technological changes, or shifts in consumer preferences. As the reallocations which cause these hardships often imply increases in GNP, the "gainers" of the reallocations should be able quite easily to "afford" compensation to those who suffer from the process by having to shift profession, to move or even to leave the labor force. Several interesting research topics are suggested by these experiences:

Topic 26: Studies of how the tariff structure and other protectionist devices in various countries influence the distribution of income within countries—an application of inter alia the Stolper-Samuelson theorem. In other words, are tariffs in general implemented on labor-intensive (or capital-intensive) products— implying that labor (or capital) is helped in terms of the distribution of income? It might also be fruitful to see the tariff structure in relation both to types of disturbances and to the "power structure" in various countries.

In view of the "nondesirable" effects of tariffs, another interesting research topic is:

Topic 27: Studies of alternatives to tariffs for achieving income compensations to domestic groups that are being hit by changed trade patterns, exchange-rate changes, changes in terms-of-trade, etc. Examples of such instruments are social transfer payments, labor training programs, etc.

All this raises the whole issue of the possibilities for influencing the distribution of income and wealth by deliberate policy actions: (1) investment in human capital; (2) progressive taxation; (3) redistribution of wealth; (4) price regulation; (5) transfer payments and social security systems; (6) collective consumption, etc. However, all of these approaches raise problems which go far beyond the problem of internal adjustments to external disturbances.

Research topics about domestic income distribution policies, to cope with the effects of external disturbances, can of course be divided into a number of subproblems for different sectors, regions, and types of employees as well as different types of policy instruments. Only a few examples will be mentioned here:

Topic 28: The domestic effects of agricultural protection, mainly in Europe. This is a "classical" field where internal measures have been taken to protect the domestic distribution of income from external disturbances. What are the effects on the distribution of income within countries of the present form of agriculture tariffs as compared to alternative techniques to protect the incomes of farmers, such as "deficiency payments" in systems when international agriculture prices are accepted on national markets?

Topic 29: The effects of such protection on exports and revenues for potential exporters of agriculture products, such as the U.S., Canada, Australia, New Zealand, and a number of LDCs. There are already a number of partial estimates, for instance for sugar.

Topic 30: The effects of agricultural protection on the domestic allocation of resources, on the international allocation of resources, and hence on the international trade pattern.

Topic 31: The possibilities of developing policy instruments that protect incomes of the individuals in agriculture without necessarily introducing protection of production in the sector: transfer payments, retraining, etc.

Topic 32: Methods to increase the efficiency of declining sectors—in the case of agriculture by amalgamation of farms, professional training, agricultural credit, etc.

Topic 33: Methods to increase the income of, and the income-earning capacity for, specific types of people in sectors hard hit by international competition. It is clear that quite different types of measures are relevant for different types of people: elderly people (pensions or subsidies during their lifetime), younger people (training in the old profession for those who are expected to stay, retraining for other professions for those who are expected to move to other sectors), etc. Similar types of projects would be relevant for other sectors of the economy with dramatically increased international competition, such as coal, textiles, etc.

An extremely important field of research, finally, is:

Topic 34: Cost-benefit studies of the costs and returns of alternative adjustment policies to protect incomes of people in declining sectors, particularly of the two main alternatives: to subsidize people to stay, and to subsidize them to move.

As many new developments in economic policy in recent years seem to have been caused by regional problems within countries, it is also important:

Topic 35: To study empirically regional differences in income and employment within countries, and alternative methods to reduce such differences, with a minimum of "disturbances" to the optimum international allocation of resources and trade patterns.

How much the ambitions in adjustment assistance have increased during the last decades can quite dramatically be illustrated by experiences from agriculture. During the last one hundred years, the labor force in agriculture in the developed countries has fallen from approximately 70-80 percent of the total labor force to the present level of 3-20 percent. Not many attempts were made during this long and dramatic process to assist those who had to carry the main burden of adjustment. Now, when a much less dramatic reduction is expected to take place, with much better employment opportunities in other sectors, great concern is expressed in the political discussion about the adjustment problems— even in countries where the agricultural population is already down to about 5 percent of the labor force. This is hardly a paradox: it is only in a generally rich society, where only small groups of people have to take the adjustment inconveniences, that compensation from other groups is possible to bring about. These circumstances have also made research about internal adjustment policies a central issue for economic and social research.

General Problems About Disturbances

A number of specific external disturbances, and policies to counteract them, have been discussed in this chapter. The discussion raises some general questions about what is really meant by "a disturbance" and which criteria should be used to distinguish between disturbances that should be counteracted and which should be "accepted." For instance, in the case of changes in the balance of payments and the reserve position of a country, it is quite clear that the direction of the disturbance is regarded as important by governments. For instance, a reduction in reserves is obviously regarded as a kind of disturbance that requires more counteraction than an increase in reserves. Similarly, disturbances on trade accounts are interpreted differently than disturbances on capital accounts. Intervention on these two accounts is also evaluated very differently in different countries. (In the U.S., direct regulations on the capital accounts seem to be regarded as less acceptable than regulations on the trade accounts—and the reverse preferences seem to prevail in most countries in Western Europe.)

Similar problems about what disturbances require counteracting policy measures exist in the context of the allocation of resources and the distribution of income. For instance, why should some external disturbances of the domestic allocation of resources be accepted but others counteracted? Should "temporary" disturbances be counteracted and "permanent" disturbances (trends) accepted? What are then the criteria for regarding one disturbance as temporary and another as permanent? Similar problems exist for disturbances of the distribution of income. Why are certain types of changes in the income relations regarded as acceptable, or "natural," whereas others are regarded as "undesirable" and calling for counteractions? All these problems indicate a final research project:

Topic 36: To study different types of disturbances to the domestic economy, to discuss criteria for interventions, and to study empirically what types of disturbances governments seem to worry about, and not worry about, respectively.

3 Research on Internal Adjustment to External Economic Disturbances: An American View

Robert M. Stern
University of Michigan

Introduction

This chapter focuses on the adjustments that nations may make in response to external economic disturbances. We begin in the first section with a general typology of disturbances that is meant to demonstrate their diversity and the difficulty of distinguishing them as to source because of the many interactions present. After noting the objectives of adjustment, we then examine in the next four sections the ways in which nations may adjust to disturbances that are manifested via the balance of payments, changes in comparative advantage and trade policies, the operations of multinational corporations, changes in East-West trade and investment relations, and externalities. In each instance, we offer a brief assessment of the state of current thinking and the questions that may require additional research. Finally, in the sixth section, we offer by way of summary an agenda for research on the issues treated in the preceding sections.

Types of Disturbances and Objectives of Adjustment

It may be fruitful to begin by characterizing the various kinds of disturbances that countries face and to which they must adjust. The following typology of disturbances is suggested by Bhagwati's work (1964, pp. 56-57; 1971) on domestic distortions:

1. Market disturbances
   a. Behavioral disturbances
   b. Technological disturbances
2. State-imposed disturbances
   a. Autonomous
   b. Instrumental

I am indebted to Alan V. Deardorff, Gary Saxonhouse, Charles Staelin, and members of the Research Seminar in International Economics at the University of Michigan for their helpful suggestions and their comments on an earlier draft of this chapter.

By market disturbances, we have in mind such things as changes in prices, income, and employment that are the consequence of private market forces.[a] Behavioral disturbances involve changes in consumer and producer behavior due to a shift in underlying parameters. Changes in consumer tastes or in attitudes towards work would be considered behavioral disturbances. In addition, we could include here changes in market imperfections that imply nonmaximizing behavior, as when there are factor-market imperfections or when firms are imperfectly competitive. Technological disturbances refer to such phenomena as the realization of increasing returns, the occurrence of externalities, and changes in factor productivity.

State-imposed disturbances can arise when government policies instituted in the past for some given purpose turn out to have effects that may not have been intended. Examples here include tariffs and nontariff barriers imposed originally to accomplish some objective that has since receded in importance. These autonomous state-imposed disturbances can be distinguished from the instrumental variety that stem from changes in government policy in response to the desire to accomplish certain economic or noneconomic objectives.

Market and state-imposed disturbances do not of course exist in isolation. That is, the government will respond to market disturbances in the light of its various objectives. And similarly, consumer and producer units will respond to changes in government policy. Thus, there are important interactions that must be taken into account. When we allow for interdependence through foreign trade and investment, countries will both transmit to and receive from other countries the effects of domestic disturbances and policy adjustments. Further repercussions will then ensue as the economies adapt to these various forces.

In formulating adjustment policies with respect to disturbances, countries evidently have certain objectives in mind with respect to economic efficiency, the rate of inflation, the level of unemployment, and the balance-of-payments position. While the efficiency objective cannot in actuality be separated from the internal-external balance objectives, it is nevertheless conventional to do so for analytical purposes. Thus, in what follows, we shall treat internal-external balance considerations primarily in macroeconomic terms and efficiency considerations primarily in microeconomic terms.

Adjustment Policies for Internal and External Equilibrium[1]

As just mentioned, internal equilibrium refers to some socially acceptable rate of inflation and level of unemployment. Countries may also have other internal objectives, such as attaining a "satisfactory" rate of growth and some desired

---

[a]The operations of governmental units involved in market activities could also be included here.

distribution of income, but we shall abstract from these objectives here. Defining external equilibrium in balance-of-payments terms requires that we specify the kind of exchange-rate system to which countries adhere. Thus, if exchange rates are flexible and not tampered with by the authorities, a country's external objective would presumably be achieved automatically via adjustments in trade and capital transactions. Alternatively, under the adjustable peg, balance-of-payments equilibrium means that there is no net change in a country's international reserves, assuming that total world reserves are constant.[b]

How then do countries adjust to disturbances? With exchange-rate flexibility, the answer is simply that they vary their domestic monetary and fiscal policies for internal purposes and the balance of payments takes care of itself, so to speak. This presumes, among other things, that domestic factor and product markets can be adjusted smoothly, that the authorities abstain from exchange-rate manipulation, and that exchange-rate changes do not exacerbate domestic price movements. The situation is more complex when exchange rates are to be maintained, as in the system of the adjustable peg, for then the question arises about the extent to which payments imbalances are to be financed or corrected.

In designing the pegged-rate system, the conception was that short-run payments imbalances were to be financed by variations in a country's international reserves while fiscal and monetary policies were to be used for internal stabilization purposes. A problem could be created, however, if reserves were not adequate and if countries were constrained from altering their exchange rate for adjustment purposes. Thus, as Meade (1951, pp. 114-24) pointed out, policies for internal and external balance might conflict, as, for example, when one country was experiencing underemployment and a balance-of-payments deficit and the rest of the world was experiencing inflation and a balance-of-payments surplus. The implication was that other means for adjustment might then be warranted, such as controls over trade and payments, so long as the prior assumptions concerning reserve availability and exchange-rate adjustment continued to hold.

In the early 1960s, however, Mundell especially (1962) suggested that a policy dilemma like the foregoing could be dealt with if fiscal and monetary policies were treated as separate policies and differentiated according to their impact on the level of income and the balance of payments. Thus, fiscal policy could be "assigned" to achieve internal balance and, because short-term capital movements were responsive to interest-rate variations, monetary policy could be assigned to achieve external balance. Mundell's work spawned a whole new literature on the analysis of stabilization policies in an open economy. Among other things, this further research has clarified the conditions under which particular policy assignments may be valid, and attention has been drawn to the sensitivity of policy assignments to longer-run forces that may run counter to the internal policy impacts.[2]

[b]We thus rule out here countries striving to increase their reserve levels as a matter of policy.

While the theoretical analysis of stabilization policies in an open economy has thus yielded many important insights, it must be remembered that, in the adjustable-peg case, the focus has been on the financing rather than the correction of payments imbalances. In recent years, however, reserves have been abundant to the point that authorities in several countries have been unable effectively to employ domestic stabilization policies to withstand inflationary pressures while at the same time keeping their exchange rates unchanged. The emphasis on financing payments imbalances has thus given way to the need to correct imbalances.

One might think that the case for greater exchange-rate flexibility would be more persuasive in a world in which domestic objectives frequently dominate national policies and there are important differences among nations with respect to rates of change in national incomes, prices, and productivity. It is patently difficult to maintain exchange rates in such circumstances without at times resorting to controls over trade and payments that may be detrimental to economic welfare. Yet many government officials and private bankers view greater flexibility with apparent trepidation. Thus, it is often contended that if exchange rates were permitted to fluctuate freely, the effects would be to: (1) increase the costs of international trade transactions and deter international investment; (2) create conditions for destabilizing speculation; (3) increase domestic adjustment costs; (4) create incentives for exchange-rate manipulation to accomplish domestic employment or monopolistic objectives; and (5) increase domestic inflationary pressures.

While the first two contentions have been examined at length in the literature,[3] the others merit more attention than they have received to date.[4] Thus, it may be that *if factor markets function imperfectly, fluctuating exchange rates could give rise to more difficult domestic adjustment problems as compared to a situation in which rates were fixed or adjustably pegged.* As for exchange-market intervention, it might be justified if it enhanced exchange-rate stability, but not if it constituted a beggar-my-neighbor policy. Finally, especially in countries with a sizable foreign trade sector, there might be some question as to whether fluctuating rates were more conducive to inflation than fixed or pegged rates. In order to clarify further some of these issues, it would be useful to review once again the major historical experiences of fluctuating exchange rates during the interwar and postwar periods. It would be interesting in particular to assess the most recent experiences since the late 1960s when countries permitted their exchange rates to float outside of their support limits.

The difficulty in analyzing many of the experiences with flexible rates is that expectations were often dominated by the imminent return to exchange-rate pegging. We do not therefore have much of a factual basis that would permit an evaluation of the efficacy of a worldwide system of flexible exchange rates. It might be interesting nevertheless if a code of behavior were to be spelled out that would govern the behavior of nations under conditions of exchange-rate flexibility. A comparable code of behavior already exists for the adjustable-peg system, although this code will presumably be modified as discussions proceed on international monetary reform. If these codes of behavior were set side by side and supplemented by the factual studies suggested above, the major issues involved in choosing between the alternative exchange-rate systems would become more clearly evident.

European Monetary Integration

The foregoing discussion is pertinent in analyzing the policy of monetary integration initiated by the Common Market countries in the late 1960s and presumably to be extended to the U.K. and other new member countries. Monetary integration raises the difficulty alluded to above of whether and how domestic policies can be harmonized among the countries seeking to maintain given exchange rates. Insofar as the requisite extent of policy harmonization is beyond the present economic and political capabilities of an expanded Common Market and the availability of or willingness to absorb additional reserves is limited, the member countries will have to decide between permitting greater exchange-rate movements, and imposing controls especially over capital transactions to keep exchange rates within narrow limits. The former choice could well mean slowing down or even abandoning the movement towards monetary integration. If recent (1971-72) indications are any guide, the inclination has been towards controls, although it is far from obvious what the welfare costs of these controls in fact are and how these costs might differ for alternative exchange-rate policies.[5]

The Reform of the Pegged-Rate System

A consensus among nations must be reached on the form and functioning of the international monetary system if for no other reason than to forestall unilateral national actions that are harmful to other nations. Should it be decided that the pegged-rate system is to be continued, albeit in modified form, there are certain obvious things that require attention. Foremost is the need to improve the adjustment mechanism by encouraging countries to let their exchange rates respond more continuously to market pressures. Exchange-market disturbances and adjustments would thus occur more gradually and be depoliticized, in contrast to the present system which has become so prone to crisis and international political acrimony. It is also imperative to centralize international reserve creation and distribution and to consolidate existing reserve assets into a single form, such as Special Drawing Rights.[6] This would similarly insure the dimunition of disturbances to the international monetary system by avoiding the excessive creation of reserves and forestalling incentives for nations to alter the composition of their reserves.

Adjustment to Changes in Comparative Advantage and Trade Policies

In the previous section, we focused on national adjustment policies for internal and external equilibrium with respect to disturbances in general. Effective adjustment policies are of the utmost importance not only in attaining macroeconomic objectives, but also because these policies will help at the same time to resolve many of the difficulties that may arise from particular kinds of disturbances, such as changes in comparative advantage and in trade policies.

It should be evident from the typology of disturbances presented earlier that changes in world trade may stem from a myriad of market- and government-related forces. These forces are both domestic and foreign in origin, and they may operate indistinguishably in individual countries with respect to production, consumption, and investment. Countries might be advised therefore to design internal adjustment policies to deal with the effects of disturbances in general rather than with the effects of particular kinds of disturbances.

Changes in Comparative Advantage

The composition of goods and services that a country buys and sells in foreign trade will change over time in response to the various influences that we have noted. If the adjustment process works effectively, these changes can be made with a minimum of disruption and countries will receive maximum benefits from optimal use of their resources. It may of course happen that the adjustment process functions imperfectly and that resources in particular industries become unemployed. In such an event, the authorities may wish to implement policies designed to alleviate the adjustment costs of output foregone that are being borne by underemployed and unemployed factors.

The policies chosen may depend, among other things, on whether the disturbance is temporary and will thus reverse itself or whether it is permanent and irreversible. Thus, for example, in the case of labor, a program of unemployment compensation could deal with temporary disturbances, whereas subsidies to encourage labor mobility and special training programs to enhance skill acquisition would be more appropriate for the permanent and irreversible disturbances that occur. There may also be distributional grounds for such policies, especially insofar as the benefits from increased consumption are enjoyed by groups other than those that become unemployed.

Adjustment policies like the foregoing are meant to deal directly with an ongoing and observable problem, without there being any need initially to relate the action to certain designated causes such as foreign trade. While some judgment as to causation may be required to distinguish temporary from permanent disturbances, the policy action should not be made contingent upon demonstrating the importance of various causes. That is, it may be exceptionally difficult and time consuming to establish causation, and in the meantime nothing may be done to ease the resource adjustment required.[c]

Changes in Trade Policies

Instead of a general policy of adjustment assistance, an alternative way of handling disturbances that are ostensibly trade related is to erect a trade barrier.[d] While such barriers are in fact commonly employed for adjustment and many other purposes, they have the unfortunate side effect of imposing added costs on consumers so as to reduce their economic welfare. Trade barriers may also be relatively less efficient devices than adjustment assistance policies when there are specific factor-market problems that are identified as being in need of correction.[7]

In our discussion of internal-external equilibrium and exchange-rate systems, we noted that unilateral actions by some countries could affect other countries adversely. This same point applies to the international trading system and it has been manifested in the consensus on trade and tariff matters articulated especially in the General Agreement on Tariffs and Trade (GATT). The GATT as an organization has served a useful purpose in monitoring commercial policy developments since World War II and in acting as the focal point for negotiated reductions in trade barriers. At the same time, however, the GATT has not been able to cope effectively with a number of important questions, in particular agricultural protectionism, the formation of customs unions, the imposition of "voluntary" export quotas, and the use of commercial policy for balance-of-payments purposes and to foster economic development.

Given the economic importance of many of these restrictive measures, it is remarkable that governments have refrained on the whole from retaliating in kind. This reluctance of countries to take action may in part be a matter of goodwill and understanding of the problems of others and perhaps implicitly a reservation on their part that they might behave similarly if the situation warranted it. Also, retaliatory action has been forestalled when there were

[c]This further implies that there will be no need to identify specific foreign countries (e.g., Japan) as being responsible for particular domestic problems. Changes in comparative advantage and trade can thus be taken for granted and policies focused appropriately to assist domestic adjustment.

[d]We include here tariff and nontariff barriers to imports as well as "voluntary" agreements whereby exporters are subjected to restraints.

important political issues at stake that appeared overriding, as in the formation of the Common Market or in dealing with domestic agricultural interests. Thus, countries have voluntarily absorbed the impact of these changes, although often without full realization of the costs involved.

Opportunities have arisen at certain junctures in the past to moderate the effects of various restrictions by means of international negotiations. Such a juncture may presently be at hand in view of the impending enlargement of the Common Market that we have noted earlier. Since tariffs on many manufactured goods have been reduced already to relatively low levels, it would be desirable for negotiations to embrace nontariff as well as tariff barriers. Moreover, the United States and other agricultural exporting nations might seek to obtain negotiated increases in trade in agricultural products in exchange for the further liberalization of trade in manufactures.

Developments in the international monetary system will have a direct bearing on the climate for trade negotiations. If balance-of-payments adjustments can be made more effectively and smoothly and if the major industrialized countries are able to maintain full employment with reasonable price stability, there would be comparatively little difficulty in absorbing the domestic resource shifts that further trade liberalization might engender. Some further actions may be necessary nonetheless to avoid backsliding in the event that domestic adjustment problems arise. In this regard, the members of GATT might agree to abstain from imposing additional trade restrictions and, instead, rely on adjustment assistance policies.

We have already alluded to the question of whether these policies should be applied generally to all kinds of disturbances or whether they should be framed specifically with trade-related disturbances in mind. The main argument in favor of a policy of trade-related adjustment assistance is to stave off protectionist policies because of the losses in welfare that these policies entail.[8]

Granting the point just made, the question then is how far countries should go in singling out trade-related disturbances when there are many other causes of displacement that are equal or greater in impact.[9] More specifically, should a program of trade-adjustment assistance be more liberal and provide greater benefits than a comparable program of general adjustment assistance? To assess this issue, we would want to determine the increases in economic welfare that would be realized presumably if resources were shifted to more highly productive uses and increased consumption occurred. The problem is, however, that an overly generous program of trade-adjustment assistance might not provide sufficient incentive for resources to shift to more highly productive employment.[10]

The granting of preferences for LDC exports raises the same kinds of questions that we have just discussed.[e] If preferences are to be meaningful, the

---

[e]If LDCs are to take advantage of preferences or multilateral trade liberalization, many of them will be forced to restructure their economies in order to remove the disincentives to exports that have been created by their policies of protection and foreign exchange control.

industrialized countries should impose no exceptions. They should also agree to abstain from restrictive measures and rely instead on adjustment assistance if needed to deal with domestic resource displacements. Again, while a special program of adjustment assistance might be required to make preferences appear more palatable, the difficulty of designing and implementing such a program and the net effects it may have upon welfare merit consideration.

Adjustment to the Impact of Multinational Corporations[11]

The impacts of MNCs have attracted a great deal of analytical attention in recent years, and there has been considerable discussion of the policies that governments should follow with respect to MNCs. The analysis has been concerned with a variety of market- and government-related impacts that MNCs may have in both the home and host countries. These impacts relate to: (1) the balance of payments; (2) domestic employment and investment; (3) static efficiency and monopolistic influences; (4) technology transfer and dynamic efficiency; (5) domestic capital markets; (6) developmental impact; and (7) creation of conflicts between governments and between MNCs and governments.

The Balance of Payments

The impact of direct foreign investment on the balance of payments can be analyzed in terms of the traditional transfer problem, which focuses on the process of adjustment mentioned earlier, the extent to which the transfer is completed, and possible terms-of-trade effects. There has also been some concern, particularly in the U.S., with the question of whether direct investment constitutes a net drain on the balance of payments. This involves the extent to which the trade balance may be worsened due to export displacement and increases in imports as compared to the reflow of investment income and favorable trade effects induced by increases in foreign income. As might be expected, the length of the balance-of-payments recoupment period is quite sensitive to the assumptions made concerning investment in the host country and to the parameter values assigned to the various production and trade effects. These same issues can also be examined of course from the host country's standpoint.

Domestic Employment and Investment

Closely related to the foregoing is whether direct foreign investment means exporting jobs and foregoing increases in the home country's domestic capital stock. With respect to job displacement, we have already noted that it may stem from many sources, thus making it difficult to disentangle them as to cause. There may also be no reason to distinguish the employment effects of shifts in intranational investment from those that take place between nations, unless there is reason to believe that the home country's welfare is harmed on balance by foreign investment. While a case can be made theoretically along static lines that welfare reduction may occur,[f] this conclusion is not inevitable especially when dynamic productivity effects, reduced import costs, and externalities are taken into account. There are also many empirical issues that require examination before a firm conclusion can be reached on the welfare effects of foreign investment.[12] Another question that has been raised is whether MNCs should bear some part or all of the adjustment cost in the home country if their foreign investment results in home-country job displacement.[g] Again the point is whether to single out the job-displacement effects of MNC foreign operations from the effects that result from their operations domestically.

Doubts have sometimes been expressed as to why MNCs invest abroad instead of exporting or using other devices such as licensing. A frequent answer is that direct investment is required to counteract some change in foreign commercial policy that would have restricted exports in any case. Direct investment has also been justified as a more effective way to serve expanding foreign markets, especially because it permits the parent company to exercise and maintain control over production and distribution. Finally, it is often alleged that if the foreign investment were not made, opportunities would be lost to competitors or foregone altogether. Controls limiting foreign investment have been criticized accordingly on one or more of these grounds.

Efficiency and Monopolistic Influences

The static and dynamic efficiency effects stemming from direct foreign investment have been of concern to host countries especially. In assessing static efficiency, it is important to determine the extent to which MNCs behave competitively or monopolistically and the impact that they have on efficiency elsewhere in the host country. These same considerations can also be posed dynamically and are of great interest, particularly in view of the role that MNCs may play in the international transmission of technological change both with

---

[f]What is involved is showing that foreign investment may be excessive from the home country's standpoint because of a divergence between private and social returns that arises because the foreign investor considers only his own returns and not the returns to home labor.

[g]In outlining proposed legislation on economic adjustment in a speech before the American Insurance Association in New York City on May 17, 1972, Senator Ribicoff suggested that companies deciding to transfer production facilities abroad "should defray the costs of assisting the laid-off employees they are leaving behind."

respect to their foreign affiliates and in the form of spillovers to other domestic firms in the host country. Another important issue is the MNC impact on the capital market in host countries, in particular whether MNC market dominance enables them to raise funds locally on more favorable terms than domestic firms. These issues involving efficiency and monopolistic influences raise important questions of public policy, which unfortunately admit of no easy answers. Without more facts at hand, it is therefore difficult to pass judgment on these various considerations and to determine what the appropriate policy responses should be.

Developmental Impact

The developmental impact of foreign investment in the host country is bound up closely with the efficiency considerations just discussed. But there may be additional aspects of concern especially to LDCs. These involve the extent to which foreign firms enhance the productivity of local resources by providing training programs and opportunities for indigenous workers and entrepreneurs, adding to or improving the infrastructure, and affecting the general business climate in a beneficial way to the host country. Some of the factors just mentioned may be carried out in conjunction with the foreign firm's operations, although where dynamic externalities are involved, as in the case of training effects, the host government may have to take special measures to insure that the externalities are realized.

Conflicts

The last of the various effects mentioned earlier concerns the possible conflicts that MNCs may creat between home- and host-country governments and between themselves and governments. Some of the contentious intergovernmental problems that have arisen involve whether foreign affiliates are subject to home-country laws, as, for example, the U.S. statutes relating to antitrust and trading with the enemy. There have also been questions about the effects on foreign affiliates of home-country controls imposed for balance-of-payments purposes, as in the case of the U.S. programs restricting foreign direct investment and bank lending. In LDCs especially, turmoil has been created when MNC profits have been subjected to higher taxes or royalty payments and when expropriations have been threatened or actually carried out. In much the same way that codes of behavior have been developed for the international monetary and trading systems, these various sources of conflict suggest that there may be a need for a code covering international direct investment.[13] Some potential conflicts may thus be defused, although there are several that are likely to smolder in view of the dictates of national policy that are unavoidably brought to bear on particular issues from time to time.

Conclusion

Because of the many diverse effects that MNCs have, it may be difficult to devise policies to deal with their operations. A case might be made for home countries to restrict foreign direct investment for balance-of-payments and employment purposes, but there is no guarantee that these restrictions will improve economic welfare. The realization of static and dynamic efficiency gains from foreign investment has to be set against the possibility of monopolistic exploitation. The developmental impact of MNCs requires analysis of how countries can best realize the benefits of various externalities. Finally, MNC operations can give rise to different kinds of governmental conflicts. Some of these might be recognized in advance and steps taken to forestall them, but others may remain unpredictable. It thus appears that there are few simple answers concerning how countries might best cope with MNC-related disturbances.

Adjustment to Changes in East-West
Trade and Investment Relations

East-West trade has not been of great importance to most Western countries, but a significant expansion of this trade and a furtherance of investment relations may well be in the offing as a result of recently expanded diplomatic initiatives. The implementation of these changes in policy raises the same issues discussed earlier. That is, *if the Western countries are to guarantee market access for imports from the centrally planned economies, this will mean relying on domestic policies of adjustment assistance and abstaining from import restrictions in case there is labor displacement due to imports*. It also means clarifying policies concerning dumping, given that the cost and price structures of the centrally planned economies are not directly comparable with those of market economies. Finally, restrictions imposed by the Western countries for strategic reasons would be in need of review.

As for international investment, the extension of export financing by Western countries does not pose any unusual problems. Some MNCs are already operating in the Soviet Union and Eastern Europe and more are likely to follow. Because there are so many sensitive issues involved, there are bound to be protracted negotiations concerning the operation and behavior of MNCs in the centrally planned economies.

Adjustment to Externalities

The significance of externalities has become of increasing concern in many countries. In particular, governments have spent substantial amounts on research and development and on education in order to foster the production and distribution of knowledge and to enhance the quality of the labor force. Environmental use and control have also been given much attention. As the examples just mentioned imply, there are many different sources of externalities and impacts therefrom. International trade and investment can thus be looked upon as creating their own externalities and being influenced by those created in other sectors, including changes in government policies. There are also externalities that stem from the provision of public goods, such as national defense and public health measures, and from national uses of common property resources, such as water networks and the atmosphere. These latter groups of externalities may operate transnationally.

The major problems involving externalities will most likely stem from differences in national policies with regard to the use and control of the environment.[14] These policy differences are bound to affect national cost structures and there will be consequent shifts in the structure and geographic distribution of trade and investment. These impacts should not in themselves be cause for concern so long as the environmental measures are not protectionist motivated and the international adjustment mechanism operates effectively. If temporary disruptions nevertheless occur, they should be dealt with by general measures for domestic adjustment rather than by trade restrictions. In cases where problems stem from the use of resources jointly by nations, there will be a need for intergovernmental cooperation to promote equity in use and control.

An Agenda for Research

In light of our foregoing discussion, an agenda for research is set out below. This agenda is arranged according to the issues identified in the preceding sections.

The International Adjustment Mechanism

1. While the need for greater exchange-rate flexibility is widely recognized, there is nevertheless substantial opposition in official government and private banking circles to a system of market-determined rates. The basis for this opposition may lie in the fear that, in comparison to a system of fixed or pegged

rates, fluctuating rates may make domestic adjustment more costly, governments may manipulate exchange rates to their advantage, and inflationary pressures may be exacerbated. It would be worthwhile therefore to review the major experiences with flexible rates during the interwar and postwar periods to determine how important the foregoing considerations may have been. Special attention might be given to the experiences with flexible rates in 1971-72.

2. Parallel with the redrafting of a code of behavior for the adjustable-peg system, it would be useful to draft a similar code for a worldwide system of flexible rates. The juxtaposition of these codes of behavior in conjunction with the factual studies just suggested would be helpful in identifying the major issues in choosing alternative exchange-rate systems. It might then be worthwhile to categorize countries and regions by the type of exchange-rate system that would be most beneficial to their welfare.

3. More work should be done on the welfare costs of maintaining disequilibrium exchange rates and how these costs might differ for alternative exchange-rate regimes. The industrialized countries, in particular the Common Market, should be a prime focus for this research.

4. If a modified pegged-rate system is to be maintained, work should be continued on such topics as automatic and presumptive criteria for exchange-rate changes and the optimal creation and distribution of international reserves.

*Changes in Comparative Advantage
and Trade Policies*

1. The nature and magnitude of adjustment costs are in need of further clarification, particularly with reference to the job displacement and losses that industries and firms may experience due to market- or policy-related disturbances of domestic and foreign origin. Such research may be helpful in identifying the sectors that are most vulnerable to economic change. It is also important to determine how adjustment costs may vary, depending upon national objectives with respect to the stability and growth of income and employment and how successfully these objectives are in fact attained. These findings may have a bearing upon the nature and timing of protectionist pressures.

2. The potential welfare gains from removing or reducing existing trade barriers need continually to be assessed, especially in relation to the adjustment costs that may be encountered in the advanced industrial countries. This research should encompass all types of trade barriers with respect to both manufactures and agricultural products. There might be grounds, however, for concentrating on temperate-zone agricultural products, especially in view of the widespread restrictions affecting production and trade in these products in such important regions as the Common Market. The welfare implications of encouraging LDC exports to the advanced countries are also worth pursuing.

3. The foregoing investigations should provide the raw material for assessing the details of particular national programs of adjustment assistance insofar as the major elements of welfare gain and adjustment costs can be identified and estimates made of the budgetary implications involved in alleviating these costs. It would also be of interest here for comparative purposes to make welfare calculations for other types of adjustment policies, in particular those involving trade restrictions.

The Impact of Multinational Corporations

The greatest need here is for continuing factual studies of the various impacts mentioned earlier that MNCs have on home and host country employment, investment, and production and on their international monetary, trade, and investment relations. It is difficult to single out individual issues for emphasis because of their interdependence. The ultimate objective is to enhance the understanding of the behavior and consequences of MNC operations in order to provide a sounder basis for evaluating various policies that home and host countries may consider with respect to MNCs.

East-West Trade and Investment Relations

The issues here are mainly practical ones, involving the revision and reinterpretation of antidumping laws, the review and revision of embargoes and other restrictions, and ground rules for MNC operations in centrally planned economies.

The Impact of Externalities

1. National differences in policies towards externalities should be reviewed, with special emphasis on how these policies are reflected in cost structures and what the consequent impact on trade and investment may be.

2. The major instances of transnational externalities should be identified and research done on how these externalities can be realized and controlled.

Notes

1. For a more detailed treatment of the issues presented in this section, see Stern (1973, esp. Ch. 10) and the references cited therein.

2. An important innovation was to cast the analysis in a portfolio-adjustment framework and thereby to distinguish the effects of stock shifts in existing portfolios from flow effects with growing portfolios. The buildup of interest payments is an example of a long-run force that could counteract a favorable initial impact of an interest-rate change. For further discussion, see Stern (1973, esp. Ch. 10).

3. See Stern (1973, Ch. 3).

4. Issues (3) and (5) have been emphasized especially in the theoretical analysis of optimum currency areas, which was first developed especially by Mundell (1961) and McKinnon (1963) and subsequently elaborated by a number of different writers. For further discussion and references, see Stern (1973, Ch. 3).

5. Some theoretical analyses and calculations of the welfare costs of disequilibrium exchange rates and controls are to be found in Hause (1966), Johnson (1966), Cooper (1968a; 1968b), Fieleke (1971), and Willett and Tower (1971). See also Stern (1973, Ch. 9).

6. There are two important points concerning SDRs that merit attention. These are (a) how to handle the distribution of seigniorage from the creation and distribution of the SDRs, and (b) the interest rate that SDRs should bear in order to induce optimal holdings. See Stern (1973, Ch. 12) for further discussion and references.

7. This conclusion follows from the theory of domestic distortions and welfare according to which policies should be addressed directly to offsetting the distortions involved. See Bhagwati (1971) for details.

8. It is interesting to note the equivocal recommendations of the Commission on International Trade and Investment Policy (1971, pp. 9-10) with respect to adjustment assistance and temporary protection of U.S. firms and industries. Small businesses are supposed to be afforded adjustment assistance while large firms are presumably to be given temporary protection by means of the escape clause or an orderly marketing agreement. It is difficult to see why such a distinction should be made since imports might have a favorable competitive effect domestically, especially in industries with an oligopolistic market structure.

9. Some calculations are presented in UNCTAD (1972) suggesting that productivity changes may be of far greater importance than trade liberalization in creating job displacement in the industrialized countries. For the United States in particular, Krause and Mathieson (1971) have shown that trade-related unemployment in the late 1960s was quite small in relation to the unemployment arising from the inadequacy of domestic demand.

10. This concern has been expressed especially in UNCTAD (1972, p. 47) where the distinction is drawn between adjustment assistance policies designed to promote domestic resource reallocation and those designed to salvage and upgrade resources in their present use.

11. For further discussion and references, see Stern (1973, Ch. 8).

12. See Hawkins (1972) for some calculations for the United States suggesting that job displacement from direct foreign investment has been very small in relation to other disruptions in the labor market.

13. Some suggestions along these lines are made in Kindleberger (1969, pp. 201-7.

14. For a review of some of the major issues involved in environmental control, see especially Walter (1972).

Bibliography

Bhagwati, J. 1964. "The Pure Theory of International Trade: A Survey," *Economic Journal* 74 (March): 1-84.

———. 1971. "The Generalized Theory of Distortions and Welfare," in J.N. Bhagwati et al. (eds.), *Trade, Balance of Payments, and Growth: Papers in International Economics in Honor of Charles P. Kindleberger*. Amsterdam: North-Holland Publishing Co.

Commission on International Trade and Investment Policy. 1971. *United States International Economic Policy in an Interdependent World*. Washington, D.C.: Government Printing Office.

Cooper, R.N. 1968a. "The Balance of Payments," in R.E. Caves and Associates, *Britain's Economic Prospects*. Washington, D.C.: The Brookings Institution.

———. 1968b. *The Economics of Interdependence: Economic Policy in the Atlantic Community*. New York: McGraw-Hill Book Co., for the Council on Foreign Relations.

Fieleke, N.S. 1971. *The Welfare Effects of Controls over Capital Exports from the United States*. Essays in International Finance, No. 82. Princeton: International Finance Section, Princeton University.

Hause, J.C. 1966. "The Welfare Costs of Disequilibrium Exchange Rates," *Journal of Political Economy* 74 (August): 333-52.

Hawkins, R.G. 1972. "Job Displacement and the Multinational Firm: A Methodological Review," Occasional Paper No. 3, Center for Multinational Studies, Washington, D.C. (June).

Johnson, H.G. 1966. "The Welfare Costs of Exchange Rate Stabilization," *Journal of Political Economy* 74 (October): 512-18.

Kindleberger, C.P. 1969. *American Business Abroad*. New Haven: Yale University Press.

Krause, L.B. and Mathieson, J. 1971. "How Much Unemployment Did We Import?", *Brookings Papers on Economic Activity*, 2, 417-27.

McKinnon, R.I. 1963. "Optimum Currency Areas," *American Economic Review* 53 (September): 717-25. Reprinted in R.N. Cooper (ed.), *International Finance*. Harmondsworth: Penguin Books Ltd., 1969.

Meade, J.E. 1951. *The Balance of Payments*. London: Oxford University Press.

Mundell, R.A. 1961. "A Theory of Optimum Currency Areas," *American Economic Review* 51 (September): 657-65. Reprinted in R.A. Mundell, *International Economics*. New York: Macmillan, 1968.

_____. 1962. "The Appropriate Use of Monetary and Fiscal Policy under Fixed Exchange Rates," *IMF Staff Papers* 9 (March): 70-79. Reprinted in R.A. Mundell, *International Economics*. New York: Macmillan, 1968.

Stern, R.M. 1973. *The Balance of Payments: Theory and Economic Policy*. Chicago: Aldine-Atherton.

UNCTAD. 1972. "Adjustment Assistance Measures," Report by the UNCTAD Secretariat. TD/121/Supp. 1 (January 14).

Walter, I. 1972. "Environmental Control and Consumer Protection," Occasional Paper No. 2, Center for Multinational Studies, Washington, D.C., (June).

Willett, T.D. and Tower, E. 1971. "The Welfare Economics of International Adjustment," *Journal of Finance* 26 (May): 287-302.

4

A Program of Research on Foreign Direct Investment

Raymond Vernon
Harvard University

The branches and subsidiaries that are owned and managed by large enterprises outside of their home countries have been growing at so rapid a rate in the past decade or so that by now they may well involve $200 billions or more of assets. The international trade in which the units of these large multinational systems are involved has become a major element in world trade as a whole; in fact, it would not be unreasonable to assume that these units are parties on one side or another of nearly one-half the world's trade, outside of agriculture. Yet the present state of understanding of these multinational systems as economic units is still incomplete, even rudimentary.

The Basic Data

To begin with, the simple dimensions of the activities of large multinational enterprises are not well recorded nor well known. This is not always a paralyzing problem from a policymaker's point of view, but it is serious enough.

The U.S.-based Enterprise

The U.S. Department of Commerce reports certain basic data for U.S.-owned branches and subsidiaries located abroad. Quarterly figures are provided for five broad industry groups by major foreign countries, covering aggregate book value of investments, earnings, dividends, interest, and royalties. On a sporadic annual basis, according to a crude industrial breakdown, one can also get the sales of overseas manufacturing facilities, as well as a crude analysis of the sources and uses of their funds. Finally, for the years 1957 and 1966, there is a more detailed census which presents not only figures of the sort described about, but also data on employment and on the local transactions of the branches and subsidiaries involved.

Data of this sort suffer not only from their sporadic timing and their gross classifications but also from other limitations.

One group of limitations results from the fact that these activities are reported as if they were first and foremost investments, that is, activities whose economic importance derives mainly from the fact that they are financial claims by a U.S. parent on a foreign asset. In my view, the economic significance of these overseas subsidiaries and branches derives mainly from the fact that they are elements in a going global business, rather than from their quality as financial investment.[1] To evaluate a foreign subsidiary as a separate entity, apart from the global system of which it is a part, can be grossly misleading. It may mislead as to the nature of the capital resources that the subsidiaries are employing and the nature of the benefits that the multinational system may be deriving. As a result, it may create a misleading base for gauging such things as trade effects, payments effects, and employment effects of a given subsidiary, since those effects may well appear elsewhere in the international system to which the enterprise belongs. A major research objective, therefore, is to find the means of describing and monitoring the activities of these global enterprises according to a perspective which recognizes that each subsidiary is a fragment of a larger multinational enterprise.

The most comprehensive effort to remedy this lack so far is that undertaken by the Harvard Multinational Enterprise Study. The main data bank generated in connection with the study is organized according to multinational systems, each consisting of a U.S. parent and its foreign subsidiaries. The bank contains in crude and skeletal form a chronology of each of the several thousand foreign subsidiaries of 187 U.S.-based multinational enterprises. Various compilations from that data bank have been published,[2] and numerous analytical exercises have been undertaken from unpublished data drawn out of the bank.[3] But the details covered in the bank for each of the 187 systems are relatively rudimentary and the chronology ends in any case in 1967. So this source, besides being incomplete, is rapidly losing its current quality. One major research objective should be to institutionalize the maintenance and improve the coverage of data of this sort.

The second source of distortion associated with the Commerce data arises from the use of standard accounting concepts in reporting the activities of the foreign subsidiaries and branches. The Commerce data report the accountant's version of "earnings," "dividends," "interest," "royalties," "equity," and "long-term indebtedness." That version is often far removed from economic reality. Two or three illustrations may serve to highlight the nature of the problem.

1. U.S. accounting practices require the write-down of certain categories of assets carried in a foreign subsidiary whenever a devaluation occurs in the country of the subsidiary. The write-down bears only the most tenuous relationship to the real economic effects of the devaluation upon the reporting enterprise.[4] The net effect of the requirement is not easily generalized. As a rule, however, it reduces recorded profits and investment below their economic levels. For example, official U.S. records regarding direct investment in Latin America probably by now substantially understate the economic value of U.S. commitments in that area.

2. In transactions between affiliated firms, the distinction between dividends, interest, royalties, and administrative charges are often quite arbitrary, and are greatly influenced by a variety of internal considerations, notably questions of tax impact.[5] Generalizations that take these official distinctions literally, therefore, are subject to major error.

3. The balance-of-payments effects of the interaffiliate transactions are especially subject to misinterpretation. In U.S. official balance-of-payments compilations, it is assumed that the dividends and interest remitted by U.S.-owned foreign subsidiaries represent returns to the parent's investment in the subsidiaries; that royalties are a payment for the U.S. export of technical services; and that administrative charges are a payment for the U.S. export of administrative services. None of these assumptions stands up very well under close examination. As a result of naive assumptions of this sort, major errors may exist in U.S. balance-of-payments data. There are grounds for the view, for instance, that the "export" of U.S. central office and technical services by U.S. parents to foreign subsidiaries may be understated in the official figures by as much as several billion dollars a year.[6] Part of this understatement may be offset by the overstatement of some other item such as dividends or interest or debt repayment; but, for some policy purposes, the misclassification may be important. Part of the understatement also may be found in profits retained overseas, so that neither the debit nor the credit entry normally associated with international transactions is reflected in the payment accounts.

As a practical matter, official agencies may not be in a position to adjust reported data of this sort, since the data so reported are in accord with current accounting practice. Accordingly, the research that is needed in order to generate better data may well have to be undertaken by private entities. The need to get on with this sort of research is pressing.

The Foreign-based Enterprises

Inadequate as the U.S. official data may be, the data of other countries are poorer still. Most countries record in some form or another the existence of the foreign branches and subsidiaries of their own parent enterprises. But as a rule these reports are a by-product of the balance-of-payments recording system of the country. As a result, the data most often available are the annual increments in investments by parents in their foreign subsidiaries, with some sort of crude breakdown by the industries and areas in which the subsidiaries operate. The IMF and OECD have taken some steps to introduce consistency in the various national data, but these efforts are limited in scope and effect. The result is that the data suffer from most of the deficiencies described for the U.S. figures, plus some added weaknesses unique to each of the national reporting systems.

Many countries, as it turns out, keep some record of foreigners' investments in their own economy; indeed, for some countries, these records are better than the official figures for the overseas investments of their own enterprises. The U.S. Department of Commerce, for example, records the subsidiaries and branches controlled by non-U.S. firms in the U.S. economy. In addition, Canada, the U.K., and various other countries provide data of a similar sort. Moreover, there have been various privately conducted surveys in many countries of the world which also generate this sort of information.[7] But no one, so far as I know, has yet tried to put these diverse sources together in order to generate a world picture.

The Harvard Multinational Enterprise Study is in process of piecing together a world picture by other means.[a] The study's data bank, when completed, will cover about 200 large non-U.S. enterprises and other several thousand subsidiaries located outside of the home country. The figures for each such subsidiary will be more descriptive than those in the study's earlier survey of the subsidiaries of the U.S.-based firms; for instance the new data will include various measures of the size of these subsidiaries' operations, and they will carry the record up to the year 1970. Various compilations drawn from this bank will be published in 1973 and the bank itself will be available to scholars for analytical purposes. But there is no present decision to maintain the bank beyond its 1970 terminal date, so that a lacuna will quickly develop.

More data on various specialized aspects of the operations of multinational enterprises also are needed but these are best discussed in the context of a series of researchable issues presented below.

Analysis of Investment Behavior

Studies of the motivations of multinational enterprises in the establishment of overseas subsidiaries are so voluminous by now that it is futile to try to offer a complete list of citations. The evidence is persuasive that the investment process is a relatively rational phenomonen—rational in the sense that it is consistent with an effort to maximize profit and minimize risk. The environment in which these activities take place, however, is one in which oligopoly is the normal state, scale factors are very large, and uncertainties of various sorts dominate the calculation.

Despite the cumulatively impressive nature of the evidence, a considerable amount of energy is being expended by researchers in order to demonstrate that, in gross macroeconomic aggregates, multinational enterprises actually behave as one would expect portfolio investors to behave. The temptation to engage in this sort of analysis is very strong. For one thing, the gross aggregates are easily at hand; for another, the portfolio approach is in accord with the mainstream of neoclassical investment analysis as taught in most graduate schools today.[8]

---

[a]G.Y. Bertin among others is reported to be developing a data bank of a similar sort, but the contents of that bank at the time of this writing were undisclosed.

For many years, analyses of this sort went their way unchallenged in the journals. The fact that the enterprises concerned seemed to be responding to wholly different rules of behavior when they were viewed at close quarters seemed to be having little impact upon those who preferred to test their hypotheses with highly aggregated data. Eventually, however, the issue was joined. Since the early 1960s, some elements of a new theoretical approach have been falling into place.[9] Since the new emphases rely on oligopoly theory much more than on the competitive model, the generalizations are less complete, less elegant, and less deterministic than the theory they purport to displace. Nevertheless, the efforts to relate the investment behavior of multinational enterprises to received oligopoly doctrine are fairly well developed.

Despite the advances made so far, however, the theoretical structure for analyzing the investment behavior of multinational enterprises is still far from satisfying. As in oligopoly situations in general, innovation and product differentiation loom large in analysis; individual investments represent a marginal act associated with a going concern; and speculation by the decision maker about the behavior of others in the oligopoly dominates the calculations.[10] Accordingly, one is repeatedly drawn to dynamic theories, in an effort to define, explain, and elaborate sequences of behavior.[11] That emphasis in turn suggests the use of simulation and game-theoretic exercises as an aid to understanding and generalization. Some imaginative efforts on these lines are being undertaken by J.W. Vaupel. In one series of computer operations, individual firms are run through a sequence that simulates the production, investment, and trade of multinational enterprise, from the innovation of a new product to its senescence. Factor costs, transport rates, scale considerations, and the timing of rival threats are varied in order to measure the model's sensitivity to these factors. Some effort also is being made to develop aggregate industry models rather than individual enterprise models. It may be that some added mileage can be gained by encouraging more exercises of this sort.

On the other hand, there are stages in the process of developing new theory when it pays to emphasize the inductive rather than the deductive phase of the cerebrating process. Though a considerable amount of observation has been done concerning the factors affecting the decisions of U.S. firms as they establish themselves overseas, much less has been done regarding the behavior of European and Japanese firms.[12] Work in progress by the Harvard Study should fill in a portion of this gap, but there is a long distance still to go.

In order to cover the theoretical and empirical aspects of direct investment, it will pay also to make a strong research commitment to the neglected phenomenon of disinvestment. Multinational enterprises are continually taking on new products but they are also sloughing off old products. The factor that leads them to drop old products is not simply a decline in aggregate demand for the product. There also appears to be some unarticulated notion of comparative advantage and disadvantage in the minds of the multinational enterprises, as they measure themselves against locally owned firms. There are indications, for instance, that products in which differentiation will no longer work and in which economies of scale are no longer very important are likely to be given up by multinational enterprises to their local competitors. The research problem is to measure the disinvestment process to the extent that it exists, and to find the underlying rationale for the process. Research of this sort would have to be done in the first instance at the firm level, but it could contribute richly both to the formulation of theory and the formulation of policy regarding multinational enterprises.

As more progress is made in describing and in predicting the investment behavior of the multinational enterprises, it will probably prove a good deal easier to understand the trade, payments, employment, and growth implications of their operations. Below, I take a closer look at each of these areas, in order to sharpen the issues and to suggest the lines of needed research.

Analysis of Trade Behavior

Public policy in the field of tariffs and exchange rates is based, as a rule, on some fairly explicit assumptions about the price elasticity of supply and demand relating to imports and exports. Both the theory and the measurements of these elasticities have proceeded placidly on their course, almost untouched and undisturbed by the growing phenomenon of the multinational enterprise. Yet a priori there is a strong case for the view that international trade conducted at arm's length between independent parties should be viewed in different theoretical and empirical terms from international trade conducted between affiliates pursuant to some central optimizing strategies; and further that these differences should have a substantial effect on the role of tariffs and the nature of existing price elasticities. If scale economies and the cost of information are also introduced in the mix of variables, the anticipation of different outcomes of the two types of situation is exceedingly high. If the labor-relations variable and the government-relations variable are introduced in the hypothesis-building exercise, the anticipation of a different pattern of behavior becomes even larger.

At this stage, the existence of a theoretical issue is just beginning to be acknowledged. Some highly imaginative pioneering work has been done.[13] Some interest has been shown in trying to incorporate the work into the main body of the economic theory.[14] But a large gap still has to be filled; the Heckscher-Ohlin and Marshallian framework, based upon factor availabilities and factor costs and upon some relatively simple assumptions regarding the role of economies and diseconomies of scale, still provides the backbone of theoretical analysis. When technology is recognized as an element in the analysis, its presence on the input side is usually reduced to the economic equivalent of a capital investment; and its market effect is usually expressed through the assumption that the technology has the effect of reducing costs and prices, rather than the much more realistic assumption that the technology is expressed mainly in new products. The problem of optimal behavior in markets where oligopoly and technology change prevail is accordingly finessed.[15] The encouragement of efforts to enrich international theory so that it more systematically incorporates oligopoly and the other elements associated with multinational enterprises is strongly indicated.

Meanwhile, once again, a strong case can be made for the encouragement of more empirical work on the trade patterns of multinational enterprises. Though U.S. patterns have been studied and though some industrywide analyses have been undertaken, the subject as a whole has barely been opened up. It is particularly important to test the results against the key assumptions that underlie public policy prescriptions, notably the assumptions regarding the size of price elasticities of supply and demand. Even without a well-developed body of underlying theory, findings that suggested the existence of relatively low elasticities, as I think would be the case on the export side of the U.S. economy, would be of critical importance in the development of investment, exchange rate, and tariff policy.

Analysis of Payments Behavior and Payments Effects

With investment behavior and trade behavior better understood, those concerned with public policy would be on firmer ground for estimating the balance-of-payments implications of the operations of multinational enterprises. But there would be several major obstacles still in the way of credible estimates of such effects.

There have been a number of ambitious systematic efforts to estimate the balance-of-payments implications of foreign direct investments.[16] None has been quite credible in its results.[17] Part of the problem has been to develop a plausible estimate of what would have occurred in the affected economies if the direct investment had *not* taken place. That exercise, as it turns out, brings the researcher flat up against the need for a theory of international investment. Confronting that need, the studies thus far turn out either agnostic or dogmatic; they either make alternative estimates on the basis of a series of mutually inconsistent assumptions, or else they plump for some simple universal proposition.[18]

Another weakness common to such studies has been their assumption that the economic consequences of a direct investment could be estimated as a function of the amount of capital in the enterprise.[19]

Still another difficulty has been that the dynamic implications of direct investment for both lending and borrowing country have been so elusive. Being elusive, these effects have been disregarded as a rule; but to disregard them in any medium-term or long-term measurement exercise runs the risk of overlooking the most important elements in the picture.

Finally, there have been the special difficulties of measurement that arise when dealing with strongly oligopolistic industries. Foreign investments in these industries are often made in order to counter a threat to the stability of the oligopoly structure itself, that is, in order to protect and prolong an existing oligopoly rent. Any exercise that is aimed at measuring the effects of the investment, therefore, requires the researcher to describe an alternative state in which the oligopoly is assumed to be much weaker. When translating this assumption into quantitative balance-of-payments terms, the researcher is obviously confronted with formidable difficulties.

Despite these problems, it is indispensable that efforts to measure the payment effects of direct investment on the basis of macroeconomic modeling should go on. Indeed, it is almost certain that it will go on, in view of the powerful intellectual attraction that such modeling exerts. What needs to be borne in mind in this connection is that exercises of this sort will probably prove quite costly in terms of their results, at least in the short- and medium-term. The inherent difficulties of the task will not readily be overcome. Accordingly, while the work must be encouraged, a certain restraint in the use of resources will have to be exercised at the same time.

Apart from the aggregate balance-of-payments effects of foreign direct investment, there is also a strong need to understand more about the financial short-run behavior of multinational enterprises. The conviction is fairly widespread that multinational enterprises play a considerable role in the hot money flows that have been associated with currency instability in recent years. Convictions of this are rarely based on hard evidence; for the most part they simply stem from a priori assumptions. For instance, it is commonly assumed that these enterprises engage heavily in covered interest-rate arbitrage, and that they react sensitively to the anomalies in interest rate differences and forward rate discounts. It is also assumed that multinational enterprises react to exchange rate risks by accelerating or decelerating foreign payment and collections. Finally, it is occasionally assumed that these enterprises react in even more uninhibited fashion, by buying or selling spot and future currencies in anticipation of changes in par values. A number of studies suggest that these opinions are not wholly without factual support.[20] The evidence is not strong enough, however, to indicate the relative importance of each of these different sources of hot money flow. In short, the factual basis for effective public policy is largely lacking.

Still another issue links direct investment with the international payments mechanism. This is the question of the effects of variable exchange rates upon such investment. The near unanimity of the economics profession in supporting more flexible exchange rates does not mean that the implications of such a regime are well researched or well understood. The research problem is to compare the investment behavior of direct investors in a regime of putatively fixed rates that suffer from sporadic breakdowns, with an alternative regime in which such rates are understood to be subject to continuous change.

Analysis of Employment Effects and Growth Effects

Employment

Like the question of payments, the question of the employment effects of multinational enterprises proceeds at several different levels. One such level involves macroeconomic estimates of employment effects; another level concerns the behavior of individual enterprises in labor relations.

In order to measure the aggregate employment effects that are associated with the existence of foreign subsidiaries, one has to grapple with many of the problems that were discussed earlier in connection with the measurement of balance-of-payments effects. There is the inevitable problem of describing a world as it would have been without the foreign investment, and measuring the employment situation in that alternative world. Then there are the difficulties associated with isolating the dynamic effects of the investment decision on employment, including the effects on productivitity and the production function. Moreover, since labor is mobile to some extent across certain international boundaries and since certain key types of labor are very mobile indeed, questions of migration also have to be included in the approach wherever they may be relevant. The chances are that models in this field, like those relating to the balance of payments, will prove in the end to be costly in execution and unilluminating in results. But some added work on such models is still justified, in the hope that stronger methodologies can be developed.

Somewhat more likely to yield useful results are studies of employment practices and labor relations at the individual firm level. Several different kinds of issues are involved. One of these—the effect of the multinational enterprise upon the capacity of labor unions to bargain effectively—is already the subject of numerous speculative tracts, as well as a few serious investigations.[21] Another issue of major importance is whether and to what degree the multinational enterprise exercises its apparent capacity to shift its sourcing patterns; if in fact such shifts take place and if the shifts are greater in speed and amplitude than those to be anticipated in a world of unrelated producers, labor's problems become particularly obvious. Studies concerning the character and consequences of labor relation practices of multinational enterprises so far have generated such useful and provocative results that more analyses of a similar kind are clearly indicated.

A closely related issue is the wage payment policies of multinational enterprises; though that question clearly impinges on the bargaining issue, it is also an independent subject in part. Here and there, comparisons have been made of the wage levels of subsidiaries of multinational enterprises as compared with those of local enterprise.[22] There is a suggestion in the data that multinational enterprises tend to pay wages that are somewhat higher than their local counterparts. The reasons for that difference, if it exists, are still obscure. And the policy implications are even more so. Nevertheless, the importance of the subject in political relations and welfare analysis is sufficiently great to justify some additional effort, so that the underlying facts and the forces behind those facts can be more firmly established.

Growth

It may seem a small step from a study of employment effects to one of growth; but conceptually the step is very large.

The problem arises from the fact that the process of growth itself is so poorly understood. As long as one is prepared to accept the validity of growth models based on some simple gap concepts—such as the two-gap model that postulates aggregate savings and foreign exchange as the operational restraints on growth—the problem may be manageable with the economist's present kit of tools. But that kind of model is widely recognized as highly inefficient for some types of policy problems. It is especially inefficient, in my opinion, if the object is to formulate policies regarding the multinational enterprise. As a conduit for the transmission of information and as a mobilizer of resources on a large scale, the multinational enterprise fits awkwardly into the standard growth models. It may be that the principal growth implications of the multinational enterprise are to be found in activities of this sort. For instance, the information introduced in the economy may prove to be a stimulant or a depressant on terms of growth; and the capacity to mobilize local labor and capital in large aggregations may have benign or distorting effects on growth.

As a result, I am pushed to a disconcerting conclusion. Despite the central nature of the question of growth, I am not at all sanguine that the macroeconomic modeling of which economists are presently capable will have much to offer on this issue. As I see it, resources devoted to this approach should be committed with considerable discrimination.

Analysis of the Technology Issue

The phenomenon of the multinational enterprise and the subject of technology interrelate at numerous points. There are several clear clusters of issues which are especially important from a policy viewpoint.

One such cluster centers on the question: In what sense can the multinational enterprise be seen as an agent in the transfer of technology; and what can be said of its relative efficiency as compared with other conduits?

One rich source which provides an important building block for hypothesizing in this field is the stream of empirical studies on the subject of communication.[23] Another such source is the series of studies that deal with the nature of the innovation process.[24] My impression is that these two fields are moving ahead at a lively pace, needing no special encouragement. Already, they have produced a wealth of ideas and partially tested propositions that have been well and fruitfully used in the development of hypotheses regarding the role of foreign direct investors as purveyors of technical information. In this area, my main concern is that so many economists and policymakers seem unfamiliar with this important work and its implications.[25] Some more effective bridgebuilding is needed in this area.

On the other hand, economists have placed great stress on an issue with which they feel much more at home, namely, the question of the choice of technologies. There is fairly widespread recognition of the fact that the choice of technologies which best serves the private interest of the multinational firm may differ from the choice which best serves the social interests of each the national economies in which the subsidiaries of such enterprises operate; and there is a common assumption that this difference is greater than would be found in the operations of comparable local enterprises.

So far as I am aware, however, the theoretical basis for that conclusion has not been completely worked out. Presumably the conclusion is based on the recognition that the cost of capital will be figured by each enterprise at a rate which differs from the social cost of capital in the economy in which it operates; and there is a general assumption that this difference will be greater for the multinational enterprise than for the local firm. That assumption arises in part out of the fact that multinational enterprises have relatively easy access to capital markets outside the countries in which they establish their subsidiaries. As a result, the relevant cost of capital for such enterprises may be little affected by the relative abundance or scarcity or capital in any one country. Moreover, there may be some recognition of the possibility that the marginal cost to a multinational enterprise in introducing a technique which is already being used by the enterprise elsewhere will be low relative to the cost of introducing a new technique; hence techniques developed elsewhere may represent least-cost solutions for the multinational enterprise. Whatever the assumptions may be, they need explicit articulation and development.

In the further development of theory, however, certain neglected dimensions need to be introduced. One of these, once again, is the introduction of the variable exchange rate issue. If capital is drawn from international sources and labor is drawn from local sources, what effect does the anticipation of a variable exchange rate have upon the relative propensity to substitute one factor for the other?

Another neglected question has to do with the fact that labor is a very heterogeneous input. Most models in this field are confined to two-sector analyses, notwithstanding the fact that the labor inputs associated with many of these technologies are extremely varied. Unskilled labor is usually plentiful; supervisory and technical labor very scarce. Nevertheless, scarce types of labor and surplus types of labor are usually treated as if they were a common factor. Another neglected aspect of these analyses—one that is much more difficult to handle from the theoretical point of view—is the problem of supply elasticities associated with different technologies. The supply elasticity of a labor intensive operation probably can be assumed to differ in systematic ways from the elasticities associated with capital intensive operations; this characteristic can be seen by comparing the problems that a capital intensive operation encounters when expanding from single-shift to multi-shift operations, with the problems that a labor-intensive operation encounters when engaged in the same process. Since this sort of consideration is known to weigh heavily at times in the choice of technologies, theoretical work on the question is strongly indicated.

Hand in hand with the development of the underlying theory, it will be useful to extend and to reinterpret the observable facts. To the extent that data exist, they seem to suggest that the subsidiaries of multinational enterprises commonly do adjust their uses of the productive factors in the direction suggested by the local conditions of cost and supply, and that the degree of adjustment depends on certain systematic and seemingly rational forces.[26] There are indications also that although the plants of foreign-owned enterprises are more capital intensive than those of local competitors, they are more efficient as measured by the use of local resources;[27] and that the differences in capital intensivity may be due to a greater investment in structures rather than to a greater investment in machinery per unit of output.[28] In any case, none of these tendencies is unequivocally confirmed. The research needed for confirmation and further analysis is reasonably straightforward thanks to some of the studies previously undertaken, and substantial added effort would seem justified.

Analyses of International Competitive Behavior and Industrial Structure

The development of multinational enterprises has been having a considerable impact upon the geographical scope of the oligopolies that engage in international trade and investment. Time was, before World War II, when many of the oligopolistically structured industries confined themselves principally to national markets. When firms in such industries did make contact with one another in international trade, there was a tendency to develop cartel agreements based on the principle of the geographical division of markets.[29]

That generalization, of course, has not applied to all oligopolistically structured industries. Even before World War II, for example, the oligopolies in oil and in copper were global in nature; enterprises originating in different countries were located side by side in many areas of the world. Nevertheless, even though that kind of situation could be found in some industries before World War II, it was not nearly as widespread as it has become in recent years. As a result, the competitive situation in world markets has been going through some profound changes.

Despite these changes, systematic research in this field has been relatively limited. There have been a few comparative analyses of industrial structure in national economies.[30] There have also been a number of industry studies which have thrown light on the international oligopolistic play of some specified industries.[31] But the surface of the problem has been barely scratched. A much more solid grounding is needed for determining whether and to what extent the principles of oligopoly behavior—principles explored heretofore mainly at national levels in the context of studies in industrial organization—need be extended to the field of international trade. This sort of work ought to be directed not only at analyses of the genre that Bain has pioneered,[32] directed mainly to industry structure, but also at the implications of that structure. In short, such studies should aim at throwing light on various economic implications, notably, pricing behavior, output behavior, and innovation behavior.

Analyses Associated with Acquisitions, Joint Ventures, and Organizational Structure

Acquisitions

Among the widespread convictions regarding the multinational enterprises which greatly affect public policy is the view that the acquisition of a going concern by a foreign investor is less advantageous to the economy that receives the investment than the establishment of a new concern would be. In theoretical terms, of course, the outcome would seem indeterminate; certain key factors that affect the outcome are the subsequent performance of the local entrepreneur who sold the going concern, as well as the subsequent performance of the foreign investor. Any extensive theoretical analysis would also have to address some other difficult issues, such as the consequences of complementarity between the facilities of the acquiring enterprise and those of the acquired enterprise, as well as the consequences of the changes in the competitive situation associated with the acquisition. Despite these difficulties—perhaps because of them—more theoretical analysis is warranted.

The same can be said of the empirical work on the subject of acquisitions. Apart from the study of "take-over bids" in Canada,[33] almost nothing has been published on the subject. One doctoral thesis now in progress under the Harvard aegis may cast some light; but it can hardly be expected to do much more. On the other hand, the existing Harvard data bank for U.S.-based multinational enterprises and those now being compiled for foreign-based multinational enterprises are rich sources for a beginning on the subject.

Joint Ventures

Tracking back over the research issues raised in this chapter so far, one can restate practically every issue in an added dimension: what difference does it make if the subsidiary involved in the investment is a joint venture? The question is of major importance for public policy, largely because of a common assumption that a joint venture somehow conforms more satisfactorily to the needs of the recipient countries than does a wholly owned subsidiary. Needless to say, the theoretical structure associated with that conclusion is no better developed than that for any of the other areas discussed in these pages.

A certain amount of research, however, has already been done regarding joint ventures.[34] The work so far suggests that the pattern of ownership is more a consequence than a cause of the business behavior of multinational enterprises, reflecting a complex but rational pattern of response to opportunities and needs. Nevertheless, the joint venture structure also plays a fairly significant causal role in determining parent-subsidiary relationships. The completion of the new Harvard data bank on non-U.S. multinational enterprises will provide a basis for more work on the subject. My estimate is that more fruitful work can be done; but the problem at the moment is much less one of inadequate research than it is one of the ignorance of policymakers concerning the existence and the meaning of the research results that have been produced to date.

Organizational Structure

As far as the main body of economic theory is concerned, the organizational structure of multinational enterprises is regarded as a non-problem. Enterprises are seen as decisionmakers with a single optimizing function; the choice of structure is simply a means of approaching the optimum.

For those concerned with questions of public policy, however, this means of finessing the problem cannot stand. True, there are strong grounds for assuming that the structure of an enterprise is mainly a consequence of its choice of strategy, thereby conforming to theoretical expectations. But there are also grounds for the view that the structure which is chosen determines the strategic choices which can be expected to follow. For instance, firms that are organized on a product-centered basis can be expected to make decisions which are systematically different from those that are organized on a geographical basis;

the propensity to develop a global oligopolistic structure, for instance, will probably be greater for those organized on product lines than for those organized on geographical lines. This choice, in turn, will affect competitive behavior and impinge on issues of public policies.

This point having been made, it is extraordinarily difficult to delineate the issues that most require added research. So far, studies in the field of organizational structure have been largely descriptive and largely concerned with the improvement of managerial efficiency from a private point of view. Efforts to relate these structures to questions of public policy are only beginning.[b] The only point to be made at this stage is to recognize that, despite the relative indifference of economists, the relationship between organizational structure and public policy may be very real. Accordingly, proposals that seek to relate these two issues should not be excluded from consideration in any adequate research program.

The Political Economy of Multinational Enterprises

Most of the serious studies that have sought to appraise the economic effects of multinational enterprises upon the countries in which they operate have been agnostic in their findings.[35] On the whole, they have concluded that these enterprises were contributing to the economic welfare of the economies in which they operate. At the same time, however, two caveats generally have been attached to the conclusions: first, that the multinational enterprise seemed especially strong and flexible in the eyes of the interests they confronted in a bargaining situation, such as labor unions and government agencies; second, that the multinational enterprise was a major source, actual or potential, of instability in foreign exchange crises.

These caveats do not appear to be enough, however, to explain the high level of tension that has so often accompanied the presence of multinational enterprises. The anatomy of that tension has been explained in numerous ways: as a reaction to the clash of interests and status between indigenous elites and the managers of multinational enterprise; as a reaction to the fear of interference and dominance by the U.S. government or by U.S. culture; as a reaction to the alleged indifference or insensitivity of foreign managers to local values; and so on.

The systematic research that has been done on this set of issues so far does no more than nibble at the edges of the problem. My own work leads me to suspect that though the tension is strong and deep, it does not necessarily lead to measures curbing the multinational enterprise. The probability that such measures will be applied is greatly affected by how badly governments feel they need

[b]One volume in the Harvard Multinational Enterprise Study will deal with the issue, under the authorship of Lawrence Franko.

the enterprise. When enterprises are perceived as no longer contributing either capital or technology or markets to the economy in which they operate, the probability of repressive measures against the enterprise is sharply increased. But that conclusion is still based on fairly casual empirical impressions.

Various researchers have attempted systematically to isolate and define the nature of the tensions involved.[36] Efforts of this sort are still going forward on a number of fronts.[c] It is hard to know how to discriminate among alternative approaches in this field; the problems are so amorphous and difficult to research. However, qualitative general surveys based on open-ended interviews probably will not pay off at this stage. And large scale quantitative surveys cannot shake off a certain aura of unreality, as if the methodology introduced a wall between the researcher and the phenomenon to be studied.

A number of case studies in depth, on the other hand, have proved exceedingly valuable.[37] To the extent that individual studies can illuminate general propositions, they seem to indicate that the multinational enterprise which tries to identify with local aspirations and local values does not reduce the tensions associated with its presence very much; and the enterprise which actually takes on the task of social modernization may be running high political risks. But observations of this sort do no more than open up the subject.

On the whole, my disposition would be to encourage political scientists and sociologists to conduct added case studies concerning the sources of tension. This is a preference *faute de mieux*. Case studies can be costly in execution and unrepresentative in results. But for the moment, I see no better way of improving existing impressions concerning the anatomy of the tensions associated with the multinational enterprise.

Notes

1. For an elaboration of the distinction and some of its implications see Vernon *Sovereignty at Bay*, pp. 152-55; also Robbins and Stobaugh.
2. Vaupel and Curhan.
3. For instance, Stopford and Wells; Knickerbocker; Vaupel.
4. Robbins and Stobaugh.
5. Ibid.
6. Vernon, "Skeptic."
7. For instance, INTAL; DIVO; van den Bulke.
8. Illustrative of this sort of analysis is Scaperlanda and Mauer; Goldberg.
9. Hymer, Ph.D. thesis; Aharoni; Caves.
10. Vernon, *Sovereignty at Bay*, pp. 65-77.
11. Wells (editor); Stobaugh; Knickerbocker.

[c]For instance, Walter Goldstein under the aegis of the Twentieth Century Fund, Karl Sauvant for the Foreign Policy Research Institute, J.J. Valenzuela at Georgia State University. The Valenzuela effort is expecially interesting for its attempt at analytical rigor.

12. Nevertheless, see Dunning, *Studies*; Tsurumi, *Profiles*; Brooke and Remmers; OECD Studies; NIERS Studies; Stobaugh. See also Wilson; Neufeld; and similar studies of individual firms.

13. See especially: Hufbauer, *Synthetic Materials*; Stobaugh; Wells (editor); Horst.

14. Vernon (editor).

15. Johnson; Baldwin.

16. Hufbauer-Alder; Reddaway; Netherlands Institute.

17. Cooper; Vernon, *Financial Executives*; Dunning, *Studies*, pp. 107-17.

18. But see Stobaugh et al., which tests the effects on a case-by-case basis, against explicit alternatives that seem plausible in light of the facts of each case. Also see Lall.

19. The assumptions discussed in this paragraph and preceding paragraphs are also implicit or explicit in many of the theoretical treatments of the economic consequences of direct investment. See Kemp; Corden; Baldwin.

20. Jadwani; Robbins and Stobaugh; Brooke and Remmers, p. 190.

21. In the latter category, see Steuer and Gennard; Kujawa.

22. Brash; Lall; Safarian; Steuer and Gennard; van den Bulcke.

23. For instance, Nelson and Pollock.

24. For instance, Mansfield et al.

25. For a group of economic essays that do manage to draw on this kind of work, albeit ever so lightly, see Raymond Vernon (ed.), *The Technology Factor in International Trade* (New York: Columbia University Press, 1970).

26. Yeoman; Strassmann, pp. 149-94.

27. Brash, p. 175; Dunning (1958), p. 186.

28. Mason; Reuber; Dunning (1958).

29. Hexner.

30. Bain; Hymer and Rowthorn.

31. Canadian Royal Commission on Farm Tractors; Freeman Studies; Harman; Tilton.

32. Bain.

33. Reuber and Roseman.

34. For instance, Kapoor; Bivens and Lovell; Uyterhoeven; Tomlinson; Deane, pp. 104-06; Franko; Brash, pp. 76-79; Stofford and Wells; INTAL.

35. The studies are summarized in my *Sovereignty at Bay*, Chap. 4.

36. For instance, J.N. Behrman, *National Interests*.

37. Goodsell; Peru; Moran.

Bibliography

Aharoni, Yair. *The Foreign Investment Decision Process.* Boston: Harvard Graduate School of Business Administration, Division of Research, Harvard University, 1966.

Bain, Joe S. *Industrial Organization.* New York: Wiley, 1959.

Baldwin, Robert E. "Determinants of the Commodity Structure of U.S. Trade." *American Economic Review*, March 1971.

_____. "Determinants of the Commodity Structure of U.S. Trade: Reply," Communication, *American Economic Review*, June 1972.

Behrman, Jack N. *National Interests and the Multinational Enterprise.* Englewood Cliffs: Prentice-Hall, Inc., 1970.

Bivens, Karen, and Lovell, Enid B. *Joint Ventures with Foreign Partners.* New York: National Industrial Conference Board, 1966.

Brash, D.T. *American Investment in Australian Industry.* Cambridge: Harvard University Press, 1966.

Brooke, M.Z., and Remmers, H.L. *The Strategy of Multinational Enterprise.* London: Longmans, 1970.

Caves, Richard E. "International Corporations: The Industrial Economics of Foreign Investment." *Economica*, February 1971.

Cooper, Richard N. "Book review of Hufbauer and Adler." *Journal of Economic Literature* 7 (December 4, 1969).

Corden, W.M. "Recent Developments in the Theory of International Trade." Special Papers in International Economics, No. 7. Princeton University, 1965.

Deane, Roderick S. "Foreign Investment in New Zealand Manufacturing." Ph.D. dissertation. Victoria University at Wellington, 1967.

The DIVO Institute for Economic Research. *American Subsidiaries in the Federal Republic of Germany.* New York: Commerce Clearinghouse, 1969.

Dunning, John H. *American Investment in British Manufacturing.* London: Allen and Unwin, 1958.

_____. *Studies in International Investment.* London: Allen and Unwin, 1970.

Franko, Lawrence G. *Joint Venture Survival in Multinational Corporations.* New York: Praeger, 1971.

Freeman, Christopher. "Three Industry Studies," *National Institute Economic Review* 26 (November 1963); 34 (November 1965); 45 (August 1968).

Goldberg, Murray A. "The Determinants of U.S. Direct Investment in the EEC: Comment." *American Economic Review*, September 1972.

Goodsell, C.F. "American Corporations and Peruvian Politics." Unpublished manuscript, 1972.

Harman, Alvin G. *The International Computer Industry: Innovation and Comparative Advantage.* Cambridge: Harvard University Press, 1971.

Hexner, Ervin. *International Cartels.* Chapel Hill: University of North Carolina Press, 1945.

Horst, Thomas. "Firm and Industry Determinants of the Decisions to Invest Abroad: An Empirical Study." *Review of Economics and Statistics*, August 1972.

Hufbauer, G.C. *Synthetic Materials and the Theory of International Trade.* London: Gerald Duckworth, 1965.

Hufbauer, G.C., and Adler, F.M. *Overseas Manufacturing Investment and the Balance of Payments.* Washington, D.C.: U.S. Treasury Department, 1968.

Hymer, S.H., and Rowthorn, Robert. "Multinational Corporations and International Oligopoly: The Non-American Challenge." Economic Growth Center Discussion Paper, No. 75, Yale University, 1969.

Hymer, S.H., "The International Operation of National Firms: A Study of Direct Foreign Investment," unpublished Ph.D. thesis, MIT, 1960.

Banco Interamericano de Desarrollo (INTAL). *La Empresa Industrial en la Integracion de America Latina.* Buenos Aires: 1971.

Jadwani, Hassanand. "Some Aspects of the Multinational Corporations' Exposure to Exchange Rate Risk." D.B.A. thesis, Harvard Graduate School of Business Administration, Harvard University, 1971.

Johnson, Harry G. "The Efficiency and Welfare Implications of the International Corporation." In Charles P. Kindelberger (ed.) *The International Corporation.* Cambridge: MIT Press, 1970.

Kapoor, Ashok. "Foreign Collaborations in India, Problems and Prospects." *IDEA* 9, 2 (Summer 1966), and 9, 3, (Fall 1966).

Kemp, M.C. "Foreign Investment and the National Advantage." *Economic Record*, March 1962.

Knickerbocker, F.T. "Oligopolistic Reaction and Multinational Enterprise." D.B.A. thesis, Harvard Graduate School of Business Administration, Harvard University, 1972.

Kujawa, Duane. *International Labor Relations Management in the Automotive Industry: A Comparative Study of Chrysler, Ford and General Motors.* New York: Praeger, 1971.

Lall, Sanjaya. "Balance of Payments Effects of Private Foreign Investment in Developing Countries." UNCTAD TD/134 Supp. 1, April 1972.

Mansfield, Edwin, et al. *Research and Innovation in the Modern Corporation.* New York: Norton, 1971.

Mason, R. Hal. *The Transfer of Technology and the Factor Proportions Problem: The Philippines and Mexico.* UNITAR Research Reports, No. 10, 1971.

Moran, T.H. "The Multinational Corporation and the Politics of Development: The Case of Copper in Chile." Ph.D. thesis, Harvard Department of Government, Harvard University, 1971.

Nelson, C.E., and Pollock, D.K. *Communication among Scientists and Engineers.* Lexington: Heath Lexington Books, 1971.

Netherlands Economics Institute, "A Quantitative Study on the Macro-Economic Evolution of Private Foreign Investment in Less-Developed Countries." Unpublished manuscript, May 1972.

Neufeld, E.D. *A Global Corporation.* Toronto: University of Toronto Press, 1969.

OECD. *Gaps in Technology Between Member Countries: Sector Report, Plastics.* Paris: OECD, 1968.

Pinelo, A.J. "The Nationalization of an International Petroleum Company in Peru." Ph.D. thesis, University of Massachusetts, 1972.

Reddaway, W.B. (in collaboration with S.J. Potter & C.T. Taylor). *Effects of United Kingdom Direct Investment Overseas: Final Report.* Cambridge, England: University Press, 1968.

Reuber, G.L. Untitled study presented to Conference on Private Foreign Investment: O.E.C.D., Development Center, Paris, June 8, 1972.

Reuber, G.L., and Roseman, Frank. "The Takeover of Canadian Firms, 1945-1961: An Empirical Analysis." Mimeograph, 1968.

Robbins, S.M., and Stobaugh, R.B. *Money in the Multinational Enterprise.* New York: Basic Books, 1972.

Royal Commission on Farm Machinery. *Report of the Royal Commission on Farm Machinery.* Ottawa: Information Canada, 1971.

Safarian, A.E. *Foreign Ownership of Canadian Industry.* Toronto: McGraw-Hill Company Limited, 1966.

Scaperlanda, A.E. and Mauer, L.J. "The Determinants of U.S. Direct Investment in the EEC." *American Economic Review,* September 1969.

Steuer, Max, and Gennard, John. "Industrial Relations, Labor Disputes and Labor Utilization of Foreign Owned Firms in the United Kingdom." In John H. Dunning (ed.), *The Multinational Enterprise.* London: Allen and Unwin, 1971.

Stobaugh, R.B. "The Product Life Cycle and International Investment." D.B.A. thesis, Harvard Graduate School of Business Administration, Harvard University, 1968.

Stobaugh, R.B., et al. "U.S. Multinational Enterprises and the U.S. Economy." In *The Multinational Corporation: Studies on U.S. Foreign Investment.* Washington, D.C.: Department of Commerce, March 1972, vol. I.

Stopford, John M., and Wells, Louis T., Jr. *Managing the Multinational Enterprise: Organization of the Firm and Ownership of the Subsidiaries.* New York: Basic Books, 1972.

Strassmann, W.P. *Technological Change and Economic Development.* Ithaca: Cornell University Press, 1968.

Tilton, John E. *International Diffusion of Technology: The Case of Semiconductors.* Washington, D.C.: The Brookings Institution, 1971.

Tomlinson, James W. *The Join Venture Process in International Business.* Cambridge: MIT Press, 1970.

Tsurumi, Yoshihiro. "Profiles of Japan-Based Multinational Firms." *Journal of World Trade Law,* 1972.

Uyterhoeven, Hugo, E.R. "Foreign Entry and Joint Ventures." D.B.A. thesis, Harvard Graduate School of Business Administration, Harvard University, 1963.

Valenzuela, Juan J. "Political Determinants of Direct, Private, U.S. Manufacturing Investment in Latin American Countries." University of North Carolina, mimeograph, July 21, 1972.

van den Bulcke, D. *Les Entreprises Etrangères dans l'Industrie Belge.* Ghent: University of Ghent, 1971.

Vaupel, J.W. "The Multinational Expansion of U.S. Manufactures." Unpublished manuscript, Kennedy School of Government, Harvard University, 1972.

Vaupel, J.W., and Curhan, Joan P. *The Making of Multinational Enterprise.* Boston: Harvard Graduate School of Business Administration, Division of Research, Harvard University, 1969.

Vernon, Raymond. *U.S. Controls on Foreign Direct Investments—A Reevaluation.* Research Foundation of Financial Executives Institute, April 1969.

_____ . "A Skeptic Looks at the Balance of Payments." *Foreign Policy*, No. 5, Winter 1971-1972.

_____ . *Sovereignty at Bay: The Multinational Spread of U.S. Enterprises.* New York: Basic Books, 1971.

_____ . (ed.) *The Technology Factor in International Trade.* New York: Columbia University Press, 1970.

Wells, L.T. (ed.) *The Product Life Cycle and International Trade.* Boston: Harvard Graduate School of Business Administration, Division of Research, Harvard University, 1972.

Wilson, Charles. *Unilever 1945-1965.* London: Cassell, 1968.

Yeoman, W.A. "Selection of Production processes for the Manufacturing Subsidiaries of U.S.-Based Multinational Corporation." D.B.A. thesis, Harvard Graduate School of Business Administration, Harvard University, April 1968.

5

World Politics and the International Economic System

Robert O. Keohane and Joseph S. Nye
Stanford University and Harvard University

The substance of international politics is conflict and its adjustment among groups of people who acknowledge no common supreme authority.
—William T.R. Fox and Annette
Baker Fox, "International Politics,"
*International Encyclopedia of
The Social Sciences* 8 (1968): 51.

Now economics is what most governments are talking to each other about. . . . This movement of emphasis in the colloquy of nations reflects a growing sense that, in the atomic age, effective power, power which can be used, may have more to do with money and goods than with bombs.
—*New York Times*, September 12, 1972.

It is not commonplace to observe that international politics and economics are closely linked to one another, and that sophisticated analysis of either requires some understanding of both. Nevertheless, few writers actually relate the two. Economists tend to assume the political structure, ignore politics entirely, or at best, attempt to analyze its effects on economic processes through the use of highly simplified political notions. Political scientists are even more guilty of disciplinary tunnel-vision. Most professional students of international politics know relatively little about international economics. Generally, like neophytes at three-dimensional tic-tac-toe, political analysts take formal cognizance of economic planes of power, but in fact succumb to the habit of playing the game on the familiar military-diplomatic plane.

This chapter draws some connections between world politics and international economic processes. The second section develops conceptual arguments about change in the nature and role of force, power, "balance of power," interdependence, complexity, and leadership. The third section surveys five specific problem areas in which politics and economics intersect. The fourth section addresses the questions of research and training in the interdisciplinary understanding of international political economy.

One difficulty in undertaking this type of enterprise lies in the slipperiness of the words and concepts involved. Casual efforts soon bog down in the ambiguities of common usage. Economic activities are generally thought of as having to do with the production and exchange of goods, services, and wealth.

The term "political activities," however, is used to refer to the actions of governments, partisan activities, controversial activities, public activities, exercise of "power," activities involving force, inefficient activities, and a variety of other confusions. Thus we begin with a brief exercise in clarification of concepts.

Economics and Politics in World Affairs

A discussion of the relationship between politics and economics should distinguish, however imperfectly, between the goals of a set of activities and the means that are used to achieve them. Economic means may be used to achieve political goals and vice versa. We will consider an actor's *political goals* to be those having to do with improving its position in conflicts with other actors, or more broadly, those having to do with the establishment of an order of relations, a structure, that it favors.[1] *Economic goals* are those that center on the possession and consumption of goods, services, and wealth. *Political means* involve political behavior: that is, the conscious use of resources (material or symbolic) to induce others to behave differently than they otherwise would.[2] *Economic means*, on the other hand, involve increasing the efficiency of one's production and exchange mechanisms in order to achieve either political or economic goals.[3]

In practice, both goals and means are likely to involve mixtures of political and economic factors. Thus, although in the short run it may be possible to identify tradeoffs between economic and political goals, over longer periods it may be impossible to settle disputes over whether the manifest goals of activity were the "real" goals of the actors involved. For example, a country that excludes foreign investment to avoid dependence can be said to trade economic for political goals. But "when the United States, for over twenty-five years, lends support to European integration because it wants Europe to be strong, it is not making a distinction between economic and political strength."[4] Insofar as economic and political goals are compatible, it is impossible to distinguish clearly between them, either in theory or in practice. Nevertheless, if we keep in mind the analytic distinctions between political and economic goals and means, we may be able to avoid undue ambiguity in language, if not always in empirical substance.

The fact that a particular activity is characterized by nonpolitical behavior—for instance, when transactions are carried on through a competitive price system—does not imply that politics was unimportant in establishing the structure of relations within which the activity took place. The impact of politics may be indirect, in the sense that political behavior is consciously used to determine the *structure* of relations within which day-to-day processes take place. Critics of pluralistic approaches to the study of local and national politics have pointed out that this second "face of power" is extremely important in determining what issues are raised for political decision and what issues are not.[5]

There can be little doubt that the major economic features of the 1960s—rapidly expanding and relatively nondiscriminatory trade, large-scale and rapid movements of funds from one center to another under fixed exchange rates, changed only rarely, and the emergence of huge multinational enterprises—could only have developed within a political environment favorable to large-scale internationalized capitalism. As Robert Gilpin has pointed out, the United States has played a crucial role in creating the requisite political structure:

Just as the Pax Brittanica provided the security and political framework for the expansion of transnational economic activity in the nineteenth century, so the Pax Americana has fulfilled a similar function in the mid-twentieth century. Under American leadership the various rounds of GATT negotiations have enabled trade to expand at an unprecedented rate, far faster than the growth of gross national product in the United States and Western Europe. The United States dollar has become the basis of the international monetary system, and, with the rise of the Eurodollar market, governments have lost almost all control over a large segment of the transnational economy. Finally, the multinational corporation has found the global political environment a highly congenial one and has been able to integrate production across national boundaries.[6]

The importance of this aspect of power leads us to distinguish between two levels of analysis, a "process-level," dealing with short-term allocative behavior (i.e., holding institutions, fundamental assumptions, and expectations constant), and a "structure-level," having to do with long-term political and economic determinants of the incentives and constraints within which actors operate. At the structural level, we are interested in how the institutions, fundamental assumptions, and "rules of the game" of political systems support or undermine different patterns of allocation for economic activity, as well as in the converse—how the nature of economic activity affects the political structure.

In some systems at some times, the levels of structure and process are relatively well insulated from one another. Basic institutions and practices are accepted as legitimate by all major parties. Economic activity in these systems may involve very little direct political intervention, and on the international level, there may be only minor and infrequent attention paid to economic affairs by top government leaders. At other times, however, allocative decisions, and the rules of the game themselves, are called into question by major participants. In the terminology that we will use in this chapter, the system becomes "politicized" as controversiality increases and depoliticized as it decreases. In highly politicized systems, attention of top-level decisionmakers is focused on the system, and nonroutine behavior dominates routine behavior. Insulation between the structure of the system and particular processes breaks down: specific quarrels become linked to macro-level arguments about appropriate institutions and permanent arrangements.

To understand political-economic changes, it is necessary to understand both the level of structure and that of process, as well as politicization and depoliticization, which link the two. Failure to do so leads to hopeless disputes about the relative importance of economic and political factors in world affairs.

The Politicization of International
Economic Activity

Ultimately, the parameters of economic activity are determined by governmental action or inaction; in that sense, economic activity always has a political dimension. Likewise, the structure of the international economic system is necessarily determined largely by governmental policies and power relationships among governments. Nevertheless, the day-to-day operation of the system can be more or less subject to controversy, and therefore more or less politicized in the sense in which we use the term.

It is when accepted structures, with their associated "rules of the game," become called into question that controversiality, and therefore politicization in our sense, is likely to increase most rapidly. During these periods, questions of who will exercise political control, and how, become dominant. Thus one observes increasing disagreements among a larger number of important contenders, over a broader range of issues, and an increase in the attention devoted to the issues by heads of government and cabinet ministers.

We are now witnessing increasing politicization of international economic affairs. To some extent, this seems to be the result of secular trends toward more governmental intervention in the economy, with important implications for international as well as domestic politics. It is also, however, a product of other long-term changes that have affected the political relations among states, the effective means at their disposal, and other aspects of their political-economic milieu. Transnational economic relations, for instance, as symbolized by the multinational enterprise acting as investor, trader, employer in several countries, and monetary speculator, create important and frequently novel problems for governments.

This politicization of economic issues is reflected by the topics of summit meetings among leaders in the United States, Europe, and Japan; in the elevated prominence of the U.S. Treasury over the last several years; in the attention paid to economic issues by newspapers and journals dealing with foreign affairs; and in the difficulties in reaching agreement on monetary, trade, or investment issues among the parties involved. Where once it was possible for political scientists to use the term "high politics" to refer simultaneously to security policy and to important matters dealt with at high levels, the increasing attention to economic questions and the close relationships between these issues and traditional political questions make the term confusing at best and seriously misleading at worst.[7] De Gaulle's delightfully anachronistic view that "l'intendance suivra" should be remembered in connection with the fact that it was partly the baggage train that ultimately did him in.

This section will outline, in broad terms, some of the changes in political relations among governments, as well as within those governments and between them and nongovernmental actors, that have contributed to this politicization. In the third section, we will consider developments in a number of issue-areas involving close economic-political interaction.

The Relative Utility of Force and of Economic Power

Political scientists for the past three decades have generally emphasized the role of force, particularly organized military force, in international politics. Force dominates other means of power in the sense that *if* there are no constraints on one's choice of instruments (a hypothetical situation that has only been approximated in the two world wars of the century), the state or states with superior military force will prevail. Thus American economic sanctions against Japan in 1940-41 could be countered by Japanese military action; to the military challenge, the United States had to answer in military terms.

If the security dilemma for all states were extremely acute, military force and its supporting components (which, of course, include a large economic dimension) would be clearly the dominant source of power. Survival is the primary goal of all states, and force is ultimately, in the most adverse situations, necessary to guarantee survival. Thus military force is always a component of national power. But insofar as the perceived margin of safety for states widens, other goals become important;[8] and there is no guarantee that military force will be an appropriate tool to achieve these goals. Furthermore, as the nature of military force and the consequences of its use change, it has become less efficacious even for achieving the goals that it formerly served. The disproportionate destructiveness of nuclear weapons limits the utility of this type of force for achieving positive goals (Schelling's "compellence") as compared to deterrence. In addition, as Hoffmann argues, prevailing norms and the costliness of ruling alien populations that have become socially mobilized increases the cost of using conventional force.[9] As these changes in goals and the nature of force take place, the roles of other instruments of power and influence tend to increase.

Force is of negligible importance in relations among the nonnuclear developed countries—for instance, between Germany and Japan, Italy and Holland, or New Zealand and the United Kingdom. Yet nonnuclear developed states are often very interested in influencing each other's policies; if force is not a useful tool of policy, other instruments are sought. With changes in instruments, patterns of world politics are therefore developing that are quite different from those typical of the first postwar quarter century. Intense relationships of mutual influence are developing in which force is ruled out as an instrument of policy—and these are not limited to common markets or members of a politico-military bloc. This is certainly an historic change of great magnitude, with implications, as noted below, for the political relevance of economics.

For other actors in world politics, on the other hand, nonnuclear force remains applicable for achieving some foreign policy aims. Small and middle powers may employ force against enemies, as one can observe on the Indian subcontinent and in the Middle East. Certain transnational groups such as the Palestinian movements rely on force to achieve their goals as well. The .superpowers, of course, have also used force to control situations about which their leaders were concerned. In some cases, such as the intervention of the United States in the Dominican Republic in 1965, and the Soviet intervention in Czechoslovakia three years later, the use of force was effective, at least in the short run. In others, such as the American internvention in Indochina, the policy of force led to disastrous results. Each superpower has also used the threat of force to deter attacks by the other superpower on itself or its allies. Yet even for the superpowers, the use of threat of force has been a declining asset in recent years.

As the efficacy of force has declined, the threats to state autonomy have also shifted, from the security area—in which the threat is defined largely in terms of territorial integrity—to the area of economic interdependence. Government policies increasingly impinge on one another, as mutual sensitivities increase as a result of the collapse of natural barriers that used to insulate economies from one another.[10] Thus the purpose of exercising power may be less to prevent another state from taking military action than to prevent it from shifting costs of its own domestic policy actions onto oneself—for instance, through trade restrictions, maintenance of an undervalued exchange rate, or nontariff barriers of one kind or another. Economic sources of power, which are more easily applied incrementally than threats of force, and which do not raise the same affronts to national prestige and dignity, are often the most applicable means for dealing with others' policies that impose significant costs on oneself.

Yet we must go beyond these observations about relative increases in efficacy of economic as opposed to military sources of power to look at the interaction between the two—for it is here that some of the most important foreign policy tensions of the contemporary world are threatening to arise. Since each superpower protects its allies against the threat of attack or political pressure from the other superpower, the importance of these nuclear weapons for deterrence is a valuable resource which can be used by alliance leaders in their own bargaining on other issues with their alliance partners. Insofar as the leaders of a state perceive their country as less dependent than its partners on their military alliance, it may be tempted to use its lesser dependence in the military field to gain economic advantages. The United States has behaved in this way on the issue of troop levels in Europe, sometimes through calculated executive actions, sometimes through congressional initiatives contrary to executive preference. The tacit linking of Okinawa reversion to a textile agreement is a sign of similar activity in American relations with Japan, now that the United States feels less dependent upon Japanese bases for the defense of Southeast Asia.

Such inter-issue "linkages," however, can carry heavy costs insofar as they create uncertainty or resentment that lead allies to reorient their fundamental policies. The linking of economic and security issues is both powerful and dangerous, since it represents a linking of economic processes with the political structure that underlies them. It may be true in the short run that the militarily dependent state has no alternatives. Repeated structural linkages, however, may create an incentive for militarily dependent but potentially powerful states to change the structure over the longer run, particularly (as is the case with Japan) if a sense of dignity is a highly important motivation.

The basic point here is that linkage strategies generate counter-strategies. The focus of these counter-strategies may be either military, as suggested above, or economic. As economic interdependence grows, so do political levers. For instance, the growth of American direct investment abroad increases the range of strategies open to other states, since they may be able effectively to threaten, implicitly or explicitly, to nationalize American-owned assets. As the relationship between Russia and France before World War I illustrates, debts may give influence to debtors as well as to creditors.[11] American investments, however, may serve in some situations to increase U.S. government influence, particularly were a decision made consciously to manipulate them for political purposes. This would further broaden the scope of political-economic linkages, and their potential danger.

Insofar as there is less than perfect congruity between the relative economic and political power of states involved in close and complex relations, structural linkages between security and economic areas are probably inevitable. In a period of transition such as the present, they are likely to become particularly pronounced. The extent to which they are employed infrequently and judiciously, only on important issues and in the service of reasonable demands, will determine the extent to which they are useful rather than destructive as tools of diplomacy.

Asymmetrical Interdependencies as
Sources of Power

One of the implications of the preceding analysis is that international political power cannot be considered as analogous to money in a domestic economic system. It is neither homogeneous nor highly fungible. Sources of power are diverse. Different forms of power are applicable to different situations, are of different strengths, and carry different costs of use. "The exercise of power" in one issue-area may look quite different than in another.

This variability in what we call "power" has long been a source of confusion and frustration to political scientists and political theorists, since it makes systematic and consistent analysis so difficult. Defining power as "the ability of one actor consciously to affect the behavior of another" helps to indicate what we mean by the concept, but it does not necessarily bring unity to its analysis. We suggest that a parsimonious way to conceptualize diverse sources of power—and therefore to explain distributions of power-resources among actors in world politics—is to regard power as deriving from patterns of asymmetrical interdependence between actors in the issue-areas in which they are involved with one another. This notion by no means solves any theoretical problems of power, but it does draw our attention to the link between power, a basic concept of the political scientist, and interdependence, which has become a focus of concern for students of international economic systems.

Where actors are asymmetrically interdependent, we expect the less dependent to be able to manipulate the relationship as a source of power, within the issue-area and perhaps in other issue-areas as well. We will focus primarily on states in this analysis, but this applies to other relationships as well: between for instance, a state and a multinational enterprise. Patterns of interdependence can vary along two dimensions, intensity of relations and relative power of resources of actors, as indicated in Table 5-1, although the most interesting relations, on which we will concentrate, are all of relatively high intensity.

Many relationships of interdependence in the contemporary world remain highly asymmetric, although intense. This is true of relations between the major developed states and many less developed countries. On the other hand, relationships of interdependence among major developed states (and between them and some less developed states, such as the oil producing countries) are frequently relatively symmetric when taken as a whole. One state or group is more dependent in certain issue-areas, but this is countered by the reverse holding true elsewhere. These high-intensity, symmetric relations of interdependence are particularly interesting for our purposes, not only because they are characteristic of relations among major developed countries, but also because they tend to give rise to a complex and fascinating politics of cross-issue linkage and bargaining.

Yet "interdependence" is an exceedingly vague term, even when the distinction between symmetry and asymmetry is made. As one author defines the term, it refers to "the extent to which events occurring in any given part or within any given component unit of a world system affect (either physically or perceptually) events taking place in each of the other parts or component units of the system."[12] One can begin to refine this by making a distinction between two loci of interdependence: the societal level and the policy level. In the former case, events taking place elsewhere in the system affect a society directly. This is

Table 5-1
Two Dimensions of Interdependence*

| | | Relative Power-Resources of Actors: | |
		Symmetric	Asymmetric
intensity of relations:	high	(Germany-France)	(US-Guatemala)
	low	(W. Germany-China)	(USSR-New Zealand)

*Percentage is a third (and crucial) dimension left out of this simple portrayal.

most striking in the monetary area. Before 1914, changes in Britain's Bank Rate directly affected Argentina's economic conditions by influencing that country's money supply, quite in the absence of deliberate governmental policy intent on either side.[13] As Richard Cooper and Lawrence Krause have pointed out, during the 1960s the economies of major Western countries were affected significantly by interest-rate and other financial changes abroad, *despite* the existence of governmental policies to control these effects.[14] Many other kinds of transnational transactions, whether involving migration, electronic communications, or multinational business, have direct effects on other societies.

At the policy level, by contrast, we are concerned with how governmental policy is affected by events elsewhere in the system: policy, rather than socioeconomic indicators, becomes the dependent variable in the interdependence equation. As governments have become increasingly involved in national economic planning, they have frequently attempted to take measures to prevent their objectives at the national level from being undercut by transnational influences. During the 1930s this took the form of competitive devaluations, bilateral trade agreements, and "beggar my neighbor" policies: during the 1950s and 1960s, it led to increasing intergovernmental coordination of economic policy in organizations such as the European Economic Community (EEC) and the Organization for Economic Cooperation and Development (OECD). The key point in either case, however, is that the burden of adjustment to change was taken to some extent off the society—or those members of it most vulnerable to change—and made the responsibility of the government. In a number of areas, societal interdependence therefore decreased—with an effective Central Bank, Argentina could control its own money supply to some extent—but policy interdependence increased.

From our political point of view, only policy interdependence is relevant to questions of power distribution among states in the short term. If governments are not concerned with the sensitivity of domestic basket-weavers to foreign competition—or, in the extreme case, with their domestic money supplies—threats to affect trade in baskets or flows of funds are not likely to carry much weight with them. Only when issues appear on governmental agendas do the transnational aspects of those issues take on direct and immediate relevance for power relations among states.

Having focused on policy interdependence, we can refine our use of the term by making what we consider to be a very important distinction between *sensitivity interdependence* and *vulnerability interdependence.* . Young's definition, quoted above, and Cooper's usage of the term in *The Economics of Interdependence*, imply the notion of interdependence as sensitivity. Transactions have effects on societies and therefore on policies, which become sensitive to one another through the effects of these flows. Under this conception, interdependence is created by interaction within a framework that is established and generally taken for granted. This conception of interdependence is often appropriate for the analysis of state behavior when the structure of relations is well established and generally accepted but where marginal effects of changes in flows within that structure can have significant effects. Thus, given the structure of international monetary relations existing until August 15, 1971, European governments were dependent on (that is, sensitive to) changes in American monetary policy, and the United States was dependent on (that is, sensitive to) European decisions to continue to hold dollars without demanding that they be exchanged into gold.

Yet as Kenneth Waltz has pointed out, this usage of the word "interdependence" may obscure some of the most important political facts.[15] To analyze the monetary system of the 1960s, one needs not only to ask about the effects of actual or potential transactions, but about the effects of disrupting or unilaterally changing the system itself. Who was capable of that, and what were the opportunity costs involved? Thus our second form of policy interdependence rests on the opportunity costs of action: the less dependent state incurs relatively lower costs from the termination or drastic alteration of the relationship. Insofar as it is relevant as a source of power, this *vulnerability interdependence* always reflects potential rather than actual costs. Its efficacy depends on mutual perceptions that state A would lose less by disrupting or continuing to disrupt a system than would state B.

Vulnerability interdependence is particularly relevant for the analysis of the *structure* of relations in an issue-area. In a sense, it asks which actors are the "definers of the *ceteris paribus* clause," or in game theoretic terms, which actors can restructure the payoff matrix.[16] It is clearly more relevant than notions of sensitivity interdependence in the discussion of the politics of raw materials, such as oil. In this issue-area, the analyst must know who would be hurt least by a suspension of oil shipments from one country, or a group of countries, to one or several consumers, and, even more important, what the major actors believe about which parties would be hurt most severely. American sensitivity to European decisions about their gold-dollar portfolio balance was virtually eliminated in August 1971 when the United States changed the rules of the game, thus negating the ceteris paribus clause upon which European attempts to use this sensitivity as a source of influence had depended. These examples are further developed in the third section.

We noted above that military power, although more costly (often prohibitively so) to exercise than economic power, "dominates" economic power in the sense that economic means are likely to be ineffective against its serious use. There is a similar relationship between vulnerability interdependence and sensitivity interdependence. Exercising the former involves threatening by word or deed to disrupt a system. Since such disruption is likely to nullify existing sensitivities—and may be planned or threatened precisely for such purposes—it can hardly be countered by attempts to manipulate those sensitivities themselves, but must be met on its own, or even more drastic, terms.

Yet threatening to disrupt a system is inherently risky, and may call into being counter-strategies. Japan countered American exploitation of greater Japanese vulnerability to embargo in 1940-41 by attacking Pearl Harbor and the Philippines. At a less extreme level, a threat to disrupt a system may threaten one's own power base. Were the OPEC countries seriously to threaten an embargo against Western countries, the search for oil substitutes and safe, non-OPEC sources of oil (even expensive oil) would presumably become much more urgent. Eventually, oil might become no more effective as a political weapon than rubber is today.

We can therefore order our three types of asymmetrical interdependence into a hierarchy according to the effectiveness of the power resulting from each of them, as well as its costs. This can be schematized as shown in Table 5-2.

Table 5-2
Asymmetrical Interdependence and the Applicability of Forms of Power

Source of Interdependence	Effectiveness Ranking	Cost Ranking	Areas of Contemporary Applicability
Military-vulnerability (differing opportunity costs of conflict)	1	1	Only in extreme situations or against very weak but recalcitrant foes
Economic-vulnerability (differing opportunity costs of system-disruption)	2	2	As the virtual ultimate weapon in a number of areas where force is ruled out—although may be countered also by linkage strategies or long-term autarchic strategies
Economic-sensitivity (different sensitivities to system processes)	3	3	As the most frequently available and usable form of power resource for wide range of low- to medium-intensity issues

There is no guarantee that patterns of interdependence on one of these three dimensions will be congruent with patterns of interdependence on the others. In the contemporary system, the United States retains great power even where a given set of relations may be adverse to it, because of its ability to sustain the costs of increased autarchy, if necessary, as well as its great military potential. Extensive American-owned foreign investments increase the potential costs of economic autarchy to the United States, but do not eliminate its superiority on this dimension. Thus in the economic as well as in the military area, the United States retains an "escalation option."

A movement from using one power resource to using a more effective, but more costly, resource, is only likely to take place where a substantial incongruity exists between the relative distribution of power resources on one dimension and those on another. If a state finds itself in a disadvantageous position within a given system of economic relations, it is likely to attempt to change the rules of the game *if* its leaders judge that the patterns of interdependence on this level are substantially more favorable to it. Likewise, if a state feels harmed by the behavior of others that appear to control the rules of the economic system, it may, like Japan in 1941, attempt to use military force to redress that unfavorable situation—but only if its leaders are rational, if it estimates the costs as relatively low compared to the status quo, and its own relative position militarily more favorable than in the economic area. The first of these conditions is rarely met for important states in the post-atomic world, as indicated above.

The analysis in this section has assumed a rational, unitary-actor model of foreign policy-making in major states. On this basis, we can explain some linkages among issues, and some behavior designed to change the power-resources relevant to a conflict. These assumptions are crude simplifications of actual behavior. We will therefore return to the problem of linkages under "Structural Change and Leadership Log," after having explored issues of policy coherence.

The "Balance of Power": Economic and Political

This discussion of the sources of power in the current international system may help us to evaluate recent characterizations of the current era as one of a "new balance of power" among the major actors. It is evident from traditional political analysis that this terminology is at best loose, since bipolarity continues to exist in the nuclear deterrence aspects of the security issue-area. Only the United States and the U.S.S.R. have invulnerable deterrent forces with credible second strike capabilities, and given the necessary political cohesion and level of expenditure to develop such a force, this will probably continue to be true for at least another decade. The United States and U.S.S.R. together account for nearly half of world GNP and some 70 percent of world military expenditure.[17] Thus in military terms, as Brzezinski has recently pointed out, "we have something which might be called a 2 1/2 powers world, although certainly not a stable balance."[18] Alternatively, the world can be seen in terms of two triangles—a military triangle involving the United States, Russia, and China; and an economic triangle involving the United States, Europe, and Japan. Two triangles do not form a pentagon, and this imagery is less misleading than images of a five-power balance.

Yet even these triangles do not properly encompass political reality. Power at the nonstrategic level is much more dispersed than at the strategic level. As a coalition-leading state, the United States developed a strategy and an accompanying ideology of anticommunism in the years after 1947 that made it susceptible to the appeals and blandishments of its allies.[19] In our terms as developed above, the development of alliance systems created networks of interdependence that were not wholly asymmetrical: the United States depended on its small allies for the attainment of its purpose as well as vice versa. Fragmentation of policy, and the consequent squandering of potential power resources, may result from the size and diffuseness of attention of a great power: Small states can often focus their attention on the U.S. government more effectively than the latter, with its many concerns and diffuse organizational structure, can do in return. Finally, great powers need to be concerned more than small states about the effects of their actions on the system as a whole. Insofar as this is true, it serves as a constraint on the exercise of power. United States dealings with Canada, for instance, have generally reflected a desire not to destabilize the structure of relationships that exists by pushing an advantage in a specific issue-area too hard.[20]

These arguments suggest that if there is a new balance of power, it does not imply, as did classical balance of power politics, subordination of small powers to great ones in a rather strict hierarchy. But if we focus on economic relations, particularly in the United States-Europe-Japan "triangle," the balance of power analogy seems even less applicable. The recent relative increase in the importance of economic power—far from heralding a return to balance of power politics—actually indicates a rather different phenomenon. On economic issues, while governments are to some extent motivated by status and power considerations, they are also strongly influenced by domestic demands for resources, which focus primarily on *absolute* gains as reflected in national income and employment, rather than on gains relative to other countries.[21] Governments may compete economically and take pleasure in doing better than their counterparts, and to some extent, economic performance abroad affects domestic economic demands. But by and large, the public and electoral pressures are for prosperity as measured by national criteria. These criteria vary from country to country, as is clear from the different tolerances of the German and English publics for inflation, or the United States and most major European countries for unemployment. Where this is the case, it is even more true that "doing better than the past" is more important to governments than "doing better than other countries" in economic activities. Relative gains in economic power come largely as by-products of successful national performance undertaken to satisfy domestic requirements.

This is quite the opposite of the traditional military-political model of the balance of power, in which absolute gains in military power are sought not at all for themselves, but entirely for the relative advantage they may confer vis-à-vis one's potential opponents. The economic game is therefore much farther than the strategic game from a "zero-sum" model in which gains and losses cancel out. Thus a chief prediction of classical balance of power theory—that states will act to protect themselves by limiting the capabilities of strong states or coalitions[22]—will not necessarily hold where this objective conflicts with the goal of a substantial gain in wealth or employment. The political pressures domestically will certainly push governments toward a willingness to sacrifice relative power, if necessary, for the sake of real economic gains that can be translated into jobs, incomes, and votes.

Thus, although Europe and Japan may not be unhappy to see American economic power reduced, they are hardly likely to take steps to achieve that goal if that would lead to significant declines in their own prosperity. Conversely, I.F. Stone's characterization of U.S. policy of rapprochement with "China as a counterweight to Japan, and . . . Russia as a counterweight to Europe" as part of "the old balance of power game," is mistaken—because it fails to perceive the positive sum aspects of the rise in European and Japanese economic strength.[23] The metaphor of a balance-of-power among strong economic powers is therefore potentially quite misleading if it implies anything more than the obvious: that the distribution of economic power is no longer hegemonial, with the United States in a dominant position, and that, *in the absence of other costs*, states will act to improve their relative power positions.

Increased Complexity of Actors and Issues

These shifts in the relative importance of military and economic power are paralleled by an increasing complexity of actors and issues in world politics. From the perspective of this chapter, four elements in this complexity stand out: (1) the increasing diversity of types of actors, particularly non-state actors, in world politics; (2) the broadened agenda of foreign policy as a result of increased sensitivity of societies to one another in areas that were formerly considered purely domestic; (3) the increasing difficulties faced by states in maintaining policy coherence; and (4) the increasing possibilities for linkages between various types of issues.

Types of Actors. If we simply count the number of states with competitive political systems, as opposed to authoritarian or mass mobilization systems, we find a relative decline over the past two decades in the former. It could therefore be argued that there is a greater diversity of types of states in the contemporary system than in the past.[24] Yet if we focus on the major trading and investing nations, we find a remarkable degree of political homogeneity: all of them have competitive political systems (with the single exception of the Soviet Union, if it is included as a major trading state).

Yet homogeneity among states could be misleading. Recent years have also seen the rise of new actors in world politics, both transnational and intergovernmental, with a bewildering variety of characteristics. Multinational enterprises and transnational guerrilla movements both complicate the patterns of interaction among states and pose problems for foreign policy, whether these have to do with complex effects of direct foreign investment or Olympic hostages in Munich. Intergovernmental organizations such as the Commission of the European Community or the secretariats of organizations such as the IMF, World Bank, GATT, OECD, or UNCTAD, have developed a certain degree of autonomy, however precarious, and ability to exercise leadership on important politico-economic issues. Outcomes in an issue-area such as international monetary policy, for instance, cannot be understood solely as the result of state action and interaction: the behavior of multinational enterprises and multinational banks, as well as the activities of international civil servants and the effects on national policies of institutionalized forums for discussion, must also be taken into account.

These actors are not likely to surpass the major states in importance during the next decade, although some of them already have greater resources at their disposal, and greater impact on outcomes in key issue-areas, than a number of members of the United Nations. Yet the new actors will co-exist with states and their importance will be felt by states. Though they lack the legitimacy and ultimate recourse to the territorial police power or international exercise of force that remain significant resources of states, and though states will generally continue to prevail over the new actors in cases of open clashes, the costs to governments of such victories can be expected to rise, and the influence of the new actors will be felt as an important constraint on state policies.[25]

Broadened Foreign Policy Agendas. One of the important effects of the new actors in world politics is their role as transmission belts that transmit policy sensitivities across national boundaries. As the decision domains of corporations, banks, and (to a lesser extent) trade unions transcend national boundaries, a wide range of domestic policies come to impinge upon each other. These effects are further reinforced by transnational communications, which occur even in the absence of organizations. This growing policy sensitivity means that foreign economic policies touch a wider range of domestic economic activity than has been true in the past quarter century, thus blurring the lines between domestic and foreign policy and increasing the number of issues relevant to foreign policy.

As the agenda broadens, policymakers are faced with an increase in the number of their objectives and frequently in the contradictions between the achievement of one objective and the attainment of others. A natural response is to increase the number of bureaucratic instruments to match the increased number of objectives. Bureaucracy is an instrument, however, that involves high costs of coordination, particularly in terms of the scarce resources of top policymakers' attention. When there are powerful simplifying myths that help top policymakers maintain the hierarchy of collective over particular interests, the bureaucratic instrument is part of the solution. When such myths are absent and the sense of overriding purpose breaks down, normal compartmentalized bureaucratic behavior often adds to the problem. Bureaucratic subunits may become competitors for influence rather than instruments of a coordinated strategy.

Difficulties of Policy Coherence. Faced with a broader policy agenda and a more varied set of actors, major Western powers have confronted great difficulties in maintaining a capacity for sustained, consistent action on a range of issues. This is particularly true for the United States, but there are indications of similar difficulties, generally not so acute, for governments of other large states.

The difficulties experienced in maintaining coherence can partly be traced to the increasing difficulties in maintaining the traditional hierarchy of goals, under pressure both from changes in the issues on the agenda and from improvements in communications and transportation technology that permit greater contact between governments at the level of bureaucratic subunits rather than at the top of the pyramid.

When a state is treated as a unit, it has been common to admit the existence of various domestic interests but to assume their ultimate subordination in a hierarchy of "national interests" with national security in the paramount position. When security does not appear to be threatened, but other objectives are in question, it becomes harder for foreign policymakers to maintain the predominance of security goals—witness, for instance, the changing pattern of politics on trade issues in the United States from the Kennedy Round to the August 1971 surcharge.[26] With the disappearance of an overriding security threat, the ambiguous but powerful symbol of national security declines.[27] With the symbol tarnished, if not completely obliterated, various interests can compete to control various aspects of foreign policy, and the hierarchy is likely to break down. Economic goals are, after all, to a considerable extent capable of being disaggregated and appropriated by particular individuals. By and large, force is applied to aggregate units, but asymmetrical interdependencies in economic areas are experienced quite differently by different social units. Thus in the absence of serious and immediate concern over security, this differential experience of the impact of interdependence will lead trade unionists in a declining industry, or marginal farmers in the European Community, to use what political power they have to challenge the assumed "normal" hierarchy of national goals.

This challenge from within may be coupled with a challenge from the outside. Diminished costs of travel and communication provide greater opportunities for transnational activities and the development of interests and perceptions of interest that transcend the boundaries of government or nation-state. Transnational actors such as oil companies and automobile firms may lobby in a variety of capitals, attempting to build transnational coalitions in defense of their interests; secretariats of international organizations may attempt similar strategies for different purposes.[28] Government bureaucrats and officials may also come together, realize the extent of their common interests, and develop tacit coalitions for the pursuit of those interests—whether those be in areas of defense, agriculture, or weather forecasting.[29] International contacts between officials may create common perceptions and approaches within particular functional bureaucracies in different states—but the perspective of one set of bureaus may conflict with that of another. At the national level, this can lead to interbureaucratic conflict and policy incoherence.

Strategies of Issue Linkage. One of the major effects of the particular structure of economic activities in the first postwar quarter century was a relative isolation of day-to-day international economic activity from other foreign policy concerns. Cooper characterizes this as a "two-track" or even a "multi-track" system (since commercial policy was often separated from financial policy), and argues that deliberate restriction of the agenda of bargaining among countries was helpful in achieving cooperative and mutually beneficial relations in the economic field.[30] In one of the apparent paradoxes that abound in social life, this separation seems to have been largely the result of the hierarchy of goals discussed above: economic issues were kept at a relatively low place on the policy totem pole and in the bureaucracy, and the separation of "high" from "low" politics was thus relatively easy to achieve.[31]

The current transition period in world political-economic affairs has created a fluidity and complexity—as well as a sense of frustration—that are conducive to linkage strategies, particularly by the United States. Thus, when the attention of a top American executive official is attracted to a set of problems, or when congressional leaders focus on them, linkage strategies come quickly to mind. The U.S. linkage of monetary matters and a defense presence in Europe, or American demands in 1971 for Japanese measures to improve the U.S. balance of payments, are cases in point. Not only will states be tempted to make such linkages, but so also will relatively strong national subunits that are in a relatively poor position in a particular relationship of interdependence—for instance, the U.S. Department of Agriculture vis-à-vis the European Community.

On a general level, our argument is that linkages among issues, as well as shifts from one power-level to another as discussed under "Asymmetrical Interdependencies" above, should be explained largely in terms of incongruities in the systems involved. That is, insofar as outcomes on a given issue taken in isolation are different from expected outcomes if the issue is linked to another question; or insofar as outcomes at one level of power are different from expected outcomes at a higher level, linkages and/or shifts of power levels should be expected. Two secular trends described in this chapter promote this: increasing numbers of issues (which makes more linkages possible), and the existence of a variety of more or less asymmetrical relations of interdependence among states. On the other hand, insofar as large states are characterized by bureaucratic fragmentation and policy incoherence, they may have difficulty taking advantage of the potential for linkage inherent in a situation; and insofar as various sources of power cannot be used effectively on some kinds of issues, the possibilities for issue-linkage are limited.

On the whole, it appears to us that the net effect of the secular trends favors increasing linkages. It is more difficult to be sure of this, however, than to be confident that the complexity and flux of the present will mean that for the next decade, strategies of issue-linkage will play an extremely important role in world politics, quite in contrast to the situation during the first postwar quarter century.

Structural Change and Leadership Lag. Earlier we distinguished between day-to-day allocative processes and the framework or structure within which they occur. The maintenance of structure requires leadership, and this involves the willingness of a state or states to forego short-term gains in day-to-day allocative bargaining when this is necessary to preserve the structure. These investments in structure may be supplied when a state is (a) preponderant in an issue and sees itself as a major consumer of the benefits produced by the structure over the long run, or (b) when a large state with broad objectives sees itself as compensated for sacrifices in one issue-area with benefits over a broad range of issues.[a]

The United States filled this leadership role in the postwar period, but more recently its leadership has begun to ebb. To some extent this is a function of domestic politics, partly stimulated by high U.S. rates of unemployment and by the introspective attitudes engendered by the Vietnam War. But it is also a result of such international political trends as the relative decline in U.S. power and the rise in power of Europe and Japan, and the weakening of the hierarchy of goals.

Kindleberger has underlined the destabilizing features of a period of changing leadership, by drawing the analogy of the transition from British to American

---

[a]To some extent, the problems of leadership are problems of any collective good, though the case does not entirely meet the assumptions of the theory.

leadership in trade and monetary affairs earlier in the century. The United States assumed de facto preponderance after 1918, but was unwilling to pay the costs of leadership until the 1930s and 1940s.[32] Similarly, the European Community holds a greater share of world trade today than the United States, yet it may be some time before it is internally capable of taking the leadership. Such periods of leadership lag create politicization because problems of day-to-day bargaining are not insulated from questions of structural change; no actor is willing to pay the necessary costs to satisfy specific demands in order to maintain confidence in the legitimacy of the system as a whole. Even if leadership is forthcoming, its thrust is likely to be, at such periods, toward proposals for reform of the structure itself. Such structural questions cannot be isolated from larger security and foreign policy concerns.

We are now in a period in which other states still look to the United States for leadership, due to the inchoate state of policy coordination in the European Community and the lack of self-confidence of the Japanese, who have moved to the forefront on an economic power basis so recently. This American leadership is currently directed toward changing the present structure of monetary and trade relations. Thus in the next decade, or until structural alterations are completed, international economic activity is bound to claim a high degree of political attention.

Major Political Problems in
International Economic Activity

The previous section focused on some changes and trends in the international political system that are tending to politicize international economic activity. In this section, we look at the political effects of international economic activity in five major problem areas.

Relations Among the Major
Market Economies

In the international monetary system of the 1960s, transactions were usually carried on in a nonpoliticized fashion according to IMF rules. The predominant mode of behavior was the defense of convertibility by central banks at fixed exchange rates by interventions within a narrow range from formal currency parity. This structure of relations had, of course, been created by political action; but when the system functioned smoothly, the attention of top decisionmakers in major states was rarely focused on it.

From time to time, however, serious adjustment problems arose for major powers. Monetary relations when this occurred were highly politicized, since international pressure was exerted on particular states to change their exchange rates or to alter their fiscal and monetary policies. States did not, in general, wish to adjust as rapidly or effectively as system-equilibrium would seem to require.[33] One interpretation of the political problem in this situation was that the "positive dimension of power"—the capacity to affect the behavior of others and therefore change outcomes—was much less effective than the "negative dimension of power"—the ability to resist international pressures to change one's behavior. Thus one found, increasingly, that the monetary system had some of the attributes of a "stalemate system" increasingly ascribed in the 1960s to relations of strategic interaction among the great powers.

Yet the effects of stalemate in the monetary area were adverse to stability, whereas stalemate in territorial and strategic terms probably enhanced stability by promoting the acceptance of existing reality and reducing the incentives for adventures. Policy stalemate in the monetary area did not lead to equilibrium, but rather to a rapidly escalating disequilibrium, in part because of the dynamic transnational activity in the sector, but also because the asymmetry in the process was not congruent with the underlying structural asymmetry. Without radically changing the structure of the Bretton Woods System, the United States was unable to change the parity of the dollar and thus to restore balance of payments equilibrium. As long as the United States remained unwilling to attack the Bretton Woods structure, holders of dollars acquired considerable leverage vis-à-vis the United States government.[34]

Within the framework of this structure (with which the United States was not fundamentally dissatisfied until it lost its surplus on current account), American balance-of-payments policy included attempts to twist allies' arms, and ingenious financing devices that to some extent were based on the threat of the use of the American "financial deterrent," that is, the threat to disrupt the system by unilateral action.[35] Yet it does not appear that its creditors really believed that the United States would overthrow the system to redress the political balance, although, as Henry Aubrey pointed out in 1969, "surely a creditor's influence over the United States rests on American willingness to play the game according to the old concepts and rules. If the United States ever seriously decided to challenge them, the game would take a very different course."[36]

Here the comparison of the "financial deterrent" to the "nuclear deterrent" of the strategic system was highly favorable to the United States, since the "financial deterrent" was not merely an instrument for negative influence—preventing another state from taking specific adverse action toward the United States—but a device for inducing changes in behavior as well. It was, as President Nixon and Secretary Connally showed in 1971, a *usable* power resource. Thus the natural (i.e., nonpoliticized) workings of the strategic system in the 1960s were stabilizing, although very little could be done about them by particular states. The natural workings of the monetary system, on the other hand, were destabilizing, but for the United States, an instrument was at hand to correct that tendency. As one might expect from these differences, there were in some ways more opportunities for politics—the deliberate manipulation of outcomes—in the monetary than in the strategic area.

Apart from its repercussions in other issue-areas, therefore, politicization was the appropriate strategy for a basically powerful state disadvantaged by a structure of relations and a set of common assumptions that dated from an earlier era. Although some economists have a tendency to lament the acrimony, crises, and losses of confidence that may have resulted from the American tactics,[37] a case can be made that "facing the brink" was as salutary in monetary affairs as it seems to have been in the Cuban missile crisis of 1962, without being equally risky. A loss of confidence in some of the specific institutional aspects of a system may well lead not to collapse of the general structure, but to new specific structures. The high degree of strategic tension between the United States and the Soviet Union in the early 1960s did not result in eliminating the strategic system, or "balance of terror," but it did lead to attempts to improve its stability through hot-line agreements, the nuclear test ban, and the strategic arms limitation agreements.

Similarly, the high degree of economic interdependence among the Western countries makes it unlikely that statesmen will abandon efforts to improve the system for the sake of pursuing policies of short-term national advantage; yet without the clearly perceived danger of system disruption, the political energy needed for reconstruction was hardly likely to emerge. This is, after all, a key problem of international politics: how to keep situations *unstable* enough that long-term solutions can be found, without lapsing either into short-term stability that provides the illusion that nothing need be done, or producing system breakdown. In much more difficult circumstances than apply in the international monetary area, this has been the problem of United Nations peacekeeping efforts in the Middle East and elsewhere.

In the monetary and trade areas, we are witnessing the belated response on all sides to a shift in objective power positions from a hegemonial situation, dominated by the United States, to an oligopolistic pattern of three main actors, one of which, the EEC, is by no means entirely united. The necessary concomitant of this shift is for attitudes of leaders to change in accordance with changes in reality. As Cooper points out:

Countries that are small relative to the Community of Nations, or that perceive themselves to be small, take the international system governing political and economic relations among countries as beyond their influence, hence they take little responsibility for its evolution.[38]

The relatively passive attitude of the United States until 1971 encouraged the perpetuation of such attitudes; insofar as smaller actors can be certain that the hegemonial power will maintain the structure of a system under almost all circumstances, they are quite free to act in self-centered and even irresponsible ways. A movement toward narrowly self-interested, system-disregarding or system-disrupting behavior by the large state will be profoundly destabilizing if it represents a permanent change of orientation toward neo-mercantilism; but if (as seems to have been the case with the United States) it is a short-term or partial change in behavior, it may provide a useful warning that maintenance of the system depends upon the behavior of all the "oligopolists," rather than simply on that of the leader.

The question now is whether the abrupt politicization of the system by the United States—to the point at which the old rules were broken unilaterally—can lead to the kind of system that many economists prefer: that is, a *depoliticized* system, free from crises and able to be sustained by routine behavior without the attention of top decisionmakers. Such a system would involve lower political costs than the present one, imply fewer risks of stimulating conflicts that could expand from the monetary issue area to others, and might be economically closer to optimal by avoiding what economists often regard as "arbitrary" political decisions.[39] Most such schemes involve greater flexibility in exchange rates with a set of "presumptive rules" to guide states in their actions. The basic dilemma is to combine some degree of international influence over exchange-rate changes with significant national autonomy; the former is necessary to avoid international policy competition, the latter to conform to the structure of political realities. It is evident that a high level of cooperation and mutual responsiveness will be necessary to make any such system work, and that a highly respected International Monetary Fund or similar international institution will be needed to provide policy coordination and to help find agreed solutions.[40] Yet there are four other political conditions for such a system of depoliticized policy-making that have often been overlooked.

Any system whose processes on a micro-level are to remain depoliticized must be structured so that there is consistency in outcomes among its various levels. That is, the results of following routine behavior, thus keeping issues at the depoliticized level, must not be radically worse for any major state than the anticipated results of a politicization strategy. If incongruity exists, the result will be eventual political crisis ranging from the difficulties raised by France in the mid-1960s to the large-scale controversy occasioned by the United States actions in August 1971. The power to make small adjustments in the system must be congruent with the power to force large changes, or to destroy the system entirely.

The second condition of a smoothly functioning and depoliticized international monetary system is that power relations within it have to be more or less consistent with power relations in other important issue areas such as security. Since power is not as easily transferred across issue areas as money is from one use to another, the alignment of power relations across issue areas need not be as precise as the alignment of triangular exchange rates. Nevertheless, if huge disparities exist from one area to another, the result will be re-politicization of the monetary system, and the re-creation of crisis, since states with a relative advantage outside the monetary area will attempt to use some of this influence to affect monetary outcomes. It is clear to everyone that trade and money are linked very closely, on a functional basis. Both trade and money are linked, more loosely, to security relations through the need for consistency: if trade and money are to be depoliticized, states must not be given great incentives to shift substantive influence-resources from one area to another. Richard Cooper makes a similar point in a more specific context when he argues that "as Europe asserts its independence in other areas, continuing dependence on the United States for strategic security will become a more aggravating source of frustration."[41] Unless cross-issue politicization is to continue, and probably expand, changes in relations of dominance and dependence in one area will require compensating changes on other questions as well.

The third condition that a new, depoliticized, system of monetary relations must fulfill is that it must be compatible with relations of political power among domestic groups in the various societies affected. This means that the net benefits of the system must be seen as satisfactory by key groups able to change national policies. Where there is ambiguity as to how to evaluate benefits—such as was the case in the 1960s regarding the reserve-currency and intervention-currency roles of the dollar in the United States, as well as elsewhere—policy is likely to be indecisive and inconsistent. Different political power constellations in different countries must also be taken into account: international bankers' interests do not necessarily coincide with those of export industries or industrial labor, and none of these is necessarily identical with consumers' welfare. Patterns of politics or the development of elite networks within countries, such that one group or another has a dominant or highly influential position in one country, at a particular time, will necessarily have ramifications for the system as a whole. "Behind the Veil of International Money" there may be national political interests; but behind those interests are the interests of groups in power,[42] or at least their perceptions of interest. Prompt deliberation on structural reform is important, because although perceptions of group interest may change slowly, they are difficult to reverse after having become fixed.[43] A malfunctioning monetary and trade system may therefore lead to changes in attitudes and political outlook domestically—and eventually even to vested interests in piecemeal measures of protection—that take on the characteristics of structural realities that must be dealt with rather than changed.

The connections between monetary and trade issues are especially worth noting in this context, since the domestic political impact of monetary decisions is felt, for most sectors, through effects on trade, upon which employment and profits in export-oriented or import-sensitive industries depend. Thus when congressional hearings are held on monetary issues, the questions, and the statements by representatives of labor groups particularly, quickly come to focus on trade, and even more narrowly on the situations of specific industries.[44]

The fourth condition for smooth depoliticization, and perhaps the most important, is that policy interdependence among the countries involved not be allowed to increase at such a rapid rate that national autonomy is seriously and dramatically eroded. As Bergsten points out, "it would be politically naive as well as highly undemocratic to attempt to force all countries into any single policy mold."[45] A monetary scheme that implies a high degree of political as well as economic integration without providing the necessary conditions for that is doomed to failure.[46] The key issue if demands for substantial national autonomy are to be taken into account as reflecting political reality, is how to *restrain* the growth of interdependence without seriously jeopardizing the goals of world efficiency and growth that may be served by closer economic ties.

The political problems that will arise from relations among the major market economies will center around the costs of interdependence in terms of social goals as compared with the benefits. As the absolute level of affluence in industrial and postindustrial societies increases, greater attention may be paid to national goals that do not involve economic maximization—such as protection of the environment, greater equality of incomes, maintenance of national control of industry, and population dispersion as opposed to concentration of a large majority of the population in a few densely populated areas. Insofar as these goals are not shared widely in the world or conflict with policies of transnational or other state actors, they may be difficult to implement on a national scale, especially where they involve some economic inefficiency, in a thoroughly open and integrated world economic system.

If possible, systems should be designed consciously to reduce interdependence at politically sensitive points as a means of protecting not only national autonomy in the short term, but adverse politicization as a result of the actions of disgruntled groups. Over the next decades, it seems likely from what we have observed about the slow transfer of loyalties in federations and common markets, that allegiances to national structures and symbols will remain strong enough that large developed states will not allow national autonomy to be utterly eroded in the interests of *global* integration.[47] Too rapid increases in interdependence in the short term are likely to lead, not to the passive dismantling of national sovereignty, but to conflict and reaction against integration that could result in politico-economic regression.

Good examples of the effects of interdependence on social priorities and values in a society are provided by the reactions of then-Secretary of the Treasury Connally and Chairman of the Federal Reserve Board Burns to congressional questions about America's international economic condition in 1972. Connally argued that in addition to a monetary realignment, the United States needs "a renaissance of responsibility in this country . . . a resurgence of spirit, a rededication of will:"

When you walk into the plants and see the assembly lines in Japan and Germany or any of these industrial nations and see what these people are doing, you see the manifest pride that they have. They are not working for just the buck in their pocket or to buy beer on Saturday night, they are working not only for themselves, they are working for Japan, they are working for Germany. They have a national pride in what they are doing.[48]

Later he commented on the "adversary position between governments and labor and industries":

Now, that adversary position, that antagonism between these three elements does not obtain to the same extent in any other industrial nation in the world. On the contrary, they have a running thread of coordination and cooperation and in some cases almost direction between government, industry, and labor, and this is the world in which we compete. This is the world in which we find ourselves. And frankly, I think it means that we not only have to go back to work, from the standpoint of labor and management, but it means we are going to have to develop new ways of doing things, and new philosophy and a new understanding in the United States about the role government itself must play in trying to restructure this Government, its policies and its programs. . . ."[49]

The obvious implication was that internal labor-management relations in the United States, for all their deep basis in American history and political culture, would have to be drastically altered because of pressure from an international economic system whose practices are geared to maximizing economic efficiency. Similarly, Burns argued in the same hearings that the United States should not pass restrictive legislation on foreign investment by American-based firms, but that American practices would have to adjust to the decision-making practices of the multinational enterprise. After observing that he was "sad" that "so many of our corporations, instead of doing their investing here and producing here, have been going abroad," he remarked:

The way to correct that is to create an economy that will be so prosperous, so attractive to investors, that they would keep their capital at home, and not only that, so that foreign investors would bring their capital here and build factories here and invest here and thereby create employment here.[50]

The implications of such a policy for social welfare, tax reform, or environmental protection measures are obvious. In much the same way that American states have been forced by competitive pressures and the mobility of capital to restrain their taxation of corporations, thus eroding the tax base, the United States as a whole is asked to respond to similar forces. The interests of some groups in American society may indeed call for such a restriction of governmental autonomy in an open, interdependent economic world; but this hardly conforms to the interests of many less mobile members of the society with less control over the conditions of their own lives.

The liabilities of interdependence may be reduced somewhat by more flexible arrangements for exchange-rate adjustments: Such a system could reduce the interdependence between various countries' fiscal and monetary policies and undercut arguments for pursuing economic efficiency above all other values. Even so, the danger exists that in responding to demands for the exercise of national power to attain sectoral or social goals, states will resort increasingly to arbitrary restrictions and ad hoc adjustments, many of which may be justifiable only in very narrow terms. Consideration should therefore be given to writing a code of permissible behavior (and developing the consensus to make it effective), indicating the conditions under which special restrictions on politically and socially sensitive transactions could be considered internationally justifiable. The objective would not be another "great leap forward" toward liberalization, but rather the rationalization of a system of limited interdependence that would be consistent with political reality. The resulting agreement would have to include nontariff barriers and problems of capital flows, particularly those involving direct foreign investment, as well as the quota and tariff guidelines now provided (however arbitrarily and ineffectively) by GATT.[51]

Multinational Enterprises and Interstate Politics

Direct foreign investment has reached a huge scale in the contemporary world. With a book value of $67 billion in 1969, American foreign direct investments alone probably produced in at least $130-$140 billion worth of goods—more than that of any national economy except those of the United States and the Soviet Union.[52] The value of overseas production by all MNEs is more than twice the value of trade among the major developed economies. Of similar significance, in 1965, according to one authority, "approximately one-third of U.S. nonagricultural exports was intracompany trade of enterprises with direct foreign investments."[53] Finally, multinational firms control and move large sums of liquid capital, contributing to gigantic movements of funds across boundaries, as in the spring of 1971, and helping sometimes to destabilize and sometimes to integrate world capital markets.[54] Thus it is clear that in the areas of production, trade, and money—as well as, obviously, in long-term invest-ment—multinational enterprises are highly significant in the contemporary world's political economy.

Even if their own actions involve pure economic means directed at purely economic ends, multinational firms tend to attract the attention of governments, since it is clear that their decisions can exert significant effects on national societies. Governments act to restrain, tolerate, or stimulate enterprises on the basis of perceptions of national interests. Perhaps more important, domestic interests that consider themselves adversely affected by activities of multinational firms—either materially or, in the case of nationalists, symbolically—are likely to protest the foreign incursions. Since governments may well become involved with one another over issues raised by the behavior of multinational firms and of governments reacting to those firms, domestic and international politics become intertwined with one another on these issues, just as they do in other politicized fields of economic activity.

These effects of multinational firms on political control assume that the firms' own objectives are entirely economic. Yet as Kindleberger points out, the distinction between power behavior and market behavior becomes ambiguous when the goal is "long-term profit maximization." Because of their ability to take long-term views, corporation goals are frequently not "purely economic," but tend to be of more mixed character—with power and survival as well as profit entering into managers' calculations.[55]

We will focus here on the effects of multinational enterprises on the international political structure. This implies two questions: (1) What is the effect of these enterprises on the structure of power in contemporary world politics? and (2) What is the effect of these enterprises on the nature of the actors in world politics, including effects on their goals and policies?[56]

Effects of Multinational Enterprises on the Structure of World Politics. The recent emergence of multinational enterprises to prominence does not imply that they are new; apart from older enterprises such as the East India Company or the Hudson's Bay Company, U.S.-based corporations have been spreading abroad since the middle of the last century. The value of U.S. direct foreign investment in 1914 is estimated at more than $2.6 billion.[57] Nevertheless, the great bulk of U.S. direct investment dates from after 1950. Even more important is the trend toward centralization of strategy, which means the creation of effective decision domains broader than the decision domains of either the home or the host state.[58]

The first effect of these actors on world politics, then, is simply their presence. They are actors with large resources and great mobility, although without significant quantities of the *ultima ratio*, force. In view of their size, their likely strategies must be taken into account by the states with which they deal. This is particularly true in light of the fact that multinational enterprises make use of a new and somewhat imponderable source of power: the mobility of their financial resources, their management skills, and their technology across state boundaries. It provides a partial counterweight to the formidable resources of loyalty, territorial jurisdiction, legal sovereignty, powers of taxation, and access to force which underlie the power of states. If nothing else, the firm may threaten to leave the country, and insofar as it is providing real resources for which it is difficult to substitute, this may be an effective bargaining weapon. The power resources of enterprises are generally not sufficient to allow the enterprise to "prevail in the crunch" in a public confrontation with a government, but they can prevent issues from coming to a "crunch" by increasing the costs of the showdown to the state sufficiently that advantageous arrangements are made.[59] With these new sources of power, the multinational enterprises of the world may marginally alter the distribution of power among actors in world politics by arrogating some to themselves, at least in the issue-areas within which they are active.

The question of effects of multinational enterprises on the distribution of state power, although a more traditional question, may be more significant. Do large developed countries such as the United States, which serve as the home bases for most multinational enterprises, gain in power at the expense of others, or is the pattern more complex than that would suggest?

In attempting to answer this question we are confronted by a problem of evaluating indirect effects. Investments of American-based enterprises abroad contribute to the industrial structures of other countries, and may well improve their productivity and abilities to compete in world markets. Indirectly, or over a longer period, American power relative to other states may well be adversely affected by the activities of multinational firms. The direct short-term effects, on the other hand, seem to contribute more to home than to host country power.

In the first place, the existence of multinational enterprises provides significant channels for influence on host governments or societies by home governments. On a relatively few but highly publicized occasions, the United States has exercised its extra-territorial jurisdiction over U.S.-based enterprises to affect the behavior of their subsidiaries for political reasons, whether this involved sales of computers to France or trucks to China.[60] As Jack Behrman puts the problem:

Its existence provides the means whereby unilateral action by the United States is transferred into host countries, through the affiliates. The existence of such a channel into the host economy inevitably raises diplomatic problems among the two governments, with the enterprise in between.[61]

Apart from the role of the multinational firm as a channel of influence from one state to another, its own actions may affect relative state power. Governments that are able to deal successfully with multinational enterprise are likely to develop a relatively greater reputation for competence and power than governments that fail to do so or have no opportunity to do so. The successful exercise of power may create power resources, both economic and political (for instance, prestige) that will aid in its repetition. Thus the political dynamics of country-company interaction are likely to have the characteristics of an unstable equilibrium: countries that are strong because of size (e.g., Japan) or control of natural resources (e.g., Libya) can strike favorable bargains with large firms. Weak countries such as Ceylon or poor, large countries such as India may find themselves in much worse situations, which may then become cumulative.[62]

Situations in which countries have become penetrated by multinational enterprises to the extent that their elites become dependent upon the enterprises are, of course, the worst for the societies involved.[63] Clear-cut cases of "imperialist" relations of this type are, however, relatively difficult to find in an increasingly nationalist world.

One should note some caveats and countervailing influences to these direct effects. When a foreign enterprise invests significantly in a small or less developed country, that country's government may acquire bargaining advantages as well as liabilities. Once made, the corporation's investments become hostages of the government's goodwill. How much power this confers on the host government depends, at least in part, on the credibility of the government's threats. If governments develop capabilities that decrease the scarcity value of such corporate resources as management and technology, the terms of a bargain shift in the government's favor. Even incompetent governments, however, can play with hostages. Since nationalization may often be expected to produce net economic costs, those threats may only be effective insofar as the government can convince its adversaries that it does not follow exclusively economic logic. As the prospects of overt political intervention by home states decrease, this power over firms may become a form of interstate power.

Poor countries are not the only ones to use foreign enterprises as a form of leverage against the home state. In several instances, Canada has been able to extract concessions from American enterprises (such as recognition of her 100-mile pollution zone) which she could not obtain from the U.S. government. In a less deliberate sense, U.S. direct investment in Europe is sometimes viewed as a hostage (complementary to ground forces) enhancing the credibility of the American nuclear guarantee.

Over the longer run, we have already noted that multinational enterprises may reduce economic disparities and thus political disparities as well. Equally important is the rise of foreign direct investment in the United States to a rate of nearly $1 billion per year.[64] This may eventually have the effect of shifting U.S. attitudes more in the direction of host country attitudes. Finally, and perhaps most important in the long run, would be the development of truly geocentric enterprises with their own central strategies but with virtually no home country affiliation. This "common threat" might tend to increase the congruence of governmental attitudes, at least among the developed countries, sufficiently to enable the development of international institutional monitoring and controls.

Effects of Enterprises on Actors in World Politics. Apart from changing the nature of actors in world politics by the fact of their own existence, multinational enterprises have stimulated the development of some other non-state actors, although no interstate organization has yet been created to oversee or regulate them. The most prominent of the transnational organizations or associations that have developed in response to enterprises have been labor unions and labor secretariats. Despite some examples of transnational trade union cooperation against multinational firms, progress has generally been relatively slow. Differences between unions based in different countries, and conflicts of interest between national, often government-controlled, and international unions have hindered the development of a coherent labor counter-strategy to the multi-nationalization of production.[65]

Multinational enterprises have also affected the goals and coherence of state actors. The *salience* of state goals may change: strain on such goals as autonomy may increase with foreign direct investment, and these goals may therefore become more important on the operational hierarchy, even though basic state values may not have been altered. Insofar as efforts to regain autonomy may affect other states as well as enterprises, interstate friction may be created.

Multinational enterprises can serve as catalysts for conflict between states, insofar as home governments object to the practices, such as nationalization or discrimination, engaged in by governments of the countries where investments were made. As they touch politically sensitive spots, the activities of the multinational enterprise create issues for government-enterprise relations, which may "spill over" into government-to-government relations. The agenda of state policy,and of interstate politics, thus becomes broadened as a result of these transnational business endeavors; this provides the necessary (but not sufficient) condition for inter-issue linkages as well as acrimony among governments.

Multinational enterprises may also affect the coherence of home country governments whose large bureaucracies tend to be fragmented and to make decisions to some extent by a process of horizontal bargaining among agencies. In the United States questions of applying the Hickenlooper Amendment have occasioned disagreements within the Executive Branch and between the Executive and Congress; large firms in industries such as oil and minerals have exerted themselves to get the support of particular agencies or elected officials; ITT in Chile apparently attempted to enlist the local CIA operative and embassy factions on behalf of its designs there.[66] On questions relating to jurisdiction over the seabed, major oil companies in alliance with the Interior Department tried unsuccessfully to secure a presidential policy that would promote their interests. Having failed to do so, they reportedly began to lobby with foreign governments against the official United States position.[67] Large governments, although capable of being extraordinarily powerful when following a coherent strategy, are quite vulnerable to fragmentation under the pressure of competing interests in alliance with various governmental subunits. As large and wealthy organizations, directed by sophisticated leaders, and with interests that may coincide with those of some, but not all, government agencies, multinational enterprises are likely to pose a threat to the coherence of governments at home as well as abroad.

In conclusion, the political effects of multinational firms in the short run of a decade will probably accentuate some conditions that already exist such as significant asymmetries between strong and weak states; a proliferation of state agendas relevant to foreign policy; shifts in the relative salience of state goals away from concern with territorial security toward a stress on autonomy from the impact of economic interdependence; and a trend toward increased incoherence in government organization. The emergence of multinational enterprises has probably played the primary role, furthermore, in the diversification of actors in the world political system and the politicization of transnational economic relations themselves, quite apart from state action. Over the longer run of several decades, however, as they redistribute resources and become increasingly "anational" in identity, multinational enterprises may stimulate more congruent attitudes in major states by posing a common, subtle "threat." Whatever the fate of enterprises in their struggles with each other and with nation-states, their effects on world politics in the coming era will be significant, even though there is little evidence that they represent an irresistible "wave of the future" that is likely to sweep everything, including states, in its path.

Natural Resources and Political Power

A great deal of attention has been focused recently on possible scarcity of natural resources, particularly energy, and the international political consequences that will result. Even those who are not alarmist about long-run supply sometimes project a shift in international power. For instance, Walter J. Hickel argues that there is no world energy crisis:

By the end of this century we will have a half a dozen alternate sources to draw on, such as oil shale, solar heat, nuclear power (hopefully fusion) and geothermal energy. . . . The only thing we might run out of is imagination.[68]

But he argues from the projection that the United States may be importing more than half its petroleum by 1985 that the United States will be vulnerable to blackmail and it will be difficult "to pursue a policy not consistent with Arab goals in the Middle East."[69] Other writers project increasing conflict and rich country penetration of poor countries to ensure resource supplies.[70]

It is important in discussing the political aspects of resources to distinguish the input and output side, and to distinguish sensitivity dependence from vulnerability dependence. Many of the projected conflicts on the input or supply side are an artifact of static analysis based on existing reserves and technologies. Many of these conflicts may be averted in the long term by new technologies (e.g., deep-sea mining of manganese of which the United States now imports over 90 percent of its consumption) and substitution stimulated by normal market processes (e.g., the use of shale oil, some of which is now available at $4/barrel).[71]

On the output side, however, new technologies and market forces may not be sufficient. The earth's carrying capacity for the waste products of resource use presumably involves certain absolute thresholds. For instance, a certain amount of heat and carbon dioxide waste could raise the earth's temperature and melt the polar ice caps. More efficient technologies of resource use can delay such effects (some say for thirty years maximum) but not escape them.[72] In other words, there may be real long-term international political problems associated with resource uses. The scientific consensus thus far, however, does not judge these problems as likely to be the dominant ones in the time frame (up to twenty-five years) of this chapter.

The following pages will focus on the input side, examining for illustrative purposes some features of the political economy of oil.

The last several years have witnessed a dramatic shift in prices and bargaining positions in the international oil industry. Producing countries, joined together in OPEC, have succeeded in substantially raising their returns from oil production in negotiations with major oil companies. The companies, in turn, have managed to raise prices sufficiently to pass their increased costs on to consumers, apparently with a margin to spare.[73] The principal losers have been the consumers of oil, mostly located in developed market-economy countries, but including consumers in less developed countries without significant petroleum reserves.

The situation in oil is not typical of trade in minerals generally. Prices of iron ore and aluminum have been under serious pressure in recent years; the export of tin is regulated by an agreement to which importing as well as exporting states are parties; the Intergovernmental Council of Copper Exporting Countries (CIPEC) is only in its infancy. Yet even though the OPEC example is not representative of the situation in other mineral trades, there are good reasons to focus on it. Producers of other commodities have looked to OPEC as a model for emulation, and CIPEC in particular has explicitly attempted to achieve for copper what OPEC has helped to achieve for oil.[74] Thus we are likely to see attempts, as long as OPEC continues to appear successful, to form organizations of exporters with the purpose of raising prices received by producers of a wide range of primary products, including but not limited to minerals.[75]

Apart from this, however, oil is extremely important in its own right. As Odell points out:

By any standards [the oil industry] is the world's leading industry in size; it is probably the only international industry that concerns every country in the world; and, as a result of the geographical separation of regions of major production and regions of high consumption, it is first in importance in its contribution to the world's tonnage of international trade and shipping.[76]

It is hardly necessary to add to these measures of gross economic importance the strategic importance that has been attached to oil ever since, shortly before

World War I, the British Admiralty replaced coal with oil as the basic fuel upon which the British navy ran.

Modern arrangements for the production and distribution of oil comprise a complex system involving, as the major actors, producing states (using OPEC as a coordinating body), consuming states, and the international oil companies. Although this oil system, as we may call it, concerns economic activities (of production and exchange), with economic goals (profit or royalty maximization, or at least satisficing, in particular), the allocative processes have traditionally been highly political. Before 1945, the generalization could be fairly made that the major international oil companies, and the governments with which they were often associated, often held the upper hand over the governments of producing countries; royalties tended to be low and restrictions on company practices relatively few in the major oil-exporting areas of the Middle East and Venezuela. Competitive market conditions did not prevail: an international cartel, with various degrees of formalization, controlled prices and output. Although transnational actors rather than states were most involved in these pricing and producing decisions, their behavior was highly political.

Power relations within the oil system were therefore congruent with power relations in world politics generally, since both were dominated by developed states and actors associated with them. After World War II, as restraints on the use of force by Western states increased and as the oil business boomed, some changes were made that increased the funds available to the producing countries. It has only been in the last several years, however, that the countries have been widely perceived as having the advantage in bargaining. OPEC members have displayed a fragile yet remarkable degree of solidarity and a highly developed sense of political possibilities; despite the huge amounts of oil available for pumping in the Middle East and elsewhere, and the new discoveries that continue to be made, they have been able—most spectacularly at Teheran in March 1971—to raise prices, and their share of these prices, at an extremely rapid rate. Demand has been increasing, but only at a moderate pace; the reallocation from consumers to producers represented by price rises has been political in the sense that it was achieved by a process of bargaining in which solidarity of producing countries (and the symbiotic relationship with the industry oligopoly) were essential elements.

The result as of 1972 is that power relations in the oil system seem strikingly incongruent with power relations in world politics generally. When we pass onto the oil chessboard, the pawns of world politics suddenly become queens, or at least rooks, with the capacity—at least within the rules of the game as now played—for coordinated and decisive action. Yet insofar as power is fungible, such a situation seems unstable: the analyst is immediately led to ask about developments that could alter the incongruity in one way or another. In the following pages, we will discuss three possible directions of development: (1) resolution of the incongruity in favor of greater systemwide political power for the producing countries, as a result of their oil profits; (2) resolution of the incongruity as a result of reduced advantages for the producing countries within the oil system; and (3) changes in the arrangements that could contribute to the perpetuation of the incongruity and perhaps its stabilization.

Increased Power for Producing Nations? The Premier of Libya has been widely quoted as declaring that his government was supporting "Irish Revolutionaries," American blacks, and Philippine Moslems against their enemies, presumably with funds derived from the sale of oil.[77] There seems little doubt that funds for Palestinian terrorists also come, directly or indirectly, from oil revenues. On a more conventional level, purchases of arms by Iran and by Arab states such as Libya, have often been financed in the same way. Thus the funds derived from oil are certainly exchangeable into the means of violence, and into power-resources for objectives (such as the control of the Persian Gulf or the retrieval of territories lost to Israel) that require such means. On a local or regional level, therefore, money is power.

Yet it is evident that none of the major oil-exporting nations has the capacity in the next decades to become a world power on a scale to rival contemporary Britain, France, or Germany, much less the superpowers. The necessary resources of population and technology are simply not present. Indeed, the danger to weak states of emphasizing force is that they will clearly lose to the major powers in a forceful showdown. The probabilities that the present incongruity between power in the oil system and in the world political system generally will be resolved by a great leap forward in world military power by the oil exporting countries can be safely dismissed as negligible.

It is much more likely that their currently strong bargaining position in oil will provide the OPEC states with other forms of *economic* power that could reduce incongruities between their positions in the oil system and in other economic systems, such as the world monetary system. If the governments of major exporting countries were to accumulate liquid monetary reserves of $50 to $100 billion—which is by no means inconceivable by 1980 if oil prices continue to rise—they would then possess the means at least temporarily to disrupt financial arrangements among the major developed countries by initiating speculative runs on various currencies, particularly if they were willing to incur some financial losses for the sake of political objectives. Joint action by major developed countries could probably be devised to nullify such a tactic, since the structure of the system, thus the rules of the game, would remain under these states' control. Nevertheless, the threat to disrupt money markets might still have some political value; and certainly the use of contingent promises to place funds with one developed country's banks or another could be an effective means of influence.

The Exercise of Countervailing Power by the Large Consuming Countries. It is clearly more plausible that the incongruity will be resolved in favor of those who are strong in all subsystems but one, than in behalf of those whose only leverage is in oil. And indeed, upon analysis it appears that the strategies available to developed consuming countries to regain advantages in the oil system are much more diverse than those that can be taken advantage of by producing states to increase their general level of power. Furthermore, these strategies seem to hold much higher probabilities of success. Six different consumer-state strategies can be distinguished and discussed.

The first of these would be straightforward: to intervene by military force to overthrow regimes in oil-producing countries that demand too much for their products. This strategy would have been viable certainly through 1945, and perhaps until the late 1950s in many areas. It can now safely be regarded as obsolescent *in all but the most critical cases*. Indigenous nationalism and superpower competition have combined to make this a very costly course of action. The British and French were driven to such measures when they thought their vital interests threatened in 1956. The United States retains a greater capacity to intervene in the 1970s than those two former great powers possessed in 1956, although in the Mediterranean, American ability to intervene is increasingly undermined by Soviet naval strength. Barring perceptions of impending catastrophe by U.S. leaders, however, direct military intervention is unlikely.

A more subtle political strategy available to the Western great powers, particularly the United States, would be to use American influence with allies and clients to split the OPEC coalition. Conservative elites in Iran, Saudi Arabia, Kuwait, and the sheikdoms of the Persian Gulf might be responsive to concerted political inducements, perhaps including guarantees of military intervention to oppose revolutions against their rule. This would be a Metternichian strategy of political repression, followed for politico-economic reasons. It would validate the arguments of the neo-Marxist writers on imperialism and would impose some costs on any United States administration that undertook it in terms of public opinion at home and abroad. Eventually, it could lead to involvement on the losing side in wars of national liberation. Nevertheless, as a short-term strategy, particularly if the Saudi and Iranian leaderships were fearful of losing power, it could hold some prospects of success.

A third strategy would be more subtle: to make "concessions" to the producing countries that could actually undermine their bargaining positions and reduce—or at least prevent increases in—oil prices. M.A. Adelman and Theodore H. Moran have argued that the OPEC cartel is protected by the fact that an oligopoly of privately owned, transnational firms produce the oil, as well as transporting and distributing it. The effect of this is to discourage price-cutting, since given the arrangements made between governments and companies in the oil-exporting areas, companies cannot make a profit if they reduce prices below the sum of remittances due to the governments and the cost of production of the oil. This sets a "floor" under prices and guards the oligopoly against unrestrained price-cutting. Were national oil companies to produce and sell oil, on the other hand, their "price floor" would only be the cost of production—now an almost negligible percentage of oil price. Thus the scope for downward price movements, and consequent destruction of the cartel's power, would be much greater.[78]

An obvious problem with this strategy from the viewpoint of the countries in which large international oil firms are based is that these companies' interests would be adversely affected, at least in the short run. Furthermore, the argument that removal of the companies from production—leaving them involved in distribution and marketing—would put strong pressure on the cartel of producing countries is untested and, indeed, speculative.

The other three strategies are less directly political, since all involve developing alternative sources of supply; nevertheless, all would have significant political effects and are likely to be taken at least partially for political purposes. (1) The first technique is to develop new foreign oil fields, such as those along the coasts of Southeast Asia, and in Australia, and Canada, not only to assure "security of supply" but to undercut the power of the producing countries' cartel. The larger and more heterogeneous the group of major oil-exporting countries, the harder it will be for OPEC to concert policies. If countries such as Australia and Canada are members, OPEC's unity is likely to be affected, whereas if they remain outside the organization, its power to dictate pricing policy will decline insofar as their production capacity is relatively large.[b] (2) A related strategy is to engage—in the United States' case with government subsidy—in more intensive exploration and development at home. This has been evident for the United States in Alaska and for northern European countries in the North Sea. It has also been reflected in experimentation in the United States with the use of underground nuclear devices to free oil, or with techniques to exploit oil shale deposits. (3) Finally, developed countries have subsidized attempts to find substitutes for oil or to develop new technologies that will not rely on oil so intensively. In this category are research programs ranging from breeder reactors to substitutes for the internal combustion engine. Some of the motivation in the latter case is to reduce pollution; but the effects on the international politics of oil would be substantial.

The last three strategies are all compatible with each other and with any of the three more overtly political strategies. Their variety, and the limits that they place on the extent to which producing countries can raise oil prices at will, help to indicate the extent to which fundamental asymmetries in international

[b]In aluminum, for instance, or iron and steel, producer cooperation has been made more difficult by the diversity of producing countries.

politics constrain developments in contradictory directions within functionally specific systems such as oil. Large technologically developed countries have more alternatives available to them. Thus even without a resort to force, their vulnerability dependence may be far less than appears if one assumes a particular structure as constant.

The Maintenance of Incongruity. Up until now the United States and other major oil-producing countries have not taken vigorous action to thwart the producers' cartel. Indeed, it could be argued that the U.S. government has identified its interest with stability and the status quo. This could simply be the result of a lag in governmental reactions to a new situation. Until a few years ago, after all, the situation must have seemed well in hand. If this lack of activity simply stems from lack of attention, therefore, it is likely to be changed in the near future.

The relative inertia of the United States could also be explained on the grounds that a tradeoff between oil price and political affiliation is inherent in the political bargains that have been struck: the United States agrees to higher payments in order to keep certain major exporters (Saudi Arabia, Iran, Kuwait, Nigeria, Indonesia, Venezuela) politically favorable to it, and perhaps to give others (such as Iraq and Libya) some incentive not to let their actions be as radical as their rhetoric. Surely there is something in this, but in an era of declining American concern about the alignment of less developed countries (see below), this policy could rapidly appear unattractive as economic costs of oil imports rose. Change to some mix of the strategies outlined in the last section might be slowed by political considerations, but would hardly be likely to be halted by this factor alone.

The third, and most intriguing, reason why incongruity might be maintained over a long period of time between control over outcomes in the oil system and in world politics generally, is related to the high cost energy policies of Western governments. Not only large international oil companies, but small producers in the United States, coal miners in Western Europe, and promoters of nuclear power all want high-cost power. Few governments have a primary goal of minimizing prices to their consumers. In short, one could see a transnational producers' coalition consisting of domestic interests, parts of the U.S. government, oil-producing governments, and multinational enterprises at the expense of consuming countries and groups.[79] Certainly the American import quota policy between 1957 and 1973 hardly lends support to the view that United States policy puts consumers' interests first.

From this perspective, one might expect the producers' cartel to continue to be strong primarily as a result of a transnational alliance of convenience between the producing countries and the international companies, with the United States government a silent but willing partner. The spectacle of Teheran—where prices were raised in such a way that the companies were not hurt, with the acquiescence of the United States government—could provide a model for the future. Even more of an augury would be the recent co-participation scheme promoted by Saudi Arabia, by which not only would Saudi Arabia own 25 percent, at first, of production facilities on her soil, but would invest oil profits in American firms.[80] This would presumably strengthen the company-country alliance by making the actors more interdependent; indeed, as foreign governments acquired larger stakes in American oil firms, they might come to exercise some control as well as to gain a greater interest in firm profits. At an aggregate level the situation would remain asymmetrical in favor of the producing states: prices would remain far above competitive levels. But the explanation for this would lie not in superior state power but in the combination of a transnational coalition and the domestic political influences inside major consuming countries.

On the other hand, if guerrilla activity or rising nationalism pushes the producing countries to full takeover of production, there is a strong probability that the increased number of producers and the incentives for political leaders to increase revenues by shaving prices to increase sales will destroy the oligopoly structure (or push it downstream). Adelman suggests that a change in U.S. government tax treatment of oil companies' payments to OPEC countries might hasten such an effect. Or if for any other reasons the number of oil producers increases, the oligopoly will become more difficult to maintain, and the basis for large transfer payments from consumers to producers will be weakened if not destroyed.[81]

The possibility is thus raised that complexities of transnational relations and domestic politics, in combination, may intervene between the interstate system as a whole and its functional subsystems, to preserve or destroy incongruities between political patterns based on the economics of natural resources and political patterns on a systemwide basis.

Unequal Development and North-South Relations

Equality is today, and will continue to be, one of the prime political values in modern society. Yet the 70 percent of the world's population living in "poor states" consumes only 10 percent of the world's production of energy and mineral resources.[82] Economic development trends have run counter to egalitarian values when interstate comparisons are made. Rosenstein-Rodan estimates differences in per capita income between the poor and rich countries at around 1:2 at the beginning of the nineteenth century and around 1:20 today (in real terms). Using optimistic assumptions about population and economic growth rates, he projects that by the year 2000, today's poor nations will have 18.3 percent instead of current 15.3 percent of world GNP. On these assumptions, the GNP per head gap between the United States and India may shrink slightly from 1:40 today to 1:36. However, the absolute gap in annual income will increase tremendously from \$3,500 to \$9,380 per person.[83] Even using optimistic assumptions about economic change in the poor countries, there will continue to be a tension between egalitarian values and world distribution of income.

It is important to distinguish the relative and absolute dimensions of international income distribution, because the relevant political assumptions are quite different. It is frequently argued that this relative gap will breed resentment that will lead to violent conflicts between poor and rich countries. Such simplistic projections tend to overlook several important factors. As Galtung points out, elites in poor states are often closer (economically, politically, psychologically) to elites in rich states than to their own people.[84] The relative income gap between the rich in many poor states and the rich in rich states may be slight. Second, even independent, revolutionary elites in poor states will confront preponderant military force on the other side. It is sometimes argued that nuclear proliferation will provide poor countries with a military means of threatening and punishing rich states. Unless one assumes suicidal motivations on the part of elites of poor states, they should be more easily deterred than the superpowers are today. They would face the same limited utility of large-scale force for achieving economic goals that we discussed in the section "The Politicization of International Economic Activity." In short, these projections of interstate wars arising out of uneven income distribution are valid to the limited extent that it is valid to assume suicidal motives of intense resentment and willingness to initiate negative sum games.

One way to limit the probability that negative sum games will develop is to focus on alleviation of the absolute effects of poverty rather than on the psychic effects of relative international inequality. For example, given the practical impossibility of closing the gap, Bhagwati suggests that rich and poor concentrate less on closing "gaps" as appropriate goals and focus instead on a "minimum income target" such as raising all countries to a \$200 per capita income level.[85] Or elites may, as in Tanzania, emphasize the creation of an internally egalitarian society even if it involves some tradeoffs in raising GNP and thereby closing international gaps.

One need not think in terms of gaps, however, to project political instability accompanying economic development. Economic change stimulates social change (e.g., urbanization, education, literacy) which is often politically destabilizing, and in some cases leads to violent internal conflicts that can attract outside intervention or spill over borders. Even without economic growth, rapid population growth may have similar destabilizing effects. Although the relationship between simple figures on population density and violent conflict is imperfect,[86] rapid population growth places burdens on the weak polities of poor states. For example, open unemployment rates in Third World cities are estimated at around 20 percent. Moreover, new entrants to the labor force for the next fifteen to twenty years will expand in number about 30 percent faster in the 1970s than in the 1950s, reflecting the accelerated birth rates of the 1950s.[87] Regardless of gaps, many poor countries will be the scene of turmoil in the coming decades.

The extent to which such turmoil will spread will depend upon the policies of the great powers. In the past, bipolarity has led to a relatively high degree of great power intervention in Third World conflicts, and local conflicts have had global repercussions. In recent years, however, there has been a trend toward "deglobalization" in the political-security area.

As Buchan points out, the current system is no longer like Waltz's 1964 description of a world in which superpower competition knew no geographical boundaries, the smallest losses of territory were inadmissable, and even minor crises had to be settled at the superpower level. Buchan argues that tight bipolarity (i.e., at all levels of the system) with its consequent broadening of the arena of political competition was the product of special circumstances between 1956 and 1963 when the polar powers were less dependent on the facilities of their allies for deterrence of each other, and had not yet mastered the technological and conceptual flux, thus devoting full attention to its antagonist in any part of the world.[88]

Even without the Vietnam experience, the stabilization of the deterrent relationship and the subsequent partial détente would have led to nearly the same downgrading of attention paid to the poor countries. If one compares the attitudes of both Eastern and Western delegates to the first and second UNCTAD conferences, one can note a major political downgrading of the importance of the Third World between 1964 and 1968.[89] Bilateral aid flowing from many rich countries reflect a similar pattern and timing. There are two important implications of this trend. First, many local conflicts in the Third World are less likely to have broad repercussions. Second, poor countries will be less able to gain economic concessions as a result of great power security concerns.

Although the political-security competition for the allegiance of poor countries is declining, it is possible that great powers may intervene politically for *economic* reasons. Both Europe and Japan carry on larger proportions of their trade and investment with poor countries than the United States does. It is possible that politically restricted access (e.g., for France in former French Africa; for Japan in Southeast Asia in the future) to such countries could create resentments that would affect political relations among the developed market economies. Two factors, however, are likely to limit the impact of such politically restricted economic competition in the Third World. First, as we argued earlier, unlike security competition, economic competition can be a positive-sum game. Gains are divisible, and institutional forms exist (particularly multinational enterprises) for evading political restriction. Second, contrary to simple images about rich and poor countries, half of world trade (and a higher proportion of direct investment) is among the rich countries. The share of the poor countries in world trade has dropped from 33 percent in 1950 to 18 percent today.[90] Nor do these trends merely illustrate the marginal proliferation of consumer choices in affluent societies. The proportion of capital goods (which often embody technology, an important factor in growth) traded among the rich has increased.[91] In other words, it is not true that intra-West trade reflects only sensitivity interdependence while North-South trade reflects vulnerability interdependence (as we have defined the terms in the section on "Politicization"). If these trends continue, rich countries will be less likely to let economic competition in poor countries dominate their other relationships. A possible exception may be Japan, but this will depend on the extent to which Europe and America facilitate her integration in the global economy.

A second possible source of great power intervention in the Third World might come through desire to ensure control of increasingly scarce raw materials. Choucri argues that despite deglobalization in the security area, rich states may increase their political penetration of some poor states to ensure the flow of resources,[92] which poor states might deliberately withhold, or which might be disrupted by turmoil. As we argued above, we do not see as imminent the extreme resource dependence that would justify costly political intervention. In special cases, such as oil, we argued that the dependence is partly an artifact of rich countries' definition of their interest as coinciding with that of domestic groups favoring high-cost energy and with the preservation of international order through supporting an oligopolistic structure. We argued furthermore that it might be less costly for the rich countries to rely on developing technologies that reduce their dependence on foreign raw materials than to engage in extensive attempts at political penetration.

Although the rich countries may limit their direct political intervention in the Third World in the next decades, they will continue to affect the structures that largely determine the economic development activities of poor countries. Exports are vital, and account for 80 percent of foreign exchange earnings of poor countries, and rich countries provide the major markets. Indeed, annual growth rates in poor countries are highly correlated with growth in rich countries—a fact sometimes neglected by those who argue for zero growth in rich countries in order to preserve resources for the future use of poor countries.[93]

Isolation from the world economy may be a relevant development strategy for large countries such as China. It is less effective for Burma and the ninety less developed countries whose income level and populations under 15 million imply domestic markets in which many economies of scale cannot be achieved, and opportunities for import substitution are rapidly exhausted. Unfortunately, an obvious solution of increasing market size through regional and other trade arrangements among poor countries turns out to be difficult to implement given the political problems involved.[94]

Another problem with isolation from the world economy is that it excludes transnational actors which are able to transcend the irrational patchwork quilt of post-colonial frontiers. Whatever else may be said of them, multinational enterprises *do* relocate industrial production in the Third World, and foundations like Rockefeller and Ford *do* bring techniques and technologies (such as "miracle" grains) which provide *parts* of solutions to development problems. Of course, many effects of transnational systems are not benign. Value added may be slight; human resources may be drained away, the periphery country may become even more peripheral. Institutional and technical assistance must be provided to enable the poor countries to make distinctions between benign and malign effects and to enforce relevant policies.

In some ways the greatest political problem in economic development and in North-South relations in the next decade will arise from the *lack* of political importance of the poor countries to the rich countries. The rich countries may disengage politically, but the poor cannot disengage from the political-economic structure that largely determines their development. Policies of rich countries will continue strongly to influence development, but the power that shapes those policies will arise largely from the interplay of domestic politics in rich countries. The tendency will be to export the costs of adjustment to socio-economic change to poor countries. The first workers fired when there is a recession in European states tend to be among the bottom part of the proletariat "imported" from poor countries. Rather than properly implement adjustment assistance, the United States finds it politically easier to exclude textile imports from poor (as well as rich) countries by "voluntary quotas." Even well-intentioned legislation like prohibition of importation of goods made under inferior pollution standards deprives the poor countries of the ability to exploit their natural resource of relatively unused "sink" capacity. Preventing "pollution havens" also means preventing export of jobs.

In short, policies in rich countries will continue to influence economic development in poor countries, but poor countries will have very little political influence over them. At the same time, there are no strong signs of a growing constituency for increasing aid to poor countries either as the basis of compensation or of compassion. The danger is not that the rich will depend on the poor in the next decade, but that they may ignore them. And while it is false to assume in relations among states that benign behavior brings forth a benign response, it is possible that neglectful behavior that offends peoples' sense of dignity can breed a willingness among some elements in poor states to indulge in zero-sum games, and to retaliate in issue-areas (some resources; access to seacoast; air pollution) where the interdependence may be less asymmetrical over the longer run.

East-West Economics and Politics

Of the areas of economic activity surveyed in this chapter East-West trade is the most highly politicized. Both Communist and non-Communist governments have devoted considerable attention to the issue, and both have intervened on a number of occasions to block, promote, or redirect trade for political reasons.[95] As a result of governmental decisions on both sides of the so-called "Iron Curtain," East-West trade as a percentage of world trade fell from 6.4 percent in 1938 to 2.6 percent in 1948 and 1.3 percent in 1953.[96] In part, East-West trade reflects the primacy of politics in cases of intense ideological and security competition. The United States, in particular during the height of the Cold War, practiced a broad and inclusive form of political linkage by relating a trade embargo to a renunciation by socialist countries of the international political objectives they were thought in the West to hold. With détente, these broad and diffuse political linkages are somewhat relaxed. Another characteristic of East-West trade, the difference of economic systems, ensures continued, if more specific, political linkages. Though less overtly political in declaration, the de facto effect of central planning and autarchic policies in the Eastern countries was to create a total embargo on Western trade except insofar as Eastern governments chose to relax that condition.

Since 1953, East-West trade has grown rapidly: between 1953 and 1967, at a rate of 13.3 percent annually, compared with a growth rate of 6.2 percent for trade among the Western developed countries, and 5.6 percent for trade within the Eastern bloc.[97] By 1967, East-West trade accounted for 2.8 percent of world trade. Although the United States engaged in only a small proportion of this trade, agreements signed in October 1972 were expected to help Soviet-American trade triple from $200 million per year within a few years and to exceed one billion dollars by 1980.[98]

A number of economic problems exist which constrain the growth of East-West trade. Foremost among them is the system of central planning under which foreign trade can vary arbitrarily from year to year. Administered prices often bear little relation to domestic costs of production and make comparative advantage and consistent trade behavior hard to predict. Closely related problems are the meaninglessness of tariff reductions in the absence of internal markets, and the inconvertibility of currencies. It appears that economic liberalization and devolution of decision-making power is regarded as too politically threatening by party elites to project great new progress for "Libermanism" in the near future. This is less true for Hungary than for the U.S.S.R., but the political boundaries of economic experimentation in Eastern Europe will continue to be set by the U.S.S.R. for some time.

These economic problems create obstacles to the participation of the centrally planned economies in world economic institutions (GATT, IMF) as well as constraining the expansion of East-West trade. The important point, however, is that devices exist to alleviate some of the effects of these differences if the political will to overcome them is present. Undertakings to increase imports have been treated as counterparts to tariff reductions in the GATT. Barter and swap arrangements exist in commodities, particularly oil.[99] And coproduction schemes between Eastern governments and Western enterprises both in Eastern Europe and overseas have been increasing.[100] In short, where there is a political will, there is an economic way. But where the economic ways are very different, the amount of political will required is that much greater. We concentrate in the rest of this section on the political will.

In the words of one expert, writing in 1969, "trade is being increasingly dictated by economics rather than politics."[101] Somewhat more precisely, one might say that political disincentives to trade—both ideological and instrumental—have declined sufficiently to allow the economic incentives to exercise more effect. Nevertheless, the issue-area remains highly politicized, as the continuing linkages between trade and other questions—such as lend-lease settlements or the treatment of Soviet Jews—indicate. The contrast in those two examples taken from 1972 trade relations between the United States and U.S.S.R. indicate that political linkages are not simply a function of a hierarchy of issues rationally controlled by the executive. Much of the current politicization is a function of "actor incoherence" and not easily controlled.

What has occurred seems to be less a depoliticization of the issue-area than a change in the political orientations of the major actors and therefore in the types of linkages that they are willing to insist on and the agreements that can be reached. This has been particularly pronounced on the Western side. In late 1947 and 1948, the United States moved to implement a strategic embargo against the Soviet Union and its allies, whose legislative manifestations culminated in the Battle Act of 1951, which provided

that no military, economic, or financial assistance shall be supplied to any nation unless it applies an embargo on such shipments to any nation or combination of nations threatening the security of the United States, including the Union of Soviet Socialist Republics and all countries under its domination.[102]

This "ferocious" language was never fully implemented, yet at American urging a Consultative Group Coordination Committee (COCOM) began to function in Paris in January 1950, and considerable American pressure was exercised to secure the support of its European allies.[103] From 1954 on, however, the embargo was liberalized greatly, so that one authority argues that by about 1956 the embargo "was no longer a dominant factor in East-West trade."[104] West European countries were generally more reluctant than the United States to sacrifice trade with the East for political reasons. The policy distance between the United States and its allies was even sharper throughout the late 1950s and 1960s on the question of trade with China and, for the 1960s, on trade with Cuba.

The relaxation in Western political conditions on East-West trade has resulted from an increase in the costs considered to result from making large demands, and a decrease in the benefits perceived to flow from such a decision. The costs of imposing political conditions increase, for instance, whenever there is a surplus of a product, such as wheat, in Western countries, particularly when the commodity in question is important in domestic politics. Australia in the 1960s and (it seems) the United States in 1972 did not impose strict political conditions on Soviet wheat purchases. Indeed, in both cases, Russian buyers purchased the wheat at bargain prices.[105] Costs of imposing political conditions also rise insofar as particular capitalist countries have balance of payments or employment problems: Thus Britain, for instance, has been particularly reluctant to use trade as a political weapon.[106]

On the Socialist side, the economic significance of trade and other economic relations with the West has been emphasized increasingly in recent years.[107] The Socialist states are anxious for Western technology as well as Western grain. In the past, it has seemed that the Soviet Union and its allies would be able to sell little to the United States, but American shortages of natural gas and other mineral resources may be changing that. Reports on the 1972 Soviet-American trade agreement indicate that by 1980 Siberian natural gas may account for 7 percent of American consumption.[108]

Writers on East-West trade often emphasize the advantages that state-trading countries possess in "enlisting politics and trade in each other's support."[109] This may well be true on the level of process: that is, given the political decisions to construct a framework within which trade takes place, the greater centralization of trading in socialist countries, and the direct links with the government, surely make coordination easier for them. However, on the structural level—on the big decisions that set the framework for day-to-day activities—the West, particularly the United States, is equally and perhaps even better placed to demand concessions in other areas for agreement to increase trade flows. In the early years of the embargo, the political concessions demanded were vague and sweeping. As political conditions have changed, they have become more specific and manageable. During the 1972 trade negotiations between the United States and U.S.S.R., it seems clear, from the composition of delegations and from press accounts,[110] that the United States was at least tacitly linking progress on trade to help in ending the Vietnam War.

It is possible that this may be the exception rather than the rule. It is interesting to note, for example, that there seems to have been little linkage between progress in the SALT talks and progress in the trade talks, despite the impression of linkage that was created at the May 1972 summit conference. Moreover, as the salience of politico-military conflict and potential conflict between West and East declines, it seems less valuable to foreign policy to retard the industrial growth of the Socialist bloc, particularly since it is no longer widely believed that an embargo can have a decisive effect in any case. Moreover, there is also a collective action problem here. America's allies have quite naturally reached a different balance than did the United States regarding the collective benefit—when it was considered a benefit—of denying the Soviet Union and its allies "strategic" goods, and the individual benefit of trade. Thus the natural tendency of smaller members of a coalition to break ranks in pursuit of individual ends reinforced their greater skepticism about the merits of an embargo in general. Once a few states engage in trade on a considerable scale, it seems quixotic for others not to follow suit. In such circumstances of intra-West competition, commercial motives tend to prevail over political ones.

Nevertheless, it seems likely that relatively specific political linkages will continue to be important in East-West trade for three reasons: (1) It is clear that trade is not equally valued by both sides. (2) It is also clear that regardless of détente, trade decisions remain highly politicized by the very nature of central planning. (3) Residual ideological and security differences remain significant; witness recent problems over extension of credits and ownership of LNG tanker fleets.[111] George F. Kennan held in 1965 that "Communist countries are not going to pay for normal trade with us by any specific political concessions,"[112] but he was wrong. In 1972 the Soviet Union agreed to pay a lend-lease debt of $722 million after protracted bargaining, and there were indications that it might relax its policy on granting exit visas to Soviet Jews in the face of a proposed U.S. Senate amendment, cosponsored by seventy-two senators, that would block key elements of the Soviet-American trade agreement unless Soviet policy toward Jews wishing to emigrate were changed. Through a policy of linkage by members of Congress, under the stimulus of the transnational sympathies felt by American Jews for their Soviet coreligionists, East-West trade was used politically to affect Soviet domestic politics. The difference between 1972 and 1952, therefore, is not so much in the degree of politicization of the issue of trade, but in the character and extent of the demands being made on the Soviet Union: The demands in 1972 are of a limited enough nature that they may be met, at least in part, whereas the demands of 1952 were so sweeping as effectively to consist of an almost absolute bar to trade.

It can be anticipated, therefore, that East-West trade will continue to be politicized, as long as strong political and economic differences between countries in the two areas continue. Yet the extent to which trade will be capable of being used effectively as a bargaining level will depend on the degree of asymmetry in interdependence between the two states. Recently, the United States has been exploiting the asymmetries in its favor effectively by linking other issues to trade; it can be expected to do so as long as those asymmetries continue to exist. Insofar, however, as the Soviet Union and its allies gain on the West in their degree of technological sophistication, or the West comes to rely on the East increasingly for energy, the asymmetries will be narrowed, although not for some time reversed. As Harry G. Johnson has pointed out, the economic situation of the planned economy states is "very similar to those of the less developed countries of the world."[113] As long as that continues to be the case, they are likely to be more dependent on trade than their Western partners, therefore potentially vulnerable to the use of political linkages and on the short side of the economic power equation. They may expect some advantage from the competitive disunity of the West on trade issues, and a few windfalls where politically motivated subsidy policies give them the chance to negotiate low prices for the import of commodities; but they can hardly expect an overall political advantage in the area. Their economic as well as military strength places limits on the demands that can be made of them; but their need for trade, particularly in technologically sophisticated products, ensures that those limits do not approach zero.

Implications for Research and Training

If the arguments made in preceding sections are correct, the political economics of international relations will continue to be highly important over the next decade or more, barring a reversion to military insecurity as a result of technological surprises or other unforeseeable causes. Research on international affairs will have to include a high political economy component if it is to enable us to understand developments, both on a theoretical and policy level. Yet most current research is highly compartmentalized by disciplines. Likewise, training programs will be required that help individuals to become literate in more than one discipline, both for college and university programs as well as for government service.

If the world is as we described it, policymakers will have to be able to answer such empirical and normative questions as:

1. Who is providing leadership to maintain the structure of economic relations?
2. Given the potential costliness of "structural linkage," what special circumstances should they be reserved for?
3. To what extent is a position of relative weakness a function of sensitivity dependence or of opportunity cost dependence?
4. Who (not just which state) profits and who loses from a transnational system?
5. As societies become more sensitive, how do apparently domestic decisions substitute for, complement, or countervail international institutional forms?
6. How do apparently domestic decisions shift the burden of adjusting to socioeconomic change into other countries?
7. When and how is it best to politicize and when and how best to depoliticize a set of economic activities?
8. Which interdependencies should be institutionalized and which curtailed? When should you build bridges and when should you build dikes to avoid international conflicts arising out of situations of changing domestic values?

Obviously this is only a partial list. The important point is that our research and training programs must develop capacities to answer such questions.

Research Orientations

Four major directions for empirical research that should be undertaken by political scientists or organization specialists with a sound grasp of economics can be distinguished as follows: (1) analysis of political-economic dimensions of international politics, as in this chapter; (2) analysis of transnational organizational behavior of multinational enterprises, trade unions, or other actors in this field; (3) analysis of transnational elite networks and interactions; and (4) analysis of patterns of international organization that could appear in this area of activity.

1. Political-Economic Aspects of International Politics. Students of international politics have tended until quite recently to focus almost exclusively on what they considered "political" relations and particularly on strategic matters, leaving economics to the economists. The problem with this has been that often the economists have not addressed the political questions, or recognized that the processes they studied were fundamentally affected by the political framework; in other instances, they have attempted to deal with political issues but have done so in a naive or crude way—for instance, by attempting simply to apply Morgenthau's conceptions of power politics, or notions of the balance of power, to politicized economic relations. This chapter has attempted to illustrate what we consider a more relevant approach to the politics of economics. Whatever our success, or lack of it, this is an important research task that requires further work.

Careful studies of these questions must be more detailed than in this chapter, and must involve systematic empirical research, including field work. Analysis can be fruitfully done along two dimensions: by issue-area, and by country relationships. The first dimension has the advantage of allowing the researcher to focus on a functionally linked system of relations, such as that in the monetary area, or in oil, and to explore the political conditions and implications of that system. By focusing on a problem area, the analyst can resist the temptation to fall merely into the description of institutions or the listing of state policies. He or she can assess the power resources and nature of the interdependencies among relevant actors in the issue-area. He or she must probe the responses of the actors to one another, and the effects of multipurpose actors, such as states—whose concerns and influence span a number of issue-areas—on patterns within the area.

More significantly, a number of such studies, done along consistent research lines and with appreciation for the political dimensions exogenous to the issue-area as well as vice versa, would allow us to begin to answer some crucial but largely unresearched questions of world politics. What bargains are struck across issue-areas, and under what conditions? How fungible are resources in a given issue-area? Under what conditions does dominance in the security area provide a state with leverage in another area in which it may be weak? To what extent are all issue-areas politicized, and to what extent can some of them be insulated from political competition? Answers to such questions—about which we have only been able to conjecture in this chapter—would shed light on the elusive concepts of "power" in world politics. If the various "poker games" in different issue-areas are not closely interconnected and resources are only fungible at the discount, we may need to reevaluate the usefulness of the homogeneous conception of power, which rests heavily on the analogy with money in an economic system.

The country approach, either on a multilateral or bilateral basis, also has advantages. Questions of interaction between issue-areas can be confronted clearly within a limited political context. Thus, in a careful study of strategic and economic interactions between Germany and Britain, or the United States and Japan, implicit and explicit tradeoffs between values can be examined in depth, relying on interviews as well as on written primary and secondary sources. Furthermore, it may be easier in this context to disaggregate the state in the analysis, and to focus on the policies of agencies, departments, and divisions, than in a broader issue-area approach. Done properly, the focus on country relationships should complement the issue-area orientation, since the two approaches look at the same phenomena from different perspectives.

2. The Analysis of Organizational Behavior. The most extensive and highest-quality work on the behavior of transnational organizations in the economic field has been done on the multinational business enterprise, by such scholars as Raymond Vernon, Jack Behrman, Charles Kindleberger, Stephen Hymer, Louis Wells, and others.[114] Hymer's theory of oligopolistic competition and Vernon's theory of the product cycle have proven to have powerful heuristic value in suggesting questions to be asked and in generating hypotheses to guide research.

Indeed, the progress that this research has shown, along with the rapid growth of interest in multinational enterprises from Congress and the public as well as the scholarly community, has attracted a number of researchers and considerable funds into this area. Studies are therefore being extended, both into new aspects of multinational enterprise behavior, and into related areas, such as the analysis of transnational developments in trade unionism.[115] Such research has already attained academic respectability, and appears to have self-sustaining momentum.

3. Transnational Elite Networks and Interactions. The interactions of states, either as unitary actors or fragmented ones, and the activities of transnational organizations do not exhaust the interesting research topics on political-economic dimensions of world politics. Some scholars, particularly those with a sociological background, are now becoming interested in what can be called "elite networks," or patterns of informal interactions among individuals holding positions that allow them to communicate with one another transnationally with relative ease.[116] In addition to providing communications channels, these networks may affect the attitudes of elites, and therefore the policies of their organizations; in some situations, informal norms to govern behavior may even arise. Analysis of this type has been undertaken by sociologists in the United States and elsewhere on domestic elites, particularly in circumscribed geographical areas, such as cities. Patterns of friendship, communication, and attitudinal responsiveness among heads of large multinational enterprises, bankers, or union leaders may be fully as interesting as similar patterns among economic leaders in Atlanta, Chicago, or Middletown. The transnational patterns, however, will be difficult to discover and involve painstaking field work and interviews.

Elite networks often exist among governmental officials as well. In such a situation, which may be described as "transgovernmental politics," actors that formally belong to a governmental hierarchy may cease to behave in conformity to roles specified or implied by the formal foreign policy structure of the state. As communications improve, the telephone becomes used even more heavily, the possibilities for informal contacts among officials increase dramatically. Officials of different nationality but similar interests in a certain problem may align themselves implicitly or explicitly with one another, perhaps in opposition to other transgovernmental coalitions with quite different interests. Indications that this happens have appeared in the literature,[117] but little systematic work has been done, particularly in the political-economic area. Yet the effects on patterns of allocation of economic activities of such interaction could be considerable, and widespread transgovernmental interactions could cast doubt on the conception of government policy as now held.

It should be said that some preliminary empirical work that has been done on these questions with respect to the politics of the monetary issue-area—particularly focusing on ministerial deputies in OECD Working Party 3 and the Group of Ten—does not support the hypotheses that transgovernmental relations are a major factor influencing monetary policy.[118] But more work would be justified, in this and other areas, to see whether and under what conditions the notion of transgovernmental interactions is useful for the analysis of contemporary economic-political reality.

4. Responses of International Organizations to Politico-Economic Problems. Political scientists interested in international organization are often disturbed by the reactions they get from their colleagues in their own discipline, as well as from economists. The notion is widespread that the field of international organization is primarily concerned with legal and institutional questions about the United Nations, or with the analysis of voting patterns in international bodies. Although it is true that much of the existing literature focuses on such questions, in recent years analysts of regional integration and political processes in international organizations have gone beyond this framework. Much of the most innovative work in the field is based on quite different assumptions about what is important and quite different research questions.

Institutional research, for instance, has proceeded recently in two directions that may be relevant to international organizations in the economic field. First, analysts have focused on "organizational development," or "institutionaliza-tion," to inquire about the growth of capacity of international organizations, of the strengthening of distinctive habits and procedures and the development of autonomy.[119] This emphasis derives from the neo-functional literature on politico-economic integration, but the general approach can be applied to a wide variety of intergovernmental organizations—including the IMF, OECD, GATT, and the World Bank. It has already been applied, in a still-unpublished study, to the Organization of Petroleum Exporting countries (OPEC).[120]

The other emphasis in research on institutions is complementary. This approach concentrates on two often neglected aspects of international organiza-tions: their output and effects on their environment.[121] This mode of analysis, which is familiar to economists, promises to yield a methodology that could be applied to economic organizations with interesting empirical results, which could then be used as a basis for policy prescription, particularly in conjunction with findings about organizational development or institutionalization. To what extent, for instance, are highly institutionalized organizations, or organizations with significant capacities for autonomous action, appropriate for various types of politico-economic tasks? What effects are various patterns of membership and various ways of forming secretariats and structuring state interaction within the organization likely to have on organizational outputs? We cannot answer such questions now, and it may be some time before we can do so even with considerable research; but without more energy and resources devoted to the problem than are now at hand, these potentially valuable discoveries will be relegated to the distant future. One area where the study of process and impact have been closely related has been in research in the field of politico-economic integration, which has largely concentrated on the politics of common markets, but can also offer insights into contemporary politico-economic issues of the international system.

A third direction in the study of international organization is represented particularly in recent work by John Ruggie, who suggests that we are more likely, in the future, to witness new forms of coordination of state action through international agencies than to see the development of increasingly autonomous, supranational organizational structures.[122] According to this contention, the role of international organizational secretariats on many issues may be to engage in coalition-building with sympathetic elements of national bureaucracies, thereby building collaborative constituencies of officials engaged in solving joint tasks in consistent ways.[123] This perspective fits nicely with the study of transgovernmental relations as discussed in the last section. One of the major roles of international bureaucrats is to facilitate, coordinate, and partici-pate in transgovernmental interactions. International organizations would not supplant the state system, but rather facilitate a process that changes its character. In the political-economic area, research is badly needed on the extent to which informal coalition-building and coordination take place in this way. If they do, and particularly if this tendency were becoming stronger, future patterns of international policy-making on economic issues could take quite different shapes than one would expect under the assumption of a state-centric, states-as-unitary-actors world—or under the conventional alternative assumption of clear supranational powers for international institutions.

The relevance of this issue can be illustrated in regard to the question of a "world central bank" that has been raised by some economists as part of a possible solution to world monetary dilemmas. Given political differences and sensitivities about sovereignty, it is highly unlikely that an institution with that or a similar name will be established in the next decade or two. On the other hand, one would be foolish to predict a return to strictly national banking arrangements, or to project merely a continuation of existing and IMF-related patterns of banking that we have seen. Rather, we may see an evolution of more or less institutionalized arrangements among central banks, such as are represented by the General Arrangements to Borrow and the Basle Agreements, coupled with coordinative mechanisms among finance ministries. The networks of expectations, communications channels, and direct interactions in these evolving arrangements may not take the tangible institutional form of a bank building of stone with bars on the windows and gold in the vault, but they will be crucial in understanding developments in the monetary area. SDR arrangements are more formalized and do focus on the IMF, yet the political scientist is led to suspect that the ongoing political coordination required to maintain or increase the value of those arrangements in a changing world taxes the ingenuity and the resources of the IMF secretariat. Since there are no major published studies of the IMF from the point of view of a political scientiest interested in international organization, it is hard to reach conclusions. But that is just the point: students of international organization have developed skills and approaches that are appropriate to the study of international economic arrangements and institutions, but the applications are infrequent. A serious research program in international political economy will have to include political scientists interested in organizational questions.

Conditions for Successful Training

To some extent, patterns of research will determine the success of attempts to train sophisticated students of world political economy. Graduate students in Ph.D. programs tend to gravitate toward areas where exciting, yet topically relevant research is being done, as well as toward areas where funds for field work and maintenance are available. Thus in the early 1960s, area programs were extremely important at the graduate level, largely under the stimulus of Ford Foundation grants. Studies of international organization, by contrast, were in the doldrums, with the exception of regional integration studies, since many of the approaches appeared to use outdated theoretical and methodological tools to study increasingly irrelevant organizations. Until students of international organizations devised more interesting and relevant approaches to the subject matter that they could properly claim, it was quite fair that they should attract few students and little research money. In our judgment, this situation has now changed.

We are less competent to comment on the situation in the economic discipline. Certain respected economists (Richard Cooper is a good example) have made political analysis of international economics an interesting field, but it is unclear to us to what extent this has challenged the traditional "pecking order" of the economics profession that puts mathematical theory at the top of the hierarchy. We suspect that training programs for graduate students will not be successful without being coupled to research efforts that have gained status in the discipline. With exciting research programs and sufficient funds for Ph.D. candidates, a field such as international political economy should have considerable "drawing power" over the next decade.

Student motivation is a key consideration around which to design a training program. There is no point in requiring a set of courses in both economics and politics if economics-oriented students regard the political science as irrelevant or uninteresting, and vice versa. Thus along with the need for good research programs, one requires strong market demand for graduates of programs that emphasize political economy at both the graduate and undergraduate levels. As Figure 5-1 indicates, the primary sources of demand are three: the federal government, nongovernmental economic organizations (particularly private businesses), and universities or colleges. Since the system is mutually interdependent, efforts to build training programs without continuing government attention and business activity relevant to the area are likely to collapse, as happened to some extent in the past few years to programs in African studies at American universities. If the main body of this chapter is correct, however, business activity in the world economy is likely to increase and the political problems of such activity will remain acute or become more so. The same will probably be true of government attention, although this may be somewhat more difficult to predict with confidence.

Attention must be given to strengthening the capacities of the press and other media in the area of political economy. For instance, a program on the order of the Nieman Fellows program to retrain journalists to deal in a sophisticated way with international economic issues would not only be valuable in its own right, but could contribute to maintaining a high level of government attention. Any program that would help to get important international economic news off the financial pages onto the front pages would be helpful in developing public awareness of the connections between politics and economics in contemporary international relations.

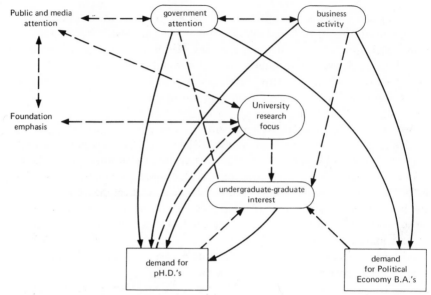

Figure 5-1. A Schematic Representation of Influences (----) and Demand Forces (——) Affecting Training of Graduates in Political Economy

Programmatic and Policy Suggestions

On the specific level of what to do, we havesuggestions in three topics: (1) research institutions and modes of operation; (2) training programs, particularly in universities and colleges; (3) measures to encourage a wide variety of organizations involved with the government to explore political-economic issues in a sensitive way.

1. Research Institutions. When changes occur in socio-political-economic reality, and the need to study them is perceived, the most obvious response is to establish new institutions for that purpose. Thus one could attempt to set up an Institute for Analysis of International Economic Problems, perhaps along the lines of the Institute for Strategic Studies in London. In our view, however, this approach is sub-optimal. First, it involves heavy organizational startup costs. Second, and more important, it would continue fragmentation of analysis. Institutes with a strategic emphasis and institutes with an economic emphasis would go their separate ways. Problems that involve linkages between the two areas, or the effects of one set of processes on another, might very well continue to be overlooked, and unfortunate disciplinary barriers could be duplicated on the institute level. The best solution would be to stimulate the reorientation of organizations such as the Institute for Strategic Studies toward serious work in the political-economic area that is relevant to their continuing work on strategic problems. If this were not possible, or were only possible in a limited way, the establishment of a new institute could be undertaken as a second-best approach to the problem.

Whatever way arrangements are made, research should be encouraged along interdisciplinary but problem-oriented lines. Faced with a problem, and in informal proximity with other professionals, it does not take long to discover that one's own paradigm is insufficient. Conversely, a difficulty with inter-disciplinary organizations, such as the International Studies Association, is that their purposes are rather diffuse. Thus it becomes difficult to involve first-rate researchers, particularly from fields other than political science, in the enter-prise. The search for an "interdisciplinary approach" often becomes an end in itself rather than a means to the solution of important problems. Insofar as broad organizations such as the ISA are engaged in activities touching on the political-economic area, their emphasis should be on serving as organizational and communications networks to facilitate the work of groups of creative people engaged in problem-oriented research tasks. ISA has recently moved in this direction with its various subgroups and the organization of its panels. In our view, this orientation should be encouraged and carried further.

The third dimension of organizing research and communications about research refers to the development and evolution of academic journals. Once again, the problem is not a lack of journals, but a lack of integration of political and economic analysis, or political and economic readership, in the journals that do exist. On the whole, economists do not read "political science journals," even when some of those, such as *International Organization* and *World Politics*, include economists on their editorial boards and publish a number of articles on economic subjects or employing economic analysis. Likewise, few political scientists follow major economics journals closely. An important step to consider, which would be both less expensive and more useful than the development of yet another journal, could be taken by supporting an annotated bibliography of works relevant to international political economy, which could appear regularly on a quarterly basis both in a journal read largely by political scientists, such as *International Organization*, and in a journal read primarily be economists, such as the *Journal of Political Economy*. If this were done well, it could make a major contribution to the reintegration of this field at very low cost.

2. Training Programs. Training should follow the same general pattern as research: interdisciplinary but problem-oriented. This leads us to regard as insufficient two sets of approaches that could be adopted. One of these would be to concentrate on training mathematical economists who might later be expected to gain political sophistication, á la Marshall Plan, by government service. While this approach, which was suggested to us by a prominent political economist, has merit, it is insufficient because it entirely discounts the value of political science as a discipline and a way of looking at politics, implying that one can equally well learn from being part of a policy process. Despite the existence of some rare individuals, this is an overly conservative approach, since an economist in a policy advising position in the government must necessarily take the political framework and constraints laid down by his superiors as given. *Good* graduate training in political science, by contrast, should impart a skeptical, even critical, and analytic as well as a pragmatic and constructive approach to power and interest in international politics of foreign policy. Furthermore, such training can include competence in, or at least familiarity with, research approaches, such as those outlined earlier, that can be useful in studying relations between world politics and economics.

The other approach about which we are skeptical is the construction of "programs," at the graduate or undergraduate levels, that simply represent adding additional requirements to those normally set for degrees either in political science or economics. Without coordinated interdisciplinary programs, involving courses *taught jointly* by economists and political scientists, seminars or tutorials designed to integrate political and economic material, or other devices to ensure that relations between the two sets of variables were clarified, students could easily find themselves in the unhappy situation of knowing too little of either discipline and of being unsure, in addition, about the connections between them.

The Oxford program of Philosophy-Politics-Economics, the attempts at integrated undergraduate education represented by the College of the University of Chicago in the 1940s, by the Swarthmore Honors Program, or by some experiments in international relations teaching at Stanford, and some of the programs at the Woodrow Wilson School or the John F. Kennedy Institute, represent attempts at interdisciplinary training. A frequent problem with such programs, however, is a failure to integrate. As Susan Strange says of the British programs:

In each case, the chief weakness of the parallel course solution is that it inevitably tends to develop divergence rather than confluence of the component parts. The economics taught by the economists and the politics or international relations (and come to that the philosophy) have less and less relevance to one another, rather than more and more. Nor is any very serious attempt made from either side to relate the courses to one another. The economists do not even try to deal with the political aspects of international economic relations and international economic problems; and few political scientists even try to explore the economic dimension of international politics or diplomacy.[124]

At the undergraduate level, we think that history-politics-economics joint degrees, with *jointly taught* interdisciplinary, problem-oriented seminars and integrated examinations, might be an appropriate response to encourage. At the graduate level, problem-oriented seminars for students from politics and economics—which might give students from both disciplines the necessary incentives to learn requisite parts of the other—offer a positive approach.

Our emphasis on the need for motivation to learn a strange field, as well as the necessity for political economists with doctorates to be thoroughly grounded in a discipline, suggest, furthermore, that a focus on programs for mid-career people, whether in government or in the universities, could be very valuable. In the State Department, for instance, a number of politically trained officers seem now to be realizing their need for economic sophistication as priorities shift. Certainly, outsiders have been commenting on the lack of high-level expertise in the State Department on political-economic problems.[125] The need for such re-training is probably no less among members of congressional staffs. Conversely, political scientists interested in international relations have something useful to impart to certain present and former officials of the U.S. Treasury Department and the Department of Commerce. The desirability of mid-career training also applies to university professors of political science and economics, who are often victims of their disciplinary blinders and the restrictiveness of their graduate educations and career paths, and to journalists, as pointed out above.

Organizationally, our orientation is not toward the construction of new departments of political economy—thus creating new barriers within the universities—but rather in the direction of teaching as well as research "task forces," encouraging interdisciplinary work on problems of training students as well as on issues in the outside world. Funds for released time for faculty, enabling them to spend substantial amounts of time and energy on retraining themselves, as well as devising new programs, would be useful.

3. Government Policy and International Political Economics. Washington, as we have been reminded recently by a member of a congressional staff, is a parochial world. Immediate problems loom more important there than they may seem in a university setting. The time horizon for anticipating future problems is probably much shorter on Capitol Hill or in the Executive Branch than in Cambridge or Berkeley. On the other hand, university observers occasionally benefit from a chastening cold shower of political realism that they may encounter in the halls of power.

As one step in bridging these two contexts, if not cultures, it might be quite valuable to schedule Washington seminars at which encounters between policymakers and university researchers could take place. An interesting exercise along these lines was carried out by David Biltchik of Face-to-Face in May 1972. To be most useful, these should not be presentations by scholars of their latest research as much as sessions in which a number of outside observers could interact with insiders from the government. Having three or four representatives of the academic, institutional, and foundation worlds in a discussion with eight or ten government officials could result in a more genuine reflection of differences as well as similarities in approach among members of each group. This would discourage question-and-answer sessions in which one person or another could assume the easy role of expert, and would encourage joint problem-solving on issues far enough removed not to be on today's action agenda, but important enough that they would be likely to appear tomorrow.

We would hope that some sessions might have the beneficial indirect effects of reorienting some of the work that is being done within the government—for instance, in the Bureau of Intelligence and Research of the Department of State, or on congressional staffs—toward emerging political-economic problems. This would help to create a self-sustaining dialogue in which government officials could contribute to the academics' world-views fully as much as vice versa.

In conclusion, we wish to reiterate our concern over the incongruence between the fragmented institutional arrangements in our society and the close intertwining of political and economic problems as described in our analysis. The powerful processes of specialization in professional disciplines, university departments, academic journals, daily newspapers, government bureaus and congressional committees all tend to create compartments where different people think separately about the economic and political components of problems. Professional specialization is important and will continue. Our institutional suggestions are designed to complement, not replace, it. To deal with the complex world of international political-economy we need both professional specialists who are technically competent economists and bridge-building generalists who are literate in both economics and political science. Despite the existence of rare individuals, good economists are often no better analysts (and frequently worse) than political scientists when they sally forth onto the messy side of their protective ceteris paribus clauses. Most political scientists, on the other hand, are economic illiterates. Fortunately, both these problems have remedies. The problem will be in implementing the remedies.

Notes

1. This definition follows Sheldon Wolin, *Politics and Vision* (Boston: Little Brown, 1960) and is somewhat broader than definitions of political goals as relating to the security of decision-making structures. The latter definition traditionally characterizes discussions of international politics.

2. This definition is discussed in Robert O. Keohane and Joseph S. Nye, Jr. (eds.), *Transnational Relations and World Politics* (Cambridge, Mass.: Harvard University Press, 1972), p. xxiv.

3. Harry Johnson, following Robbins, defines economics in terms of the problem of allocating scarce means among given ends. "The Economic Approach to Social Questions," in David Mermelstein (ed.), *Economics: Mainstream Readings and Radical Critiques* (New York: Random House, 1970), p. 15.

4. William Diebold, "The Economic Issues Between the European Community and the United States in the 1970's," in Steven Warnecke (ed.), *The European Community in the 1970's* (New York: Praeger, 1972), p. 95.

5. See Peter Bachrach and Morton Baratz, "Decisions and Nondecisions: An Analytical Framework," *American Political Science Review* 57 (1963), pp. 632-42. Reprinted in Roderick Bell, David Edwards, and Harrison Wagner (eds.), *Political Power* (New York: Free Press, 1969).

6. "The Politics of Transnational Economic Relations," in Keohane and Nye.

7. "Economic issues are high politics for the governments involved." Testimony of Francis Bator, House of Representatives, Committee on Foreign Affairs, Sub-Committee on Foreign Economic Policy, July 25, 1972.

8. Arnold Wolfers, *Discord and Collaboration: Essays on International Politics* (Baltimore: Johns Hopkins, 1962).

9. Stanley Hoffmann, *Gulliver's Troubles, or the Setting of American Foreign Policy* (New York: McGraw-Hill, 1968), Ch. 2.

10. See Richard Cooper, "Economic Interdependence and Foreign Policy in the Seventies," *World Politics* 24 (January 1972).

11. Herbert Feis, *Europe: The World's Banker* (New Haven: Yale University Press, 1930).

12. Oran Young, "Interdependences in World Politics," *International Journal*, Autumn 1969, p. 726.

13. A.G. Ford, *The Gold Standard, 1880-1914: Britain and Argentina* (Oxford: Clarendon Press, 1962), p. 191.

14. Richard Cooper, *The Economics of Interdependence* (New York: McGraw-Hill, 1968); Lawrence Krause, "Private International Finance," in Keohane and Nye.

15. "The Myth of National Interdependence," in Charles Kindleberger (ed.), *The International Corporation* (Cambridge, Mass.: MIT Press, 1970).

16. See Anthony Lanyi, "Political Aspects of Exchange-Rate Systems," in Richard Merritt (ed.), *Communications in International Politics* (Urbana: University of Illinois Press, 1972).

17. George Modelski, *Principles of World Politics* (New York: Free Press, 1972), p. 134.

18. Zbigniew Brzezinski, "The Balance of Power Delusion," *Foreign Policy* 7 (Summer 1972).

19. See Robert O. Keohane, "The Big Influence of Small Allies," *Foreign Policy* 2 (Spring 1971).

20. See K.J. Holsti, "Canada and the United States," in Steven Spiegel and Kenneth N. Waltz (eds.), *Conflict in World Politics* (Cambridge, Mass.: Winthrop, 1971).

21. An exception was De Gaulle's use of monetary policy as a diplomatic instrument to weaken U.S. influence. See Edward Kolodziej, "French Monetary Policy in the Sixties: Background Notes to the Current Monetary Crisis," *World Affairs* 135 (Summer 1972).

22. Morton Kaplan, *System and Process in International Politics* (New York: Wiley, 1957), p. 23.

23. I.F. Stone, "The Flowering of Henry Kissinger," *New York Review of Books*, November 2, 1972, p. 26.

24. Robert Cox and Harold Jacobson (eds.), *The Anatomy of Influence* (New Haven: Yale University Press, 1973), Appendix C.

25. See Keohane and Nye, "Conclusions," for elaboration.

26. Harold Malmgren, *International Economic Peacekeeping in Phase II* (New York: Quadrangle Books, for the Atlantic Council of the United States, 1972).

27. Arnold Wolfers, op. cit.

28. Robert Cox, "The Executive Head," *International Organization* 23, 2 (Spring 1969).

29. For examples, see Keohane and Nye.

30. Richard Cooper, "Trade Policy is Foreign Policy," *Foreign Policy* 9 (Winter 1972-73).

31. Malmgren, op. cit.

32. Charles Kindleberger, *Power and Money* (New York: Basic Books, 1970).

33. Lanyi, op. cit., pp. 428-29, indicates some reasons for this reluctance.

34. Raymond Vernon has pointed out that alarm about "balance of payments deficits" was to a great extent generated by the convention of treating direct investment as illiquid, thus obscuring the fact that U.S. claims on other economies were far larger than their claims on the U.S. economy. As Britain showed in two world wars, such claims can be made liquid. Vernon's view was that the "run on the bank" was "induced largely by the fact that the banker has kept insisting, repeatedly and stridently, that his institution was going bankrupt." *Foreign Policy* 5 (Winter 1971-72).

35. C. Fred Bergsten, "Reforming the Dollar: An International Monetary Policy for the United States" (New York: Council on Foreign Relations, 1972).

36. Henry Aubrey, *Behind the Veil of International Money* (Princeton, Essays in International Finance, No. 71, January 1969), p. 9.

37. Bergsten, op. cit., p. 47.

38. Richard N. Cooper, "The United States and the Enlarged European Community: Britain Must Keep Her Global Perspective," *The Round Table*, Issue 244 (October 1971), p. 570.

39. For an interesting discussion of similar issues from the perspective of game theory, see Lanyi, op. cit., especially pp. 431-43.

40. For instance, see the discussion in Bergsten, op. cit., pp. 44-47.

41. Cooper, "The United States and the Enlarged European Community," p. 574.

42. The phrase is Aubrey's, but for a fuller discussion of interests of groups, see Fred Hirsch, *Money International* (Penguin Books, 1969); and William I. Wadbrook, *West German Balance of Payments Policy* (New York: Praeger, 1972).

43. On this point see C. Fred Bergsten, "Crisis in U.S. Trade Policy," *Foreign Affairs* 49-4 (July 1971).

44. For instance, see the House and Senate Hearings on the Par Value Modification Act of 1972. Committee on Banking and Currency, House of Representatives, Ninety-Second Congress, Second Session (March 1, 2, 3, and 6, 1972); Committee on Banking, Housing and Urban Affairs, United States Senate, Ninety-Second Congress, Second Session (February 22, 23, 24, 1972).

45. Bergsten, "Reforming the Dollar," p. 44.

46. The work of Hans. O. Schmitt is important on this point. See his "political Conditions for International Currency Reform," *International Organization* 18, 3 (Summer 1964); and "The National Boundary in Politics and Economics," in Richard Merritt (ed.), *Communication in International Politics* (Urbana: University of Illinois Press, 1972).

47. See Leon Lindberg and Stuart Scheingold, *Europe's Would-Be Polity* (Englewood Cliffs, N.J.: Prentice-Hall, 1970); J.S. Nye, *Peace in Parts* (Boston: Little Brown, 1971), Chs. 2, 7.

48. House of Representatives, Committee on Banking and Currency, Ninety-Second Congress, Second Session (March 1, 2, 3, 6, 1972), *To Provide for a Modification in the Par Value of the Dollar*, Hearings, p. 36.

49. Ibid., p. 43.

50. Ibid., p. 79.

51. For the most comprehensive study of GATT, see Kenneth W. Dam, *The GATT: Law and International Economic Organization* (Chicago: University of Chicago Press, 1970). For a fuller discussion of the need for and problems of linkages such as those suggested here, see William Diebold, *The United States and the Industrial World* (New York: Praeger, for the Council on Foreign Relations, 1972).

52. Estimates of production of foreign subsidiaries of U.S. corporations abound. See, for instance, John Fayerweather, "The Internationalization of Business," *Annals of the American Academy of Political and Social Science*, September 1972, p. 2.

53. Werner Feld, *Nongovernmental Forces and World Politics: A Study of Business, Labor, and Political Groups* (New York: Praeger, 1972), p. 76.

54. Lawrence B. Krause, "The International Economic System and the Multinational Corporation," *Annals*, September 1972, pp. 93-103.

55. See Richard D. Robinson, "The Developing Countries, Development, and the Multinational Corporation," *Annals*, September 1972, pp. 67-79; Stephen Hymer and Robert Rowthorn, "Multinational Corporations and International Oligopoly: The Non-American Challenge," in Charles Kindleberger (ed.), *The International Corporation* (Cambridge, Mass.: MIT Press, 1970); John Kenneth Galbraith, *The New Industrial State* (Boston: Houghton Mifflin, 1967).

56. The following discussion draws on an essay by Robert O. Keohane and Van Doorn Ooms, "The Multinational Enterprise and World Political Economy," *International Organization* 26, 1 (Winter 1972), pp. 84-120.

57. Mira Wilkins, *The Emergence of Multinational Enterprise: American Business Abroad from the Colonial Era to 1914* (Cambridge, Mass.: Harvard University Press, 1970), p. 201.

58. See Raymond Vernon, *Sovereignty at Bay: The Multinational Spread of U.S. Enterprises* (New York: Basic Books, 1971); William Diebold, *The United States and the Industrial World*, op. cit.; Richard N. Cooper, *The Economics of Interdependence: Economic Policy in the Atlantic Community* (New York: McGraw-Hill, for the Council on Foreign Relations, 1968).

59. For a general discussion of the problem of bargaining between transnational actors and states, see J.S. Nye, Jr., and Robert O. Keohane, "Transnational Relations and World Politics: A Conclusion," in Robert O. Keohane and Joseph S. Nye (eds.), *Transnational Relations and World Politics*

60. See Vernon, cited, pp. 232-36; Jack N. Behrman, *National Interests and the Multinational Enterprise: Tensions among the North Atlantic Countries*, (Englewood Cliffs, N.J.: Prentice-Hall, 1970), Chs. 6-8.

61. Behrman, p. 98.

62. For support for this generalization, see Edith Penrose, *The Large International Firm in Developing Countries: The International Petroleum Industry* (Cambridge, Mass.: MIT Press, 1968); Michael Tanzer, *The Political Economy of International Oil and the Underdeveloped Countries* (Boston: Beacon Press, 1969).

63. See Jonathan Levin, *The Export Economies: Their Pattern of Development in Historical Perspective* (Cambridge, Mass.: Harvard University Press, 1960); Harry Magdoff, *The Age of Imperialism: The Economics of U.S. Foreign Policy* (New York: Monthly Review Press, 1969).

64. Diebold, op. cit., p.

65. See Robert W. Cox, "Labor and Transnational Relations," in Keohane and Nye; David H. Blake, "Trade Unions and the Challenge of the Multinational Corporation," *Annals*, September 1972, pp. 34-45.

66. *Boston Globe*, March 21, 1972; *New York Times*, March 23, 24, 1972.

67. See Edward Miles, "Transnationalism in Space: Inner and Outer," in Keohane and Nye.

68. *New York Times*, October 25, 1972.

69. Ibid.

70. Nazli Choucri, with James P. Bennett, "Population, Resources and Technology: Political Implications of the Environmental Crisis," *International Organization* 26, 2 (Spring 1972).

71. Edmund Faltermayer, "The Energy Joyride is Over," *Fortune*, September 1972).

72. Donella Meadows et al., *The Limits to Growth* (New York: Universe Books, 1972); Robert Heilbroner, "Growth and Survival," *Foreign Affairs*, October 1972.

73. M.A. Adelman, "Is the Oil Shortage Real?", *Foreign Policy* 9 (Winter 1972-73).

74. See Theodore Moran, "Raw Deal in Raw Materials," *Foreign Policy* 5 (Winter 1971-72), pp. 119-136.

75. See, for instance, Bart Fisher, *The International Coffee Agreement* (New York: Praeger, 1972). Also see Steven Krasner, "The Politics of Primary Commodities: A Study of Coffee," Ph.D. dissertation, Harvard University, 1971.

76. Peter Odell, *Oil and World Power: A Geographical Interpretation* (Middlesex, England, and Baltimore, Md.: Penguin Books, 1970), p. 11.

77. *New York Times*, June 12, 1972.

78. Adelman, cited; Theodore Moran, "Coups and Costs," *Foreign Policy* 8 (Fall 1972), pp. 129-137.

79. Adelman, op. cit.

80. *The Economist* (London), October 4 and 14, 1972; *New York Times* October 3, 1972.

81. Adelman, op. cit.; Moran, "Coups and Costs."

82. Nazli Choucri, with James P. Bennett, "Population, Resources, and Technology."

83. Jagdish Bhagwati, *Economics and World Order from the 1970's to the 1990's* (New York: Macmillan, 1972), pp. 29-32.

84. Johan Galtung, "A Structural Theory of Imperialism," *Journal of Peace Research* 2 (1971).

85. Bhagwati, op. cit., p. 13.

86. See Choucri, op. cit.

87. Uma Lele and John Mellor, "Jobs, Poverty, and the 'Green Revolution'," *International Affairs* 48 (January 1972), p. 21.

88. Alistair Buchan, "The End of Bipolarity," in *East Asia and the World System* (London: Adelphi Paper 91, 1972).

89. J.S. Nye, "UNCTAD: Poor Nations Pressure Group," in Robert Cox and Harold Jacobson (eds.), *The Anatomy of Influence: Decision-Making in International Organization* (New Haven: Yale University Press, 1973).

90. Malmgren, op. cit., p. 183.

91. Andrew Shonfield, *Modern Capitalism* (London: Oxford University Press, 1969), Ch. 3.

92. Choucri, op. cit.

93. See Edward J. Woodhouse, "Revisioning the Future: An Ecological Perspective on Development," *World Politics* 25 (October 1972).

94. See J.S. Nye, *Peace in Parts*, pp. 99-103.

95. For reference in writing this section, we have relied particularly on the following: (1) Josef Wilczynski, *The Economics and Politics of East-West Trade* (New York: Praeger, 1969); (2) Alan A. Brown and Egon Neuberger (eds.), *International Trade and Central Planning* (Berkeley and Los Angeles: University of California Press, 1968); (3) Nathaniel McKitterick, *East-West Trade: The Background of U.S. Policy* (New York: Twentieth Century Fund, 1966); (4) Gunnar Adler-Karlsson, *Western Economic Warfare, 1947-1967* (Stockholm: Almquist and Wiksell, 1968); and (5) Samuel Pisar, *Coexistence and Commerce* (New York: McGraw-Hill, 1970).

96. Wilczynski, op. cit., p. 52.

97. Ibid., p. 56.

98. *New York Times*, October 19, 1972.

99. See Marshall Goldman, "Red Black Gold," *Foreign Policy* 8 (Fall 1972).

100. See Pisar, op. cit.

101. Wilczynski, op. cit., p. 269.

102. McKitterick, op. cit., p. 15.

103. Adler-Karlsson, op. cit., pp. 22-82, contains an extensive treatment of the formation of the American embargo. Yet it should be recognized that, due to presidential reluctance to alienate American allies, "no other country, in the last analysis, actually had to do anything as a result of the Battle Act." McKitterick, op. cit., pp. 15-16.

104. Morris Bornstein, "Discussion," citing Frederick Pryor, *The Communist Foreign Trade System* (Cambridge, Mass.: MIT Press, 1963), in Brown-Neuberger, p. 128.

105. Wilczynski, p. 142, for the Australian case, *New York Times*, September 29, 1972, for that of the United States.

106. Wilczynski, op. cit., p. 230.

107. Ibid., p. 62. See also Marshall Goldman, "More Heat in the Soviet Hothouse," *Harvard Business Review*, July-August 1971, pp. 4-11, for an excellent treatment of the Soviet need for technology.

108. *New York Times*, "News of the Week in Review," October 22, 1972.

109. Wilczynski, p. 241.

110. "The Scent of Honey: A Survey of East-West Trade," *The Economist*, January 6, 1973.

111. See *New York Times*, January 9, 1973.

112. The quote is from Wilczynski, p. 268. The citation is to U.S. Senate, *East-West Trade*, Hearings before the Committee on Foreign Relations, 1965, Part II, p. 148.

113. Harry G. Johnson, "Notes on Some Theoretical Problems Posed by the Foreign Trade of Centrally Planned Economies," in Brown-Neuberger, p. 394.

114. Works by Vernon, Behrman, Kindleberger, and Hymer have been cited above. See also Louis T. Wells, Jr., "The Multinational Business Enterprise: What Kind of International Organization?", in Keohane and Nye.

115. Cf. the studies by Cox and Blake, note 65, above.

116. Preliminary work is being done along these lines by Ivan Vallier, at Santa Cruz, and Ernst B. Haas, at Berkeley. See Vallier, "The Roman Catholic Church: A Transnational Actor," in Keohane and Nye.

117. For a discussion of this problem see Robert O. Keohane and Joseph S. Nye, Jr., "Transnational Systems and International Organizations," unpublished manuscript. See also Richard Neustadt, *Alliance Politics* (New York: Columbia University Press, 1970); Robert O. Keohane, "The Big Influence of Small Allies," *Foreign Policy* 2 (Spring 1971); Leon N. Lindberg and Stuart A. Scheingold, *Europe's Would-Be Polity* (Englewood Cliffs, N.J.: Prentice-Hall, 1970).

118. Robert W. Russell is engaged in some very interesting work on this subject at the Harvard Center for International Affairs.

119. See, for instance, Robert O. Keohane, "Institutionalization in the United Nations General Assembly," *International Organization* 23, 4 (Autumn 1969); Philippe Schmitter, "The 'Organizational Development' of International Organizations," *International Organization* 25, 4 (Autumn 1971).

120. Study in progress by Zuhayr Mikdashi. For a more traditional analysis of OPEC by the same author, see *The Community of Oil Exporting Countries* (Cornell University Press, 1972).

121. Research along these lines is projected by Harold K. Jacobson, Robert W. Cox, and Lawrence Sheinman.

122. John Gerard Ruggie, "The Structure of International Organization: Contingency, Complexity, and Post-Modern Form," Peace Research Society, *Papers* 18 (1971): 73-91.

123. For earlier work along these same lines see David Mitrany, *A Working Peace System* (Princeton, N.J.: Princeton University Press, 1943); Robert W. Cox, "The Executive Head," *International Organization* 23, 2 (Spring 1969).

124. Susan Strange, "International Economics and International Relations," *International Affairs* 46, 2 (April 1970): p. 313.

125. Testimony of Francis Bator, House of Representatives, Committee on Foreign Affairs, Sub-Committee on Foreign Economic Policy, July 25, 1972.

6

Minerals Trade and International Relations

Samuel Schurr
Resources for the Future

The belief that international trade and investment is conducive to the establishment of better political relations among nations, or to a desirable pattern of economic development within nations, is probably under more serious attack in respect to trade in mineral raw materials than in any other phase of trade among nations. Skepticism concerning the beneficial effects of raw materials trade is rooted, to a considerable extent, in two underlying circumstances:

1. The commodities traded originate, in the main, in less developed countries, whereas consumption occurs mainly in countries that are comparatively rich and well developed; and
2. Ownership of the companies which search out the mineral deposits, develop the mines, produce the raw minerals, and process and transport the refined minerals to market lies, in the main, within the rich, developed countries.

The problems affecting international relations that grow out of the unique characteristics of the minerals trade are treated, in the first section of this chapter, in terms of several broad issues of policy, and in the second section, with specific reference to the international oil industry.

The Broad Issues of Policy

The Pace of Economic Development in the Raw Materials Exporting Countries

There is an extensive literature, some of it polemical, dealing with the economic effects of foreign-owned mining activity in the less developed countries. It is unnecessary to do more than summarize the main elements in the economic argument.

Let us deal first with the direct economic effects of mining. The major argument (here paraphrased) is that the activities connected with the exploitation of minerals are all outward oriented (i.e., away from the country), so that except for the particular enclave surrounding the mine and its related processing plants, the domestic economy enjoys few spillover effects. The material inputs required in the extraction process are of small importance compared, for example, with manufacturing, but even those required are usually imported. At the other end of the production chain, the mineral product is sent elsewhere for further processing and subsequent manufacture. Thus, there is a distinct absence of direct linkages, either forward or backward, between the mineral activity and the rest of the economy. Even transportation facilities, which must be provided, are essentially oriented to getting the minerals out of the country on their way to further processing and consumption centers elsewhere.

Nor are substantial spillover effects achieved through the payment of wages and salaries. To begin with, the industries are not labor-intensive, and, for the most part, the subsequent operations of smelting, refining, etc., which could employ additional workers, are located in the consuming countries. Also, the jobs held by native personnel are mainly at the manual level, whereas technical and managerial employment is mainly preempted by nationals of the home country of the parent company. Consequently, the direct employment and income effects of the mineral activity are even smaller than they might otherwise be. (The failure to employ native personnel in managerial functions is also criticized on other grounds; e.g., no basis is provided for the subsequent assumption of management functions by the host country [see below].

Yet, for all the failings of the *direct* economic effects, the financial and fiscal effects of minerals activities are extremely important. In raw materials exporting countries foreign exchange earnings and government revenues are heavily dependent upon mineral exports. Consequently, there is a perennial struggle between host country governments and international companies concerning the amount of revenues that accrue to the exporting countries and the means by which these revenues are determined. Much of the persistent tension between international companies and host governments arises from conflicts over the setting of price and, in particular, over relative shares in the economic rent generated by minerals exports. (See the second section of this chapter for particulars pertaining to oil.)

An associated aspect of prime concern is the behavior of raw materials prices in international trade as compared with those of manufactured products. The minerals exporting countries argue that they are placed at a disadvantage in relation to the industrialized importing countries by (a) the sharp short-run fluctuations in raw materials prices; and (b) secular changes in the terms of trade which are said to favor finished products over raw materials.

As a consequence of the features that are said to characterize minerals extraction, the idea that mining will generate enough *direct* effects to serve as a springboard for economic development has been seriously questioned. An industrialized enclave with minimal linkages to the remainder of the economy is, almost by definition, a poor vehicle for initiating a process in which one thing leads to another in such a way as to foster economic development on a broad front. The proceeds which a government earns from mineral exports are a completely different matter, however. These earnings will frequently exceed all other funds available for investment. They are a sine qua non for economic development in many countries of the world. It is, therefore, deemed axiomatic that every effort must be made to maximize the size of the country's share of these proceeds, within the constraint of not killing the goose.

All of this is familiar terrain within the field of economic development and no new directions for study are indicated. What is required, however, is a far closer articulation than heretofore between research on economic development and studies of specific commodity markets and of the structure of the particular industries producing the various raw materials, in order to achieve an improved understanding of commodity price behavior and of the economic limits on profits (and profit sharing) set by market forces and industrial structure.

The Conflict Between Nationalism and the
Foreign Ownership and Management of
Mineral Enterprises

The Legacy of Colonialism. The lingering memories of colonialism must be contended with throughout the less developed world in connection with foreign ownership of mining enterprises. The point is that in the colonial system raw materials were shipped from the colony to the mother country for transformation there into manufactured products (some of which were later sold back to the colony). The continuation of such a pattern after countries have thrown off their colonial status can easily be interpreted as the persistence of the old relationship in a new guise.

If memories alone were not sufficient to plant this conception in the minds of people in the raw materials exporting countries, ideology is ever present to hammer the point home. The belief that capitalism in the advanced countries depends upon the existence of colonialism elsewhere, an idea which traces its origins to Marx and Lenin, is a constant theme in the politics of the less developed, raw materials exporting countries. No matter how weak the hold of Marxist doctrine in other respects this aspect appears to hold undiminished sway in many places.

The idea of colonialism gains additional credibility because of the manner in which foreign investment in minerals is *perceived*, as compared to the perception of investment in manufacturing or in service activities. A hypothesis that needs to be investigated is that there is a general tendency within countries in which foreign investment in minerals occurs to regard such investments as serving solely to exploit the natural wealth of their own country for the benefit of consumers in other parts of the world, particularly in those countries in which the investing company is domiciled. A simplistic view would have it that foreign investment in minerals does not create capital in the exporting country but instead only transforms and depletes natural capital that is already present for the exclusive benefit of the exporting companies and the importing countries. Investment in manufacturing, on the other hand, although it, too, may be resented, can be regarded as wealth-creating in that capital is being established in a situation in which previously there was nothing, i.e., natural capital is not being transformed, and certainly not depleted. What is more, investment in manufacturing (and service activities) can be said to be undertaken in order to produce for the indigenous market, unlike mining which sends essentially all its output away from the producing country.

Local Participation in the Ownership and Management of Minerals Enterprises. It is becoming increasingly evident from developments throughout the world that the continued viability of a system of international exchange in mineral raw materials depends upon the establishment of arrangements that will serve to reconcile foreign investments in minerals with strongly-held local attitudes that are antagonistic to such investments.

One important route to such a reconciliation lies in the direction of doing those things which will help build up local participation in the ownership and management of the minerals enterprises in conjunction with the continued investment of foreign funds. A major subject for study is of the techniques that will bring about large-scale local participation in ownership and management without stopping the flow of needed foreign investment capital and of foreign technical expertise. Participation in existing concessions along the lines now being pioneered in the oil industry (discussed below) may turn out to provide a useful model in some respects. However, there are numerous other possibilities which should be studied for their comparative effectiveness in reconciling these apparently conflicting sets of objectives as well as protecting the legitimate economic interests of consumers of raw materials—something which the oil agreements fail to do (see below).

Nationalism and Economic Development. Foreign investment in minerals, involving as it often does the control of the most important assets of a country, is a direct infringement of a nation's desire to manage its own affairs. This is a sentiment that would be encountered in respect to any set of economic activities—mining, manufacturing, public utilities—which loom large within a particular country (and, indeed, rankles even where no international extraterritorial issues are involved—witness Appalachian resentment at "absentee" control over its development). However, the legacy of colonialism and the unique characteristics of minerals exploitation strengthen this sentiment where the minerals extractive industries are concerned.

It is important to recognize that there may be more than mere sentiment in the desire to be master in one's own house. A hypothesis in need of study is that there is a strong connection between uncorking the ability to run a nation's own affairs and the broad process of economic development of the country. It is altogether possible that running the show is an important way to find and harness energies within the country which would otherwise remain dormant.

Combined economic, political, and behavioral research is needed to determine whether nationalism can activate an energizing potential that may be of overriding importance in the process of economic development. The comparison with the domestic situation within the United States, in which there is growing recognition of the importance of self-esteem and local control to the emergence of minority groups, should also be kept in view in such research.

Also in need of study are the dangers (and how to avert them) of the destructive features of nationalism that will never be far removed from its positive side. The destructive aspects pose a potentially grave threat to the United States and other Western nations because in various parts of the world the colonial legacy contains a heavy anti-Western, anti-capitalist, and anti-white component.

Is Expanding Raw Materials Trade Compatible
With the Lessening of International Frictions?

An issue of overriding importance to international order which must be faced squarely is whether heavy foreign trade and investment in mineral resources is basically compatible with friendly relations among nations.

The necessary ingredients for a mutually beneficial international exchange would appear to be present in raw materials: the dependence of the industrialized nations on imports of essential raw materials such as petroleum, copper, iron ore is growing, and the LDCs earn large amounts of foreign exchange, essential to capital formation and economic development, through the sale of these materials. And yet, for reasons already indicated, although the exchange may be mutually beneficial it does not appear to be contributing to a reduction of international political friction. What changes can be introduced that will lessen the sources of political friction?

Meeting the Objectives of the Exporting Countries. The discussion to this point has been concerned entirely with the issues that give rise to deep dissatisfaction within the exporting countries. To meet the objectives of the exporting countries a minimum step would appear to require (a) participation by these countries in the ownership and management of resource industries, and (b) arrangements for increasing their share of the profits resulting from the export of minerals.

Meeting the Objectives of the Importing Countries. The importing countries want dependable supplies of essential raw materials at prices which are not exorbitant. The basis for fears within the importing countries in respect both to the security of supply and the imposition of monopoly prices are well illustrated in the case of oil (dealt with in the second section of this chapter). Devices to neutralize the coercive power of the exporting countries, and needed research on the subject, are also identified in that discussion. It needs to be recognized that such devices (e.g., large stocks of oil within consuming countries sufficient to withstand supply interruptions), which give the appearance of being directed against the exporting countries, may in fact be essential to the viability of the present international trading system.

The Distribution of Use of the World's Mineral Resources. The per capita use of all types of mineral resources in the United States and in Western Europe is far above that of the less developed countries of the world. This fact, inherent in the comparative levels of economic development in the Western world and in the less developed countries, had led to the playing out of many scenarios that carry frightening implications for the entire non-Western world. A frequent exercise is to multiply U.S. per capita consumption levels by the present and expected population levels of Asia, Africa, and Latin America in order to demonstrate that the world's known reserves of many essential materials will not be adequate to the task.

There are many things wrong with so simplistic a calculation, but its persuasive power is great in depicting the Western world, led by the United States, as consuming more than its share of the world's wealth of mineral resources. Although purely a hypothetical construct, this idea adds greatly to the exacerbation of political frictions that already result from the present patterns of international trade in raw materials. The Western countries are depicted as building themselves up by depleting the earth's resource base (much of it within the LDCs), with the result that not enough resources will be left when the poor countries try to raise themselves to Western standards.

There is an urgent need for research on the outlook for world mineral supply and demand in the future that would place this subject in more realistic perspective. The topics that need to be studied on the supply side include the outlook for developing additional reserves of raw materials as a result of continuous exploration, aided by changes in prices and costs and technology; the possibilities for substituting more abundant for less abundant raw materials, and for replacing natural materials by synthetics, etc. On the side of demand, the real possibility that the road to economic development for the LDCs is likely to be radically different than the coal-steel-railroad patterns of the United States and Western Europe needs to be examined in a realistic, convincing manner.

A major effort to engage this range of topics on a world basis is badly needed. It is by no means clear what such an investigation would show in respect to the world's raw materials future: a frightening picture would point the way to new plans and institutional arrangements for conservation and for sharing in a severely diminished bounty; a hopeful picture could lay the foundation for a thriving pattern of international raw materials trade.

Alternatives to Present and Projected Trade Patterns. The possibility that existing and indicated trade patterns in energy and mineral raw materials are essentially incompatible with the minimization of international political friction needs to be considered. The antagonisms that result from trade and investment in this sphere are so strong and so deeply ingrained to make it conceivable that no amount of institutional adjustment can undo the damage to international relations.

Research is badly needed on the possibilities that exist for the Western world, or for specific countries or groups of countries, to satisfy their raw material needs with a declining instead of a growing dependence on exporters within the less developed countries. Possibilities along these lines are described for energy materials in the next section dealing with international oil. Deep study of the subject is needed not just for the energy materials but also for other clusters of mineral raw materials—the ferrous metals, the non-ferrous, the light metals, the fertilizer minerals, etc.

Such research is not altogether dissimilar to that suggested for the preceding topic. It may point the way to means for the Western world eventually to go it alone if the frictions inherent in raw materials trade are judged to be essentially intractable to improvement. On the other hand, knowledge that there may indeed be a feasible alternative to growing interdependence between the Western world and the less developed countries could serve a salutary purpose on both sides and thereby obviate the need for so radical an upheaval in trading patterns.

International Oil: An Illustrative Case

Oil is the preeminent commodity in international trade by any standard, whether economic, political, or strategic. Key elements in this trade are: (1) The export-import relationships between countries in the Middle East and North Africa and the industrialized nations of Western Europe, Japan, and (in the future) the United States; and (2) The dominant role of a handful of international companies, most of them U.S. corporations.

In considering future conditions and problems of the international oil trade a few propositions, examined below, should be kept in view:

1. The countries of the Middle East and North Africa stand unique, for the next decade at least, in their capacity to satisfy the liquid fuel requirements of the major importing countries. There will be very large oil flows from this region

to Western Europe, Japan, and the United States, and a very large monetary flow in the reverse direction.

2. The revenue flows may prove too large for many of the oil-exporting countries to absorb within their own economies. The monetary, financial, and political implications of such a situation could be of fundamental importance. Attempts must be made to envisage their shape and scope.

3. Oil from the Middle East and North Africa is being sold at a price which far exceeds its real costs of production. The international companies, under present and foreseeable circumstances, appear to be essential to the continuing ability of the exporting countries to maintain this large margin between costs and prices.

4. Participation by the governments of oil-producing countries in the ownership of major producing concessions is now a certainty. Such a development carries vast, but uncertain, implications for oil prices, oil company management, and the future of company-government relations in raw materials producing countries throughout the world.

5. Brinkmanship in the form of a threatened embargo on oil shipments has been (and could again be) an effective commercial weapon of the exporting countries in exacting higher prices for their oil. Supply interruptions, threatened or actual, could also be used as a coercive weapon to achieve political and military ends.

6. Long-term, heavy dependence on oil imports from the Middle East and North Africa is *not* an unavoidable future, at least for the United States and some of the countries of Western Europe. New resources of oil, some of them indigenous, may be developed, and other domestic fuel alternatives to imported oil supplies may be achieved. Problems encountered in drawing on Middle Eastern supplies may hasten the development of alternative sources.

Supply Capability of the Middle East and North Africa

With proved oil reserves (as of December 31, 1972) of about 440 billion barrels, out of a world total of approximately 530 billion barrels (excluding the U.S.S.R. and the United States), the Middle East and North Africa contain an overwhelming proportion of the resources upon which the importing countries of the world must rely. The countries of Western Europe and Japan already depend upon these resources for more than 80 percent of their total oil consumption; the United States has in recent years depended upon the Middle East and North Africa for less than 5 percent of its oil consumption, but this dependence has been projected to grow to perhaps 35 percent by 1980, and to an even higher percentage in subsequent years.

The physical ability of this exporting region to satisfy all the demands which may be placed upon it over the next ten to fifteen years (as far ahead as most current projections go) seems well assured. The National Petroleum Council, in a report to the U.S. Secretary of the Interior, states that there is no problem of physical capability on the basis of the figures shown in table 6.1 (in billion barrels).[1]

The figures may be read in the following way: (1) On a world basis there are already sufficient proved reserves to satisfy cumulative consumption for the next fifteen years, but there would not be enough oil to sustain required production levels at the end of this period in that the (then) reserves-to-production ratio would drop to a too-low level (less than 5 to 1 in 1985); (2) However, new amounts will be added to proved reserves during the period and there is every reason to expect that they will be at least as large as those added during a recent 15-year period. The reserves added during 1955-1970 were themselves larger than the cumulated consumption estimated for the period 1971-1985; (3) The estimated cumulated U.S. consumption is well beyond present proved reserves *plus* the amounts discovered over a recent 15-year period, i.e., additions to reserves would need to exceed the recent record by a substantial amount if the United States were not to become as heavily dependent upon imports as projected.

Mere physical capability does not guarantee that the exporting countries will agree to allow their oil reserves to be depleted at the rate required for the satisfaction of growing world needs. Hostile attitudes toward maximum exploitation may take hold as a result of concern about the conservation of supplies for these countries' own subsequent needs; or for a time when it is thought oil may be more expensive; or for environmental reasons which have not yet permeated these countries to any major extent. If supplies from a few Middle Eastern countries continue to gain in importance in world energy consumption it will be essential to prepare for the possibility that such attitudes may prevail in the future; the situation will need to be kept under surveillance for early warning signals.

Table 6-1
World Supply of, and Demand for, Oil: 1971-1985

	Cumulated Oil Production Required for 1971-1985 Inclusive to Meet Forecasted Demand	Estimated Proved Oil Reserves as of 12/31/70	Gross Additions to Proved Oil Reserves Over 15-Year Period, 1955-1970
United States	110.6	37.0	42.2
Rest of "Free World"	241.1	474.4*	407.2*
	351.7	511.4	449.9

*Predominantly Middle East and North Africa.

Implications of the High Monetary Flows

The governmental oil revenues of Middle Eastern and North African countries came to about $9 billion in 1971. (Earnings in other major exporting countries were: Venezuela, $1.8 billion, and Nigeria, just short of $1 billion.) By 1980, Middle Eastern and North African export earnings from sales to Western Europe, Japan, and the United States have been projected at about $20 billion or more. Looking ahead to 1985, it has been estimated that for the eleven OPEC countries revenues could amount to about $50 billion/year, implying a cumulative flow of funds between 1970 and 1985 of as much as half a trillion dollars.

The implications of these huge monetary flows is a subject which deserves attention both in terms of the balance-of-payments situation of the importing countries, and of the uses to which the funds could be put by the exporting countries. If many of the countries are unable to absorb funds at this level within their own economies what problems are indicated for the stability of the world monetary system? To look in another direction: to what extent could such amounts of money, if partly directed to armaments, serve to alter the balance of military power within the Middle East?

One of the possible consequences of these monetary flows which has recently become evident is that the oil-exporting countries might become large equity holders in companies in the United States and other industrialized countries. An offer has already been made by Saudi Arabia, through its Minister of Petroleum and Mineral Affairs, that there be a commercial agreement between the United States and Saudi Arabia providing for a preferred place for Saudi oil in the United States and the investment of Saudi capital in the marketing of oil in this country. The economic, political, and strategic implications of such investments by oil exporting countries, perhaps embodied, as in this case, in broader arrangements, calls for careful analysis.

Oil Prices: The Role of the Oil Companies

During recent years oil-producing countries have engaged in a persistent drive to increase the revenues received from concessionaire companies. The Organization of Petroleum Exporting Countries (OPEC) has played a key role in coordinating the activities of the countries in this regard. Indeed, its establishment—in 1960—was brought about by the collective resistance by the countries to the lowering of posted prices that had already occurred. From the beginning the function of OPEC was conceived of as promoting the interests of the principal oil-producing countries by parallel lines of national policy and by cooperative action.

As oil product prices declined in world markets in the late 1950s, the foreign-owned producing companies began to lower the posted price of crude oil, thereby reducing the tax revenues of governments which were based upon a 50-50 share in company profits as calculated on the basis of the posted price of oil. Governments resisted, and succeeded in preventing further declines of posted prices. The latter, held constant, consequently lost their relationship to market prices and became simply a nominal base for calculating the tax liabilities of the companies. Given this base, although taxes were still levied on what was called income, this had become a mere formality. Instead, taxes in effect became a fixed charge per barrel, and thus an inescapable cost to the companies. In the late 1960s the per-barrel tax (including royalties) to the companies had been running on the average between 80 cents and 90 cents at the Persian Gulf, and about $1 in Libya.

As a result of several rounds of negotiations in 1971, the tax recently stood at about $1.25 to $1.30 per barrel at the Persian Gulf, and—barring further escalation—will rise to about $1.45 in 1975. In Libya, the tax is slated to rise to more than $2.00 per barrel by 1975.

Also, as a result of the 1971 negotiations, oil prices on world markets have shot upwards, reversing their earlier declining trend. Prior to the 1971 price negotiations the costs of oil to the companies, i.e., their tax-paid costs, stood at about $1.00 per barrel at the Persian Gulf, composed of real production costs of between 10 and 20 cents per barrel and government taxes of around 90 cents. As a result of the negotiations, this figure has increased to about $1.45 per barrel, and will increase by another 15 to 20 cents by 1975.

It is important to observe that the concessionaire companies have been vital to the success of these efforts by the producer countries to earn high, and increasing, taxes per unit on their oil exports. There is a legitimate question—severely in need of study—whether the producing countries could maintain the wide margin between oil prices and real production costs without the international companies to serve as their tax collectors (see below).

Participation by Producer Governments
in the Major Concessions

Higher per-barrel earnings is one of two major objectives that have received serious attention in OPEC councils in recent years. The other is the eventual attainment of majority ownership in the major concessions—perhaps through the setting up of new companies in which the foreign concessionaires and national firms of the producing countries would both hold an interest. Negotiations pointed toward this objective have already yielded their first results—an agreement on participation between four Persian Gulf states (Saudi Arabia, Kuwait, Abu Dhabi, and Qatar) and a group of twenty three oil companies. Only Iraq had not negotiated a participation agreement as of early 1973. The general agreement provides for 25 percent participation by the producer governments in existing concessions, rising in steps to 51 percent by January 1, 1982, at which level it would remain until the expiration of the concessions.

As the producing countries expand their ownership role they will face the problem of how to dispose of their oil without undermining the international price structure on which their oil revenues depend. Unlike the situation that confronts the concessionaires, the per-barrel tax need not be a fixed cost item for a producer-country national company. They are, in other words, in a position to cut prices (that are topheavy in producer-government tax take) in order to achieve enlarged markets.

When "participation" in ownership of the existing concessions began to emerge as a producer-country objective, some students of the world oil industry suggested a scenario for the future with the following major elements: (1) producer-country national companies entering the international market on a large scale and seriously eroding the price structure; (2) the countries at the same time attempting to maintain or even increase their tax take from the concessionaires. As a result of thus being ground between higher taxes and lower prices, it was reasoned that some concessionaires would reach the point of no longer being able to obtain an acceptable rate of return on development investment. They might then, so the scenario ran, abdicate their concessionarie status and simply become contractors or purchasers of oil produced by national companies.

If national companies were then to take over a major portion of oil production, the scenario continued, they would have to look to the international companies as purchasers of their oil. Only these companies would have the necessary marketing and transportation network, and, consequently, they would be in a position to strike hard bargains. With countries competing in the sale of oil, prices could be driven downward, with no bottom limit except the low real cost of oil production, ex tax. The countries would have overreached themselves and suffered a collapse of oil revenues as a consequence.

Responsible officials in the oil-producing countries, it is now apparent, were considering ways of avoiding the predicted consequences (perhaps because they were paying close attention to the speculations of Western students of the oil market). In the participation agreement they have therefore included a provision for "buy back" by the international companies of specified portions of the country's share of crude at prices which are *above* the tax-paid cost of the crude. These buy-back prices have been estimated as equivalent to an extra cost of between 9 and 18 cents per barrel over the entirety of the concessionaires' crude output.

Thus, not only would country revenues not collapse under the weight of the sale of country-owned crude on world markets, they would instead be higher and the concessionaire companies would continue to serve as the instrument by which the taxes imposed by the producer governments were passed along to consumers in other countries.

It is not surprising, therefore, that participation has been characterized as a device to restructure the oil trade so as to give expression to producing country interests through the good offices of the oil companies.

Participation is a development of major importance that promises to cast its shadow over the entire area of international relationships in the raw materials field. It will be worthy of the most careful continued surveillance and study, particularly on the following key questions:

1. How will the price of oil be affected? Will effective and enduring devices be found to continue the oil companies in their role of tax collectors for the producing countries? Or will country competition eventually erupt, if and when national companies enter the international oil market on a significant scale?

2. If oil prices are held up by reason of arrangements between the companies and producer governments, what will be the response of the importing countries? The latter have, on the whole, made no persistent attempt to modify the existing market structure which permits producing countries, and to a diminishing degree companies, to enjoy the great economic rents which arise from oil production at going prices. It remains to be seen what effect they could have on cutting into the very wide—and ever-growing—margin between real production costs and market prices if they were to use the bargaining power they possess.

3. How will the companies and the producer countries work out their relationships in the vital area of managerial prerogatives? At levels of participation below 51 percent, the deciding voice will still be that of the companies. However, as country participation moves towards the 51 percent level to be achieved in 1982, it will be important to study the frictions that develop in management decisions and the means that are worked out for resolving difficulties.

4. What will be the broader effects of participation in pioneering a new institutional arrangement that, on the one hand, goes a long distance towards giving the countries the opportunity to manage their own affairs, but, on the other, avoids the extreme solution of nationalization and its resulting disruptions? Arrangements that will stabilize relationships between foreign-owned companies and producer governments are badly needed if the mechanism for satisfying world raw materials needs through international trade is not to be threatened with collapse.

The Threat of Supply Interruptions

The Middle East is, of course, a region marked by a high degree of instability. The threat of international hostilities is ever present, as is the threat of internal strife. Eruptions of this sort could of course lead to interruptions in the flow of oil supplies to consuming countries.

Supply interruptions can also result for political reasons. At the time of the Arab-Israeli war of 1967, there was a concerted effort by the Arab countries, both before and during the hostilities, to use an export embargo, both threatened and actual, as a weapon to coerce the Western powers, particularly the United States and Great Britain. Continuing political tensions in the Middle East suggest that the coercive use of an oil embargo might be tried again at another time.

What is now coming to be recognized as an equally, or perhaps more, important prospect in the future is the use of the oil embargo threat as a *commercial* bargaining weapon by the exporting countries. This was clearly demonstrated by events during the 1970-71 tax and price negotiations between the international oil companies and the producer countries. These were carried out under the threat of an embargo on oil shipments, first by Libya in the initial round of negotiations, and then by the Persian Gulf producers in a subsequent round. Such threats played a part in bringing about agreement to the terms that led to substantially higher oil prices for importing countries.

The threat of supply interruptions can be neutralized, for example, by the maintenance of oil stockpiles in consuming countries large enough to ride out an actual stoppage in oil supplies from the exporting countries. How large is large enough, particularly as the exporting countries accumulate huge monetary reserves that would enable them to withhold oil for long periods of time at no economic pain to themselves? Alternatively, what is the best way of providing protection against threatened supply interruptions—aboveground stocks; underground storage in depleted oil fields; the maintenance of unused capacity in secure areas; some combinations of these? How much safety can be bought by diversifying oil imports among a large number of supplying countries? Questions of this kind require study, preferably on a joint basis, by the major importing countries. Plans for restricting consumption, if an embargo does occur, and for allocating reduced supplies among the various countries and various uses within countries require simultaneous study.

Concern has also been expressed about the possibility that the U.S.S.R.—particularly if it gains greater political control in the Middle East—may see the manipulation of oil supplies as an attractive weapon to be used against Western countries. According to current energy projections the U.S.S.R. may within a decade be the only major world power that is self-sufficient in energy raw materials. Deep study of the political and strategic implications of the projected situation is required.

*Alternatives to Imports from the
Middle East*

Two major possibilities are known to exist for greatly enlarging oil (and natural gas) supplies in areas that are far closer to the United States and Western Europe, and that pose far fewer political, strategic, and commercial problems than are involved in drawing upon Middle Eastern sources. One of these is the North American Arctic, the other is the North Sea.

Developments in the North American Arctic, which started with the large oil discoveries on the Alaskan North Slope, have, of course, not proceeded nearly as rapidly as had been expected as a result particularly of delays occasioned by concern for the adverse environmental impacts of oil production and transport developments in Alaska.

Despite this, it is important not to lose sight of the probable existence of very large oil reserves in this region. The original North Slope discoveries have been set at 10 billion barrels, but some estimates of recoverable oil reserves now run to 75 billion barrels in Alaska and to more than 100 billion barrels in the Canadian Arctic, in addition to very large recoverable reserves of natural gas in both Alaska and Northern Canada. And it is altogether possible that if and when commercial development really gets under way, considerably larger amounts will be found.

In the North Sea, recoverable reserves have been estimated at between 30 and 40 billion barrels of oil, with sizable reserves of natural gas. Some analysts have estimated that production of oil and gas from the North Sea could by 1980 result in a substantial decline in Western Europe's percentage dependence on oil imports as an element in total energy consumption. If this were to happen, it would constitute a remarkable turnabout in Western Europe's energy fortunes. As recently as five years ago so radical a change in what was regarded as oil-barren Western Europe would have been utterly unthinkable.

Estimates of future discoveries in new oil and gas provinces and of the production that may result from such discoveries are subject to a high degree of uncertainty. The foregoing figures should therefore be regarded as no more than illustrative of judgments about possibilities that exist. The realization of these possibilities requires that, in addition to the physical availability of the resources, there exists a set of policy and economic circumstances that are favorable to their commercial development. Careful study of the geological prospects and related policy and economic requirements for commercial development are badly needed.

Apart from future developments that are dependent upon new discoveries, there exist in the United States vast known reserves of coal and oil shale that could be converted into liquid and gaseous forms. Investments in R&D are required in order to achieve commercial technologies for such conversion. In Canada there are huge known resources of tar sands, already being exploited commercially, for which substantial expansion would be possible.

U.S. policies may in the future be shaped to encourage the discovery of new oil and gas reserves at a much faster rate than in the past. Policy in the United States may also be geared to the development of technologies for achieving early commercial success in conversion processes for going from coal and shale to liquid and gaseous fuels.

Questions which need to be studied are how rapidly the future possibilities for developing new supplies can be realized. What policies would serve to bring about a faster rate of development? How will policies to encourage rapid growth of alternative sources in the United States, Western Europe and elsewhere be affected by the stance adopted by Middle Eastern countries on the production and price of oil and the security of supply? What are the possibilities for coordinated development policy in respect to new supply sources by all of the major oil importing countries? What are the prospects and problems of a coordinated approach to oil and gas energy supply in the United States and Canada? What new institutional approaches are required for those lines of policy that are international in scope?

Notes

1. National Petroleum Council, *U.S. Energy Outlook, An Initial Appraisal, 1971-1985*, Volume Two (Washington: November 1971), pp. 43-45.

7

The Developing Countries in a Changing International Economic Order: A Survey of Research Needs

James W. Howe, Project Director*
Overseas Development Council

The Changing North-South Relationship

The last half of the decade of the 1940s was a remarkable period. As it emerged from its greatest war, the Western world found the intellectual and political energy not only to organize for reconstruction and development, but also to create the international monetary and trade systems as well as the United Nations and its related family of organizations. These systems have served us well, but some of them are now showing their quarter century of age. The widely recognized need for their reform makes a thorough examination of the need for scholarly work on the institutions, systems, and conventions that compose the "international economic order" particularly timely. It is important, moreover, that such an examination pay particular attention to the interaction of the international economic order and the poor countries; for by the end of the century, four out of every five of the earth's inhabitants will be living in these countries, and numbers alone require that they not be left out of account.

The success of development efforts in the poor countries depends both on their solution of their own internal problems and on the correction of problems in the international economic order that militate against their development. Yet relatively little is being done to support scholarly work in the latter area. Outside financing available to developing countries has concentrated on the problems *within* the less developed countries themselves—in fields such as planning, budgeting, taxation, housing, transportation, industry, health, agriculture, and education. Essentially all of the official development assistance (ODA) provided by the sixteen rich countries which comprise the Development Assistance Committee is devoted to such internal development problems. Much of this assistance, which amounts to about $7.7 billion annually, is for the transfer of resources or technical know-how. Although some is for the development of knowledge and understanding about the internal development problems of the poor countries, very little of this amount is for scholarly work in the international economic order. Because foundations have more flexibility than do

*This chapter was prepared by the Overseas Development Council, under the direction of James W. Howe, Senior Fellow, in association with Guy F. Erb, Senior Fellow; Mildred Weiss, Staff Associate; Susan Sammartano, Staff Associate; and John W. Sewell, Vice President for Council Affairs. The opening section was prepared by James W. Howe. The authorship of subsequent sections is indicated in the notes.

197

public bodies to finance scholarly work on the international economic order, this may be a particularly appropriate field of activity for their consideration.

The Importance of the North-South Dimension

Even as colonialism was the great moral issue of the first half of this century, so the great moral problem of the last half is the gap between rich and poor nations. It is illustrated by the fact that the 20 percent of the world's people who live in the so-called "developed countries" consume 80 percent of the world's product, and the gap between rich and poor is growing. But in a world that is becoming more dependent on international cooperation as each year passes, this moral problem may in the long run have practical implications for the well-being of the rich as well as the poor: the world systems will not forever work for the rich unless they work also for the poor.

A half century from now, scholars' views of the important issues of the twentieth century may change. While it now seems paramount to many to repair the monetary, trading, and investment systems so that they will meet the needs of the score or two industrialized nations which dominate these systems, the scholar of 2025 A.D. (or even of 2000 A.D.), may consider this of small importance if no progress is made during the twentieth century on the great moral issue of that period. While a half century—or even a quarter century from now—seems distant indeed, the scholarly community, if no other community, should give serious consideration to that time frame. And in that time frame, these two unmistakable trends of the present—the growing disparity of income and growing dependence on international cooperation—make it evident that the development of the poor countries is one of the central issues of the century.

The Need for Research by
Developing-Country Scholars

In the course of preparing this survey of research, the Overseas Development Council consulted a great number of experts. Questionnaires were also sent to over 200 institutions which we believed were to some extent working on the problems of developing countries. Of the 100 institutions which responded, however, only twenty-six were located in developing countries. (The Appendix to this chapter, pp. 255-264 summarizes the responses.) In addition to the questionnaire, the Council also held several meetings with experts who were chiefly, but not exclusively, from the United States. Although we sought both written and oral views from scholars and officials in developing countries, we are not satisfied that those views have been adequately represented. We hope further work will be done to explore more fully the views of representatives of developing countries on this important topic.

In our survey, we have found that, with a few exceptions, developing-country scholars are working on internal, not external problems. They are not looking at the international economic order. Thus developing-country scholars are not in a position to advise policymakers in their own countries on how to relate to the international economic order. Should rich-country scholars undertake to do so?

In our view, it is not satisfactory over the long run for developing-country policymakers to have to rely exclusively, or even largely, on rich-country scholars for advice on how to relate to the international economic order. They lack not only the credibility but also the credentials, including, especially, a sense of what it is to be underdeveloped. Another missing credential is an intimate understanding of the goals of the particular developing country. Moreover, it is an almost universal goal to reduce dependency on the outside or at least to increase national control over external events. In acting as a surrogate for the missing developing-country scholar, the rich-country adviser is a constant reminder of the fact of dependency. The obvious analogy is that of the American white liberal who, in leading the civil rights movement on behalf of the American blacks, kept the blacks from one of their most cherished goals: doing it for themselves.

What is the answer to this dilemma? We believe it is to support research on the international economic order by developing-country scholars and institutions—research that will equip developing countries to make their own judgments about their relationship to such systems. This is not to say that rich-country scholars should not work on the same subjects. But the focus of foundation support should be on the work of developing-country scholars—working jointly with scholars from developed countries where appropriate.

Admittedly, in many developing countries, the ranks of scholars are thin, and asking them to spend time on the international economic order may reduce their work on domestic matters. But we believe that this problem may be overstated, since (1) the skills for scholarly work on international matters are often not interchangeable with those on internal matters, and (2) financing scholarly work would increase the supply of scholarship. Moreover, some of the harmful competition between international and domestic scholarship, for example, might in some cases be avoided by scholars who have migrated from poor to rich countries to work on the impact of the international economic order on development, and thus return to the subject of development—and possibly to their home countries.

The Interdependence of Rich Countries, Poor Countries, and the International Economic Order

Two interrelated sets of factors suggest that the rich, industrialized nations have a considerable stake in making certain that *all* countries benefit from the international economic order.

First, the rich countries themselves are becoming increasingly dependent on the several international systems. In the United States, the solution of several important concerns depends upon effective international action. For example, full employment will benefit from a smoothly functioning world trade and monetary system, which, by increasing U.S. exports, would create jobs and raise average wages. The current U.S. approach to the control of narcotics—and of its close companion, crime in the streets—depends heavily on control of the illicit international drug trade, which in turn requires international cooperation. Protection of the environment also will gradually require international cooperation on an uncommon scale. And the so-called "energy crisis" and growing dependence on a wide range of raw materials from abroad underscore the need for preserving and strengthening the international trade, investment, and monetary systems. Second, there is evidence that the security of the United States (and of the other great powers) is becoming increasingly dependent on economic and technological factors. Thus today many people feel more threatened by the energy crisis than by the chance that a misunderstanding with Russia or China will set off a nuclear interchange.

How do these concerns involve the developing countries? These countries are majority members of most of the international systems on which *all* countries depend. Each of these systems is more likely to function well if its member nations are disposed to cooperate, have a high capability to cooperate, and generally have a common view of the purposes and methods of each international system. Unless the poor countries believe they are reasonably well served by this system, they may not give the kind of cooperation needed.

The Impact of Rich-Country Values
and Techniques on Developing Countries

The values and basic economic techniques of the rich countries have had a pervasive influence upon the less developed countries. Thus, for example, the convention of individual private property, common in the industrialized countries, has largely superseded more communal or familial attitudes toward land and even capital prevalent in certain parts of the developing world. Individual achievement, once viewed by some societies in terms of performance in tribal warfare, is now widely reckoned in Western terms of a job, home, and bicycle or car. The idea of progress itself, which is common in the industrialized world, is not an indigenous concept in many poor countries. Women, who until recently were considered the property of their husbands in many countries, are now emerging as politicians, writers, and entrepreneurs.

But beyond such fundamental values, the West has superimposed upon many developing countries its own choice of methodology: the profit system; the notion that levels of national saving and investment depend largely on the rich; the preference for capital-intensive investment and for investment in import-saving industry and raw-material exports; and belief in the efficiency of large-scale enterprise.

Thus over the past two decades, for example, the rich countries have led the poor to emphasize capital-intensive investments through their educational and aid programs and through their private investors. Since the developing countries are long on labor, short on jobs, and short on capital, this was the wrong development emphasis. In part this was simply a thoughtless process, but in part it reflected the desire of aid donors to increase their exports of capital equipment to the poor countries. Many aid programs continue to tie procurement to the donor's exports and in some cases (the United States is not the only offender), aid is blatantly used as an export promotion scheme. In such cases, the intent of aid together with the investment policies of rich-country private corporations is to mold the recipient's economy so that it complements that of the donor country. Viewed through one prism, this approach has an attractive efficiency about it, but as the developing-country critics see it, it deprives them of the right to make basic choices affecting their values and their political and economic systems. They also believe this locks them into a position of dependence on the rich countries.

Another example of the superimposed goal is the controversial Western notion that the predominant goal of development is growth. It was long thought that if a vigorous rate of growth could be achieved, the benefits of development would "trickle down" to all concerned. The Western view has been that to achieve a high rate of growth, it is necessary to accept a considerable degree of inequity in the distribution system.

This notion is increasingly subject to challenge. Several countries have deliberately followed policies designed to achieve several goals simultaneously instead of focusing on growth alone. For example, although Taiwan and South Korea have borrowed much Western technology and have attracted Western private capital, they have organized agriculture along cooperative lines, have radically reduced inequity in the distribution of income, and have emphasized *labor*-intensive investment, especially in products for export. Growth was not their single objective, but only one of several goals including distributive justice, full employment, and population stabilization. Nevertheless, spectacular and sustained growth was achieved. Similarly, although details are not known, it appears that China has achieved remarkably equitable distribution of income and of social services while continuing to grow.

The Negotiating Strategies of the Developing Countries

Like all other countries, the poor countries frequently find themselves in bargaining situations with outsiders—whether rich-country governments, multinational enterprises, or international institutions. For the most part, individual poor countries bargain alone, seeking their national advantage in a competitive world. Sometimes they bargain in groups, seeking specific deals, such as those recently negotiated by the petroleum-exporting countries. In some cases, forums exist which offer several developing countries a chance to bargain as a group to reform an international system. An example of this is the International Monetary Fund's new Committee of 20, which is working out proposals for the reform of the international monetary system. Nine developing countries are members of that committee.

The developing countries often complain that they lack bargaining leverage. They have little influence on major trade negotiations and little retaliatory power to use as a threat to counteract protectionist moves by the rich countries. Often they feel powerless with respect to negotiations by the major shipping conferences, handicapped in negotiations with giant corporations, or frustrated by the difficulties of effecting changes in the world's investment rules, patenting and licensing practices, or patterns of rich-country investment in research and development. With respect to use of the ocean, some poor countries with long seacoasts have attempted to muster leverage by claiming up to 200 miles of the adjacent ocean. In the field of debt and debt renegotiation, the accepted rules by and large leave the poor countries feeling apprehensive at the prospect of debt renegotiation, despite the considerable debt relief resulting from past negotiations. Many developing-country spokesmen feel that until their countries can organize themselves to mobilize such bargaining strength as they do have, they will be unable to achieve either structural change or specific improvements in their economic environment.

Despite this widespread feeling of relative weakness vis-à-vis outside economic interests, responses to the questionnaire that the Overseas Development Council sent to research institutions in developing countries revealed that very little scholarly work is going on in developing countries on their relationships to international economic systems. It is our view that a great deal of scholarly work needs to be done by these countries themselves on the various systems that compose the international economic order. A fuller understanding by developing countries of these systems, and of the true extent of the asymmetries within each of these systems, should be beneficial. It should give developing-country policymakers practical advice about reforms that are politically feasible and beneficial. Until these policymakers have access to local experts who understand the complexities of each international system, they will be at a disadvantage. They will also be at a disadvantage unless those developing countries with common interests can agree on certain common goals for negotiation. From the point of view of any developing-country policymaker, it is not enough that a proposal for reform be sponsored by a fellow developing country and buttressed by careful scholarly work in that country. He may want to seek advice from experts in his own country to ascertain that the proposal is in fact also in his own nation's interest. Thus each poor country seeking a common negotiating target must have access to experts whom it trusts. Usually that will mean indigenous scholars.

But who should select the potential negotiating targets for study, and who should design and manage the network for the coordination of developing-country research on these priority issues? If this is done by the Western foundations which furnish the money, it may not fit the priorities of the developing countries and it is unlikely to be trusted by them. Unlike research on animal diseases, research on negotiating strategies is too sensitive to be directed by rich "Northerners." Both the initiative and participation in such efforts should come from scholars and perhaps policymakers from developing countries—with special care taken the research be sound from the point of view of professional credibility and practicality.

Suggestions for Research:
The Interdependence of Rich Countries,
Poor Countries, and the International
Economic Order

1. Global Priorities. As the world becomes increasingly interdependent, "ideal" global priorities for the use of public resources need to be identified and studied. The sum of national priorities does not add up to a rational set of global priorities. For example, global military expenditures in 1970 totaled $204 billion dollars—a sum exceeding the combined income of the poorest one-half of mankind. Studies of the contrast between an ideal set of global priorities and the priorities resulting from national action are needed, as well as studies of possible gradual ways to introduce global considerations into national decisions on priorities.

2. New Social Theory. The convergence of three broad ideas promises to gradually transform many of the world's dominant values, attitudes, and institutions. First is the controversial idea that global economic growth cannot expand indefinitely. Growing out of that idea is a new concern for social justice. If the demands of the poor cannot be met by indefinitely expanding the world "pie" of resources, the focus of world concern shifts to the question of how to divide these resources. The third idea is the rising acceptance of transnational solutions to many world problems and of transnational political authority to administer those solutions. These three powerful ideas pose questions regarding the allocation of scarce resources among nations. Work on these questions should include an examination of the validity of each of the ideas and of changes needed in existing patterns of distribution of wealth among and within nations.

3. Population. As the collective claims of society begin to strain some of the earth's natural capacities, the crucial role of population growth comes into sharp focus. In our interdependent world, we depend on common global resources— including energy, minerals, marine protein, and waste-absorptive capacity. In those instances where resources are finite, the more of us there are, the less each of us can have. The need to stabilize world population thus assumes a new urgency. There is now increasing evidence that birth rates are not reduced voluntarily in countries and areas where the income level of the majority of the population is extremely low, where food supply is uncertain, where even rudimentary health services are lacking, and where illiteracy is prevalent. The experience of a growing number of poor countries indicates that development policies combining growth with more equitable distribution of income and services are also more effective in providing parents with the *motivation* for limiting family size.[1] We need to know much more about this interaction of development and the birth rate.

4. Objective Measurement of Rich-Country Support for Development. Research is needed to construct and test measures of the relative performance of the several industrialized countries in support of development. The OECD's Development Assistance Committee (DAC) has done this for official development assistance (ODA) and other official flows. But these flows account for only a small portion of the foreign exchange available to the developing countries. Other areas requiring objective measures of performance include: trade, monetary reform, debt relief, government policies on a variety of other international issues that affect development, increased access of developing countries to private money markets, and domestic production policies (such as those concerning agricultural production) that have an impact on the developing countries. In constructing these measures, some means should be found to credit those rich countries with vigorous public education programs to acquaint their people with development problems in the poor countries. The goal of this project would be to develop a model of a "report card" similar to the DAC annual report on development assistance, but on a much more comprehensive basis.

Suggestions for Research:
The Impact of Rich-Country Values and
Techniques on the Poor Countries

5. Comparative Development Models. Studies of the Chinese, Cuban, and North Korean models of development are needed in order to learn the extent to which they are applicable to the development policies of individual developing countries. Similarly, additional studies are needed of the development experience in such countries as Brazil, Taiwan, Tanzania, South Korea, and the city-states of Hong Kong and Singapore. On the basis of these studies, developing-country scholars should be encouraged to examine the applicability of such developmental experience to the solution of problems in their own countries. The object of all of these studies would be to increase the alternatives open to the developing countries and to contribute information to help them make the best choices. Thus the international economic order would encourage individual developing countries to draw on the more successful elements from several models—instead of dictating one model or another according to current power relationships.

6. Impact of Western Values. Case studies are needed to identify the extent to which Western values, goals, and methods have dominated development policies and scholarly work in the developing countries. In what ways has the result been beneficial in terms of the quality of life? In what ways detrimental? What indigenous systems have been suppressed that might have been adapted to modernization? What indigenous systems still exist but are endangered?

7. Income Distribution and Growth. Additional case studies are needed on the relationship between equity of income distribution on the one hand, and savings rates, growth, population stabilization, and unemployment on the other. Is the Western model, with a rich saving and investing class, essential for growth? Does increased equality decrease savings and investment and therefore growth? What changes in theoretical concepts might be necessary to explain the results of this study?

8. Need for a Historical Perspective. The rapid rate of change of factors affecting economic policy has tended to concentrate the attention of researchers and policymakers on the present, the near past, and the immediate future, with little resort to economic history to assist in the formulation of policy. There is a need for economic historians to assess the extent to which economic development has (or has not) taken place over various periods, and why—to provide a historical context and some guidance for current decisions.

Suggestions for Research:
The Negotiating Strategies of
Developing Countries

We believe it would be premature to outline here a proposal for a program of scholarly work to improve the negotiating strategies of developing countries. Reluctantly, we conclude that a special, major study is essential to design such a program in order to secure the full participation of scholars and policymakers in developing countries. The nature of the topic is such that any recommendations, however sound, would be invalidated if they came chiefly from developed-country "experts."

Therefore we propose that one or more foundations sponsor such a study. The project should involve developing-country scholars and statesmen of such stature that their recommendations would have force. Papers should be commissioned and views exchanged to develop a consensus on which topics should receive major attention (this in turn presupposes agreement on the best topics for a joint developing-country negotiating effort); as well as on the best method for administering the special research program. The developing-country participants should have the dominant role in selecting topics and should have an important part in shaping the system for managing the program.

Such a program might be managed by: (1) designating or developing several scholarly institutions to coordinate research work on one topic in several developing countries; (2) designating or developing several scholarly institutions to facilitate the work on a single topic by developing-country scholars in residence at that institution; or (3) designating or establishing one institute in each of three or four developing regions to focus that region's attention on a broad range of topics, either by working with scholars in residence or coordinating the work of scholars throughout the region.

As far as the input of foundations is concerned, it might require: (1) creating a consortium of foundations with staff to manage the special research program, with some means of representing the developing-country point of view in the decisions of the staff; (2) agreement in principle by several major foundations (a) on one of the three management systems outlined above; and (b) on the financial share of each foundation (with the funds to be paid directly to and administered by the designated scholarly institution); or (3) some combination of the first two possibilities.

International Trade*

International trade is the main link between developed and developing countries. The transmission of values, knowledge, and goods and services through trade has shaped the nature of the relationships of poor countries with the developed world. Many of the internal social and economic structures of individual developing countries have been determined by their trading relationships with developed countries.

For most developing countries, international trade is the major source of foreign exchange: more than four-fifths of their total available foreign exchange is derived from their exports. With the strong need of poor countries for imports of capital goods, intermediate goods, and essential consumption goods, inter-

---

*Prepared by Guy F. Erb.

national trade will remain a bulwark of most countries' efforts to improve their living standards, whatever their pattern of development.

The mosaic of international relationships and institutions that influence world trade has grown largely in response to the requirements of the developed countries: not as a result of a single event or international conference, but rather as the outgrowth of a series of actions and agreements that have been oriented primarily to the trading relations of the developed countries of North America and Europe, and Japan. The interests of developing countries have not been of paramount importance in the formulation of policies of individual developed countries, nor have poor countries been adequately represented at multilateral trading negotiations. The result of this pattern of concentration on developed-country interests has been evident (1) in the Kennedy Round of tariff negotiations, which in general retained higher tariff rates for products of greatest interest to developing countries; (2) in the difficulties faced by the developing countries in gaining increased access to developed-country markets; (3) in the problems encountered in negotiating and operating commodity agreements; and (4) in patterns of investment in developing countries that often reinforced the dependence of these countries on the production and export of relatively few commodities. Recently, foreign private investment in developing countries also has been questioned with regard to its appropriateness as an instrument of technology transfer to host countries in the light of their stage of development and serious employment problems.

Nor have the developing countries always adopted appropriate trade and investment policies; their own trade barriers are sometimes a barrier to the effective combination of foreign and domestic resources, and many have failed to derive the potential benefits from policies of import substitution, with the consequence that the increases in income that might have resulted from protective policies have not been fully realized.

But the trade relations of the two groups of countries are changing in response to national policies and international measures. Other factors making for change are shifts in the composition and direction of trade and in the distribution of investment, which is increasingly influenced by the decisions of multinational enterprises.

For some developing countries, entry into trade in manufactured goods implies a new form of interdependence with developed countries—including situations of potential conflict of interest when their exports impinge upon markets unfamiliar with competition from emerging exporters. An increasing number of developing countries are arriving at a stage of development and industrialization at which production of manufactured goods at competitive prices is possible for an expanding list of products.

The success of developing countries that have gained significant entry to developed-country markets has given rise to a rethinking of the "import-substitution" strategies that were the dominant development policies of many developing countries during the 1950s and 1960s. Therefore, increased attention is now directed to projects with a potential contribution to the export earnings of poor countries. This tendency will intensify demands for access to the markets of rich countries. Consideration of trade adjustment assistance in rich countries and multilateral safeguard systems may be necessary complements of more liberal access to developed-country markets. The protectionist movement in developed countries should be studied not only from the point of view of impact on possibilities for liberalizing developed-country trade through multilateral negotiations, but also as a factor affecting the trade and employment conditions of poor countries.

For some time to come, however, the exports of large numbers of developing countries will continue to be concentrated on primary commodities. Appropriate national and international policies will have to be formulated for this group of countries. Another large group of developing countries is still relatively underdeveloped and trade prospects of this group will remain poor for the foreseeable future. Limited in economic size, or at very low levels of development, these countries can be expected to enter the world trading system only slowly, and will require policies tailored to their specific situations and problems.

Trade in services—including shipping, insurance, and tourism—is an increasingly important component of the trade of developing countries. Some of these nations can now supply shipping and insurance services competitively. Others wish to enter these service fields by means of special incentives and subsidies to local firms. Tourism is also expected to become a major earner of foreign exchange for many countries in the next decades, although questions have been raised about its economic and social effects in some developing countries.

Although the trade of developing countries has grown, it has occupied a decreasing share of total world trade in the post-World War II period. One factor in this decline has been the poor performance of trade *among* developing countries. Policy measures including establishment of common markets and free trade areas, negotiating of preferential trading agreements, and export promotion have been initiated with varying results.

Actions by developed countries and their economic groupings, in particular the European Community, have a major impact on the efforts by developing countries to increase their own earnings from trade. The formation of "trade blocs" is an aspect of the evolving world trading relationships that may have great impact on trade among poor countries, and on their relationships with developed nations.

The contribution of earnings from exports of goods and services to the development of poor countries is the result of dynamic relationships among myriad economic entities. Hence, although the field has been the subject of intensive scholarly work, the coming years will see continuing needs for policy-oriented research. The following section presents some of the more important topics for research on international trade questions.

Suggestions for Research:
Access to Developed-Country Markets

1. Analysis of Trade Patterns. [2] In spite of the large number of trade barriers protecting the markets of developed countries, exports of manufactured goods from many developing countries are increasing rapidly, and, in addition, include new products that fall outside the stereotype of simple, labor-intensive consumer goods. Trade patterns in the 1970s will require continuing analysis if developed countries are to adjust their economies to changing international competitiveness. Will the semi-industrialized countries be able to continue to export increasing amounts of relatively sophisticated manufactured goods? Can the obstacles posed by tariff and nontariff measures, communications and marketing problems, and other constraints on imports in developed countries be overcome? If so, what are the prospects for other developing countries to move into the production and export of nontraditional products? Whenever possible, research in these areas should be geared to policy alternatives facing developing countries.

2. Impact of Trade Barriers on Developing-Country Exports. Effective participation by developing countries in the forthcoming multilateral trade negotiations will require knowledge of the impact on their trade of tariff and nontariff barriers (NTBs) currently in force in both developed and developing countries. Much research is under way in the General Agreement on Tariffs and Trade (GATT) and the United Nations Conference on Trade and Development (UNCTAD) on tariffs and NTBs and their effect on trade flows. After the negotiations, further work will be required to evaluate the effect of liberalization on developing-country trade as concessions are implemented. What effect will liberalization of tariff and nontariff barriers in developed countries have on the trade of the developing countries—in particular on that of the smaller countries? What has been the impact of developing-country trade restrictions on their own export performance? Can developing-country restrictions be liberalized and/or simplified in the context of multilateral trade negotiations? What would be the effect on developing countries of a zero-tariff system in developed countries, and what assumption about NTBs would be appropriate in such a study?

3. Trade Adjustment Assistance. Programs of trade adjustment assistance will be important for further trade liberalization and will have a significant impact on the degree to which imports from developing countries may be liberalized. Do imports from developing countries significantly increase existing problems arising from imports from developed countries, or due to changes in productive technology or tastes in developed countries? What aspects of adjustment assistance programs have the greatest impact on poor countries? What methods are there to determine trade disruption caused by alleged "low-wage" imports? Can adjustment assistance reduce the need for "voluntary" restraints and other NTBs? What would be revealed by a cost/benefit comparison of trade adjustment assistance and foreign assistance, taking into account effects of both types of programs on developed (donor) countries and developing (recipient) countries?

4. Safeguards. Multilateral safeguard mechanisms to temporarily restrain rapidly rising imports of specific products have been suggested as a means to reduce the disorganized growth of trade barriers. What would be the role of developing countries in a multilateral agreement on safeguards? At what rate can the United States and other developed countries accept manufactured imports from developing countries? Is it possible to devise a scheme that would apply protection through safeguard clauses only to those imports from sources actually shown to be causing a disruption of domestic markets? Could poor countries be given more liberal treatment under a system of multilateral safeguards? What special conditions might apply to protected industries in developing countries?

5. Tariff Preferences. In 1970, the developed countries agreed within the UNCTAD Board to provide lower tariffs—through a Generalized System of Preferences (GSP)—for the industrial products of developing countries. Only the United States and Canada have not yet followed up their commitments while other developed countries have implemented their preferential tariff programs. As experience is gained with the GSP, research will be required on the impact of the preferences on growth and development, possible improvements in coverage and levels of preferential treatment, and their effect on trade patterns.

In some cases, it has been estimated that national preference schemes within the GSP will not benefit developing countries and may even have a negative effect on exports of manufactures from some countries. If analysis of trade flows confirms this, what measures can be adopted to improve the schemes? Can improvements in the GSP be negotiated in the context of the multilateral trade negotiations, taking into account the fact that a long-run effect of tariff concessions will be the reduction of preferential trade margins? If no significant improvements can be made, would it be preferable to terminate the GSP after its first ten-year period, and attempt to increase export earnings of developing countries through overall trade liberalization in developed countries, together with programs of export development in developing countries?

6. Developed-Country Markets. What has been the relative performance of major developed countries—the United States, members of the European Community, Japan, and the Eastern European nations—in accepting imports of manufactured and semi-manufactured goods and traditional exports from developing countries? What factors—such as company practices, marketing systems, and restrictive business practices—underlie differing market performances? Would an improvement in importing performance by one or more of the major trading countries result in a diffusion of the imports from developing countries and thus reduce potential market disruption in certain markets?

Suggestions for Research:
Agricultural Trade

7. Agricultural Trade Policies. What is the impact on the trade of developing countries of the domestic agricultural policies of developed countries? Of the related international trade policies of developed countries regarding agricultural products? How can trade liberalization in agriculture be reconciled with national goals in this field?

8. Liberalizing Agricultural Trade. Possible measures to facilitate freer trade in agricultural products range from steps to coordinate the policies of developed countries to an improvement in the international division of labor through significantly liberalized trade in agricultural goods. The impact of possible new policies on developing-country interests—both prior to and after the introduction of such policies—should be studied.

9. Institutional Performance. Have the existing institutions concerned with agricultural trade—the GATT, the FAO, UNCTAD, commodity organizations, and various commodity study groups—been effective in furthering the agricultural trade interests of the developing countries? Should attention be given to alternative institutions in this field with the aim of improving the means of increasing developing-country trade in agricultural products?

Suggestions for Research:
Primary Commodities

10. Problems of Commodity Agreements. The commodity-by-commodity approach to international stabilization schemes has not met with notable success. What political, economic, and technical factors have hampered the operation of agreements, or prevented their implementation in the cases of coffee, tin, cocoa, sugar, and other specific commodities?

11. Producer Agreements. In view of the difficulties besetting agreements including producers and consumers, are cooperative arrangements among producers likely to become even more significant? In this regard analysis of the recent experience of petroleum, coffee, copper, and tea producers will be of interest.

12. Market Information. What improvements can be made in the market information available to developing-country producers of specific commodities to enable them to obtain sophisticated price and output data that will ensure a parity of information between buyers and sellers?

13. New Policies Toward Commodity Arrangements. What new methods of international commodity policy could be tried in the 1970s? Is it realistic to envisage generalized agreements that include products of temperate agriculture?

14. Overall Strategy on Commodity Trade. What would be the characteristic of an international commodity policy designed to deal with the complexity of commodity trade through an overall strategy and linked to the objective of equitable economic and social development in producing countries? Consideration of new approaches to commodity problems would involve: scholarly work on short-term commodity market regulation; reexamination of the operation and financing of buffer stocks; market research to promote consumption of primary commodities and to deal with problems posed by synthetic products (including a consideration of the biodegradable properties of certain commodities and the consequent environmental implications of their consumption relative to synthetic materials); improving access to the markets of both market-economy and socialist developed countries; promoting trade among developing countries in primary commodities; and consideration of alternative methods of production regulation, control, and diversification—bearing in mind their differing impacts on the distribution of income in producing countries.

Suggestions for Research:
International Trade in Services

15. Statistics. The currently compiled data on trade in services do not cover adequately the developing countries' trade, mainly imports, in such categories as shipping, insurance, technology, and tourism. Quantification of this trade is an important prerequisite for further analysis of the trends and problems in these areas.

16. Tourism. Tourism is often promoted as a potentially significant addition to foreign exchange receipts. Yet in some cases, the foreign exchange actually received from tourism by Central Banks has been far lower than the expected expenditures by foreign tourists. Hence, the question of loopholes in foreign exchange regulations causing shortfalls in tourism revenues could be examined in the light of the general economic, political, and social conditions in countries at different levels of tourism development. Consideration could also be given to: employment generation by the tourist industry, government revenues derived from tourism compared with revenues from other economic activities, the profitability of the hotel industry (government owned, private, and mixed enterprises), and the social impact of tourism.

17. Trends in Trade in Services. What are the trends in the trade in services of the developing countries? What are the effects on developing countries of the restrictions on trade in services that result from concentration of the supply of services in a few developed countries? What are the possibilities for import substitution in the field of services by developing countries? Can the anticipated increase in demand for services lead to the export of services by developing countries? Are there possibilities for significant changes in the international division of labor in the field of services over the next two decades? What form of regulation or "rules of fair play" can be established affecting trade in services?

18. Effect of Increased Rich-Country Income. To what extent will increases in income in developed countries be directed toward domestic services, thus limiting the increase in demand for the products of developing countries?

Suggestions for Research:
Export Development

19. Obstacles to Developing-Country Exports. The export development and promotion experiences of many developing countries during the 1960s should be analyzed in an effort to improve the performance in this area in the future. What successes have been achieved by individual countries in overcoming the major obstacles to successful export development? Among the obstacles often cited are: lack of entrepreneurship and "achievement orientation," unawareness of market opportunities, lack of financing, scale and quality of developing-country production, government practices and administration, commercial practices, and sales promotion. What steps can be identified to aid developing countries in overcoming these obstacles?

20. Techniques of Export Development. What techniques of development and promotion have been most useful? Which institutional approaches have yielded the best results? What information gaps are there in marketing and product analysis?

21. Foreign Assistance and Export Development. What has been the experience of bilateral and multilateral aid agencies in promoting export diversification? What is the impact of export incentives and measures linked to development finance, such as preferential bidding procedures, for developing countries that are members of integration groupings? What would be the impact of aid untying?

22. Developed-Country Reaction to Export Development Programs. What incentives can continue to be applied to exports if countervailing measures by developed countries become widespread?

23. Exports and Employment. What has been the impact of past programs of export development on employment in developing countries? How can the contribution of export development to increasing employment be maximized?

What forms of training have proved most useful in complementing export promotion activities?

24. "Least Developed" Countries. Because of their limited short-run export potential, the least developed among the developing countries will require special measures to facilitate their entry into world trading systems. Policy-oriented scholarly work might include: exploration of the export potential of individual least developed countries and the specific form of assistance needed to realize the trade possibilities identified, evaluation of the export promotion needs of the least developed countries, evaluation of their overall policies in the foreign trade sector and the subsequent recommendation of measures to improve the planning and programming of foreign trade, a review of the adequacy of the government infrastructure dealing with foreign trade and the identification of specific measures of assistance needed to rectify any deficiencies encountered.

Suggestions for Research: Trade
and Economic Cooperation Among
Developing Countries

25. Forms of Economic Cooperation. Economic cooperation among developing countries has met with various difficulties and only a few groupings are functioning at the present time. Methods of trade and industrial cooperation of more limited scope than customs unions or free-trade areas have been attempted in some subregional groupings, and an interregional preferential trade protocol was recently signed by sixteen countries. What are the factors influencing cooperation among the developing countries that will determine the success of integration or cooperation attempts in the 1970s? What measures regarding transportation, payments, trade credits, nontariff barriers, and other obstacles to trade can be taken in specific instances to encourage intra-developing-country trade?

26. Interregional Trade. Does the interregional trade protocol of the GATT represent a new and viable alternative to regional or subregional groupings? What are the prospects for limited economic and trade cooperation among developing countries? What are the most appropriate techniques for negotiating trade liberalization among developing countries? What is the impact on developed and other developing countries of the various types of cooperative arrangements among developing countries?

27. Developing Countries' Adjustment to Trade Among Themselves. To what extent could trade liberalization among developing countries be facilitated by development planning for diversification or adjustment assistance measures within the developing countries themselves?

Suggestions for Research: Trade Blocs

28. The Outlook for Trade Blocs. What would be the costs and benefits of a world system based on blocs of countries organized around the principal trading entities: North America, Japan, and the European Community? What are the factors facilitating and impeding such an outcome? What would be the effect on trade flows of a major movement toward bloc formation? On economic and social development in poor countries? On relations among developed and developing countries? How watertight are trade and economic blocs likely to be?

29. Trade Blocs and International Monetary Reform. What is the probable effect of international monetary reform on trade and economic relations among developed and developing countries? Could the net result be a strengthening of "vertical" arrangements linking developed countries with spheres of economic influence between them? Or will pressures continue toward a loosening of such arrangements as the Franc Zone?

30. Developed-Country Integration. What is the impact on developing countries of economic integration among developed countries? An examination of this issue would include consideration of systems of "reverse preferences" and commodity trade arrangements between groups of developed and developing countries. What are the costs and benefits to Associated States of trade and economic agreements with the European Community? What are the implications of these agreements for the economic and social values influencing developing patterns in the European Community's Associated States?

31. European Community Agricultural Policies. What will be the effect of the expansion of the European Community on its agricultural policies? After some years of experience with the new Common Agricultural Policy, it will be necessary to examine the policy's impact on the trade of both Associated and non-Associated developing countries.

32. Trade of Communist Countries with Developing Areas. Although it is increasing, the trade of Eastern European countries and the People's Republic of China with developing countries is still relatively low. What are the prospects for this trade in the 1970s and beyond?

Suggestions for Research:
Exchange-Rate and Credit Policies of
Developing Countries

33. Exchange-Rate Flexibility. Developing countries have been frequent users of exchange-rate variations as instruments of export promotion and balance-of-payments adjustment. Recent contributions to the analysis of this area of policy have been the work by Little, Scitovsky, and Scott,[3] and the National Bureau of Economic Research. Decisions made in the context of monetary reform on guidelines for exchange-rate flexibility and exchange-rate margins will have significant impacts on many developing countries. Within the reformed system, continuing work will be needed on the application and effects of various exchange-rate policies in poor countries.

34. Trade Credits. Trade credits granted by developed countries to poor countries have been subjected to increasing scrutiny in the context of the debt situation of recipients. Further work of a statistical nature is needed in many cases to ascertain the magnitude of this debt and its future patterns of allocation among recipient countries (see pp. 230-235). Trade credits granted by emerging exporters of industrial goods also have received greater attention recently within the international community. Many developing countries feel at a disadvantage in relation to rich countries with respect to the terms and conditions of credits they are able to extend to prospective purchasers. What is the feasibility of international arrangements designed to support export credit systems of developing countries? How many countries could benefit from such arrangements in the medium-term?

35. Export-Credit Insurance. Recently, international attention has been focused on proposals for multinational export-credit insurance schemes. Are such schemes viable contributions to the export development programs of developing countries? What are the factors governing the choice of a national credit insurance agency or participation in a regional, subregional or global arrangement?

*Suggestions for Research: Trade and
Development Theory and Policies*

36. Trade Theory. The view that trade is the leading sector of economic development in poor countries has been challenged by some economists and policymakers. Can new light be shed on this question by an examination of the experience of the 1950s and 1960s? Is the "engine of growth" theory a generalization that cannot be applied to all developing countries? What new theories of trade and development respond more adequately than traditional trade theory to the actual situation in developing countries? Can models incorporating factors such as human skills, the product cycle, and technological gaps among countries render the theory of comparative advantage theoretically and empirically applicable to the problems of developing countries?

37. Trade Policies and Level of Development. Is there a breakdown of developing countries according to their economic characteristics (such as size or level of development) that would facilitate the formulation of different trade policies according to certain criteria?

38. New Development Strategies and Trade. What are the appropriate economic and trade policies for developing countries wishing to subordinate trade to a development strategy emphasizing the eradication of widespread poverty through improvement of income distribution, increased employment, education, and other social measures? What are the political implications of such policies? What are the implications for developed countries of the introduction of such trade and development policies by developing countries?

The Effect of the International Monetary System on the Less Developed Countries*

The current international monetary system grew out of the international meeting at Bretton Woods, New Hampshire, in 1944, which led to the creation of the International Monetary Fund (IMF) and the adoption of the Fund's Articles of Agreement. The IMF presides over many of the more visible parts of the international monetary system. It issues supplements to international liquidity in the form of special drawing rights (SDRs). It counsels members about their exchange rates and their internal economic policies, and, in general, it interprets and applies the articles of the Fund.

The international monetary system affects the poor countries in a number of ways. Most important, by constituting a workable means of paying for trade, it has encouraged the expansion of international trade which has benefited the poor countries. However, some of the operations of the international monetary system appear to have worked to the detriment of the poor countries.

Control of the Monetary System

Many of the operations of the system are controlled predominantly by the rich countries. The decisions of the IMF are controlled by a weighted voting system in which the twenty-five rich countries have about 70 percent of the voting power, and the remaining nearly 100 members have only about 30 percent. Most important monetary decisions in the past actually have been made by a caucus of rich countries, called the Group of Ten, and then merely confirmed by the Fund.

There is now pressure from the poor countries for a greater voice in major decisions. At least tentatively, a "Committee of 20" nations has replaced the "Group of Ten"; the new, larger group includes nine poor countries. In addition, there has been pressure from the poor countries for a larger voting share in the IMF.

*Prepared by James W. Howe.

Special Drawing Rights (SDRs)

In August 1969, the IMF agreed to expand the supply of international liquidity by issuing $9.5 billion of SDRs over a three-year period. These reserve assets are distributed free of charge according to a formula that coincides with members' quotas; thus about three-quarters of the SDRs have been allocated to the rich countries and one-quarter to the poor. Many proposals have been made to revise this distribution system to increase its benefits to the poor countries.

Reserve Assets

Reserves held by governments consist of gold, dollars (or other foreign currencies), SDRs, and reserve positions in the Fund. A great debate is under way as to which of the three largest items (gold, foreign currencies, or SDRs) should predominate. This debate has involved chiefly the rich countries. Poor countries have not been as certain as to where their interests lie.

Exchange-Rate Flexibility

Under the Bretton Woods system, there was limited flexibility in the exchange-rate system. Each country's exchange rate was supposed to be fixed in relation to gold—and therefore in relation to the rates of other countries. Under the Bretton Woods system, nevertheless, frequent changes in exchange rates were made, with some domestic political cost.

At present the system appears to be changing so that rates are not fixed at all, but "float" more or less freely, according to the decisions of the money markets and a certain degree of Central Bank intervention. Some proposals have been advanced suggesting that exchange-rate realignments be undertaken more casually and frequently, allowing individual rates to float with respect to each other within wider margins than heretofore. The developing countries have frequently been cool to suggestions for greater flexibility. The emerging flexible system will present problems of uncertainty, and it is not yet entirely clear where their interests lie.

Exchange-Rate Alignment

The developing countries have frequently maintained their currencies at somewhat overvalued rates, although outsiders typically have advised them to devalue. There is currently a debate among the rich countries as to the correct alignments among themselves. As decisions are made, they may have a profound effect—for good or ill—on the developing countries.

The Balance of Payments

Monetary morality has long considered it "good" to achieve a balance-of-payments surplus and "bad" to suffer a deficit. But this, too, is changing, with some experts arguing that it is just as bad to get out of balance on the surplus side as on the deficit side of the ledger. Since poor countries as a whole tend to be deficit countries, they may find some reason to sympathize with this new position which is being advocated by the United States, among other countries.

IMF Surveillance

A number of proposed reforms of the monetary system would rely on additional IMF surveillance over certain economic activities of its members. Some poor-country spokesmen are questioning whether they dare risk submitting to additional surveillance by the IMF, since, historically, its decisions have been made largely by the richest members.

Suggestions for Research

1. *Control.* Policy analysis and empirical research are needed to sort out the questions relating to the control of the international monetary system. How do the various economic forums controlled by rich countries affect the poor countries? What mechanisms enable the poor countries to be heard? Is lack of representation merely an indignity, or does it have economic implications for the poor? Does the Committee of 20 represent a significant political-economic shift toward developing countries? If so, can poor countries safely agree to strengthen the IMF's powers of surveillance over its members? What alternative IMF voting systems might be defensible? Could the Fund quotas of developing countries be altered so as to give them a stronger voice in Fund decisions?

2. *SDRs.* Scholarly work on SDRs is needed to answer a number of questions. Through what channels might the funds generated by SDRs be linked to development finance—through international banks, bilateral aid, or by direct allocation to developing countries? Which method is most desirable? How much money might reasonably be expected each year? How could one solve the problem of fluctuations in SDR issuances, which might damage institutions that had come to depend on SDRs as a source of finance? How might the "dollar overhang" be linked to development finance?[a]

3. *Reserve Composition.* What criteria do developing countries use for determining the composition of their reserves? What will be the impact on developing countries of any changes in the characteristics of SDRs, including, in particular, the interest rate?

---

[a]This is such a fast-moving topic that these particular questions might be answered shortly by political negotiations. However, it seems likely that for many years there will be other questions concerning SDRs with potential effects on the poor countries.

4. *Flexibility.* Analysis is needed to guide individual developing countries on the subject of exchange-rate flexibility. What are the costs and benefits to them of a system in which realignments of exchange rates take place frequently and with little or no political odium? Can measures be introduced into the international system to ease the political problem of devaluation for the developing countries? Perhaps additional commodity studies would help to determine the price elasticities of demand, thus providing guidance on when to devalue. Case studies of successful and unsuccessful devaluations by developing countries also might help.

5. *Relation of Developing Countries to Major Currencies.* In light of the changing positions of the monetary giants, what is the best course for various developing countries? Individual country or regional studies are needed to gauge how certain developing countries should relate to the principal world currencies, including the yen. Should they form regional monetary blocs? Payments unions?

6. *Reserve Accumulation.* What is the future effect of reserve accumulations by major developing countries (e.g., oil producers, Brazil) on their own positions and on the international monetary system? What are the costs and benefits of holding large reserves?

7. *Private Capital Flows.* What is the effect of flexibility on levels of flows of private capital to poor countries?

8. *Multiple Rates.* The pros and cons of dual or multiple exchange rates as instruments to rationalize protection policies and export incentives will require reexamination in the context of the trade and monetary negotiations.

9. *Control Versus Liberalization.* The National Bureau of Economic Research study on exchange control, liberalization, and economic development is expected to provide findings in three main areas: (1) the effects of exchange controls on resource allocation, (2) the experience of various countries with "devaluation-cum-liberalization," and (3) the growth effects of exchange control regimes. After the publication by the National Bureau of Economic Research of the case studies of individual countries and the summary volume in 1973, it should be possible to determine the general applicability of the findings and to analyze the policies of developing countries and national and international bodies.

Private Foreign Investment*

Private foreign investment in developing countries is a major source of both capital and contention. Flows of private direct and portfolio investment, and private trade credits, are very important components of the total financial resources available to many developing countries. Although foreign private direct investment at any given period has tended to be concentrated on those countries

*Prepared by Guy F. Erb.

with "favorable" investment climates and on extractive industries, foreign private capital has had a significant impact in many countries, and in recent years has moved increasingly into the manufacturing sector.

Foreign firms in developing economies can provide funds for investment, technology, skills for their labor forces, employment, and access to export markets. At the same time, the outflows of investment income as foreign private firms repatriate profits to their home countries; the impact of the foreign investment on economic, social, and political systems in the recipient countries; and the problems posed by rapid shifts of productive resources by multinational companies all have given rise to considerable debate on the merits of private foreign investment.

In absolute terms, net flows of foreign direct private investment to developing countries have risen from an average of $1.8 billion per year during 1960-65 to over $3.5 billion in 1970, and to over $4.0 billion in 1971. Private flows of portfolio investment in developing countries and multilateral institutions and private trade credits also amounted to a total of over $4.0 billion in 1971. These magnitudes of capital flows and financial movements have great impact on world trade and production patterns. They have an unquestionable effect on the "international economic order," and there is a consequent need for scholarly work dealing with specific aspects of private involvement in Third World development.[4]

Suggestions for Research

Areas for further research include the effect of foreign private direct investment, and of the activities of multinational corporations in particular, on the economic, social, and political systems of host countries—including the implications of the investment for employment, consumption patterns, and income distribution. The complexity of the effects of private foreign investment on economic activity in developing economies indicates that an interdisciplinary approach to this group of problems should be adopted.

Studies of individual countries, studies focused on specific sectors of several countries, or analyses of individual firms would be appropriate methods of approaching research on foreign private investment in developing countries. Case studies are needed of specific types of investment and of different types of corporations: extractive, light manufacturing, and advanced technology enterprises. The importance of obtaining data and insights through case studies cannot be overemphasized. Features of the operations of multinational enterprises that could be included in case studies are the movements and impact of foreign capital and technology, relations with home and host governments, transfer pricing policies, and marketing policies.

Global trends in foreign private investment and the future relations between capital-exporting and capital-importing countries are also worthy of consideration. Earnings from private investment are expected to be a major component of the foreign exchange available to the United States. Analysis is also needed of variables such as investment income received from recipient countries, the levels of anticipated new investment and reinvestment, and willingness and capacity of developing countries to absorb foreign private capital and to allow the outflow of earnings on that investment.

The economic and balance-of-payments aspects of private investment in developing countries have been the subject of research for some time. Views on the utility of much of the research in this area differ widely, but there appears to be a consensus that carefully considered work still would be useful, particularly if efforts were made to improve the basic data used in policy-oriented analyses.

Although a large and rapidly growing literature exists on private investment, and in particular on the multinational corporation, much of the work has been lacking in empirical content and often has not been of high quality. Very few of the studies have gone beyond balance-of-payments and income-impact analysis based on simple economic or econometric models. There is a lack of adequate socioeconomic cost/benefit studies of direct foreign investment in poor countries. Therefore, in undertaking further scholarly work on multinational enterprises and private foreign investment in developing countries, several factors should be borne in mind. (1) One of the main deficiencies of recent work in this field has been a lack of a significant empirical basis for the analysis presented. There is a shortage of statistics on many aspects of the foreign operations of companies based in developed countries. Future work would benefit from the careful development of data that could serve as a basis for the analysis of the specific hypotheses. (2) There is a need for synthesis and analysis of existing material in several areas of investigation. (3) Means should be sought to apply the knowledge already obtained to the practical aspects of policy formulation in developing countries. (4) Future research in this field would benefit from an interdisciplinary approach and might be constructively organized through "research consortia," which could draw financial support and analysts from a variety of sources.

Some specific suggestions for further research are listed below:

1. *Efficiency.* Do the activities of multinational enterprises lead to an improved combination of productive factors and greater economic efficiency? Case studies of specific instances of multinational investment in developing countries could investigate this question. What are the factors that have contributed to mutually beneficial arrangements between foreign investors and developing countries? Analysis could be undertaken of possible gains in efficiency in the light of other aspects of a firm's operations, such as its effects on the social or political situation in the host country. Questions have also been raised concerning the relevance of the traditional economic concepts of efficiency (minimizing inputs for a given output, or, raising output with the smallest possible increment in inputs) to underdeveloped economies with a surplus of

labor and inequitable income distribution. The effect on developing countries of using technology which is based on the above assumptions also should be further explored.

2. *Transfer of Technology and Values.* The multinational corporation often transfers not only managerial skills and productive technologies, but the consumer patterns and value structure implicit in its production and research and development (R&D) for a developed-country market. What are the social, political, and economic implications of the entry of foreign corporations into a developing country? Factors to be considered in an interdisciplinary analysis of this question include the effects of direct foreign investment on: income distribution in the host country, local management and entrepreneurship, market structure, local technology, labor skills, local labor and financial markets, societal goal achievement and the political process.

3. *Balance-of-payments and Income Effects.* What are the implications for developed and developing countries of the continued growth and geographic extension of multinational corporations? It has been suggested that the balance-of-payments situations of the United States and other developed countries will become increasingly dependent on income received from foreign investment. Can the developing countries absorb an increasing share of foreign direct private investment? What are the implications for policies of income distribution in developing countries if the manufacture of consumer products accounts for a growing share of foreign investment in their economies? Can a limited market for consumer goods in developing countries support the size of multinational companies' operations that is implied in forecasts of earnings on foreign investment, or will it be necessary to envisage a deepening of the market for consumer products by explicit policies of income redistribution? How does the ability of private firms to shift technology, capital, and management among countries affect the process of international balance-of-payments adjustment?

4. *Case Studies.* Factors affecting the operations of foreign companies in developing countries should be examined on a case-by-case basis. Among the topics needing analysis are: investment incentives and their impact on corporate decisions and host-country revenues. Are such incentives useful and effective enough to offset revenue losses? Other issues are local participation in equity and management of foreign companies; the development of local managerial opportunities, including the use of management contracts, which entail use of outside managerial skills for a certain period; wage and earnings policies followed by foreign enterprises, including the effects of differential earnings of management staff; and transfer pricing, its cause, and its effects on developing-country benefits from foreign investment.

5. *Investment Codes.* Guidelines or "commonly agreed principles" for international companies have been suggested as means to replace the varied national policies affecting investment and the absence of any agreed standards. A number of problems, including treatment of investors by host countries, expropriation

and compensation, and capital control need elucidation before any such guidelines can be considered. What is the interest of the developing countries in such an "investment code"? What are effective means of enforcing such a code? Are regional differences among developing countries significant enough to indicate a need for different investment codes, or can a multilateral code be uniformly applied to investors in Africa, Asia, and Latin America? An analysis is required of the costs and benefits to the various groups that would have to accommodate themselves to such an agreement. If the obstacles to multilateral investment codes are sufficient to delay or prevent international agreement, what are the desirable characteristics of national codes which might provide guidelines for the foreign operations of a given country's firms?

6. *Exports and Foreign Investment.* Further studies should be made of the contribution to exports of developing countries made by foreign companies, particularly in the manufacturing sector, and taking into account the restrictions of foreign sales that in some cases appear to be conditions for obtaining particular investments and technology transfers. What are the net export earnings (local value added) derived from specific cases of investment for export?

7. *Foreign Sourcing.* The manufacture abroad of components for assembly elsewhere is an increasingly frequent rationale for investment in developing countries. What are the employment, training, and net foreign earnings effects of this type of investment?

8. *Cooperative Host-Country Policies.* The impact of regional or subregional policies on foreign investment—such as the program of the Andean Group—will require study as experience is gained with this and other measures.

9. *Dispute Settlement.* Experience gained with methods of dispute settlement will be a possible subject for scholarly work as future cases come up for arbitration in the International Center for the Settlement of Investment Disputes. What guidelines can be obtained for the resolution of future disputes? Can adequate incentives be devised to lead firms and countries to submit to arbitration?

10. *Expropriation.* Local take-overs of the operations of foreign firms require analysis, as do the pros and cons of undertaking a policy of "divestment." Specific cases of expropriation and the circumstances that led up to them should be examined. What are the relevant legal concepts of fair compensation? What would be the implications for expropriation proceedings of a revision of the theoretical considerations regarding international equity and property rights?

11. *Alternatives to Foreign Private Investment.* Have developing countries considered the alternatives to private foreign direct investment adequately? What would be revealed by cost/benefit analyses of the alternatives? To what extent is it possible, or desirable, to utilize trade credits, loans from other private sources, or local and foreign capital markets rather than direct foreign investment?

**Bilateral, Multilateral, and Private
Voluntary Aid Programs***

The Role of Aid

Public and private programs of assistance to development have become an important element in the international economic order. A rich-country government's aid program has come to be popularly regarded as the most important measure of its support for development. Yet quantitatively, aid programs are a substantial but not preponderant source of finance—constituting less than 15 percent of the foreign exchange that becomes available annually to the developing countries. Qualitatively, however, they have often been innovative—pioneering in technological, social, and institutional development in the developing world.

An international aid-giving community also has come into existence with the participation of such mechanisms as the OECD's Development Assistance Committee (DAC), the U.N. Development Programme, the World Bank, IDA and the IFC, the Inter-American Development Bank, the Asian Development Bank, and, most recently, the African Development Bank. Various consortia and consultative groups have been created to coordinate aid to individual developing countries. There is also now an informal network of public and private aid institutions sponsoring research on development problems that cut across national boundaries (initially, thus far, in the field of agriculture). Bodies such as the Inter-American Committee of the Alliance for Progress (CIAP) in Latin America play an important role in regional coordination. At the regional level, there are also the U.N. Economic Commissions for Latin America, Asia, and Africa.

In addition to administering or coordinating aid, some of the elements in this community have set targets for aid giving and have created procedures for measuring the volume and quality of aid. This has been done within the general framework of development goals approved by the U.N. General Assembly as part of the second U.N. Development Decade. In general, the flow of aid has fallen behind the volume targets and is not catching up. The U.S. government is having particular trouble keeping up with its share. After more than a quarter century of experience with bilateral and multilateral development assistance, some serious issues have emerged in this field.

Aid Volume

One of the sharpest issues between rich and poor nations is the *volume* of aid. In absolute terms, official development assistance (ODA) has been increasing.

*Prepared by James W. Howe.

Whereas in 1960 it was $4.7 billion, in 1971 it had reached $7.7 billion—showing an average increase of 5.8 percent per year. However, rich countries have (in varying degrees) committed themselves to official development aid programs amounting to 0.7 percent of their GNP by the mid-1970s. They are well behind on this commitment. This shortfall of aid behind the international target set for the second U.N. Development Decade is a subject the poor countries raise at most international meetings.

Quality of Aid

The quality of aid is affected by such features as how much is in the form of grants, the terms of the loans, whether the aid is tied to procurement in the donor country, and whether it is available for a wide variety of uses or is inhibited by inflexible rules. The developing countries have been pressing for softer loans and more grants of untied aid, which can be made available for a variety of purposes. Over the years, the quality of aid in general has deteriorated—growing harder, more tied, and less flexible.

Style

The developing countries would like aid to be made available as unobtrusively as possible, with no political strings and few technical and professional requirements. Aid donors, on the other hand, often tie strings to their aid, either designed to serve their own ends or to ensure that their aid is well used. This issue creates great acrimony.

Administration

The question of whether to maintain representatives of aid agencies in all recipient countries affects the issue of centralization of decision-making. The United States is centralizing its bilateral aid so that more decisions are made at headquarters in Washington and fewer in the capital cities of the developing countries. The World Bank aid program has long been centralized, as has the British, while the UNDP is making an effort to decentralize its aid. Developing countries in general would probably prefer to be able to negotiate aid programs and projects in their own countries.

Another administrative issue is whether each aid agency should carry out projects with its own personnel or contract the work out to private individuals or institutions. In the latter case, an issue which affects the developing countries is whether the donor should contract with the private entity or give the money to the developing country to make the contract.

Public Support

A central issue affecting aid programs is public support in the donor countries. In several countries, public support for aid is stronger than government support. Even in the United States, where lack of public support for aid programs has seemed to be a major obstacle, a recent ODC poll shows that there is more support than is generally believed.[5]

Non-Appropriated Sources of Finance
for Development

Partly because of problems in the United States of maintaining an adequate volume of aid, and partly because of problems everywhere with aid quality, aid style, and aid administration, a search has begun for new sources of financial flows to developing countries that would not have to rely on the appropriations process. Most modern nations have systems for redistributing income from rich to poor. Increasingly these systems are automatic governmental rather than voluntary systems. But aid is essentially voluntary, and the world has no automatic system for redistributing income from rich to poor. Those who believe there are asymmetries in the trading, monetary, and other international economic systems complain that there is actually a reverse automatic system— for redistributing resources from poor to rich.

Suggestions for Research

1. *Public Support.* Is there in fact a rationale for U.S. development aid to the poor countries which will appeal to the public? An inquiry into the reasons why there is widespread public enthusiasm for the development of the Third World in some countries and little interest in others would be useful. To what extent do the reasons lie within the aid programs? Would change in these programs make a difference? What kind of change? To what extent would a vigorous public education program make a difference? Are there popular misconceptions about the size, rationale, and nature of the aid program? Would correcting these help the program?

2. *The Burden of Aid.* A study of the burden of aid might inquire into the budgetary burden, balance-of-payments burden, and real-resource burden aspects of aid.

3. *The Volume of ODA.* A privately financed candid study is needed to deflate the somewhat exaggerated figures for official development assistance reported by DAC.

4. *Aid Style.* It would be useful to conduct a study of aid style from the points of view of developing countries on the one hand, and the doubting

publics of donor countries on the other. Is there a style and an organization for aid giving that could meet the "no strings" desire of aid receivers while still assuring aid givers that their aid will be well used? To what extent will the emerging community of aid givers above help resolve the problem?

5. *The Achievements of Aid.* Studies of the results of aid also would be useful. Does aid actually help development? Where is the proof? What political and psychological price has had to be paid—if any—by perpetuating a dependency relationship? What is the relationship of aid to private investment, trade, export promotion—and broader American economic interests in the less developed countries? Such additional studies might be modeled along the lines of the study of Taiwan done by Neil Jacoby.[6]

6. *Organization for Aid Giving.* Several issues that have arisen concerning the present organization of aid giving might be studied. Should the World Bank or the United Nations predominate? Should the Bank set up its own resident missions or rely on the U.N. Resident Representatives for leadership? Should the experience with consortia and consultative groups be extended? Should the world reach for a new global pattern of aid organization with a world development council, a world development budget, and a budgetary process requiring a greater degree of commitment from aid-giving nations than under present DAC operations? Should regional aid-giving and coordinating arrangements be extended?

7. *Non-Appropriated Sources of Aid.* Should other sources of financial flows to developing countries which do not involve aid appropriations be developed? For example:

(a) The United States may soon repeal its tax deferral on earnings by its corporations on investments abroad. Corporations will have to pay taxes on profits earned abroad when they earn them rather than only when they repatriate them to the United States. This will force a drain of funds from certain poor countries to the rich United States. Would a scheme to rebate such taxes to the governments of such countries be feasible? How large are the funds involved? What problems would such a scheme create?

(b) The United States and other rich countries collect income taxes from immigrants from poor countries. Jagdish Bhagwati has suggested that rich countries rebate a portion of these taxes to the poor country from which the immigrant came. He has also suggested that the rich country add to these rebates a grant of a matching amount in recognition of the fact that the benefits of this brain drain to the rich country are in fact much greater than the portion of income taxes collected from the immigrants that would be rebated. What problems would this raise? How much might it produce?

(c) From time to time, a world tax on multinational corporations has been suggested as part of a move by the world community to control the activities of these entities. Would such a tax generate funds that could be used for development? What problems would it create?

(d) In an effort to protect the fish harvest of the oceans, the world may one day want to impose an international tax on fish catches. Might this produce funds for development?

(e) Similarly, taxes on profits from mineral or petroleum taken from the oceans beyond national jurisdiction have been proposed. The same thing is conceivable for any commercial use of space or of the Antarctic—since these are beyond national jurisdiction. The possibility of these tax funds being used for development might be studied.

(f) The United States recently suggested a tax on too rapid accumulations of foreign exchange, with the proceeds to be used to help poor countries develop. How practical is this proposal?

8. *Requirements for Aid.* A special study should be undertaken of the capacity of the "least developed" countries to put resources to good use. What limiting factors are indigenous to these least developed countries? What can be done about them? What limiting factors are attributable to the nature of the foreign aid programs available to these countries? What corrective steps can be taken?

Access of Developing Countries to
Private Money Markets in Rich Countries*

Historically, governments have frequently borrowed in one another's large private money markets. However, only a few of today's poor countries have succeeded in doing so. Most poor countries lack access to these markets for three reasons: (1) they lack the technical knowledge needed to operate in these markets; (2) they often lack the creditworthiness to be acceptable in such markets; and (3) they cannot afford the high rates of interest they would have to pay.

Several years ago, David Horowitz, president of Israel's Central Bank, proposed that rich-country members of the World Bank open their capital markets to the placement of bonds by the Bank's soft-loan arm, the International Development Agency (IDA). As part of their contribution to IDA, such countries would also guarantee these bonds against default and would contribute to an interest subsidy fund which would reduce the effective rate of interest to developing-country borrowers below the market rate. IDA would in turn use funds from the sale of such bonds to help the poor countries develop.

A variant on the Horowitz scheme recommended that donor nations facilitate, guarantee, and subsidize the interest rate on bonds directly placed by developing countries.

Currently, borrowing by developing countries in the Eurodollar market is

*Prepared by James W. Howe.

growing. An increasing number of transactions appear to be arranged directly between banks and foreign developing-country governments.

Suggestions for Research

1. *Access to Private Savings.* Do developing countries have sufficient access to private savings in rich countries but choose not to use this source of funds? Are there real obstacles to their effective access to capital markets in developed markets? If so, what are these obstacles? How might they be removed? What kind of technical assistance to developing countries, if any, might be useful in facilitating their use of capital markets?

2. *Guarantees.* What are the procedural and technical aspects of a system of guarantees against defaults on developing-country obligations? Of a system of interest subsidies? To what extent would a guarantee of a developing-country obligation against default be better than continued access to U.S. Export-Import Bank or World Bank lending? Would a guarantee system be at the expense of operations in the capital markets by the Export-Import Bank and the World Bank?

3. *Eurodollar Market.* What are the current and prospective possibilities for developing-country access to the Eurodollar market? Could subsidiaries of developed-country firms in developing countries issue bonds on the Eurodollar market with a guarantee from the parent company?

4. *Bank-to-Government Lending.* Does bank-to-government lending provide a substitute for bond flotations by developing countries?

The External Public Debt of the Poor Countries*

The World Bank estimates that the end-1971 external public and publicly guaranteed debt outstanding[b] of the eighty developing countries reporting to it stood at approximately $74.4 billion (at end-1971 exchange rates), or double that of 1966. Half of the total debt was owed by eight countries (India, Pakistan, Brazil, Mexico, Indonesia, Iran, South Korea, and Turkey), three-quarters by seventeen (the eight just mentioned, plus Argentina, Chile, Israel, Colombia, Yugoslavia, Egypt, Spain, Algeria, and Peru).

*Prepared by Mildred Weiss.

[b]External public debt, as defined by the IBRD, "includes all debt that is owed to creditors outside the debtor country in foreign currency, goods or services, with an original or extended maturity of over one year, and that is an obligation of the national government, of a political subdivision, or an agency of either, or of an autonomous public body."

The figures used here understate the total developing-country debt outstanding; they do not include those countries to which the World Bank Group has not extended loans, and they exclude those private loans that are not guaranteed in the donor country.

For political, historical, economic, and cultural reasons, each country, and each geographic region of the world, is unique with respect to its total debt outstanding and the predominant types of that debt, long- and short-run debt service obligations, the growth rates of its debt and its debt service, the size and nature of the aid being received, per capita GNP, export earnings, and the amount and type of foreign investment that has been attracted. Some countries are relatively free of debt problems, while others find that meeting debt-service obligations can be exceedingly difficult, if not impossible.

But the growing indebtedness of the developing countries should not, in itself, be a cause for alarm. The rise indicates only that the total capital flow to them has been increasing. A country with a sizable debt is not necessarily worse off than a country without debts; the borrowed funds may have produced domestic and external returns sufficient for the debtor country to pay debt service and to import the goods and services essential to development.

However, a sizable debt can make a country particularly vulnerable to debt-service difficulties, even if its policies regarding debt management and investment have been wise. For example, fluctuations in export earnings or in aid can have a serious impact on the debtor country's foreign exchange holdings. And the bunching of debt-service obligations into a short time period can cause temporary payments problems. Finally, social or infrastructure investments, although they may be important to the country developmentally, are unlikely either to generate foreign exchange directly or to yield returns in any form before a long gestation period has passed.

Debt-Service Payments, Export
Earnings, and External Financing[c]

The total debt service of poor countries registered $5.9 billion in 1970 and an estimated $7.1 billion in 1971.[d] In the 1960s, debt-service payments grew at an average annual rate of 9 percent; but they increased by 18 percent in 1970 and by 20 percent in 1971. This recent, more rapid growth will probably continue because of an increase in the volume of loans (especially the hard, commercial variety), a diminishing volume of grants and grant-like flows, a gradual hardening of credit terms for certain types of development assistance (e.g., capital raised on the international capital market), and the expiration during this decade of the grace periods on many of the soft loans made in the early 1960s. In the absence of a significant increase in export earnings or of larger amounts of soft aid, such heavy debt-service obligations could cause serious payments difficulties for some countries in the 1970s.

Export receipts are still the primary source of foreign exchange for most developing countries and are used to meet debt-service obligations as well as to

[c]External financing consists of official development assistance (ODA), other official flows, private investment and lending, private export credits, and grants by private voluntary agencies.

[d]Debt service is made up of the interest and amortization payments on external public and publicly guaranteed debt outstanding.

pay for imports. But in the 1960s, debt service for the poor countries as a whole rose faster (at an average rate of 9 percent annually) than did their export earnings (at 7.5 percent annually); by the late 1960s, debt service was rising by almost 15 percent a year, while export earnings were increasing by an annual 10 percent. Therefore, debt service has been taking up an increasing portion of their export earnings.

Their debt-servicing and import capacities are affected also by the amount of official and private financial resources they receive from abroad. The total net flow of these financial resources from the developed countries that are members of the OECD's Development Assistance Committee (DAC)[e] to the poor countries (a flow representing approximately 95 percent of the external flow from all sources to the developing countries in any given year) has been steadily expanding since 1963 (when it equaled $8.57 billion). By 1971, it had climbed to $18.3 billion.

The greatest growth of this net external resource flow has occurred in those categories having the harder terms—those that exact a rapid and large outflow from the poor countries in the form of dividends and profits, repatriation, and debt-service payments. Moreover, in recent years, the overall terms of the aid extended the poor countries—another element of "net external financing"—have been hardening. Grants have been falling relative to loans, as well as absolutely. Primarily because of the steadily rising average interest rate of loans, their grant element has fallen;[f] and as a result of the drop in the volume of grants, the grant element of loans and grants combined has fallen also. These trends could have serious implications for a debtor country, because hard terms for external funding today mean large debt-service payments tomorrow—and if debt-service is large, even a sizable gross capital flow will yield only a small net transfer.[g]

The Dilemma of the Debtor

If debt service makes heavy demands on its scarce foreign exchange, a developing country is likely to face a dilemma: should it meet its debt service commitments and restrain its imports of goods and services for development, or should it instead continue to import—perhaps with hard credits—at its present level and risk defaulting on future debt payments (in the event that debt relief is not eventually forthcoming from its creditors if the debtor country faces severe debt

[e]Australia, Austria, Belgium, Canada, Denmark, France, Germany, Italy, Japan, the Netherlands, Norway, Portugal, Sweden, Switzerland, the United Kingdom, and the United States.

[f]"Grant element" is defined by DAC as "the face value of a financial commitment less the discounted present value of the required amortization plus interest payments (using a 10 percent discount rate)."

[g]"Net transfer" is the gross flow less interest payments and amortization.

difficulties)? Either course has hazards because of the interrelationship of debt service and domestic investment and consumption—both now and in the future.

If, on the one hand, the debtor country holds back on its imports, it will probably slow down its economic growth rate, and possibly injure its future debt-servicing capacity. More specifically, if it restrains its imports of consumer goods, severe domestic political and social repercussions may result; its economic development, too, may be adversely affected—since in a poor country expenditures on nutrition and education, for example, can have a significant impact on investment. If, instead, the country restrains its imports of capital goods, its productive capacity may prove inadequate now or at some time in the future. If it holds down its imports of raw materials and intermediate goods, it may create excess capacity in its already established industrial plant. Domestic pressures for greater allocations to consumption would prove especially strong in cases of rapid population growth or low per capita incomes; and pressures for increased investment (and for the additional employment it can bring) would intensify in step with the growth of the available labor force.

If on the other hand, the debtor country chooses to maintain, or possibly augment, its level of imports of goods and services for development, it may—by taking on too many debt obligations—jeopardize its credit rating by the donor countries; this, in turn, may reduce the level of any future capital inflows, or at least harden the terms at which such capital would be available. Should a debtor country's situation become so grave as to cause or at least threaten default, its foreign creditors may provide debt relief, if only to assure the ultimate repayment of the debts. But before such relief can be granted, there will probably be a disruption of the debtor's capital inflows and imports, with unfortunate repercussions on its domestic development program. Once the debt relief operations have occurred, however, the country's credit rating is likely to pick up almost immediately, if only for a while, and the capital inflows to expand.

Debt Relief

Since 1956, nine developing countries (Argentina, Brazil, Chile, Ghana, India, Indonesia, Peru, Turkey, and Pakistan)—countries numbering among the biggest of debtors—have undergone multilateral debt relief, in most cases more than once.[h] Before 1965, such operations had generally been limited to private suppliers' credits; since then, however, official bilateral debts have, on occasion, been included.

These multilateral debt relief exercises have tended to be ad hoc in nature—exceptional responses by creditors to an actual or imminent default. The debt covered was generally short- or medium-term commercial debt. Only short-term relief was provided, and it usually involved a relatively high rate of moratorium

---

[h]Many more countries have reached bilateral agreements with their creditors.

interest, to cover the cost to creditors of the relief operations. The debtor country was expected to resume debt-service payments soon thereafter. However, repeated reschedulings for these debtor countries became the norm.

As a rule, debt relief operations have included requirements that the developing country impose strict controls on its monetary and fiscal policies and that it limit its use of short-term credits. Thus, stabilization measures were imposed on the country while its development needs went ignored. And the short-term character of these debt rearrangements reduced the ability of the debtor country to plan ahead with any degree of certainty.

The nature of the debt relief recently accorded Turkey, India, and Indonesia represents a significant departure from tradition. Long-term government debts were included, and the consortia of the major aid givers extending the debt relief departed from the typical ad hoc approach; concessional terms were used, especially in the case of Indonesia in 1970. Because the amortization on the bilateral and multilateral official development assistance of the 1960s is now falling due, difficulties in meeting the service payments on long-term debt are becoming more common. It is possible that extended postponements, reductions, or cancellations of debt-service payments will become accepted debt relief measures.

Suggestions for Research

1. *Case Studies of Debt Relief Operations.* Individual country experiences (e.g., Turkey and Ghana) should be examined to determine the possible effects of debt relief (i.e., rescheduling, refinancing, or cancellation) on the debtor and the creditor. In doing this, long-term debt relief operations should be compared with short-term ones and extensive operations with limited ones. Did the debt relief encourage more careless debt management on the part of the developing countries? Did it undermine the sanctity of the debt contract (particularly in the case of repeated debt relief operations)? Did the debt relief deter future capital flows (by reducing the debtor's creditworthiness in the eyes of potential creditors) or did it, in fact, encourage additional flows? Did it give the debtor country sufficient time for stepping up its investment, production, exports, savings, and revenues?

2. *Debt-Servicing Capacity.* What are the major factors determining long-term and short-term debt-servicing capacities?

3. *Tied Aid and Debt Service.* Does the tying of development loans to projects or suppliers seriously reduce the debtor country's ability to service its debt? What is the real value of tied loans? Would the country have bought the tied goods and services anyway?

4. *Altering the Net Flow of Capital.* What would be the economic and political repercussions of (a) increasing the gross capital flow to the debtor,

(b) extending aid on softer terms, or (c) granting the country debt relief (rescheduling, refinancing, or cancellation) on the debtor country being helped, on its creditors, and on the other debtors?

5. *Export Credits.* Further study on private official export credits (i.e., on the forces affecting their flow, terms, and sources) would be helpful in shaping policies to avoid serious debt-service problems.

6. *The Costs of Debt-Servicing.* Individual cases should be examined to determine how the meeting of debt-service obligations has affected the debtor country's development program.

Scientific and Technological Change and the Poor Countries*

Because of the contribution that technology can make to economic development, it has become a matter of concern that the technologies now in use in the developing countries are frequently inappropriate to these countries' needs.

Technology: Its Creation, Transfer, and Adaptation

"Technology" consists of product design, production facilities and processes, and organization and marketing techniques. A country acquires it (1) through transfer from abroad (after which it is either used intact or subsequently adapted to local conditions), or (2) from indigenous innovation.

The more modern and more specialized technologies are generally the property of individuals or businesses; the devices used for their transfer include direct investment and the operations of multinational corporations, patents, or licenses, equipment importation and servicing, turnkey projects, and consultant services. Such vehicles of course presuppose (1) the willingness of the owner to offer terms that the potential buyer likes and can afford to meet, and (2) knowledge on the part of the potential buyer of the existence of the technology in question. Older or less complex technologies, in contrast, are more likely to be transferred through published material, the migration of people, programs of technical assistance, or schooling.

Internationally, there is a marked imbalance in the creation and transfer of technology. About 98 percent of all research and development (R&D) is conducted by the developed countries and is generally directed toward meeting their own needs. The existence of this technology would seem to offer an opportunity for the poor countries to telescope the stages in their development

---

*Prepared by Mildred Weiss.

by drawing upon, and possibly adapting, the knowledge and experience gained by today's industrial nations. However, the limited amount of R&D carried out in the developing world tends to emphasize innovation rather than the adaptation to local conditions of the vast amount of technology that already exists in the developed countries. Because of these conditions, most of the technologies currently in use in the developing world were created by the industrial countries for their own use. Unlike the developed countries, most poor countries have a relative scarcity of capital and technical managerial skills and an abundance of unskilled unemployed and underemployed labor. In addition, the domestic markets of the developing countries are generally too small and too widely scattered to permit full-capacity use of large-scale, mass-production technologies imported from the developed countries. Finally, the poor countries differ markedly from rich countries with respect to climate, local raw materials, and a host of other production and distribution factors.

In the past, the governments and research institutions of the developing countries, donor-country governments, and multinational corporations have not been sufficiently sensitive to the existence of these differences. The policies pursued by certain poor-country governments for a variety of political, economic, and prestige reasons have so severely distorted the market prices for capital and labor that, even though capital is scarce and labor abundant, the use of capital-intensive, labor-saving technologies has been encouraged. Government policies affecting the cost of capital include artificially low interest rates on capital, price subsidies, overvalued exchange rates, and a differential tariff structure. Those affecting the cost of labor include minimum wage laws, national social security programs, and job tenure legislation.

Some donor-country policies also have been harmful. For example, the practice of tying aid to source or product, technical advice from foreigners or natives trained to emphasize labor-saving techniques (to fit the situation in developing countries), and the promotion of modern machinery by foreign salesmen have contributed to the selection of equipment that is not wholly appropriate to the individual poor country's needs.

The practices of the multinational corporations operating in the developing world also have had some detrimental effects on the technological capability of the poor countries. These corporations are inclined to employ the technologies most familiar to them or those which must be used more extensively if the R&D which went into them originally is to yield a good return. Any adaptation they—or domestic enterprises in the developing countries—carry out is kept to a minimum, because of its cost in training, time, and risk of economic failure. The developing-country hosts have often exercised little or no influence over the multinational corporations' choice of technology or investment.

Moreover, in the developing world, the personal prestige gained by pure research often exceeds that gained by applied research. Frequently, a poor-country industry cannot afford to carry out its own research. Moreover, many

R&D institutes in developing countries are governmental or academic organizations, and hence the needs of industry often go unnoticed by researchers, while firms seldom, if ever, learn about the discoveries of the institutes. Therefore the developing countries frequently must choose between using a foreign technology to produce a given product or not producing it at all, at least for the present.

Questions Now Being Raised by the Poor Countries

Observers in both developing countries and developed countries have become critical of the wholesale importation of technology from the industrialized to the less developed countries. Developing countries are increasingly aware that the technologies used frequently have not been well suited to their needs. The technical-scientific elite of these countries—which has been growing slowly since the 1950s—perceives in this transfer of technology a new version of colonialism, especially given the weak financial-technical-commercial local bargaining position of the poor countries vis-à-vis the multinational corporations. The developing countries increasingly recognize that excessive use of foreign technology can perpetuate this external dependence by discouraging the development of an indigenous R&D capacity. Efficiency and prompt implementation of a given technology in the short run must often be weighed against the perpetuation of external dependence in the long run.[i] Finally, the price and other terms exacted by the foreign owner of the technology might be very high, much to the detriment of the balance of payments of the buying country.

Identifying Appropriate Technologies

What is it that makes technology "appropriate"? A primary consideration is that the technology should permit the most effective possible use of a country's resource endowments while economizing on its scarce resources. Its output should be of the quality, precision, uniformity, price, and quantity demanded by the domestic and foreign markets. It should have a favorable impact on future employment opportunties—and on income distribution—and it should make possible the satisfaction of future domestic and foreign demand.

Properly chosen, a given technology can be used to achieve many different ends: for example, to increase employment and redistribute income domestically, to train local workers and managers, to slow down the too rapid influx of people into urban areas, to stimulate local demand for traditional consumer

---

[i]Of course, in some instances imported technology may prove complementary to domestic knowledge, processes, management, inputs, or products, or to the development thereof, thereby promoting the growth of local technological capability. Or an imported technology may be such that it can exist side by side with domestic technologies.

goods, to expand indigenous R&D capacity, to increase output, to disperse economic development throughout the country, to encourage the creation of ancillary and subsidiary industries that provide significant job opportunities, to avoid a large need for sophisticated maintenance and repair work, and to increase output as demand expands. Without changing the processes, or the amount of capital, it is sometimes possible to create more employment openings—by using double or triple shifts of workers, by running the machines at faster speeds (and with a lower machine/worker ratio), or by using cheaper raw-material inputs (in combination with more workers to oversee the operation).

Although our knowledge of the technical constraints operating on the adaptation of specific industries and technologies to different economic environments is limited, it is recognized that the scope for adapting to some of them is significant.

Suggestions for Research

1. *Obstacles to the International Transfer of Technology.* What public policies (e.g., with respect to taxation, import controls, and minimum wage legislation) and what cultural attitudes impede the introduction of new technologies from abroad?

Studies should be made of the international patent system and of poor-country patent mechanisms, as well as of other economically restrictive practices, in order to determine their importance as deterrents to a poor country's ability to introduce or develop suitable technologies.

What are the various means of linking science and technology institutes in developed countries to those in developing countries, in order to accelerate the international flow of scientific and technological knowledge and to encourage its application to local needs?

2. *Technology Transfer vs. Indigenous Innovation.* Criteria and information sources are needed to help poor-country policymakers and entrepreneurs make more effective choices among existing (current and vintage) foreign technologies and to identify opportunities for indigenous development of more appropriate technologies. It would be useful to determine when it would be better to sustain the costs of short-term inefficiencies and delays for the sake of longer term progress in the adaptation of foreign technology and domestic research and development.

Environment and Development*

Although the most commonly recognized threat to the environment is the pollution or destruction of the air, the water, and the land within individual

---

*Prepared by Susan Sammartano. Adapted from "Environment and Development" by Susan Sammartano and James W. Howe, in *The United States and the Developing World: Agenda for Action* (Washington, D.C.: Overseas Development Council, 1973), pp. 101-108.

countries, concern is also rightly growing about transnational pollution involving such problems as the spreading of chemicals like DDT and pollution of the air and rivers across national boundaries. Today, the environment debate has at least two international dimensions. First, environmental problems in some way face every country and, where they have transnational effects, require some international cooperation. Second, the environment debate has identified some areas of potential conflict between rich and poor nations. But underlying the environmental problem everywhere is the shared need for more knowledge about its nature and extent, and the proper courses of action for nations to take in responding to it.

Worldwide economic activity has increased so rapidly during the past two decades that we have scarcely had time to identify and examine its many consequences. In 1950, world population totaled 2.5 billion, and the gross world product (GWP) was about $1.4 trillion. At that level of economic activity, the evident stresses on the world's "ecosystem" were very few. But in 1970, only two decades later—when population had reached 3.6 billion and the GWP was approaching $3.7 trillion—new signs of environmental stress in one part of the world or another, chiefly in the rich countries, were being reported almost daily.

*The Poor Countries' View of
Environmental Problems*

Many developing countries in Asia, Africa, and Latin America question the relevance of the new concern with the environment for their own major concerns. Their dominant and persistent priority is to gain freedom from the deprivations of mass poverty. For countries with few automobiles or factories, air pollution is not an issue. Where there is widespread shortage of food and housing, as well as chronic unemployment, preserving scenic vistas is often counted a luxury. Countries with an average income of $100 per person simply do not have the same perspective on environmental issues as rich countries do. As Indian Prime Minister Indira Gandhi has eloquently stated:

When (people) themselves feel deprived, how can we urge preservation of animals? How can we speak to those who live in villages and in slums about keeping the oceans, the rivers and the air clean when their own lives are contaminated at source? Environment cannot be improved in conditions of poverty.

These conflicting views on the question of protecting the environment were discussed by representatives of 113 national governments at a United Nations Conference on the Human Environment, held in Stockholm in June of 1972. The conference helped to increase official and public understanding of environmental issues and to broaden the concept of environment to include the concerns of poor countries.

In November 1972, the General Assembly voted to locate the U.N. Environmental Program (UNEP) secretariat in Nairobi. This was a victory for the poor countries. In addition, the Governing Council for Environmental Programs, which will coordinate all of the U.N. system's environmental activities, is dominated by representatives of the developing world. As a result of these two factors, the poor countries are likely to have an important voice in international decisions on environmental questions. The rich countries may now find that they will be unable to deal with some problems of direct concern to them without taking into account the priorities and interests of poor countries. It now remains to be seen whether the poor nations will use the UNEP secretariat primarily as an instrument of confrontation against the rich; or whether they will work toward a less polluted environment within the broadened environmental perspective.

Suggestions for Research

Before the United States can act responsibly on the international aspects of environmental matters, many basic questions need to be answered. In fact, apart from informed speculation, the nature of the threat to the environment and of the appropriateness of specific national and international policies for responding to that threat are largely unknown. In the economic sphere, the United States and other developed countries need to know the extent of the potential conflict between continuing our present rate and types of economic growth and safeguarding our environment, with its finite supply of natural resources and limited ability to absorb waste products. For their part, some of the developing nations are uncertain whether, to what extent, and at what cost their goal of economic development is compatible with environmental quality.

Foremost among the issues to be studied are the following:

1. *Pollution Abatement Costs.* How much will the enforcement of higher environmental standards in the developed countries raise the operating costs of pollution-intensive industries? Will the effect be short run or long run? Will certain industries be forced to relocate in areas with lower environmental standards? Will the poor countries, which at this point probably possess a greater waste-absorptive capacity, welcome polluting industries and, if so, on what terms?

Is it true, as is often alleged, that it would be cheaper for the poor countries to install "clean" technology now, while there is little industrialization, rather than wait to clean up later when the limits of absorptive capacity are approached?

2. *Availability of Technology Suitable for Poor Countries.* Since the multinational corporations already have a solid base of "dirty" technology, will their activities exacerbate pollution problems? Or, since they (a) are visible and under fire, (b) have the resources for research, and (c) are likely to use standard operations everywhere, will they develop adaptive technologies which are responsive to the environmental goals of poor countries? Alternatively, will they

develop clean but expensive technologies to meet conditions in the rich countries and impose these technologies on the poor? Is a special public effort needed to subsidize research in nonpollutive technology of interest to developing countries, or will existing research efforts do?

3. *Market Position.* Some competitive advantage will be gained by producers who do not comply with antipollution standards, as opposed to those who do. Therefore, what measures can be agreed upon among nations to prevent such differences from triggering frictions in trade relations? And how can these measures be adopted without at the same time negating the advantages that individual nations might otherwise have as the result of greater absorptive capacities or differences in priorities?

4. *Recycling.* Many rich countries are increasing their ability to recycle waste products. What effect will this have on exports of raw materials from the poor countries?

5. *Substitution.* Can pollution be reduced by substituting natural products for synthetics? What would be the effect of such a development on poor-country exports of raw materials, and on economic efficiency in the developed countries?

6. *Methods of Financing National and Transnational Pollution Control.* Another important area that requires further study is the method of financing pollution control. In the domestic sphere, arguments have been advanced for devising a system in which the cost of pollution control would be reflected in production prices —the principle of "polluter pays." What are the relative merits of such a system? What are the alternatives?

Is the principle of "polluter pays" feasible if applied to the developing world? Would another method of financing international antipollution activities be more practical, as well as ethical? Should entirely new methods of financing be considered (e.g., some kind of levy on international shipping of major polluting materials, such as oil)?

In particular, with regard to the ecological problems of the developing countries, should the United States favor the principle of compensation (i.e., a transfer of funds from rich countries to compensate developing countries in cases where environmental standards cause them to suffer export losses)? What about additionality—a concept which would require developed countries to grant funds (in addition to the 0.7 percent of GNP for rich-country economic aid accepted in principle for the second U.N. Development Decade) for the specific purpose of incorporating environmental safeguards in development projects? Are these useful constructs for furthering the goal of environmental protection on an international scale?

7. *Forms of Pollution Control.* Studies are needed of the effectiveness of various forms of direct and indirect (as well as punitive and voluntary) controls over environment to make available to developed and developing countries alike a range of specific policies from which they can choose in accordance with their requirements and preferences.

8. *Present State of Environment.* Assistance to the developing countries is needed to survey the present state of their environment, and the major hazards to which they think they are exposed.

Claims to the Wealth of the Oceans*

Unilateral claims by coastal states to jurisdiction over their adjacent waters have become increasingly frequent and extensive during the past two decades. In contrast, prior to World War II, territorial jurisdictions had been narrowly drawn and defined, leaving the principle of freedom of the high seas virtually unchallenged. Four interrelated factors lie behind these unilateral claims and behind the protests that these claims have aroused.

The Petroleum and Hard Minerals of the Sea

Rapid advances in the technology of marine exploration and exploitation have increased international awareness of, and access to, the vast petroleum and hard-mineral wealth of the seas. The world's oceans now are seen as more than just navigational routes or huge fishing ponds. Even those coastal nations that still lack the technology and financial capability for exploiting the ocean's resources already look to the waters off their coasts with interest.

The supply of subsea petroleum may exceed that on land. And its value may one day surpass that of all other marine resources. Offshore production today equals 18 percent of the 15-billion-barrel world total; by 1980, it could make up 30-40 percent of the 25 to 30 billion barrels produced, and by the year 2000, 40-50 percent of some 60 to 75 billion barrels. Because subsea petroleum is probably located primarily in the continental margins and because recovery there would be much cheaper, most drilling in the next few years can be expected to be carried out near the coast.

Little is known about the minerals under the deep sea, although exploration is already under way. Some sixty elements are believed to be held in suspension in the ocean waters; and many precipitate onto the ocean floor. The almost ubiquitous manganese nodules on the seabed have attracted much attention because of their cobalt, nickel, and copper content; their exploitation during this decade is highly probable.

Subsea deposits of petroleum and hard minerals will become increasingly important as land deposits are depleted and as prices rise enough to make the exploitation of seabed minerals economically feasible. For the most part, the necessary technology already exists. However, there remain strong legal and

*Prepared by Mildred Weiss.

political obstacles to exploitation: investors, especially those building costly, relatively permanent installations, fear the competition of trespassers, as well as expropriation or other unilateral acts by the coastal states involved.

Fisheries

Both rich and poor nations increasingly look to the oceans as an important source of protein (as well as income). The sea's fisheries—like marine petroleum and hard minerals—have generally been exploited most successfully by the richer, technologically more advanced countries. Now that the developed countries' demand for meat is exceeding the world supply, their interest in the protein of the sea is rapidly growing. Since they already possess the necessary marine technologies, they have much to gain from fishing, from seafood processing, and from aquaculture.

Some developing coastal states—having played no significant role in earlier international marine agreements, customs, or practices—are now asserting an economic nationalism with respect to the use and control of the oceans. Moreover, fish provide the people of many developing countries with the largest portion of the protein they consume. Finally, fish exports are the mainstay of some of these countries' economies.

However, at the same time that interest in fisheries has intensified on the part of many countries, there has been a leveling off in the rapid growth of the world fish catch. Without better conservation measures, the discovery and exploitation of new fish stocks, a wider use of "trash fish," improvements in marine technology, or an expansion of aquaculture, the protein (and income) actually derived from the sea will not satisfy the world's fast-growing demand.

The Precedent Set by President
Truman in 1945

In response to technological progress in the exploitation of seabed minerals beyond the traditional 3-mile national limits, President Truman issued a proclamation in 1945 asserting U.S. jurisdiction and control over the natural resources of the seabed and subsoil of the continental shelf lying off its coast. New mining installations, being costly and relatively permanent, would someday require regulation as well as legal safeguards against trespassing competitors and coastal state expropriation; traditionally, only a nation-state could perform such a role, and then only with respect to its own territory.

President Truman thus set a precedent. His proclamation was subsequently used by other coastal nations as a justification for their own, frequently more sweeping, unilateral claims. Today, almost three decades later, only twenty-nine states still claim a 3-mile territorial sea, while seventy claim 12 miles or more.

Pollution Fears

Many states increasingly fear the pollution of their coastal areas from oil spills from large modern tankers or collisions at sea, offshore mining and drilling, and marine exploration activities.

Problems to Resolve and Interests
to Accommodate

Unilateral maritime claims have diminished international certainty about the various jurisdictions of ocean space and have eroded the doctrine of freedom of the high seas. International communications, navigation and commerce, national and collective security measures, and scientific research are endangered. And the rising number of users of ocean space, together with the multiplication of the uses to which they put it, is increasing the possibility of conflict among these users and uses, as well as threatening widespread depletion of the sea's living resources and pollution of the entire marine environment.

The U.N.-sponsored Conference on the Law of the Sea scheduled for late 1973 is expected to move toward defining the "continental shelf," "territorial sea," and "high seas"; and to examine such key issues as the dissemination of technology among nations, freedom of navigation, fishing and mining rights, and conservation and antipollution measures.

At present, neither the poor nor the rich countries form a cohesive block with respect to the kind of international oceans regime they would like to establish. The problems to be resolved are legal, economic, technical, and political. Moreover, many different interests—both within and among nations—must be accommodated. If agreement on an international regime is ever to be reached, each state must believe it will somehow benefit from the existence of that regime.

Geographic considerations are one key factor in shaping a nation's attitudes toward an international regime. Because the continental margins are probably the principal location of marine petroleum, those nations controlling them would obtain an enormous economic windfall. On the basis of seabed considerations alone, there are at least five categories into which nations can be grouped:

1. Over forty countries are land-locked or shelf-locked; only rarely have they enjoyed any of the sea's many benefits. With few exceptions (for example, the Federal Republic of Germany) members of this category are less developed countries. They would be inclined to support narrow national jurisdictions and an international sharing of the wealth of the seas.

2. The concerns of those nations with relatively short coastlines and narrow continental margins—typically the African developing countries—resemble those of the nations in the first category. Even if their continental margins did contain

some wealth, these countries would probably gain more, at least for the present, from an international regime (especially inasmuch as the oil deposits in the continental margins of the Southern Hemisphere are usually much less extensive than those of the Northern Hemisphere).

3. The few nations with long coastlines and only limited access to continental margins, notably those on the west coast of South America, have tended to lay claim to some type of 200-mile jurisdiction. They would probably benefit more, however, from an international revenue-sharing scheme for seabed resources than from the exploitation of their own jurisdictional claims.

4. Those developing countries with long coastlines and extensive continental margins, such as Argentina and India, must decide, if they have not already done so (a) whether they would gain more by drilling and mining unilaterally within their respective jurisdictions or by participating in an international revenue-sharing system, or (b) whether they would be better off in dealing with foreign-owned petroleum and mining companies on a bilateral or on a multilateral basis.

5. Those rich countries with long coastlines and large continental margins, such as Canada and Australia, would gain little, if anything, from an international regime for drilling and mining, particularly if the benefits were to go primarily to the developing world. They would probably prefer large national jurisdictions, since they would possess the technologies and finances needed to exploit them.

A nation's policy on an international oceans regime might also be affected by the following considerations: its technical and financial capacity for mining and drilling; its ability to fish off its own coasts; its capacity for fishing in distant seas; its attitudes on freedom of navigation, shipping, overflight, and scientific research; the anticipated price and income effects of seabed mining on its present and potential domestic land producers and consumers; its concern about marine pollution and depletion of the ocean's living resources; its collective and national self-defense needs; and its attitude toward making unilateral agreements with foreign oil and mining companies.

Suggestions for Research

1. *The Role of an International Ocean Regime.* What would happen if no widely acceptable international agreement on an oceans regime could be negotiated? For example, what if part of the package proved unacceptable to many poor countries, thereby causing them to hesitate or even decline to sign the agreement? Would bankers be willing to put up the necessary money for deep-sea mining if the security of their investments were uncertain? What would be the effect on interstate relations? Would there still be freedom of passage through today's international straits? Would the survival of yet more species of fish be endangered?

2. *Research Advancement and Cooperation.* What are the most practical procedures for facilitating freedom of scientific research, for encouraging the development of a marine technology appropriate to the developing countries' needs and capabilities, and for ensuring the worldwide dissemination of knowledge, technology, and training? Would regional study centers and regional representation on scientific expeditions be useful to these ends?

3. *Economic Impact of Seabed Mining.* What are the economic implications of seabed mining for consumers and for land producers? What will the world demand for minerals be in the next two or three decades? Will supplies prove sufficient and dependable? What will happen to the price levels of the various minerals? Which producing countries and which consuming countries will be most affected? How can any negative economic effects be avoided or at least compensated for? At present, the emphasis of the analysis should be on the minerals found in the manganese nodules, for these are likely to be the most important of the seabed deposits recovered over the next decade or two.

4. *The Potential of the Oceans as a Source of Protein.* How can man best harvest the oceans without depleting them? Emphasis has long been on exploitation rather than on conservation. The expansion of aquaculture and the use of new processing methods for heretofore untapped marine life would boost enormously the protein yield of the sea for poor countries.

5. *Interests of Landlocked Countries.* Some of the least developed of the poor countries are landlocked. Their special situation—with respect to navigation and trade, fishing, and mining—has so far received only cursory consideration. An impartial third party should study their plight, and then make suggestions on what they might do to alleviate it; such a study might, for example, attempt to develop ideas on how the landlocked states could obtain the best possible access to the sea.

6. *Island Jurisdiction.* Still needed is a detailed inventory of the earth's half million islands—maný within the jurisdiction of developing countries—with respect to their location, size, ownership (often disputed), resources thereon and nearby, and political status. How is the jurisdiction of each island to be determined? What would be the impact on the freedom of the seas? How are the lines to be drawn in the case of disappearing rocks and reefs or shifting river beds?

7. *Marine Revenue Potential.* What is the revenue potential of the ocean's petroleum, natural gas, and hard minerals? Of its protein? Of taxation on ocean shipping or on ocean dumping to encourage better methods of waste disposal? What other good ocean revenue sources are there? What are the best ways to distribute these resources, once they have been collected?

8. *Current Capabilities of Developing Countries.* Which marine resources are today exploitable by the poor countries, in view of their financial and technological capabilities?

9. *Pollution of the Seas.* Better methods of waste disposal would reduce the

problem of marine pollution. Much more study is needed on the various marine pollutants, with respect to their source and point of entry into the sea, their effect on marine life, and their movement, build-up, and persistence over time. This is especially important for those developing countries which depend on tourism.

International Migration*

Several types of international migration have today replaced the transcontinental migrations of the past: temporary migrations of poor-country workers in response to the labor requirements of industries in developed countries, the movement of professional and highly skilled people from developing to developed countries in response to more favorable employment opportunities, and emigration (sometimes illegal) attributable to overpopulation and unemployment in some poor countries.

The most important of these migrations from the point of view of an analysis of relations between developed and developing countries have been the movements of workers from developing to industrial countries, particularly in the Mediterranean area, and migration *among* developing countries, for example in Central America and Western Africa. Workers from the littoral states of the Mediterranean—particularly Greece, Turkey, Spain, Yugoslavia, Algeria, and Tunisia—are today major components of the work forces of several European industrial nations. This movement of course has significant economic, social, and political implications for the host countries and the developing countries concerned. Migrations of peoples among developing countries have had an important impact on some African economies. Such movements among developing countries often reflect the arbitrariness of some national frontiers, which cut across tribal groupings or traditional patterns of nomadic or seasonal movement. Moreover, in Africa, Latin America, and Asia, the presence of foreign or racially distinct persons has given rise to strife and open conflict within the host country, or between the host country and the nations from which the migrants originated. Such cases include the treatment of Asians in Uganda, Chinese in Indonesia, and the migration of Salvadoreans and their assumption of an important position in the Honduran economy—which led to the war between El Salvador and Honduras, and, in part, to the disruption of the Central American Common Market.

Trade, investment, and economic and cultural relations all can be affected by these international migrations. Social developments in the developing country exporting labor can be significant. Yet little is known about the effects of these migrations, and the formulation of policies to deal with problems stemming from them lacks a sound statistical, factual, and theoretical base.

*Prepared by Guy F. Erb.

Suggestions for Research

1. *Migration from Developing to Developed Countries.* What is the magnitude of current migratory movements from developing to developed countries? What social and economic problems have arisen in host countries as a result of the entry of large numbers of foreign workers? As communities of expatriates grow, what provisions can be made for schooling, health care, and housing? What social and economic impact does the departure of large numbers of male and female workers have on the country of origin? Skilled workers often form the bulk of the emigrants. Should some form of international compensation be established to reduce the adverse impact of such emigration on the developing country concerned? How many of these migrant workers return to their home countries? Do they return permanently, or is their movement governed by cyclical conditions in the industrial countries requiring their services? What happens to workers when they permanently return to their societies? Are the potential gains from the reentry of skilled workers realized? Will the tendency for enterprises to seek new sites for production in developing countries lead to the effective use of the workers that have returned to their home countries in the Mediterranean area and in Latin American countries?

2. *Migration Among Developing Countries.* In what ways does the movement of peoples among developing countries affect the social and political stability of the countries in question? What are the magnitudes of such movements in different developing regions? How does the movement affect relations between developed and developing countries? What are its implications for the foreign economic policies of developed countries? Can development assistance policies facilitate the solution of problems deriving from migration among developing countries? Can problems and conflicts stemming from migration be anticipated so that international measures may be taken to ameliorate the situation?

Development and Public Education in the Rich Countries*

The willingness of the rich countries to assist the development of the poor countries depends upon a favorable climate of public opinion in the developed countries. Enlightened policies on the part of rich-country governments in each of the fields discussed in the appendix to this chapter, such as trade, investment, aid, and monetary policy, can only be sustained with the support of enlightened public opinion in those countries. Such opinion does not now exist. Although governments of rich countries will not always do what the public wants, they are unlikely to carry out policies that are vigorously opposed by powerful groups within their own countries. Trade policies in the United States are a good example; in this area, a vocal minority of organizations who feels American jobs are jeopardized threatens to create new barriers to trade and investment that will effectively hamper the export programs of the developing countries. Another

*Prepared by John W. Sewell.

example is the official U.S. program of development assistance to the poor countries. Although the program traditionally has been favored by the Executive Branch, it has met with increasing opposition in the Congress. This opposition is traceable, according to many Congressmen, to the combination of active opposition by various groups, based mainly on the Vietnam experience, and widespread public indifference.

Moreover, the public is generally misinformed about development assistance. Even college-educated people appear to have a wildly exaggerated idea of the size of the program. Congressional mail still contains demands that we stop giving aid to France. Many people have an image of aid as an outflow of U.S. cash that winds up in the pockets of rich members of the ruling classes in the poor countries. Clearly public education programs are needed not only about aid but about the interaction between each of the international economic systems and the poor countries.

The experience of various European countries contrasts sharply with this situation in the United States. In the Netherlands, the United Kingdom, and Sweden there is a substantial body of public opinion that supports national policies designed to meet the needs of the poor countries. Relative to their wealth, the contribution by these countries to the developing countries has been excellent and can be attributed at least partly to enthusiastic public support for such programs. To some degree this public support is due to vigorous public education programs in those countries.

Nevertheless, there is still inadequate knowledge about the state of public opinion in the rich countries, particularly in the United States, and about how attitudes concerning the poor countries are formulated. Some work has already been done in this area. A major survey sponsored by the Overseas Development Council will give Americans a much better idea of the state of public opinion in their own country. In addition, some research has been initiated, under the direction of the Kettering Foundation, on the formulation of public opinion in foreign affairs in general. However, there still remains a great need for additional research in the areas suggested below.

Suggestions for Research

1. *The State of Public Opinion.* What do Americans believe about development assistance? About trade and investment? About developing countries, poverty, and the poor in general? By and large, there have been no in-depth public opinion surveys (although the current ODC-sponsored survey will provide some of the needed information). Much can be done to find out the actual beliefs of Americans, the depth of their knowledge, and, equally important, their sources of information of development issues.

2. *How to Increase Understanding of World Affairs.* Very little is known about public opinion formulation in international affairs. Are the key determinants of public opinion the attitudes of elites, or do most Americans tend to

make their own judgments? There is much room for systematic assessment of various types of educational programs for citizens in foreign affairs if the United States is to have a citizenry knowledgeable about the subject.

3. *Creating an Educated and Aware Public.* At present, a number of groups and organizations interested in international affairs exist at the local level. There are also groups at the national level (such as the ODC, and population and environmental groups) with information and resources and a desire to cooperate with local organizations.

How can the groups at these two levels be linked? Traditionally they have come together through organizations such as the Foreign Policy Association or the United Nations Association, or through mass-membership groups such as the League of Women Voters. But in many ways the traditional foreign affairs network has fragmented and the links between national headquarters and their local affiliates are not as strong as in earlier years. National organizations are increasingly finding they must follow, not lead, their local membership as it is clear that active and vital organizations will vary widely from city to city.

We suggest therefore that the major foundations undertake to investigate the whole network of national foreign affairs educational organizations to see whether or not they can meet the needs of the 1970s and 1980s. Such an investigation should raise the question: education to what end? It also should look at whether traditional models of citizens' education and involvement are still viable or whether new models and organizations should be created. Several possibilities—not mutually exclusive—are worth further exploration:

a. Regional representatives—a network of "sales agents" who would actively stimulate cooperation between local and national groups.

b. Development Education Fund. Conventional wisdom holds that many worthwhile projects go begging because it is hard for major funding sources to make small grants. An autonomous fund able to make small contributions for local activities designed to increase American understanding and concern with the problems of the poor countries might have a major impact.

c. The Electronic Media. Perhaps modern communication provides an answer to the dilemmas of public education. Foundations have invested large amounts of capital in seeking ways to utilize television to inform the public on issues of public policy. The success so far has been small, but the need remains great. The application of modern communication techniques—video, cable, cassettes, interactive programming, simulations, etc.—could have a major impact on public attitudes concerning development.

4. *Development Curricula.* Development specialists so far have virtually ignored the main socializing body in our society—the schools. There already exists growing understanding of development among specialists; the problem is to translate that understanding into suitable materials and to introduce them into the schools. A major field for research should be how to introduce development concepts into secondary school education.

Conclusions and Recommendations*

Most existing scholarly work on the international economic order deals with problems of concern to rich countries. There is, of course, much work of interest to the poor countries, but almost all such work is based on the premise that what the poor countries need is to work more assiduously on their internal problems. While that premise has much validity, there is little recognition that important constraints on the development of the poor countries arise from the international economic systems designed by the rich countries or from the economic policies followed by the rich countries. Serious gaps exist in research on this subject even by rich-country scholars, and very little has been done by scholars in developing countries. A vigorous program is needed to upgrade the research focused on this subject by scholars everywhere, but most importantly by scholars in the developing countries.

Our study of the state of research on the developing countries in the changing international economic order leads us to the following conclusions:

1. *The international economic order is important to developing countries.* A foreign visitor remarked to us last fall that both the United States and the poor countries would be better off if the dwindling U.S. appropriations spent on helping poor countries develop were spent instead on establishing an effective program to help U.S. farmers, workers, and industries move out of the lines of production where the United States is inefficient and into those where we could excel. Without denigrating U.S. development aid, which we believe can be very useful to the poor countries, we believe our visitor had a profound insight: the success or failure of development programs in many poor countries depends not only on their own efforts, but also on what happens beyond their shores as a result of the policies of rich countries and of international economic institutions largely directed by rich countries.

We have identified ten components of the international economic order that bear on the development of the poor countries:

1. trade
2. monetary relations
3. investment
4. the transfer of science and technology
5. international public or publicly guaranteed debt
6. private money markets
7. governmental and private aid programs
8. an international regime for the use of the oceans
9. the international protection of the environment
10. migration, including the "brain drain."

Some of these components—such as trade, monetary relations, aid, and debt—involve systems with institutions and agreed rules emerging to guide their

*Prepared by James W. Howe.

operation. Others, such as the protection of the environment, are in their formative stages, with only the beginnings of a formal institutional order; while others, such as the international regime of the oceans, are still in the planning stage.

2. *Developing countries are important to the international economic order.* Our second conclusion is that the poor countries themselves are increasingly important to the successful functioning of the international economic order.

In the monetary field, the importance of the poor countries to reform efforts is indicated by the fact that developing countries have nine places on the International Monetary Fund's new Committee of 20, which is charged with developing proposals for international monetary reform. Moreover, in the IMF, developing countries have 33 percent of the vote, and four-fifths of the membership; this gives them more than enough power to block any measures that fail to take their interests into account, since major IMF decisions require approval by 80 percent of the weighted votes and three-fifths of the total membership. In the field of direct private investment, it is also daily becoming more evident that a high degree of cooperation will be required from developing countries as well as from private investors to ensure a continued flow of resources and technology to the poor countries. The same kind of competent cooperation increasingly will be required to agree on a new regime for the oceans and to protect the global environment.

3. *Study of the international economic order is needed to identify elements of unfairness to the poor countries.* The clearest evidence of asymmetry in the present global economic systems is the fact that only one-fifth of the world product is consumed by three-fourths of the world's population. This global disparity in wealth is reflected in institutional arrangements. For example, the developing countries receive only one-fourth of the total distribution of the IMF's Special Drawing Rights. We believe that similar asymmetries exist in the fields of trade, investment, science and technology, the exploitation of the resources of the oceans, and private money markets. Others disagree. Therefore one conclusion of this chapter is that scholarly work is needed to identify the extent of asymmetries in each of the components of the international economic order.

4. *Very little research on the international economic order is being conducted by developing-country scholars.* Not much work has been done by scholars in the developing countries on the components of the international economic order. Therefore these countries generally have relied largely on foreign—mostly Western—scholars to advise them. Most of the work that is being carried out by scholars of developing countries in this area is concerned with the internal problems of their national economies.

5. *There are major gaps in understanding the interaction between the international economic order and the developing countries.* This is true of scholarship everywhere, not just in the poor countries. This conclusion was

confirmed in consultations with scores of scholars, scholarly institutions, and development practitioners in both rich and poor countries. Therefore we conclude that support of study in the neglected areas by scholars in rich as well as poor countries should be a high priority for institutions financing research.

6. *Research results need better dissemination.* Much of the scholarly work proposed in this chapter would be oriented toward making specific changes in the international economic order that benefit developing countries. Its influence would depend not only on the quality of the work done, but also on the methods used to disseminate and apply the results of research. For example, the applicability of research work on developing countries might be enhanced if its prospective users participated in the preparation and implementation of such projects. The OECD Development Centre is undertaking an analysis of the methods and relative success of dissemination of research results in collaboration with the governments of developed countries that are members of OECD's Development Assistance Committee, and selected developing countries. The outcome of this project will merit careful consideration by those interested in ensuring that research conclusions are put to good use.

Action Recommendations

1. *Support for scholarly work on the international economic order by developing-country scholars.* The poor countries can do very little about the way the international economic order impinges on their development without a much better understanding of each of its components. Therefore a central theme running throughout this chapter is that developing countries should be helped to expand and improve their own scholarly work on the components of the international economic order so that they can deal more effectively with these outside economic forces and share increasingly in their control and—where appropriate—their reform.

2. *Support for mutually reinforcing scholarly work in several developing countries to help identify goals that are common to these countries as a group, and to prepare for bargaining collectively to achieve these goals.* It is not enough for developing-country scholars to know more about the international economic order. By agreeing on topics for coordinated scholarly work, developing countries can increase their knowledge and understanding of such topics and their collective bargaining power either to deal with the international order as it stands or to reform it. This is not an effort to pit the developing countries in a political confrontation against the rich countries. On the contrary, much of the present fruitless confrontation arises from lack of scholarship. While it is possible for scholarship to sharpen the conflict between rich and poor, we believe that it can in the long run reduce acrimony by helping to identify realistic bargaining goals and providing a solid factual foundation for negotiations to achieve those

goals. While some subjects are matters of ideology and not amenable to scholarly consensus, this is not true of others. In the latter cases, once the facts are widely agreed upon among scholars, political negotiations can proceed much more economically, with less wrangling over erroneous or exaggerated allegations.

3. *Support for scholarship to widen knowledge of development experience throughout the world.* Such knowledge will help developing countries design their own development policies and shape their economic, political, and social systems to fit their own values. As indicated earlier, developing-country spokesmen do not believe they have been free to make such choices for themselves. To gain that freedom will require more than acquiescence by the industrialized powers—both capitalist and socialist. It will require much hard work to examine the various methods that have been employed to solve problems in China, Taiwan, North and South Korea, Brazil, Chile, Cuba, Hong Kong, Singapore, and other countries, and to sort out whether any of these solutions might be applicable to the specific problems of other individual developing countries.

There is room in this area of research for studies by scholars in both rich and poor countries. The former are eager to examine and to document the experience of China as they are already doing in other countries. As these reports are published, resources should be available to enable scholars in each developing country to evelute the experience to see whether any of it is applicable to any of their particular problems. One hears with increasing frequency the assertion that developing countries can only free themselves from outside influences by cutting off contact with the outside and turning inward. To be sure, in the cases of some problems, outside experience may not be applicable, and indigenous solutions may have to be found. On the other hand, we suggest that in many cases, the best way for a developing country to find the solutions to its problems is to free itself from exclusive reliance on one outside model and to look over the entire range of developmental experiences around the world, selecting and adopting whatever may be applicable. Far from cutting itself off from outside experience, it can seek to deepen and vary its exposure to ideas from the outside world to assist it in setting its own policies for development. Financing institutions should give a high priority to this kind of scholarship by both rich-country and poor-country scholars.

4. *Support for scholarly work to increase our understanding of public opinion in the rich countries on the subject of the development of the poor countries.* Does public opinion in the rich countries adequately understand the extent of interdependence among all nations? What is the reason for the low priority which enlightened public opinion—particularly in the United States—assigns to the development of the poor countries?

**Appendix—Institutions with Research
in Progress or Recently Completed on
Relations between Developed and
Developing Nations***

This Appendix summarizes the results of an inventory of serious academic, governmental, and institutional research in progress or recently completed that bears on the themes explored in this chapter. Although it is not a comprehensive list by any means, it does provide a good overview of significant research activities in the developed and developing countries.

Questionnaires inquiring as to the nature of research projects recently completed and currently under way were sent to 230 research institutions and government agencies in both rich and poor countries. Replies were received from some 100 organizations, 26 of which were in developing countries.

Developed Countries

The replies from developed countries indicate that three subject areas were generating the most interest among institutions either conducting or financing research: international trade (including adjustment assistance, regional integration, and invisibles), with projects reported by 39 organizations; private foreign direct investment, with projects reported by 26 institutions; and the transfer of science and technology, with projects reported by 19 organizations.

The areas which have claimed the smallest percentage of developed-country research include: the external debt of developing countries, poor-country access to rich-country money markets, and development education in the rich countries.

Developing Countries

Our sample of institutions in developing countries was small, since only 26 of our questionnaires to institutions in this category were returned. Of these, only 14 had any research completed or under way on the international economic order. Specifically, 8 organizations indicated they had research projects in the overall field of trade; 7 were investigating foreign investment; and 6 were concerned with the transfer of science and technology between rich and poor nations. None of the 26 institutions which replied are conducting research in the

*Prepared by Susan Sammartano.

fields of private money markets, international management of ocean resources, the negotiating strategies of developing countries, the impact on poor countries of rich-country values, or development education in rich countries. A number of the responding institutions stated explicitly that most of their research concentrated on internal issues such as development strategies and planning techniques, rather than on the international economic order.

Multilateral Organizations

Questionnaires were sent to all of the larger multilateral organizations. In addition, we examined the published lists of research programs of several others. Of the 18 institutions surveyed, only 4 have headquarters located outside the developed countries.

Twelve of the multilateral organizations whose research programs we surveyed were currently conducting or had recently completed projects in the field of international trade; 10 were investigating foreign investment; and 9 were studying the international transfer of science and technology. Generally, the research of these institutions is more involved with the study of the international monetary system than are individual research and governmental institutions in both rich and poor countries.

Multilateral organizations were found to place little or no emphasis on research concerning poor-country access to developed-country money markets or development education in the developed countries.

Table 7-1

Institutions with Research in Progress or Recently Completed on Relations between Developed and Developing Nations

	Transfer of Values	Trade	Foreign Private Investment	Internat. Monetary System	External Debt	Foreign Assistance	Internat. Migration	Access to Capital Markets	Environment	An Ocean Regime	Science & Technology	Negotiating Strategies	Development Education
Argentina													
Instituto Torcuato Di Tella													
Universidad Nacional De Tucuman		X					X		X		X		
Australia													
University of Sydney, Dept. of Economics				X									
Austria													
Vienna Institute of Development	X												
Brazil													
University of Brasilia Department of Economics			X										
Bangladesh													
Bangladesh Institute of Development Economics			X										
Chile													
Catholic University of Chile (CEPLAN)	X		X								X		
France													
Institut. De Recherche Sur le Droit Des Pays En Voie De Developpement		X								X			
Societe D'Etudes Pour Le Developpement Economique et Social	X										X	X	

Table 7-1 (cont.)

	Transfer of Values	Trade	Foreign Private Investment	Internat. Monetary System	External Debt	Foreign Assistance	Internat. Migration	Access to Capital Markets	Environment	An Ocean Regime	Science & Technology	Negotiating Strategies	Development Education
Germany													
German Development Institute						X							
Hamburg Institute for International Economics		X	X	X							X		
Institut fuer Weltwirtschaft University of Kiel		X	X								X		
IFO-Institut fuer Wirtschaftsforschung, Center of African Studies		X											
Research Institute for International Technological-Economic Cooperation		X	X								X		
India													
Institute for Social and Economic Change				X	X		X				X		
National Council of Applied Economic Research			X								X		
Indonesia													
Institute for Economic and Social Research		X											
Italy													
Centro Per il Credito Agrario Nei Pasei in Via de Sviluppo				X									
Institute for Studies on Economic Development		X											
Japan													
Institute of Developing Economies		X	X			X					X		

Institution								
Mexico								
Centro de Estudio Monetarios Latinoamericanos						X	X	X
Netherlands								
Development Research Inst.	X	X		X		X	X	
Institute of Social Studies	X				X		X	
Netherlands Economic Inst.	X						X	
Philippines								
National Science Development Board				X	X			
Senegal								
Institute Africain de Developpement et de Planification		X	X	X	X	X	X	
Singapore								
Economic Research Centre, University of Singapore						X	X	
Sweden								
Institute for International Economic Studies						X	X	
Swedish International Development Authority						X		
Thailand								
Economic Cooperation Centre for Asian and Pacific Region		X				X	X	
Uganda								
Makerere Institute of Social Research		X		X	X	X	X	
United Kingdom								
Girton College, Cambridge					X			
Institute of Commonwealth		X		X	X	X	X	

Table 7-1 (cont.)

	Transfer of Values	Trade	Foreign Private Investment	Internat. Monetary System	External Debt	Foreign Assistance	Internat. Migration	Access to Capital Markets	Environment	An Ocean Regime	Science & Technology	Negotiating Strategies	Development Education
Studies, Univ. of London													
Institute of Development Studies, Univ. of Sussex		X	X			X					X		
Intermediate Technology Development Group											X		
International African Inst.		X					X		X				
National Institute of Economic and Social Research		X											
Political and Economic Planning		X											
Royal Institute of International Affairs		X	X			X		X			X	X	
Trade Policy Research Centre			X										
University of Cambridge, Dept. of Applied Economics		X	X										
University of Strathclyde, Overseas Development Unit		X	X								X		
United States													
African-American Scholars Council		X					X						
African Studies Association Brandeis University*		X	X	X		X							
Agency for International Development	X	X	X	X	X	X	X	X	X		X		
American Council of Voluntary Agencies for Foreign Service						X							
Brookings Institution		X	X	X		X			X		X		
Council of the Americas		X	X							X			
Cornell Univ. Graduate School		X											

Organization	1	2	3	4	5	6	7	8	9
Development Advisory Service of Center for Internat. Affairs									X
Harvard Univ. Business School								X	
Institute for Policy Studies						X		X	X
International Development Research Center, Indiana University					X				X
International Insurance Advisory Council of U.S. Chamber of Commerce					X				X
Kettering Foundation	X								
Massachusetts Institute of Technology		X							
Midwest Universities' Consortium for International Activities						X		X	X
National Academy of Sciences		X							
New York University								X	
Pennsylvania State Univ. School of Earth Sciences									X
Resources for the Future		X	X	X					
Social Science Research Council				X					X
Southwest Research Instit.		X						X	X
Stanford Research Instit.								X	X
United States Department of Agriculture			X						X
U.S. Department of State								X	X
University of Florida, Agricultural Experiment Station									X
University of Illinois, Agricultural Experiment Station								X	X
University of North Carolina									X

Table 7-1 (cont.)

	Transfer of Values	Trade	Foreign Private Investment	Internat. Monetary System	External Debt	Foreign Assistance	Internat. Migration	Access to Capital Markets	Environment	An Ocean Regime	Science & Technology	Negotiating Strategies	Development Education
Univ. of Pennsylvania, Wharton School			X										
Williams College, Center for Development Economics		X									X		
Multi-national Organizations													
Asian Development Bank		X				X							
FAO		X								X	X	X	
GATT		X	X										
IBRD/IDA	X	X	X	X	X	X		X	X	X	X		
ILO	X	X	X				X		X	X	X		
IMF		X	X	X	X								
OECD	X	X	X	X	X	X	X	X	X	X	X	X	
OECD Development Center		X	X	X	X	X	X	X					
U.N. Advisory Committee on the Application of Science and Technology to Development											X		
U.N. Asian Institute for Economic Development and Planning		X	X			X							
UNCTAD	X	X	X			X			X	X	X	X	
U.N. Economic Commission for Africa		X	X	X		X	X				X	X	
UNESCO											X		
UNIDO	X	X	X								X		
UNITAR											X		

U.N. Seabed Committee									X			
Developing Country Sub-Total	0	8	7	2	1	2	4	0	2	0	6	0	0
Developed Country Sub-Total	3	39	26	6	2	13	7	2	5	4	19	3	1
Multinational Organizations Sub-Total	5	12	10	4	3	7	3	2	4	5	10	4	0
Totals	8	59	43	12	6	22	14	4	11	9	35	7	1

Notes

1. For an elaboration of this thesis, see William Rich, *Smaller Families Through Social and Economic Progress*, Monograph No. 7 (Washington, D.C.: Overseas Development Council, 1973).

2. An examination of research needs in the field of trade is also found in Harald B. Malmgren, *Trade and Investment Relations between Developed and Developing Nations: A Review of the State of Knowledge*, Occasional Paper No. 2 (Washington, D.C.: Overseas Development Council, 1971).

3. *Industry and Trade in Some Developing Countries*, Oxford University Press, New York, 1971.

4. A listing of sources of information on the study of foreign private investment and multinational enterprises can be obtained from the Overseas Development Council, 1717 Massachusetts Avenue, N.W., Washington, D.C. 20036. Two recent reviews of foreign investment and the multinational corporation are: "The Multinational Corporation," *The Annals of the American Academy of Political and Social Science*, September 1972; and Harald Malmgren, *Trade and Investment Relations between Developed and Developing Countries: A Review of the State of Knowledge*, Occasional Paper No. 2 (Washington, D.C.: Overseas Development Council, 1971).

5. The results of the recent survey sponsored by the Overseas Development Council, "Survey of Attitudes and Opinions of Adult Citizens of the United States Toward International Development," will be published by the Overseas Development Council in the fall of 1973.

6. See Neil H. Jacoby, *An Evaluation of U.S. Economic Aid to Free China, 1951-1965*, A.I.D. Discussion Paper No. 11 (Washington, D.C.: U.S. Agency for International Development, Bureau for the Far East, 1966).

8 Future East-West Economic Issues

Franklyn D. Holzman
Tufts University

Introduction

The purposes of this chapter are to point out some of the major policy issues in East-West economic relations which are likely to arise over the next twenty years, to indicate present state of knowledge on these issues, and to suggest an agenda for further research.[a] Some of the economic issues to be discussed below will be important regardless of the paths taken by international politics. The importance of others, however, will depend strongly on political developments. The major political question mark, to my mind, is whether progress toward East-West détente of the past 10-15 years will continue or whether at some point in the next few decades cold war will be resumed. At this point in time, the probability of a resumption of cold war seems highly unlikely. However, it must be recognized that our sages have been notoriously myopic when it has come to predicting turning points in political trends. If cold war should resume, then it would be extremely valuable to examine carefully the political and economic issues connected with policies of economic warfare. On the other hand, a whole host of other problems gain in importance under conditions of stable East-West détente. There are other possible political trends which will affect economic policies, but these are of somewhat lesser importance and will not be separated out for special treatment. Among these are: (1) the cohesiveness exhibited in East-East and West-West political and economic relationships, respectively (e.g., Sino-Soviet relationships); and (2) the extent to which capitalist economies turn Socialist or Communist and vice versa, with particular reference to the nations of the Third World. Economic developments may also affect the political climate with subsequent implications for economic issues. For example, if Soviet food (especially grain) and Eastern European resource constraints are not satisfactorily resolved or if growth rates of GNP and productivity continue to slow up, the Communist nations will have an impetus to look to the West even more than

---

My debts in writing this chapter are too numerous to mention. I am especially indebted for helpful suggestions, however, to Harold Berman, Gregory Grossman, Charles Kindleberger and Raymond Vernon.

[a]As an economist, I plead incomplete knowledge on some of the political issues presented below.

they already do for food and resources, on the one hand, and technology on the other.

In the first section which follows, we assume a return to cold war. Subsequently, the general assumption will be détente of unspecified degree. In most cases it will be obvious how the problems being discussed are affected by the state of East-West political relations. The topics to be covered in the sections below are:

1. Economic Warfare
2. International Monetary Problems
3. Trade and Credits: Comparative Advantage and Balance of Payments
4. Commercial Policy
5. Joint Ventures
6. Technology
7. Arms Control and Disarmament
8. Environment
9. Inequality, Resources, and Population

Sections 2-6 are stock in trade topics for economists and are dealt with most extensively, especially 2-4. Sections 7-9 are dealt with much more briefly not because they are not just as important but because they are either not primarily "economic" or because they are not primarily "East-West" and are treated in more detail elsewhere.

East is defined here to include all of the Communist nations. The questions raised below regarding the Eastern nations and their economic policies will usually apply more forcefully to the USSR and to Eastern Europe than to the Asian nations including Mainland China, about which much less is known today.

Economic Warfare

Since the end of World War II, the United States has been practicing economic warfare of different degrees of intensity against the various Communist nations. In this, they have been abetted, usually reluctantly however, by the nations of Western Europe. The purpose of this economic warfare has been to weaken the Communist nations, economically and militarily. The Communist nations have, on their part, also purposively restricted their economic contacts with the Western nations, but being the smaller and poorer of the two blocs, their action has been more of a defensive than offensive operation.[b] On the other hand, the U.S.S.R. has practiced economic warfare against several nations including some other Communist nations, viz., Yugoslavia, Albania, and China, a fact which has been thoroughly documented (Freedman, 1970).

---

[b]This should not be taken to imply that American policies were entirely offensive. Certainly the introduction of export controls in 1949 were in part a reaction to the consolidation of Eastern Europe in 1947-48, the Berlin Blockade, etc.

The United States economic offensive against the Communist nations has been carried out on a broad front. American exporters have been forbidden to ship a wide variety of so-called strategic commodities to the Communist nations under the Export Control Act of 1949. Western European exporters were proscribed by the Mutual Defense Assistance Act or "Battle Act" of 1951 from shipping a similar, but smaller, list of goods to the East on pain of withdrawal of American aid. Total embargos were or still are in effect on U.S. exports to Cuba, China, North Korea, and North Vietnam. American exporters and banks have been forbidden to extend credits (other than normal 90-day commercial credits) or loans to most of the nations of Eastern Europe and to the U.S.S.R. under the Johnson Act of 1934 because of World War I debt or Lend-Lease (in the case of the U.S.S.R.) defaults. Since all other nations have been excused from these provisions of the Johnson Act by virtue of having signed the Bretton Woods Agreements in 1944, a fact not closely related to their present debt-paying abilities, it can be inferred that the continued application of the Johnson Act to the Communist nations constitutes economic warfare. Finally,[c] the United States does not grant most-favored-nation treatment to the Communist nations with the exception of Poland and Yugoslavia. This is undoubtedly viewed as economic warfare by some American policymakers but it does have other more profound roots related to the differences in the manner of conducting trade between free market and centrally planned economies and these will be discussed in a later section.

As the cold war has declined, so has the intensity of American economic warfare through a combination of legislative and administrative actions. Should there be a change in trend in the political climate, there will undoubtedly be pressures to reconstitute trade controls against the Communist nations. Against this possibility, it would seem worthwhile to study, retrospectively, the effects and effectiveness, both political and economic, of these U.S. policies since World War II. Economic warfare in general and in particular has been the subject of many investigations (Wu, 1952; Wiles, 1968, Chaps. 16-18; Freedman, 1970) as has the case in hand (Adler-Karlsson, 1968). Nevertheless much remains to be done—or redone. There is considerable question, for example, as to the rationality of our choice of potential exports to be put on the proscribed list (cf. Holzman, 1971). How were these choices made? Were the target nations' comparative disadvantages taken into account? If so, why weren't agricultural products on the list? To what extent were commodities on our (and our allies') proscribed list obtained elsewhere? To what extent were our export controls circumvented by exports of American subsidiaries in Europe and Japan? To what extent did our policy of denial force the target nations to become independent of us, thereby strengthening rather than weakening them over the medium and longer run? How were our (and our allies') export controls administered? What kind of value judgments intruded themselves at the operating levels in the U.S. Dept. of Commerce? How much business (foreign exchange!) have our exporters lost to Western Europe? to all nations? as a result

[c]Many minor practices which discriminate against the Communist nations could be listed.

of export and credit controls on the U.S.S.R. and Eastern Europe? (Cf. Montias, 1970; Harvey, 1966) By how much would our balance of payments have been improved if our controls had been no greater than those of other nations and/or limited to only the most crucial military and technologically-advanced commodities? To what extent did implementation of the Battle Act hurt the economies of our allies? How much have our policies cost the economies of the U.S.S.R. and Eastern Europe? Cuba and China? By denying the Comecon nations many products, did our policies lead to the overcommittment of resources in the early 1950s, the tensions which caused uprisings in Poland and Hungary in 1956, thence the reforms of the 1960s? What has been the balance of economic pluses and minuses of our policies? These are some of the economic questions which need further work.

The political wisdom of our economic warfare policies has been questioned many times: how these policies treated the U.S.S.R. and Eastern Europe much too homogeneously, insufficiently exploiting their differences; maintained the embargo against Mainland China for much too long a time, especially after the Sino-Soviet rift; by our harsh policy, made a hostile "Albania" or "China" out of Cuba instead of a friendly "Yugoslavia"; and so forth. In light of changing Sino-Soviet and Soviet-East European relations, what kind of political policies do we wish to follow? In view of what we know of the effects and effectiveness of economic warfare, to what extent should changes in political posture be accompanied by changes in economic policies? The whole area of the desirable interrelationships between political and economic policies in the East-West field deserves study. The temptation to use economic sanctions whenever there is a political dispute seems irresistible to some policymakers.[d] Should there be an international agreement to free international trade of politics except where national security is involved? Is this hopelessly naive? Are there any instances of serious political and diplomatic crises which have not lead to economic sanctions? If so, how do these situations differ from those which have led to sanctions?

A related issue has to do with the nationalization and expropriation of Western enterprises, investments, and properties by nations like Cuba, Chile, and Egypt. It seems inevitable that, over the next 15-20 years, some smaller nations will turn Socialist or Communist, either through evolution or revolution, or will decide to nationalize selected industries for other reasons. In anticipation of such developments, further multifaceted studies are in order which view the problem from the standpoints of international law, economics, and politics (Borchard, 1928; Katzavor, 1964; Lillich, 1965; White, 1962). The direct economic problem is what compensation, if any, is appropriate to the former owners of a nationalized industry? In this connection, not only is there a need for agreement on principles of estimation, but also a need to arrive at some

[d]The most recent instance (September 1972) is Senator Javits' proposal that the *U.S.* withhold MFN status from the U.S.S.R. until they remove the emigration tax from Soviet citizens (Jews).

agreement for international, rather than unilateral national determination of amounts of compensation. Indirectly, this raises many issues having to do with multinational firms, direct foreign investment, and imperialism—topics on which there is already a vast and well-known literature. The political wisdom of repeating our response to Cuban expropriation, regardless of the "justice" of the case, needs reexamination.

International Monetary Problems

As trade between East and West increases, particularly if the political climate warms, there will be pressures to include the Eastern nations in the International Monetary Fund and, in general, to integrate their operations into Western financial arrangements.[e] With Western international monetary arrangements presently (September 1972) in such a state of flux, some may feel that it is premature to worry about changing the financial institutions of the socialist nations. However, the differences between the two systems are, at this time, so profound that ultimate objectives are not likely to be seriously affected by the outcome of the present turmoil in the west (but see the last paragraph of this section).

The differences referred to are epitomized by the fact that, with minor exceptions, the currencies of the socialist nations are completely inconvertible and their exchange rates do not function as real prices but simply as disembodied accounting units.[f] Socialist currency inconvertibility is more dramatic than its counterpart under capitalism. Under capitalism, inconvertibility usually means that residents are not allowed to convert domestic currency into foreign currencies in order to limit imports. Sometimes the inconvertibility may be restricted to, say, capital but not current transactions. Socialist inconvertibility applies to virtually all transactions and not only to residents but to nonresidents as well. Foreigners are forbidden to take the domestic currency out of the country or, if they have succeeded in doing so, from bringing it back in again or exchanging it for other currencies. Socialist inconvertibility stems in part from ordinary balance-of-payments pressures which fast-growing, fully-employed economies often experience. It (particularly nonresident inconvertibility) is also due to the kind of central planning with direct controls practiced in all of these nations, at least until the mid-1960s. Under this system, the outputs and prices of most important commodities are determined by the central planning board and a large percentage of inter-enterprise and enterprise-organization transactions are planned in advance without the mediation of market mechanisms. Under these circumstances, foreign importers and exporters can only trade in

---

[e]Rumania was admitted to IMF membership in November 1972.

[f]By the term disembodied, I mean that when the exchange rate is used to convert a price in foreign currency into domestic currency, the price in domestic currency usually has little, if any, relationship to other domestic prices.

goods where the trade has been planned in advance. A foreign importer is not allowed to come into the domestic market and compete with domestic enterprises for goods, particularly intermediate products, because this would upset the plan and would disturb the production schedules of many enterprises. In effect, foreigners who might hold bloc currencies, with the exception of tourists and diplomatic personnel whose purchases are restricted to consumers' goods, are forbidden from spending them freely. This has been dubbed "commodity inconvertibility" by Altman (1960) to distinguish it from the more normal case of "currency inconvertibility." A second reason for "commodity inconvertibility," in addition to the need to safeguard the integrity of the plan, is the fact that the internal prices of the centrally planned economies are for the most part too irrational to allow foreigners to shop around freely. Many commodities, for example, are priced below cost and their export would involve a loss to the economy.

It is easy to understand why, under the circumstances outlined above, the exchange rates of bloc currencies do not function as real prices. The supercession of market forces by planners' commands implies that the exchange rate is unnecessary and the existence of irrational internal prices implies that no single exchange rate could do the job.

In fact, the socialist nations trade with each other and with Western nations at world prices. Among themselves, strict bilateral balancing of accounts takes place as a result of inconvertibility.[g] In East-West trade, bilateral balancing is avoided to the extent that foreign exchange earned as a result of surpluses with some countries is used to support deficits with others. As noted, unlike the case of capitalist nations, deficits are not supported by having foreigners hold one's own currency. Since domestic currencies are never exchanged for other currencies, the exchange rates need not function as real prices. The only function of the official rate is to enable a nation to report its trade balance in its own currency rather than in the foreign currencies (or prices) at which transactions actually take place. The trade balance in domestic currency so arrived at is unrelated to the value of the same products in actual domestic prices and a further conversion is necessary to include these products in the national income accounts. To facilitate decisions regarding what is to be traded and with whom, irrational prices are notionally adjusted by the planners and commodity by commodity notional exchange rates are, in effect, calculated, thereby bypassing the official exchange rate (Holzman, 1968).

The Comecon nations have striven since 1957 to eliminate the rigid bilateralism into which their trade has been confined as a result of inconvertibility. These efforts, which have been administrative rather than economic in nature,[h] have not met with success since the root causes of inconvertibility have not been

[g]Where bilateral balancing has not taken place because of credits or failures by one partner to fulfill deliveries, the creditor nation has often been saddled for long periods with an inconvertible currency which it cannot use to finance, for example, debts with the West. Czechoslovakia has recently been in this unfortunate position.

[h]As, for example, by the establishment of a Comecon Bank through which all intra-bloc transactions are recorded in so-called "transferable" rubles.

touched. That is to say, at least until "commodity inconvertibility" is eliminated, intra-bloc trade will remain bilateral. And the elimination of "commodity inconvertibility" fundamentally requires decentralized planning including opening domestic markets to foreign buyers and sellers and noncomitantly, of course, the establishment of rational internal prices organically related through a real exchange rate to external prices. East-West trade is conducted on a relatively multilateral basis through use of convertible currencies and gold. In this respect, the socialist nations are not much different from any small LDC which operates primarily with major currencies and whose own currency plays a very small, if any, role in international trade. In theory, convertible currencies might be used to multilateralize intra-bloc trade. In practice, this does not and cannot happen because convertible currencies have so much more value to the Socialist nations when spent in Western than in Eastern markets.

This stark picture is changing somewhat as a result of the internal and foreign trade reforms in some of the Eastern European nations, particularly Hungary and Czechoslovakia before the 1968 intervention (Brown and Marer, 1970). The Hungarian reform has involved considerable decentralization of internal transactions and some rationalization of prices internally; externally, a few producing and consuming enterprises are now being allowed to deal directly with Western importers and exporters. Unfortunately, the reforms in most of the other Comecon nations, particularly the U.S.S.R., do not involve much substitution of market mechanisms for direct controls.

Given these general characteristics, what kind of changes are necessary for an integration of the Socialist and capitalist international monetary worlds? The possibilities of integration will be much greater, of course, if the Socialist reforms proceed steadily and along Hungarian lines than if the Soviet reform model prevails. The U.S.S.R. reform will be crucial since the U.S.S.R. is the dominant economic and political power in the bloc. What are the prospects for a real reform in the U.S.S.R.? What are the political and economic forces for or against such a reform? How much beyond Hungary must a nation go before a convertible currency and a "real" exchange rate is possible? What light does Yugoslavian experience have to shed on the question? Is it possible for one or two countries in the Socialist group to establish convertibility through such reforms and still maintain the same degree of cohesion with the other Socialist countries? Would it not be incompatible for a "reformed" nation with convertible currency to conduct the preponderance of its trade with other Socialist nations via planned bilaterally-balanced trade? If the answer is "yes," wouldn't the U.S.S.R. oppose such reforms in the other Comecon countries?

Suppose the present Soviet model prevails over the next twenty years. It would seem impossible under present regulations for nations with nonexchange rates and inconvertible currencies (especially commodity inconvertibility) to be members in any meaningful sense of the International Monetary Fund! Are there any techniques aside from drastic internal economic reform for eliminating or bypassing commodity inconvertibility? With a minimum of disruption to the plan, the Socialist nations might open their consumers' goods markets to foreign importers using the foreign exchange thereby earned to import substitute products for the domestic market. Another possibility might be for the Socialist nations each to provide buffer stocks of standard commodities at fixed and acceptable prices into which their currencies could be converted by foreigners—in effect, the establishment of a commodity standard. Would a combination of such measures suffice to reduce or eliminate commodity inconvertibility? Would it be possible to bypass the problem by allowing the development of a free market in such currencies reflected in a fluctuating market rate of exchange?[i] Such arrangements would only be possible, of course, if the Socialist nations allowed their currencies to be held by foreigners out of the country. Are there any other devices for devaluing a non-exchange rate? In substance, (in contrast to theory) are the socialist nations *much* different in East-West trade from the LDCs and other small nations whose currencies are not much used, if at all? Could the IMF, in any case, admit this group of nations whose intra-trade relations can hardly be called "monetary"? Recently, the U.S.S.R. has established subsidiaries of its central bank in several Western nations. These banks have engaged in joint credit operations with Western banks. What implications if any would expanded operations of this sort have for the convertibility problem? To .overcome the disadvantages of bilateralism and inconvertibility in trade with Socialist nations, "swapping" (of unwanted goods) and "switching" (of unwanted currencies) markets have developed in Western Europe and these do a multimillion dollar business. What potential does this institution have for resolving the inconvertibility problem and at what cost?[j]

Trade and Credits: Comparative Advantage and Balance of Payments

Over the past ten years, the Socialist nations have played the role of the LDC vis-à-vis the major western nations in the sense that they want to import more than they can export to the West, their excess demand is concentrated on technologically advanced machinery and equipment, and wherever possible they would like to buy on medium- and long-term credits. There is considerable question in the minds of many Western observers as to whether a greatly expanded East-West trade is in the cards over the next few decades, even if all restrictions on trade are lifted, and as to how the Eastern nations will pay back substantial credits if such credits are extended.[k] East-West joint ventures have avoided this latter transfer problem, so far, by providing for profits and repayments to be made in kind in the products of the projects in question (below). Barter-type arrangements of this variety are, of course, very limited in

---

[i]It might well be impossible under posited conditions to generate a market of sufficient depth to yield meaningful prices.

[j]For a discussion of payments in convertible currency in connection with joint investment ventures, see the section "Joint Ventures," below.

[k]East Europe and the U.S.S.R. are each estimated to have already a convertible currency debt with Western Europe of some $2 billion (*The Morgan Guarantee Survey*, Sept. 1972, p. 8).

their applicability to arrangements with private traders and could not be depended upon as a means of finance in a greatly expanded East-West trade.

How will East-West trade develop; more particularly, what will the East export to the West? The U.S.S.R. will export more raw materials but, in fact, with internal demand catching up to output in petroleum, raw material exports in aggregate may not increase by too much. Some scope would appear to exist for expanded Soviet exports of manufactured products. But can this be realized without drastic changes in marketing techniques and are such changes likely to occur? Eastern Europe's prospects appear poorer than the U.S.S.R.'s. For one thing, they are a raw material short area and do not have this type of easy export to fall back on. With regard to manufacturing, all of the Eastern European nations suffer the same disadvantage noted for the Soviets. Internal and external reforms appear somewhat more probable in Eastern Europe than in the U.S.S.R. and under the proper reforms, manufacturing technology and exporting techniques may improve. Eastern Europe and the U.S.S.R., even with improved marketing techniques must face up to the fact that their manufactured products are generally regarded as inferior to those available in Western Europe because, some think, with central planning the producing enterprises do not have to meet competition either at home or in other Socialist markets. Is this likely to change with reforms? Can the Socialist nations, in any case, export more of their manufactured products to the LDCs in order to earn foreign exchange to finance their deficits with the advanced Western nations? Or is this not a solution because of (a) Western competition in these markets and (b) unwillingness of the LDCs to lose hard currency to the Socialist nations?

The sketchy picture which emerges above and which is commonly accepted is one which casts doubts on the ability of the U.S.S.R. and East Europe to balance their convertible currency accounts over the next few decades because of inability to provide sufficient hard currency exports. Is this a valid conclusion?[1] Does economic theory not tell us that every nation must have a comparative advantage in some products as well as comparative disadvantages in others? The two Leontief paradox-type studies done of the U.S.S.R. (Rosefielde, 1972; McMillan, 1972) show that that country's exports and imports, in aggregate and in particular markets, have factor proportions which make sense in terms of a Heckscher-Ohlin model. So the law of comparative advantage has not been repealed in at least this nonmarket economy with its irrational prices, a result which was not on the face of it to be confidently expected! Similar studies for the nations of Eastern Europe would be useful.

If comparative advantage is there, perhaps the fault lies in the balance-of-payments adjustment mechanism. A nation which has a deficit in its balance of payments presumably can get into balance by devaluing its currency. This option is not a meaningful one for the Socialist nations since, as noted above, their exchange rates are not real prices and they must simply trade at world prices regardless of the level or structure of internal prices. How can a Socialist country

---

[1]It is certainly reminiscent of the now disproved "permanent dollar shortage" hypothesis of twenty years ago.

perform the equivalent of a devaluation with regard to its exports? Presumably simply by selling existing exports at lower (than world) prices than before and by attempting to sell exportables abroad which previously had been deemed unprofitable for export at world prices. The latter policy might be pursued, but there is question about the former! For wouldn't selling at below-world prices run the Socialist nations afoul of anti-dumping laws? (See "Commercial Policy" below). Aren't they, in effect, precluded from really serious price competition as a result of the fact that they cannot disprove dumping charges in the way a private capitalist exporter can (or doesn't need to) after his nation devalues its currency? The answers to these latter two questions would appear in general to be "yes" although there would undoubtedly be many exceptions. If bloc currencies remain inconvertible, the extent of this problem and possible solutions should be investigated. The problem is one more serious because, at present at least, price competition is easier for the socialist nations than competition on styling, packaging, servicing, and on any of the dimensions related to effective marketing—an area in which they definitely suffer a comparative disadvantage.

Another possible explanation of the failure of Socialist nations to compete by lowering prices still further than they have is that they may feel that additional trade is not worthwhile at more adverse terms of trade. This was the Soviet view in the early thirties when, after importing from 1925-32 the machinery and equipment most essential to industrialization, they opted for autarky and virtually withdrew from the world market. It is also not inconsistent with the well-known Prebisch approach to the trade problems of the LDCs.

A final explanation of the balance-of-payments problems of the Eastern nations is their chronic practice of "taut" or overfull employment planning. Overfull employment planning means that planned demand exceeds available supply. Under these circumstances, domestic producers and consumers will fight for exportables and more imports and thereby create pressures in the direction of balance-of-payments deterioration. As the "absorption" approach tells us, even a devaluation under these circumstances is unlikely to improve the balance of payments. Questions to be raised at this point are: Why has "taut" planning persisted despite its well-known adverse effects? (Some possible reasons are given in Holzman, 1970.) Will economic reform end "taut" planning? Are Yugoslavian inflationary pressures and balance-of-payments pressures, despite economic reform, due to "taut" planning?

A thorough study of East-West payments problems under differing assumptions is in order. Some of the differing assumptions which ought to be considered are: whether or not internal reforms are promulgated and the nature of the reforms; the degree to which the bloc preferential trading system is maintained, and, conversely, the extent to which East-West trade is increased at the expense of intra-bloc trade; the extent of convertibility, if any, of bloc currencies; possible improvements in marketing, packaging, servicing, advertising, and so forth.

Commercial Policy

As East-West trade expands, the problem of how to reconcile Eastern practices with Western "rules of the game" will become a more and more important issue. Some of these "rules" are embodied in the international monetary framework in which trade is conducted and problems in this area are discussed elsewhere in this chapter. Others fall under the rubric of commercial policy. Since World War II, the advanced Western nations have been attempting to set up the conditions and institutions which would insure "fair" trade. These efforts are partly a reaction to the chaotic state of trade before World War II, brought on by the Great Depression, which took the forms of high tariff barriers, extensive use of nontariff barriers to trade, competitive depreciations, establishment of preferential trade blocs, widespread trade discrimination, and, in consequence, a severely reduced volume of international trade and investment. Fair trade in this context means, essentially, trade which is relatively free of barriers of all kinds, which is nondiscriminatory among nations, with competitive market considerations being the sole basis on which trade decisions are made, and which does not cause unwarranted disruption of markets. Considerable progress has been made in the West since World War II toward the achievement of this goal(s). In part, this progress initially resulted from the recovery of the international monetary system which was characterized in the late 1940s and early 1950s by serious balance-of-payments disequilibria, inconvertibility, bilateralism and so forth. Otherwise, most progress has been made under the auspices of the General Agreement on Tariffs and Trade (GATT), through application of generally accepted national antidumping regulations, and general commitment by most nations not to discriminate in trade. Despite substantial progress, actual trade practices are far from the ideal. Even in theory, many exceptions are made: to protect agriculture, for factors related to state trading, for customs unions, in balance-of-payments crises, and in many other cases where domestic political and economic considerations make it difficult to always stay with the "rules of the game."

Given present institutions and methods of planning, it is inconceivable that the Socialist nations could subscribe to the "rules of the game" either in East-West or (especially) in intra-bloc trade. Intra-bloc trade suffers the special handicaps of having to be rigidly bilateral because of inconvertibility and of being planned annually, in advance, and negotiated in a package by state trading monopolies. East-West trade is much less bilateral since the Socialist nations are willing to spend convertible currencies earned in one Western nation on another's goods.[m] Further, the fact that one party to the transaction is likely to be an enterprise rather than a state trader is bound to reduce the "package" character and size of the transaction and increase the importance of commercial

[m]They are unwilling to spend them in another Socialist nation because, with East-West trade so artificially constrained, a dollar spent in the West is worth a lot more than a dollar spent in the East.

considerations. Nevertheless many serious problems remain, some of which we discuss below.[n]

Trade Barriers, Trade Agreements,
and Discrimination

Under the aegis of GATT, nations regularly get together and attempt to reduce trade barriers, mainly tariffs, among themselves. These nations offer each other most-favored-nation (MFN) treatment. Since in the Socialist nations foreign trade derives from the central plan and is conducted by state agencies, there is no need for tariffs or explicit quotas–control is exerted, in effect, by implicit quotas. Socialist nations cannot, therefore, reciprocate MFN treatment in the usual ways or engage in mutual reduction of trade barriers like other nations (Malish, 1972). In an effort to simulate reciprocation of MFN treatment, several Socialist nations did establish double- and triple-column tariffs, the lower schedules being reserved for nations granting them MFN treatment (Familton, 1970). But this is inadequate reciprocity since it only divides a given amount of trade between MFN and non-MFN nations and does not allow the foreign seller to compete more favorably on the domestic market as well–as does reduction of tariffs in free market economies. Probably for this reason, GATT required Poland to agree to increase its imports from other GATT nations by several percent a year in exchange for membership and the extension of MFN treatment. Individual Socialist nations not in GATT use this same formula on a bilateral basis in negotiating for MFN. Used on a bilateral basis, of course, it is purely discriminatory and no different from the application of a lower tariff schedule described above. While the Polish formula provides an opportunity for nondiscriminatory increases in trade, it does not guarantee it. The guaranteed increase in imports from GATT nations may be at the expense of non-GATT trade and it may be discriminatory–favoring some GATT nations over others on the basis of noncommercial considerations. Clearly, operation of the Polish formula should be investigated particularly if it is likely that other Socialist nations are going to join GATT on similar terms. How can one ensure that trade increases be nondiscriminatory? How large an increase in imports from GATT does reciprocity require? Should the increase be once and for all or annual? Should the increase be adjusted for differences between nations and changes over time in growth rates? Does it make sense to insist on nondiscriminatory *increases* in trade without even investigating whether or not previous levels and patterns are characterized by discrimination? Should the Western nations really care whether or not they are formally extended MFN by the Socialist nations so long as they themselves keep to their own rules of the game? In fact, since the Socialist nations are so short of hard currencies and don't spend them in other

[n]The classic study in this area is (Gerschenkron, 1945). Professor Gerschenkron should be prevailed upon to publish all or part of his unpublished monographic study of state trading.

Socialist nations, don't their extra earnings from being granted MFN automatically return to the West just as if MFN had been reciprocated?

Suppose now that most or all of the Socialist nations have been included in GATT and have been extended MFN treatment. Under these circumstances, their trade with each other and changes in that trade would presumably come under GATT scrutiny. Undoubtedly, they would be viewed as a kind of customs union and on these grounds would be allowed to discriminate in favor of each other just as members of the EEC are. The problems which might be raised are (1) the degree of that discrimination and (2) arbitrariness in changes in the degree of discrimination. With regard to (1) it is informative to consider that when the EEC nations formed a customs union, their percentage of intra-trade grew from 30 percent in 1958 to close to 50 percent in 1970. In comparison, the comparable percentages for the nations of Comecon were less than 15 percent prewar to around 70 percent in the 1950s. If this had been accomplished by tariffs rather than by implicit quotas, I daresay that a shift of this magnitude would have required not just the elimination of tariffs between the Socialist nations but also, say, a trebling or more of the tariffs on the products of the non-Socialist nations. The nations of Comecon, in fact, constitute the equivalent of a customs union of unprecedentedly large "preferentiality," a fact with which GATT has not yet had to content. It may be a fact which GATT will prefer to ignore so long as the future trend is for Comecon to reduce its external barriers. Some thinking about this problem would seem to be warranted.

The second question, that of arbitrariness in changes in the degree of discrimination, is likely to cause more trouble in the future, particularly if political relations in the Soviet bloc pursue no more stable a path in the future than they have in the past. This is not to say that intra-bloc political relations are necessarily less stable than in the West, but simply to take account of the fact that socialist foreign trade is more reflective of political currents than is trade among capitalist countries. This is due to the obvious fact that, in the former, foreign trade is nationalized and trade negotiations between Socialist nations is conducted by large state organizations.[o] So, for example, for a number of reasons, Rumania's trade with the Socialist nations declined from 65 percent to 52 1/2 percent between 1965 and 1967 and her trade with capitalist nations rose correspondingly. Suppose, as could very well happen, these percentages were reversed again over a two or three year period! It is unlikely that such sharp changes could occur on the basis of ordinary commercial considerations. What could happen is that, reflecting a changed political climate, the Rumanian and other Socialist trade delegations would be instructed to negotiate larger percentages of their overall planned trade with each other. Rumania's capitalist trade partners would accordingly suffer just as if Rumania had levied new and large discriminatory tariffs on imports from and exports to them.

---

[o]This is not to deny the relationship between trade and politics in a capitalist nation like, for example, United States' policies toward the U.S.S.R., China, and Cuba. My argument would be that these Western trade policies are less volatile and are typically directed almost exclusively at enemies–those outside of the system.

Other factors will cause trade with centrally planned economies to change in discrete rather than continuous ways and to be based less on commercial considerations than trade with Western nations. First, there is the simple well-known fact that in most of the Socialist nations costs and prices tend to reflect inaccurately the true value of products—and this is known in these countries; and profits and losses provide less of a guide to production and trade partly for this reason. The usual profit-loss guide is bypassed also because of the interconnectedness of the parts of the aggregate central plan and the need to use trade to avoid bottlenecks and, finally, because it is easy, with nationalized industries, to grant subsidies for losses and to remove excess profits directly into the state treasury.

Secondly, when trade is conducted by state monopolies, there is often a tendency to look not just at exports or imports, separately, and to judge each transaction on its own merits, but to view exports as payments for imports or in other ways to connect the transactions. To some extent this is also true of capitalist nations with balance-of-payments problems which are motivated to achieve bilateral balances with some of their trade partners. Along these lines, Nove (p. 111) explains that there are Italian, but no British cars in Budapest because " . . . the Italians demanded a quota for cars in their bilateral agreement and the British did not. The Italians probably obtained their quotas by . . . offering quota against quota, in respect of goods which enter without quantitative restriction from non-communist countries. . . ." (He also points out, incidentally, that there are many more Polish, Czech and East German than Italian cars in Budapest.) What the Italians and some other capitalist nations have done in trade with the Eastern nations is commonly practiced in intra-bloc trade and in East-West trade by Socialist nations.

The upshot of the preceding discussion is that, in the absence of drastic economic reforms in the Socialist nations which allow decentralization of international trade, East-West trade will undoubtedly continue to incorporate a wide variety of noncommercial considerations. In many cases, Western nations implicitly compete against each other for the trade of Socialist nations in ways which flout the accepted "rules of the game"; in other cases, third Western nation buyers and sellers are supplanted by Eastern traders who could not have made it without government support. In this connection, a number of questions come to mind. We have suggested that there is a presumption that East-West trade involves more, and more flagrant, breaches in the "rules of the game" than West-West trade. Can this presumption be tested statistically? An attempt should be made to do so. A related study has been made by Brada and Wipf (1972). East-West trade currently amounts to only about 4 percent of the trade of the Western industrial nations. If this percentage increases to, say, 10 percent in the next twenty years, would the impact be much more destructive than so far of the western trade fabric? How much of the noncommercial and discriminatory character of East-West trade is the result of practices of Western nations, particularly those which have trade agreements with the East, and their traders who treat trade with the East on a different footing from West-West trade? How much could East-West trade be "cleaned up" if the Western nations agreed to adopt a common code of operation vis-à-vis the socialist nations? Do the Western nations need a special organization (with or without the Eastern nations) in order to devise and implement a code for East-West trade? (Cf. CED, 1972.)

It has just been noted that when two countries conclude a trade agreement, this agreement is almost certainly going to involve some degree of discrimination. Yet, it seems clear that because of the institutional differences between East and West, trade agreements appear necessary if a substantial amount of trade is to be generated between the nations. From the standpoint of the centrally planned economies, the agreements are desirable because they provide the planners with the kind of certainty that planners favor in constructing their plans. The Western nation with a trade agreement which projects purchases and sales will outcompete the one without such an agreement. As noted, this involves discrimination. An important question is: is there any way of defining realistically or of achieving nondiscrimination in this context of government trade agreements?

Actually, even without trade agreements, governments have been interfering with trade in ways which contravene the "rules of the game." For example, when the president of the United States met with the premier of Japan in September 1972, he was able to return home with guarantees that the Japanese would buy certain American products and would limit the competition in our market of other products. Should the keeper of the "rules" be concerned about this? Will these practices subside if the Western nations are able to develop a better set of international monetary institutions which reduce the incidence of balance-of-payments disequilibrium?

For the Socialist nations, trade agreements are important, as noted, for incorporating foreign trade into their central plans. For the capitalist nations, they provide an umbrella under which it is possible to enlarge trade with the Socialist nations. The reason this is the case is because it is virtually impossible for western exporters and importers to investigate in any depth the needs and availabilities, respectively, of the Socialist economies. Freedom of access to enterprises in these economies, to the details of the central plans, and to other relevant data are much too restricted for the conduct of the kind of market research upon which large Western firms—the kind likely to be interested in Socialist markets—depend in making their own future plans. This raises serious questions regarding the potential for expansion of East-West trade under present institutional arrangements, even with trade agreements. What are the possibilities of greater access to producing and consuming enterprises? to more data on projected trends in these economies? What can we learn from the phenomenally rapid build-up of trade between Japan and the Socialist nations over the last fifteen years? Shouldn't the principle of nondiscrimination apply to such things as facilities to do business, offered to Western enterprises from different nations, in the Socialist bloc?

Dumping

A special commercial policy problem, closely related to some of those just discussed, is dumping. Since the early thirties, when the U.S.S.R. was accused of dumping agricultural products on then depressed Western markets, the charge has been leveled many times against Socialist nations. Most Western nations have national anti-dumping regulations and the members of GATT have, as a group, condemned dumping. Dumping means exporting your goods to another country at less than the normal value of the products, i.e., either below-cost or below domestic selling price. Dumping is viewed as undesirable by Western nations when the dumped products outcompete domestic or third country suppliers. This is because those who are dumping are unlikely to continue to do so since it usually involves a loss or abnormally low profits. In effect, it is viewed as unfair competition which also eventually may even leave the importing nation worse off than before—if the dumper, having taken over the market, raises his price above the previous level.

To the centrally planned economies, dumping is no problem. If they don't want foreign competition, they simply don't import the product; if they do want the product, then having it dumped is beneficial since it reduces its cost to them.

Socialist dumping is in fact really almost a non-problem because there is very little evidence that Socialist nations are interested in dumping or that they have often dumped (Wilczynski, Chap. 9; Pisar, Chap. 12). Basically, the foreign trade combines are instructed to sell at as high a price and earn as much foreign exchange as possible in the West. There is very little evidence that they are interested in disrupting Western markets. Difficulties arise on several counts, however. First, most Western importers would prefer to and are used to dealing with Western rather than Socialist exporters. In order to penetrate these markets, Socialist exporters are forced to sell at below the going price. What would be called cutthroat competition by a Japanese exporter is likely to be called dumping when it is a Soviet exporter in question! Second, it is in the nature of the centrally planned economies to view sales at below cost as perfectly legitimate under certain circumstances. At the macro level, as noted above, the foreign trade monopoly views exports as payment for imports. It may be worth selling some product for a loss if the foreign exchange earned in the process can be used to import a product which returns a large social profit. At the micro level, while the combines are instructed to sell at as high a price as possible, they also have even higher-priority instructions to fulfill their sales plans, i.e., to export all products which have been allocated to them for this purpose. If they have to export at a loss in order to fulfill their plan, they will do so. They will receive a state subsidy to cover the loss and a bonus for fulfilling the export plan. Failure to fulfill the export plan means no bonus. Third, it is usually difficult or impossible to prove or disprove a dumping charge against a Socialist country because of the chaotic nature of their cost/price systems, the absence of equilibrium exchange rates, and the difficulty of getting relevant cost or price data were these data deemed useful.

The problem, then, is not the occasional case of true Socialist dumping which occurs but rather the fact that Western charges of dumping are numerous and that in most instances there appears to be no way of determining their legitimacy. Both at the theoretical and policy levels, this problem deserves further attention. It will not disappear unless the Socialist nations all undertake drastic reforms; it is likely to become more pressing as East-West trade expands, particularly in the United States with its strong anti-Communist public sentiments if the U.S.S.R. is granted MFN treatment in the near future. How can the United States control this problem? Assuming that the determination of dumping by Socialist nations remains obscure, should we seek from them voluntary controls of the kind exercised by Japan to prevent competition in certain of our markets?P What are the policy options?

Comparison of Diverse Forms of
Trade Barriers

A problem which faces analysts interested in problems, particularly those related to MFN, but others as well, is the fact that the many different kinds of trade barriers employed by different nations are, for the most part, not obviously comparable. How can one compare a set of tariffs with a set of explicit quotas, with exchange controls, or in the case of the Socialist nations, with a set of implicit quotas? If it were possible to measure on a single scale these different kinds of barriers, the problems of implementing commercial policy arrangements which included the Socialist nations could be made more precise and more objective, if not easier. Techniques for comparing different kinds of trade barriers have been developed (GATT, 1958; Pryor, 1966) and have been subjected to criticism. Pryor's work, in particular, was designed to compare the explicit trade barriers of Western Europe with the implicit barriers of the Socialist nations to imports of tropical food products from the LDCs. While this method provided a good first effort, it suffers from some serious methodological problems (Holzman, 1969, 1971) and cannot be relied upon. More work on this problem is certainly warranted not only because of the light it would shed on East-West issues but for its usefulness in problem analysis and decision-making in the whole area of international economics.

PThis is the approach envisaged in the U.S.-U.S.S.R. Trade Agreement of 1972.

Joint-Ventures

Joint East-West ventures is an area of great public interest at the present time. While most persons believe that joint ventures between private capitalist and Socialist state enterprises originated some seven or eight years ago, in fact quite a number existed in the early 1920s with Soviet mining and trading concerns. Present ventures take many forms from simple exchanges of licenses and designs to cooperation involving financing, construction, production, managment, and marketing of products. Motives are also manifold. For example, on the part of the West these ventures may represent ways of getting cheap labor, assured and protected markets, large supplies of scarce raw materials (especially those with the U.S.S.R.), recently even Eastern technology. Eastern motives run more to need for capital, acquisition of technology and production techniques, and assistance in marketing products in the West (Goldman, 1969). (Some Eastern nations have joint ventures in the LDCs and in Western Europe in which their role is equivalent to the usual Western role in East-West ventures.) These ventures differ from similar ventures in the West in several respects. A major difference is that in cases where the production facility is located in a Socialist country, with the exception of Yugoslavia, Western collaborators have not been allowed to hold equity. A second major difference has been that in most cases, the Western collaborator has not received payment in money but rather in kind in the form of part of the output of the project. This reflects the inconvertibility of bloc currencies and their balance-of-payments pressures and is a moderately effective second-best technique of handling the transfer problem under these conditions.

While there is some public information on these ventures today, it is far less than is available on West-West multinational corporations, and, in fact, our ignorance is considerable. A useful first step toward reducing this ignorance would be a factual survey of past and present ventures including as many nations, East and West, as possible and indicating the range of activities, financial terms, and other characteristics of these arrangements. Studies in depth of individual ventures are in order. How successful have East-West ventures been? How do they compare, in all specifics, with West-West ventures? To what extent does the substitution of "in kind" for monetary payment relations affect the nature and success of the venture? Does it not increase the costs and uncertainty involved in each relationship and thereby reduce, relatively the number of ventures? While providing a partial solution to the balance-of-payments problems of the Eastern nations, does it not, on the other hand, contribute to trade discrimination? Recently, a few ventures have provided for payments in convertible currencies to Western collaborators. This is almost unavoidable where the venture provides goods or services to Eastern consumers (e.g. hotels). What are the convertible currency limits to ventures of this nature? In light of the convertible currency problems of the Socialist nations, is it likely that they will eventually try to take over such ventures themselves?

While balance-of-payments considerations may deter the Socialist nations from arranging payments on joint ventures in convertible currency, Western nations may also prefer a barter arrangement because of what might be called an exchange risk. If payments are to be made, say, in dollars and U.S. prices double, then the real value of the payments is only half of what it should be. Clearly, before Western investors would be willing to make such an arrangement, they would have to be protected against such a risk.[q] Two possible methods of protection come to mind. First, the contract can be denominated in gold with payment to be made in an equivalent value of any convertible currency. For this to provide a good inflation hedge, the price of gold would have to fluctuate inversely with the values of national currencies. This has not, of course, been the case.[r] A second possibility is to include in contracts an escalation clause which ties the value of interest and repayments to price level increases in the country whose currency is to serve as medium of exchange. These and other techniques of hedging the exchange risk need to be explored. If payment in convertible currency rather than in kind can be made acceptable to Western investors, the choice of investments in the Communist nations will no longer be limited largely to ventures in which payments can be made from the output of the venture.

Another question of interest relates to the impact of the one-sided equity relationship which characterizes the ventures. How does this affect: the willingness of Western enterprises to enter; the type of venture; the rate of return required; and so forth?

Yugoslavia is reported recently to have passed a law allowing some Western collaborators a 50 percent equity in some projects on their territory (e.g. hotels). Does equity in this case carry the same advantages to capitalist investors as in capitalist countries or are there restrictions of one kind or another, lower allowable rates of depreciation, and so forth which negate potential advantages? For the socialist nations, at least, this appears to be a significant ideological breakthrough—like the partial rehabilitation of the interest rate in the U.S.S.R. in the mid-sixties. What are the chances of a similar breakthrough in Eastern Europe and the U.S.S.R.? (It has been reported that Rumania has just passed a law allowing 49 percent equity.) Could Western reluctance to invest and transfer technology force the issue? What would the impact of Western equity in Socialist industry be for the basic ideological constraint against private ownership of means of production by Socialist citizens? Is this the road to convergence?

Former Secretary of Commerce Peter Peterson (1972) has raised a number of questions in connection with potential U.S.-U.S.S.R. ventures in the raw

[q]The comparable Western investment problem is the exchange-rate risk. That is, if a Frenchman invests in American industry and American prices double while French prices remain stable, then presumably the dollar will depreciate to half its value. However, the French investor is largely protected against this loss by the fact that if American prices rise by this amount, in all probability so will the value of his investment and returns (cf. Friedman, 1970).

[r]For example, the German mark was recently revalued upward in terms of gold despite the rising German price level.

materials field. He points out that some of these projects require unprecedentedly large capital inputs. This raises, in his mind, questions regarding: the appropriate balance between U.S. and Soviet investment; whether or not existing credit institutions are adequate to the requirements of such ventures and whether new credit institutions need be developed; the role of the U.S. government; form of repayment; performance guarantees and recourse against nonperformance; degree of dependency on Soviet natural resources which is appropriate; and so forth. If ventures of indicated magnitude are allowed to develop, these questions need to be investigated along with the impact on our economy (e.g. balance of payments) and international policies (U.S. capital as "hostage") of the much greater interdependence between these two giant nations.

Finally, the kinds of theoretical and empirical studies which have been developed to analyze West-West multinational corporations need to be applied to the special cases of East-West ventures (e.g., Kindleberger, 1970).

Technology

The question of technology is very important in East-West economic relations cutting across, in this survey, the areas of economic warfare, trade, and joint ventures. The United States, in particular, and the advanced Western nations in general, would appear to have a comparative advantage relative to the U.S.S.R. and other Eastern nations in products requiring advanced technology. A considerable part of East-West trade and joint ventures is motivated, especially on the part of the Eastern nations, by the desire to acquire the products of advanced technology or the advanced technology itself. Correspondingly, U.S. export controls are, and have been, concentrated on products which embody advanced technology, particularly those which may have an impact, however slight, on military potential.

Despite its importance, there seems to be little research of interest in the field which might be viewed as specific to East-West trade. This may be due to general difficulty of dealing with technology issues in economics, especially on an empirical level.

An evaluation of some of the issues in the technology area would benefit from better information on the reasons for the apparent East-West lag (Boretsky, 1970). Is it because the smaller Socialist scientific and engineering community has not received adequate cross-fertilization from the larger Western community in the form of products (trade) and Western scientific visitors as a result of both Eastern and Western obstacles to intercourse? Or is it rather due to some of the mechanisms of central planning such as (a) the lack of managerial incentives to adopt innovations and (b) the separation of those working on industrial R&D from the operation of enterprises? Whichever the answer, it seems clear that where the need (from the planners' standpoint) has been great, rapid technological advances have been achieved, witness the Soviet independent achievements in space, commercial and military aircraft, atomic and hydrogen bombs, and steel.

Further study of Socialist problems in development of technology is needed. A major study of the Soviet picture by Joseph Berliner is nearing completion and this should fill many gaps. Robert Campbell's (1968) fine study of the Soviet oil and gas industry contains many insights. David Granick's (1968) retrospective study of how the Soviets adapted foreign technology in their prewar metal-fabricating industry and Sutton's (1968) study of the prewar period are also useful. Papers by Judy, Pryor, Woroniak, and Zauberman (1970), and an OECD study (Zaleski, 1969) provide further postwar information on the U.S.S.R. and Eastern Europe. But much remains to be done. Will the Eastern Bloc continue to have a comparative disadvantage in technology over the next twenty years: (a) assuming present methods of planning, (b) assuming reforms which rationalize the development and adoption of advanced technology, and (c) assuming large-scale importation of technology from the West? Should advanced technology in strategic areas (weapons, computers) be withheld from the East on security grounds? Or is it true, as some argue, that a nation which relies on imports of the most advanced equipment is importing obsolescence and a ten year handicap—the average time lag between drawing board and assembly line? This question needs resolution.

Arms Control and Disarmament

Progress in arms control and disarmament, albeit very limited so far, has been the product of the détente of the past decade. For those interested in East-West developments in this area, a number of areas of research are open.

First, there is the problem of verification. For some specialized kinds of arms control agreements, physical methods of verification (seismic detection, spy satellites, etc.), not always perfect, exist. Economic methods of verification are also possible, given sufficient data. Efforts in this direction should be made and, if successful, could facilitate further agreements. Economic methods rely on using the interconnectedness of different parts of the economic system to pin down changes in military production or expenditure, as the case may be. Input-output methods are one way of attempting to verify changes in production. Considerable work on Soviet input-output tables has been done by Vladimir Treml and his associates (Treml, 1964, 1972) but much more detailed data need to be made available before reliance can be placed on such methods. In the absence of adequate input-output data, efforts have been made by government workers and scholars to manipulate partial production data on industries which contribute to military output in an effort to deduce the latter (cf., for example, Boretsky, 1970). Efforts along these lines, so far, have left much to be desired. Finally, other scholars have worked with budgetary and other financial data to try to pinpoint military expenditures and changes therein (Holzman, 1965; Becker, 1969). Such work, if successful, would be useful in verifying general arms reductions agreements. The U.S.S.R. has proposed, for example, that both nations reduce budgeted military expenditures by 15 percent and it is agreements of this sort that we have in mind. More work needs to be done along these lines and, in particular, more data needs to be secured from the U.S.S.R. and other Socialist nations.

At present, the major nations of the world devote $200 billion to military purposes, a figure which drawfs world expenditures on education, health, and foreign economic aid, respectively, and is about as large as the total GNPs of the less developed world. Should there be a large-scale reduction in military expenditures with détente, there would be some (depending on the speed of reduction) dislocation in the major nations, particularly the U.S. and U.S.S.R., and also some question as to what to do with the resources so freed. Dislocation would probably be most serious in the market economies and some of the pressures against reducing military expenditures derive from fear of just such dislocation. Work needs to be done on the macro- but particularly on the micro-strategies to be followed to reduce economic dislocation to a minimum, as well as on making the best use of the freed resources. While considerable work has been done in the past on the micro-strategy (CLPW, 1964; Melman, 1970)—figuring out substitute uses for freed capital and labor which do least violence to former training and human dignity—this kind of work needs to be carried out on a continuing basis because military technology and substitute civilian activities are constantly changing. Aside from domestic adjustment problems, and domestic uses of freed resources, there would undoubtedly be pressures and incentives to devote some considerable part of resources to assisting the less fortunate nations of the world. Some planning for such an event would appear to be in order (see "Inequality, Resources, and Population," below).

A major East-West arms problem, disarmament or not, is the fact that the U.S.S.R. on the one hand, and the U.S., U.K., and France on the other (to name some of the major actors) supply a large part of the rest of the world, especially the LDCs, with the arms to fight their wars. "Their" in this case can be interpreted to refer to the donors and/or recipients, depending on the war in question. The exact extent of this trade in arms is not known because transactions of this character are not reported in the trade statistics, or elsewhere, by most nations. The major studies which have appeared recently (SIPRI, 1972; Leiss, 1970), while confined primarily to major weapons systems and to sales to the LDCs, nevertheless do suggest that the arms market is large and growing. Further studies are needed which are more inclusive of the present extent of the market and of the direction in which the market is going? For example, will Japan begin to enter the market on a larger scale and what impact will this have? Some suppliers (e.g. France, Sweden) are believed to be motivated by the desire to get longer runs and lower unit costs in their arms industries, others (e.g., U.S., U.S.S.R., U.K.) by political factors as well. Are these differences reflected in different terms of trade? What impact will these differential motives have on disarmament prospects? What is the economic impact of the arms trade on the recipients? To what extent is limited foreign exchange diverted from productive projects? To what extent does receipt of advanced weapons divert skilled manpower and resources from other projects? To what extent does receipt of the same weapons create a skilled manpower more rapidly than otherwise?

All of these and other questions need exploration within the context of East-West competition ·in arms markets and in terms of possible action in the direction of arms reduction and disarmament.

Environment

On September 22, 1972, the *New York Times* announced that a U.S.-U.S.S.R. Joint Committee on Cooperation in the Field of Environmental Protection had been established and that thirty joint projects had been established. On October 5, the *Times* announced a twelve nation East-West International Institute of Applied Systems Analysis which will investigate, among other things, pollution control. Ever since "external diseconomies" ceased to be an "empty box" to economists some 10-15 years ago, it was clear that environmental interdependencies were eventually going to require cooperation for effective control; and that controls were going to be necessary if rapid environmental deterioration was to be avoided.

There are a number of areas already in which East and West are in contact as a result of environment. The Baltic Sea, for example, which is bordered by the U.S.S.R., Poland, Finland, Denmark, Sweden, and the Germanys is rapidly becoming a "Lake Erie" as waste from most or all of these nations finds its way into it. Offshore oil drilling by the U.S.S.R. in the Black Sea creates pollution dangers for Turkey, and in the Caspian Sea for Iran. Soviet irrigation policies are contributing to the decline in the level of the Caspian Sea which adversely affects Iranian (as well as Soviet) fishing resources. The Mediterranean-Aegean-Adriatic complex bordered by East and West is beginning to show signs of pollution. Research on jointly inhabited seas is needed: to allocate responsibility for pollution; to devise legal and economic measures for stopping or reducing further pollution; to determine the optimum level of pollution; and to devise methods of reducing the pollution if this seems warranted and of allocating the costs of such remedial actions. In determining the optimum level of pollution, one would weight the costs of stopping or reducing pollution against the gains to the various populations concerned from less pollution. Calculations of this sort may yield different results for different countries and reconciliation of these differences may be a major problem and in need of study.

International fisheries are another area of potential conflict and need for cooperation. A major case in point is whale fishing. The U.S.S.R. and Japan in particular both engage in whale fishing to a degree which threatens the extinction of the species. Research is needed here on substitutes, on the optimal rates of harvest, and on enforceable rules of national fishing behavior. These points apply not only to whales but to all fish and other animal life threatened with extinction by man.

Environmental interaction will undoubtedly develop in many other dimensions and will increase rapidly over the next few decades. Some other possible areas of East-West conflict are air pollution and weather control. In general, of course, East-West environmental problems are just a subset of the more general set of environmental problems on which considerable work is, or will shortly be, in progress.

There are two major general problems which arise in the resolution of most pollution-type situations which require special notice. The first, hinted at above, is that the curtailment of pollution will undoubtedly involve changes in income distribution between (as well as within) nations. The second problem relates to the fact that time perspective on pollution problems is typically going to be long run. Decisions made about the optimal level of pollution today will undoubtedly have a more profound effect on the next and future generations than on present populations. In making these decisions, then, it is necessary to take account of changing income elasticities of demand for an unpolluted environment and of social rates of discount. Further, income elasticities, and changes in them, will undoubtedly differ substantially from nation to nation and between East and West, as will social rates of discount. Research on these matters would seem to be in order.

Finally, it is of interest to study the differences in approach to environmental problems which is taken by capitalist and Socialist nations, respectively. It is noteworthy that, while most people believe on a priori grounds that Socialist nations are likely to be more careful about despoiling the environment than capitalist nations because they do not have to contend with private profit, in fact it appears that the particular system of managerial incentives used in most Socialist nations is such that Socialist managers pay no more attention to environment than capitalist entrepreneurs. While there is considerable documentation on Soviet practices (Goldman, 1972), more is needed and it would be particularly interesting to investigate the practices of other socialist nations.

Inequality, Resources, and Population

The interrelated issues of this section are certainly the most important discussed in this chapter. Nevertheless, they are dealt with very cursorily below. This is because they are more properly the province of other chapters and only incidentally a matter for study in terms of East-West relations.

Over the past decade, the per capita incomes of the LDCs rose more slowly than those of either the Eastern or Western advanced nations.[s] In absolute terms, many of the more advanced nations experienced annual increases in per capita income that were considerably greater than the total per capita incomes of the people of many of the poorer nations. In terms of these vast differentials, the amount of assistance which flows from the advanced nations to the LDCs is a drop in the bucket. There are two reasons why, over the next several decades, the advanced Eastern and Western nations may find themselves in need of a common policy regarding the great inequality between the haves and have nots. First, there is a growing intolerance among the poorer nations of the present state of affairs and of the worsening trend. Second, there is the recent realization that planet earth, with its limited resources, pollution problems, and large population, may never be able to support the world population of the future at the standard of living of the more advanced nations today.

A common policy may not be easy to arrive at for ideological reasons: the Socialist nations espouse greater equality than do the capitalist nations. There is literature on international burden-sharing which needs to be expanded for the problems noted above (Kravis, 1963; Pincus, 1965). For the shorter run, there is also a need for additional comparative East-West studies on the theories and practices of aid to LDCs (UN, 1966; Vassilev, 1969) including studies in depth, like that of Desai, (1972) of very important aid projects. The relative successes and failures of the two systems may provide some clues regarding proper transitional policies for the future.

Closely related to the above are questions of the world's limited resources and growing population. These are problems of such overwhelming importance to the world of nations that their East-West facets pale into insignificance. Nevertheless, the U.S.S.R. does contain a large share of the world's resources and China a large share of the world's population. Any studies dealing with future resource and population problems would do well to reckon with these nations.

References

Adler-Karlsson, Gunnar. *Western Economic Warfare, 1947-67.* Stockholm, 1968.

Altman, Oscar. "Russian Gold and the Ruble," *Staff Papers*, 1960.

Becker, Abraham. *Soviet National Income, 1958-64.* Berkeley, 1969, Chapter 7.

Borchard, Edwin M. *The Diplomatic Protection of Citizens Abroad.* New York, 1928.

Boretsky, M. "The Technological Base of Soviet Military Power", in JEC, Congress of the United States, *Economic Performance and the Military Burden in the Soviet Union.* Washington, 1970.

---

[s]The Socialist nations in Europe all have GNPs per capita of over $600 per year; those in Asia have much lower incomes and qualify as LDCs.

Brada, J., and Wipf, L. "Export Performance of East European Nations in Western Markets," (Manuscript, 1972).

Brown, A., and Marer, P. "Foreign Trade in the East European Reforms," Paper presented to the *Research Conference on Economic Reform in Eastern Europe.* Ann Arbor, November, 1970.

Campbell, Robert. *The Economics of Soviet Oil and Gas.* Baltimore, 1968.

Committee for Economic Development (CED). *A New Trade Policy Toward Communist Countries.* New York, September 1972.

Committee on Labor and Public Welfare (CLPW), U.S. Senate. *Convertibility of Space and Defense Resources to Civilian Needs: A Search for New Employment Potentials.* GPO, 1964.

Desai, Padma. *The Bokaro Steel Plant.* Amsterdam, 1972.

Familton, R.J. "East-West Trade and Payments Relations," *Staff Papers*, March 1970.

Freedman, Robert O. *Economic Warfare in the Communist Block.* New York, 1970.

Friedman, Milton. "Discussion" in *The International Adjustment Mechanism.* Published by the Federal Reserve Bank of Boston, March 1970.

Gerschenkron, A. *Economic Relations with the USSR.* New York, 1945. (Published by the Carnegie Endowment for International Peace).

_____. *Essays on the History of State Trading.* (Manuscript).

Goldman, Marshall. *The Spoils of Progress: Environmental Pollution in the Soviet Union.* Cambridge, 1972.

_____. "The East Reaches for Markets," *Foreign Affairs*, July 1969.

Granick, David. *Soviet Metal-Fabricating and Economic Development.* Madison, Wisconsin, 1968.

Harvey, Moses. *East-West Trade and United States Policy.* New York, 1966, pp. 49-50.

Holzman, F.D. "East-West Trade and Investment Policy Issues." In *United States International Economic Policy in an Interdependent World.* Washington, D.C., July 1971.

_____. "Some Notes on Over-full Employment Planning." *Soviet Studies*, October 1970.

_____. "The Ruble Exchange Rate and Soviet Foreign Trade Pricing Policies: 1929-1961." *American Economic Review*, December 1968.

_____. *The Feasibility of Financial Verification of Reductions in Soviet Defense Expenditures.* (Manuscipt, 1965).

_____. "On the Technique of Comparing Trade Barriers of Products Imported by Capitalist and Communist Nations." *European Economic Review*, Fall 1970.

_____. "Comparison of Different Forms of Trade Barriers." *Review of Economics and Statistics*, September, 1969.

Judy, Richard. "The Case of Computer Technology." In Wasowski, 1970.

Katzavor, Konstantin. *Theory of Nationalization.* The Hague, 1964.

Kindleberger, Charles (ed.). *The International Corporation.* Cambridge, 1970.

Kravis, I. and Davenport, M. "The Political Arithmetic of International Burden Sharing." *Journal of Political Economy*, August 1963.

Leiss, Amelia. *Arms Transfers to Less Developed Countries.* Cambridge, 1970.

Lillich, Richard B. *The Protection of Foreign Investment.* Syracuse, 1965.

Malish, Anton F. *United States East European Trade.* United States Tariff Commission, 1972.

McMillan, Carl H. *Aspects of Soviet Participation in International Trade.* Ph.D. dissertation, Johns Hopkins University, 1972.

Melman, Seymour. *The Defense Economy: Conversion of Industries and Occupations to Civil Needs.* New York, 1970.

Montias, Michael. "Statement" before Subcommittee on Foreign Relations of the Joint Economic Committee, December 9, 1970.

Morgan Guarantee Survey. September 1972.

Nove, A. "East-West Trade." In *International Economic Relations*, Paul Samuelson (Ed.), New York, 1969.

Peterson, Peter. *U.S.-Soviet Commercial Relationships in a New Era.* Department of Commerce, Washington, D.C., August 1972.

Pincus, John. *Economic Aid and International Cost Sharing.* Baltimore, 1965.

Pisar, Samuel. *Coexistence and Commerce.* New York, 1970.

Pryor, Frederic. "Research and Development Expenditures in Eastern Europe." In Wasowski, 1970.

_____. "Trade Barriers of Capitalist and Communist Nations against Foodstuffs Exported by Tropical Underdeveloped Nations." *Review of Economics and Statistics*, November 1966.

Rosefielde, Stephen. *Factor Proportions and the Commodity Structure of Soviet International Trade, 1955-68.* Ph.D. dissertation, Harvard University, 1972.

SIPRI (Stockholm International Peace Research Institute). *Arms Trade with the Third World.* Stockholm, 1972.

Sutton, Anthony. *Western Technology and Soviet Economic Development, 1917-30.* Stanford, 1968.

Treml, Vladimir and others; *The 1959 Intersectoral Flow Table.* McLean, Va.: Research Analysis Corporation, 1964.

_____. *The Structure of the Soviet Economy, 1966.* New York, 1972.

U.N. (United Nations). "The Financing of Economic Development." *World Economic Survey, 1965, Part I.* New York, 1966, Chapter 4.

Vassilev, V. *Policy in the Soviet Bloc on Aid to Developing Countries.* Paris: OECD, 1969.

Wasowski, Stanislaus (Ed.). *East-West Trade and the Technology Gap.* New York, 1970.

White, Gillian. *Nationalization of Foreign Property*. New York, 1962

Wilczynski, J. *The Economics and Politics of East-West Trade*. London, 1969.

Wiles, Peter. *Communist International Trade*. New York, 1968.

Woroniak, Alexander. "Technological Transfer in Eastern Europe: Receiving Countries." In Wasowski, 1970.

Wu, Yuan-li. *Economic Warfare*. New York, 1952.

Zauberman, A. "Pushing the Technological Frontier Through Trade." In Wasowski, 1970.

Zaleski, E. and others. *Science Policy in the USSR*. Paris: OECD, 1969.

Environmental Management and the International Economic Order

Ingo Walter

New York University

Continued concern with the quality of life, as measured in ways other than real income per capita, is beginning to take on dimensions that may carry with them some major implications for the character of the international economy in the decades to come. One of these is the quality of the human environment. International trade has long served as a mask for environmental problems by distributing the consequences of imprudent economic growth and exploitation of natural resources among a variety of national political collectivities through imports and exports of depletable raw materials and pollution-intensive manufactures and semi-manufactures. International investment can serve the same purpose by permitting things that are environmentally unacceptable in one nation to be accomplished elsewhere. But the ability of trade and investment to serve this function is growing steadily more limited. And as nations increasingly build environmental factors into their calculus of social welfare there will inevitably be shifts in the international economic system.

The question is whether these shifts are really of major significance. And, if so, what types of international economic relations will be affected and what are the determining policy linkages? How will this affect the international economic order in the coming decades? These are the kinds of questions to which this chapter is addressed. There is still a great deal of uncertainty. But it is not too early to try to discern some of the principal cause-and-effect relationships that appear to be emerging, and to identify some needed and potentially fruitful avenues for future research.

Introduction

Public concern with the quality of the human environment is hardly a new departure in the definition and determination of social welfare. It has played a subordinate role, however, to the more conventional requisites of improved material levels of living; the marginal social cost of environmental degradation either was not explicitly recognized or was not considered significant in relation to the marginal benefits of the causative economic and social activity. Over time, the balance has altered in the face of the growth of population, shifts in its distribution, and a rapid rise in the level of economic activity. The biosphere—as a dynamic physical, chemical, and biological system that is at once multifactorial, multidirectional, and multidimensional—began to show its limits. Invisible damage to the environment became visible. Damage that could be safely ignored became consequential.

None of this is new. The problem of environmental despoilation has grown roughly in proportion with national and international economic advance over decades and centuries. So why the crisis? Because of slippage between emergence of the problem and its political recognition.[1] Because changes in levels of living bring changes in social values and priorities. Because of development of mass media and changing patterns of social action. Because the assimilative capacity of the environment—its ability to cleanse itself—is increasingly being attained and surpassed. Because, quite simply, when one begins to look for something what one finds often exceeds expectations.

The issue has come to a head in the United States in the early 1970s. It will not go away. Abroad, it is emerging even more abruptly in some nations, and in others more gradually. In still others—despite the best efforts of international organizations concerned with the problem—it will be some time in coming. Differences in environmental problems and in their recognition as such, both interregionally and internationally, give rise to leads and lags in their effects and in policy responses that are of major importance for the international economic order in the decades to come.

Ten Basic Issues

A fundamental characteristic of environmental despoilation and its control is *uncertainty*, both in an objective and in a subjective context. This makes it impossible to discuss the issue in any but probabalistic terms, and forecasting becomes a risky proposition, at best. Under such conditions, policy actions can easily take on vectors quite different from what would have been if everything that needed to be known was known. And since we are principally concerned with the consequences of these policy vectors for the international economy, it is often impossible to present much more than a series of alternative scenarios or possible outcomes. Uncertainty in environmental management can be traced to a variety of sources. Important among them are the following:

1. What are the sources of environmental despoilation? Generally, pollution of the environment may be considered any departure from its "natural" state caused by: (a) gaseous discharges into the atmosphere, whether toxic or not, that alter the composition of a given airshed; (b) liquid and solid discharges into bodies of water affecting their quality, particularly their ability to sustain life and to serve as an economic social resource; (c) thermal discharges affecting water quality; (d) noise; (e) radiation; (f) disposal of solid wastes; (g) degrada-

tion of natural scenery and terrain, and the elimination of recreational opportunities; (h) endangering of wildlife species; and (i) congestion. Clearly, there are differences of views on each of these in terms of the need for and desirability of maintaining the "natural" state.[2]

2. What are the consequences of environmental despoilation? In the case of each of the foregoing areas—in some more than in others—controversies rage among specialists. What are the environmental consequences of an alternative course of action intended to produce the same or similar results? What are the social, economic, and environmental consequences of abstaining altogether? Particularly in the alteration of water quality through material and thermal discharges, air pollution, and protection of wildlife, the experts are often poles apart. Without consensus or even substantial agreement, and given the time and resources that may be involved in reversing environmental damage once it occurs (if it is reversible at all) confusion may turn into extreme caution. As a result, the economic consequences of environmental management may be greatly magnified in degree, accelerated in time, and inflated in real costs, in relation to the net benefits achieved once all the returns are in.

3. Closely related to the foregoing issue, what are the environmental limits? We know that the environment can assimilate certain types of pollutants in certain volumes without raising the disharmonies in the use-reuse cycle that are associated with environmental degradation. But what kind of pollutants, and in what volumes? Again, uncertainty is paramount, and without knowing the depth of the "environmental sink" economic development can easily be restrained unduly or forced beyond its ecological limits.

4. Even if all sources of environmental despoilation could be identified and their consequences clearly delineated within known assimilative limits, there is still the question: What is an "acceptable" environment? The issue is a political one, subject to collective decision-making once the relevant tradeoffs are known.[3] Will a given river system better serve as a common-property social resource by virtue of its potential as a sewer? A source of potable water? A transportation artery? A recreational resource? A source of power? The decision has to be made. Often it is not—or not soon enough—because of imperfections in the political system, changing societal goals, and related factors. Again the question of uncertainty arises, and its impact is amplified by the tendency for costs to rise exponentially with the degree of environmental restoration required.

5. Suppose all of the foregoing questions have been answered, the outcome should be a system of coherent and mutually-consistent standards governing environmental quality. Because environmental assimilative capacity and social preferences can and do differ among political collectivities, the resultant standards may and probably *should* differ accordingly. An important exception is "transboundary pollution," when environmental damage that may or may not be consistent with standards maintained by one political collectivity spills over

to affect another.[4] Transboundary pollution may represent the least-cost manner in which Collectivity A has chosen to achieve its standards, thereby damaging Collectivity B. Or it may be a question of different standards adopted by A and B. In either instance, a strong case can be made for concerted remedial action through cooperation, establishment of a broader-based environmental authority, harmonization of standards or, in the extreme, political and economic sanctions between the affected groups. The transboundary issue may be bilateral, multilateral, or even global in nature.

6. Once environmental standards have been decided upon, they must be formulated in such a manner that they can be efficiently complied with and, where necessary, enforced. Adjustment costs may be considerable if standards vary over time or where the gap between the norms and reality is large, calling for phased implementation. Standards may be enforced on a "case-by-case" basis, with the collectivity bearing the burden of proof regarding environmental damage in each instance of pollution. Alternatively, "blanket" enforcement may be applied to *all* pollution, possibly tempered by individual exceptions, with adequate proof required of the individual polluter that environmental damage above and beyond the agreed standards is indeed not involved. There is a fundamental difference between the two approaches.

7. While adjustment to environmental control standards involves transitional costs of various kinds, they may also entail recurring costs—costs attributable to doing things in a less-than-optimum manner in order to preclude environmental damage. More inputs are required to produce the same amount of output, measured conventionally. This basically involves the internalization of externalities—the absorption of costs that heretofore were borne by society at large in the form of environmental degradation.[5] The market fails to bring this about because common-property resources generally have not been and often cannot be priced: Hence reliance on enforced standards. Assessment of environmental control costs is itself highly complex because of changing technology, economies in the reclamation of waste products, age and type of facilities involved, potential for scale economies, and so forth.

8. That environmental management generally involves costs is accepted. The question is who pays.[6] Regardless of how these costs are met, society pays. Productive resources are diverted to environmental control, and with given technology fewer resources can go toward the production of other goods and services. Society may well be better off, all things considered—and presumably is if the right collective decisions have been made—but not in terms of the conventional definitions of economic welfare. Enforced standards may simply involve the "polluter pays" principle, with relevant costs being passed forward in the form of higher prices. Or punitive taxation may be used, with assessments based on the amount of environmental damage induced, but with the same end-result. Or direct and indirect subsidies may be used to defray part or all of the EC (environmental control) costs using national fiscal mechanisms. Or some

combination of these. In any event, society ultimately bears the burden, no matter *how* the goal is achieved. But the latter does influence competitive relationships among national or regional economies, and thus bears detailed examination in that context.

9. Environmental management problems, when viewed in the light of economic structure, turn out to be highly industry-specific and product-specific. Some goods and services are extremely pollution-intensive. Others are not. Hence the impact of environmental control (EC) will not fall evenly upon individual products, industries, economic sectors, population groups, geographic regions, or national states. Moreover, the problem is highly localized in the case of most pollutants, with the deleterious social impact diminishing with geographic distance from the source. On both counts, in the light of the evident EC costs, there is a built-in bias to delay action for competitive reasons—a fact reinforced by rapidly-evolving technology and the prospect of future improvements in EC efficiency.[7]

10. A question closely related to environmental control is management of the stock of natural resources. If these resources are believed to be in long-run short supply, then they in fact assume the role of a common-property resource not unlike the environment. While the market in fact prices natural raw materials on the basis of currently available supply and demand, viewing depletable resources in this light would indicate that they may currently be vastly underpriced.[8] Just as setting a price on the previously unpriced environment has major economic implications, so will policies designed to set prices for raw materials in accordance with very-long-run supply and demand. Again, a large number of uncertainties is involved, including technological change, substitution among different materials, the economics of materials-reuse, and so forth. But the issue is a serious one. Each of the questions ennumerated above has a bearing on international economic relations and their evolution in the coming decades. In some cases the effect is immediate and direct, but in most instances the implications are longer-range in nature. And the same kinds of uncertainties that characterize the environmental issues themselves affect assessments of their emerging impact on the international economic order.

Implications for the International Economy

There are at least five principal ways in which environmental management can affect the shape of future relations between national and regional economies: (a) control of environmentally damaging processes; (b) control of products that are damaging to the environment in their normal use; (c) control of products that damage the environment as residuals at the end of their useful lives; (d) control of transboundary pollution; and (e) control of depletable natural resources. Each gives rise to a series of problems that transmit the environmental pressures to the international economy. Twelve more or less distinct sets of issues will be examined here. They are believed to be the major ones, looking ahead, but others of equal or greater significance may well emerge in time.

*1. Environmental Policy Configurations
and International Competition*[9]

The most obvious source of possible international trade dislocations arising out of environmental control is regulation of the production process itself. If the "polluter pays" principle is assumed, the cost of reducing production-related emissions will be fully reflected in final product-costs, and this will affect competitiveness. If there are no other barriers to effective competition—as within a unified national or regional market—the impact may be rather pronounced, even sufficient to induce a "go-slow" approach on the part of the political units involved and biasing the system toward a more gradual elimination of the sources of environmental despoilation. The international economy, of course, is characterized by a variety of other competitive distortions, and hence the relative importance of costs induced by environmental control may be diminished accordingly.[10]

Apart from the existence of tariffs and other competitive distortions, the impact of environmental management on trade flows will depend on several factors.

First is the extent to which EC norms will differ between national states. Existing variations in environmental assimilative capacity (EAC) and public preferences have already been noted. The question is how large these differences really are and to what extent they will be reflected in different EC standards among nations. Very little information exists to date, but if one views EAC as a supply factor and environmental quality as primarily a consumption good, the following developments are possible:

a. In the intermediate term, standards will differ very substantially, even among the industrial countries.
b. There will be a "catch-up" phase during which the gap between realized and desired environmental quality at current income levels will narrow.
c. As incomes rise, so will environmental standards, and the concept of what is an "acceptable" environment will ultimately become relatively uniform among the industrial countries.
d. Convergence on uniform standards will be characterized by significant leads and lags during the adjustment process.
e. Differences in standards, a transitional problem among industrial economies, will be a long-term factor vis-à-vis the developing economies.[11]

While coordinative efforts at the international level may succeed in accelerating the convergence of EC norms, it is doubtful that they can contain the potential impact of standards-variations on international trade flows, except perhaps where appropriate institutional machinery already exists, as in the EEC.[12] Significant competitive advantages in specific sectors may thus be available to countries with more lenient standards while these differences exist.

Second is the bearing of EC standards on production costs. This is partly a question of *how* they are implemented. The following options exist:

a. The "polluter pays" principle may be applied, forcing internalization of environmental externalities and their ultimate reflection in production costs and prices.
b. "Pollution taxes" may be used, either as fixed penalties for noncompliance with existing standards or in the form of fiscal levies that are variable with the amount of pollutive discharge—both of which may accelerate the impact of EC measures on costs but which differ in terms of their effect on the individual firm's internal economics and pricing decisions.[13]
c. Subsidies, financed out of general tax revenues, may be used to defray part or all of certain EC costs.
d. A considerable degree of latitude may be employed in enforcing standards both with respect to the degree of compliance required and the question of timing.

Again, there is as yet very little concrete evidence as to existing or emerging differences in national implementation patterns. OECD member nations have adopted the "polluter pays" principle, embodying the advantages of equity and discouraging consumption of products whose production is highly pollutive, but having the disadvantage of potentially impeding international competitiveness in the face of differing standards.[14] For this reason, strict adherence to it is still an open question, and indeed the OECD program itself provides exceptions for "hardship cases." Pollution taxes and related charges—such as the proposed Sulphur tax in the United States aimed at sulphur-dioxide emissions—seem to be relatively rare at both the national and subnational levels. Little information is available on direct subsidization, but there are clearly wide variations in indirect subsidization, both interregionally and internationally, such as favorable tax and depreciation treatment of EC hardware, government sponsored R&D, and access by industry to public sewage-treatment facilities. The gap between the establishment of EC regulations and their subsequent enforcement likewise appears to be relatively wide, once again subject to the absence of reliable information.[15]

It may be expected that the "polluter pays" agreement in principle that has already been reached among the major developed market-economy countries will eventually be extended to cover questions of enforcement and subsidies, thereby safeguarding the trade-neutrality of environmental control measures in the long run. But there will be a transitional period during which trade flows may be affected by existing differences in enforcement techniques. In most cases the resultant international competitive effects are likely to be raised in the appropriate international forums as matters for negotiation. The question of punitive taxation is not likely to come up at the international level, since industries subjected to international competitive disadvantages from this source can request relief through domestic channels. Certainly international agreement on punitive tax measures will be difficult, if not impossible, to attain.

Overall, there is at present little evidence on the extent to which trade flows are being affected by international differences in ways of implementing EC norms. In view of the aforementioned variations in the norms themselves, any attempts to assess the trade impact would tend to capture both effects at once. When these standards begin to converge, the techniques employed in their implementation will gain in relative significance, with the principal emerging issue being the use of public subsidies and assurance of trade-neutrality. This, in turn, will tend to come under scrutiny within conventional multilateral examinations of subsidies and related measures as distortions of trade in such forms as GATT, OECD, EEC, and so forth. It may also be possible, perhaps likely, that agreement between the major trading countries on uniform ways and means of enforcing EC standards will come at a relatively early stage, well before the standards themselves grow into alignment. Again, this is probably not true with respect to the developing countries, and the prospective impact of both questions on East-West trade is completely open.

The foregoing are policy inputs subject to national political decisions processes and international conciliation. Within a nation, interregional variations in EC norms and their competitive effects on trade are moderated by the existence of a strong national government charged, in principle, with minimizing their disruptive impact. Evidence in the United States suggests that it will take a decade or more to devise a coherent system of national environmental standards and enforcement procedures to attain this goal.[16] Internationally, with political sovereignty much more important and in the absence of supranational authority, the adjustment period will be considerably longer and the competitive implications for trade flows will be much more durable.

One concludes that there will be substantial differences in the effects of EC measures on competitive relations among industries, firms and products. Pollution-intensive industries producing tradable products are affected in the first instance.[17] But so are firms using the output of these industries as important raw material or intermediate inputs. For example, induced increases in (generally nontraded) electric power costs and environmental control measures undertaken in the ferrous and nonferrous metals sector will escalate costs in various manufacturing industries. Among industries that may be significantly affected are iron and steel; pulp and paper; stone, clay and glass; mining; fabricated metals; instruments; petroleum; chemicals; nonferrous metals, food and beverages; textiles; rubber; as well as nonelectrical and electrical machinery.

2. Questions of Economic Structure and Aggregate Impact

Clearly, when a country makes a commitment to the maintenance and restoration of environmental quality it must devote substantial economic resources to this task. Environmental control absorbs productive factors by using capital and technology to reduce the negative externalities of existing patterns of economic activity—or by changing ways of doing things from those most efficient in meeting primary economic wants, but are environmentally damaging, to those less efficient but less damaging as well. In the latter case, if the same degree of want-satisfaction is to be maintained, more resources must be used in the productive process. Alternatively the wants can be changed, either as a natural result of changing relative prices or by political and administrative means; and the implications of such developments are discussed elsewhere in this chapter.[18] Furthermore, even if environmental control raises aggregate social welfare (as it presumably will) it will tend to reduce overall welfare measured in any way that ignores environmental quality as a consumption or investment good. Environmental management is not a free good. It must be paid for, either by fiscal diversion of purchasing power or by its monetary diversion through increased prices.

The amounts involved are not small. Current EC spending in the United States comes to around $9.5 billion, about $7.5 billion of which is by federal and state-local governments. Estimates of future EC spending for the United States point to a doubling over the intermediate term (5 years) to 1 - 2 percent of GNP, and to a further rise to 2 - 3 percent of GNP over the long run. Estimates vary widely between nations, presumably due to differences in perceived EAC and differences in views of what is needed, ranging from 1.4 - 1.6 percent of GNP for Sweden to 4 - 5 percent for the Netherlands. Such variances are in part attributable to the uncertainties that exist, and a narrower range around 1.5 - 2 percent of GNP is likely to emerge for most industrial countries— depending on what yardstick is used for measurement and what standards are applied.[19]

The international dimensions of the issue relate to two kinds of effects. The first is a monetary question: If environmental control is enforced through the general application of the "polluter pays" principle, or if it is partly or wholly financed by government fiscal deficits, then it will result in a generally higher price level than would otherwise obtain. It thus affects the relative value of the national currency, the flow of imports and exports, and the balance of payments. If the prevailing international financial system permits reasonable flexibility in exchange rates, any such impact will be reflected in a commensurate depreciation of the national currency on the foreign exchange markets. If not, the result will be growing pressure on the current account of the balance of payments and, depending on what happens elsewhere, the eventual need for devaluation.[20]

Existing macroeconomic studies are contradictory in terms of implications of environmental control for the balance of payments and aggregate incomes. One, using an econometric model of the U.S. economy and projected future American EC measures (assuming other nations do *not* follow suit), emerges with the following results:

Over the 1972-80 period, pollution control and compensatory macroeconomic policy measures are expected to raise the U.S. unemployment rate by 0.3 percent, raise the average annual rate of inflation by 0.26 percent, reduce fixed investment not related to pollution control by an average of 2.3 billion annually, and exert a negative impact on the U.S. balance of trade in the amount of 1.9 billion. If, on the other hand, pollution control costs are 50 percent higher than current estimates, or standards are raised correspondingly, the average annual 1980 negative trade balance effect is estimated to be in the neighborhood of $3.2 billion.[21]

General price sensitivity to pollution control in other countries may, of course, be greater or lower than in the United States, depending on the availability of substitute fuels, comparative efficiency in applying environmental control techniques, and differences in economic structure. The impact on aggregate trade flows depends also on the distribution of control measures among competitive national economies and the range of affected products competing on world markets.

Moreover, the credibility of such assessments would be greatly improved if the *net* effects could be determined by means of similar analyses for the major competitor countries. Other studies come out with entirely different results, but are plagued with questionable assumptions and an even more serious lack of reliable data.[22] The concepts and analytical methodology is ready, but the poor quality of data inputs and uncertainty as to future developments render current aggregate projections of EC-impact extremely questionable.

Again, the international financial implications of environmental management center on what the specific national policies and programs are. The wider the differences, in standards and in implementational methods, the larger the potential effects. Different standards may be enforced by identical means. Or identical standards may be enforced by different means—e.g., Country A uses punitive taxation and "polluter-pays" while Country B uses subsidies financed by fiscal levies. Or different standards may be enforced by different means. The impact depends on the precise configuration that evolves. But even if identical standards are enforced by identical means, environmental management does not necessarily have zero impact on the balance of payments or exchange rates, because there may still be major international variations in the degree of *efficiency* with which productive resources are applied to the established environmental goals.

The international financial implications may or may not be important in the long run, depending on how responsive the world monetary system is to changes of this sort. Perhaps of greater importance are the trade implications of shifts in national economic structures invariably brought about by the diversion of resources to environmental control. Surface competitive effects, which can and will vary widely by industry and by product, have already been discussed. Beneath this surface lies the question of how the induced structural changes will affect a nation's comparative advantage in the world economy, and how this in turn will influence what it trades, with whom, in what volume, and what its net gains from international commerce will be.

International comparative advantage is based on a variety of factors, including availability of natural resources, labor, investment in physical capital, investment in human capital, investment in technology, and so forth, all employed in the production of tradable goods and services. The precise configuration of a nation's capabilities in supply of tradable products and services, relative to its demand for them, determines the composition, direction, volume and terms of international trade.

Environmental control tends to divert a nation's productive capabilities from things that can be traded internationally to something that cannot—from the production of tradable goods and services in demand throughout the international economy to achievement of environmental balance. As a result, its ability to produce tradables is lower than it would otherwise be. In economic terminology, the transformation function as between importables and exportables in the presence of EC-induced resource diversion falls below where it would be in the absence of environmental control.[23] The question is whether or not the reduced potential output is *symmetrical* between those goods and services that a country tends to import and those it tends to export. If it is, the EC impact is relatively neutral: a country's comparative advantage is unchanged, although the volume of and gains from trade decline. Its terms of trade (export prices relative to import prices) also will tend to remain the same, with prices of both export and import-competing goods increasing.

But suppose environmental control does not impact the trade sector symmetrically. Suppose, for example, the kinds of economic activities required for environmental management happen to absorb larger amounts of capital than labor or other productive factors, both in terms of tangible (plant and equipment) and R&D investments required, to achieve a given quantum of EC-output, however, measured. Whether or not this is true remains to be seen, but preliminary indications are that it is.[24] As a result, EC activities will employ relatively greater amounts of capital than of cooperant factors of production. In terms of conventional trade theory, if a country happens to be capital-abundant relative to other productive factors—and exports capital intensive products and services while importing those using intensively other productive factors—the impact of environmental control on trade cannot be symmetrical. That is, potential output of importables (noncapital-intensive goods and services) will decline relatively *less* than potential output of exportables, and this erodes the basis for the nation's comparative advantage in the international marketplace.

Both its comparative advantage in exportables and its comparative disadvantage in importables are reduced, and its production mix of tradable goods and services become less specialized in the export sector. Assuming balanced trade, the volume of trade declines significantly *more* than in the case of equivalent neutral-incidence environmental control, as does the country's gain from international commerce and its corresponding loss in real income.

At the other extreme, suppose the country specializes in the production of *labor-intensive* goods and services, and pollution-control techniques again happen to be fundamentally capital-intensive. The result now is quite different. Potential output in the import-competing sector is reduced substantially more than that of labor-intensive exportables. The volume of (balanced) trade may again decline, but less than in the earlier case, and the erosion of gains from international commerce may also be less serious. Indeed, in terms of economic structure the country actually may specialize to a greater degree in the production of exportables than it did before the EC measures were imposed.

From the standpoint of international comparative advantage, therefore, the factor-intensity of environment control techniques will affect the structure and volume of its international trade. It will also affect its gains from trade, both in absolute terms and in relative terms as international prices respond to EC-induced import and export price changes. One is tempted to speculate, therefore, that even if environmental control standards are identical between nations, enforced identically, using the same mix of factor inputs, the impact of environmental management will still not fall evenly upon the trading nations of the world. Those countries whose international competitive advantage is based on the same factor/resource/efficiency matrix underlying environmental control will be affected differently from those countries whose trade position relies on a fundamentally different configuration of supply factors.

The corollary to this question is whether there are any systematic relationships between what a nation imports and exports and the degree of environmental damage associated with production of those particular goods and services.[25] Conceptually, every final product or service, were it to be produced without any environmental externalities (as defined by the relevant political collectivity) would have a price higher than its prevailing market price. With a given state of the art, the difference between this hypothetical price (P_H) and the actual price (P_A) in relative terms can be called the "direct EC-loading" (DCEL) of a given product:

$$\text{DECL} = \frac{P_H - P_A}{P_A}$$

Every product and service has a direct EC-loading, and the variance among them is probably very large. But even more important is what the *overall* EC-loading of a given final product of service is once the DECLs of all of the *intermediate inputs* have been considered. The "overall EC-loading" (OECL) is therefore the sum of the DECL of the final product (*j*) and all required inputs (*i*), weighted by the contribution of each input to the value of the final product (a_{ij}):

$$OECL = \frac{(P_H - P_A)_j + \sum\limits_{i=1} a_{ij} (P_H - P_A)_i}{P_A}$$

If it were possible to compute the OECL for each internationally-traded product or service, it would be possible to gain some useful insights into the potential effects of environmental control on trade and payments flows. Suppose the OECL's of United States exports turned out to be systematically higher than (or lower than) those of its imports. Then environmental control, even if uniformly applied by all of the major competitor countries, would have a disproportionate impact on the United States—either larger or smaller—and any other countries evidencing similar bias in overall EC-loadings in one direction or the other. What scanty evidence is available so far is inconclusive, but points to the need for further research and vastly improved data.[26]

3. Trade in Polluting Products

The foregoing discussion dealt with the impact of environmental management on trade flows via its bearing on production processes; resources are used to reduce or eliminate environmental damage incurred during the production process, and this raises costs to individual suppliers and to the economy at large, thereby affecting international competitive relationships. There is also a parallel thrust dealing with products that are themselves environmentally damaging, either in their normal use or as residuals at the termination of their useful lives.

In the field of polluting products, the added cost of meeting increasingly stringent standards should clearly be reflected in final costs, the rationale being that these incremental charges fall significantly short of the added benefits of a cleaner environment. In the short run, such costs can be wholly or partially absorbed by the firm, for competitive reasons or by government dictate, but over the long term they will indeed be passed forward to the ultimate consumer, user, or taxpayer. A likely result is the potential restriction of final demand for certain goods and services, raw materials, and intermediate inputs, with market forces fostering a substitution of those elements which have lower EC-loadings for those more heavily subject to cost-increasing environmental norms. Hence, while the market normally fails at internalizing environmental externalities, the market may represent the means by which coherent public policy can overcome this inherent flaw in the system.

The term "unforseen side effects" will become increasingly important in the general issue of international trade in polluting or otherwise socially risky products. Particularly affected will be the chemical and pharmaceutical industries, as is indicated by the Toxic Substance Control Act, passed by the U.S. Senate in May 1972 and a possible harbinger of the future. In essence, no material may be introduced into the environment unless it has first been convincingly demonstrated that no ecological or human damage will occur, either in the short run or the long run, directly or indirectly. The legislation clearly reflects the public's preoccupation with environmental uncertainties and its nagging suspicion that past mistakes and ongoing heavy promotion of products with questionable ecological attributes may well indicate competition's failure to encourage socially responsible behavior—to be remedied only by stricter public controls.[27]

Nobody knows what the ultimate consequences of a new product will be for the ecosystem. But the trend clearly is toward extreme caution, a trend that has reinforced "negative proof" as the coming, generally accepted code of conduct in the introduction of new materials and the reassessment of existing ones. In practice, this means the requirement that rigorous test protocols be followed in the case of any new product, under the control of a public agency, with the same procedure applied to any existing product that becomes suspect.

The implications for the international economy are several. Costs of compliance with negative proof requirements will be high, and will vary according to the standards and procedures applied. Marketing and distribution will be impaired, both in terms of logistics and time-requirements.[28] Innovation may be dampened to some degree by shifting the cost/payoff balance, with increasing concentration in large firms with sufficient human and capital resources to operate under the new conditions. The sensitivity of supply and trade flows to shifts in individual and collective demand patterns may be hindered or stretched out in time. Major changes in industrial structure may result as increasing interfirm cooperation and collaboration is made necessary, with parallel implications for national and international rules governing anticompetitive business behavior.

The principal issue confronting international trade in the field of polluting products concerns the compatibility of national and regional standards. Even within nations, standards differ. For certain products, perhaps they should differ. For others, perhaps not. In regulating the environmental characteristics of products, where the issue of transboundary pollution does not exist, the political collectivity concerned should be able to define standards in accordance with its assessments of the various alternatives' respective social and economic costs and benefits. Indeed, to the extent that it has political sovereignty, it will insist on that right.

Within nations, due to the economic cost of interregional variations in environmental product standards—combined with asymmetries in power and interests of national vs. subnational political collectivities—a considerable degree of uniformity can be expected. Transition periods may be employed but national norms will emerge. Between nations, this conclusion does not necessarily hold, (a) because the cost of differing product standards to the world economy are not easily identified and measured; (b) because such costs may be less pronounced given large national or regional markets within which compatibility exists; and (c) because differences in norms may be upheld by virtue of national political sovereignty and in the absence of supranational authority.

International harmonization of product-standards thus may not be a legitimate goal if it leads to a divergence rather than a convergence of marginal social benefits and costs among societies demonstrating difficult preferences. But even if it is, standardization will be a drawn-out, painful process subject to intergovernmental agreement, most likely on a product-by-product level. For certain products, substantive agreement already exists or can be expected in the intermediate term. For others it is not unreasonable to expect ultimate convergence of standards, particularly among the major trading nations or blocs—as their perceptions of the relevant cost/benefit configurations evolve —with other countries subscribing to the norms that emerge. For still others, there is little prospect for compatible product standards in the foreseeable future. Much will depend on what happens in other aspects of international economic relations. Far-reaching liberalization of trade and payments and growing economic interdependence will raise the importance and the apparent costs of variations in environmental product-standards and build pressure for unified norms, while the maintenance of growth of commercial and financial distortions will obscure them.

In the meantime, nations will continue to translate their unique social values and environmental conditions into product standards which, they will (and should) insist, must be met by all goods and services sold in the national market—whether produced at home or abroad. Imports which do not meet these standards will be barred from entry. Whereas the range of products encountering this difficulty at present is limited, it will widen substantially in the intermediate term to include—besides automobiles and other less important traded products already subject to environmental controls—a widening array of manufacturers such as aircraft, engines, construction equipment, containers, detergents, synthetic fabrics, pesticides, fungicides, fertilizers, food additives and food products themselves, pharmaceutical products, petroleum products, instruments, etc. This raises three sets of problems.

First is the trade-restrictive impact of product-standard variations themselves. Meeting such standards raises costs even under a unified EC system. Producing for a global market characterized by incompatibilities in standards compounds supply difficulties and multiplies costs. The extent of the problem is highly industry-specific, however, and dependent on the particular economics encountered. Some lines may be produced efficiently for different markets in different configurations, just as they are supplied to-order for individual buyers, and incompatibilities in EC product-standards will be of little importance. Others may be geared to the strictest norms imposed in any major market and produced in volume according to those standards, with little or no competitive disadvantages in national markets characterized by more lenient or nonexistent standards, again with minimal disruption. For still others all output can only be produced one way or the other (e.g., in agriculture), and if the incremental costs or the efficiency losses encountered in supplying a given market having strict EC norms are sufficiently high, then that market may have to be sacrificed altogether, entailing potentially serious economic dislocations. Between these extremes are product lines that can be adapted to different standards with varying degrees of difficulty—including inadequate production runs, product redesign involving additional R&D expenditures, etc.—with disruptive effects likely but not prohibitive. It has not yet been determined, considering the emerging matrix of international trade flows during the coming decades, to what extent each of these supply characteristics obtains and what this implies for the overall impact of international incompatibilities in product-standards related to the environment.

Second is the problem of discrimination in the treatment of domestically-produced and imported products with respect to their environmental characteristics. While inconsistencies in standards may be disruptive of trade, they do not distort the relative cost and price advantages upon which trade is based. Indeed, they may reinforce them. However, when the standards, or their administration, are applied to imports in a manner different from import-competing goods, they may take on the role of a commercial-policy device—a nontariff barrier (NTB) that is applied for reasons not related primarily to protection of domestic industry, but that may easily be employed as a trade-distortive device.[29] This kind of discrimination has proven to be an important source of NTBs in such closely related questions as packaging and labeling regulations, health and safety requirements, industrial standards, and so forth.

Third, on the demand side it is clear that the cost and quality changes brought about by product-related EC standards will shift purchasing patterns. Consumers and industrial purchasers will be induced to adopt less-pollutive products in place of those that are inherently more damaging to the environment, and hence more costly to bring up to standard. Substitution between different kinds of fuels, food products, fertilizers, and other products is well underway, and this trend will intensify and spread, with potentially important implications for patterns of international trade.[30] Then too, desirable characteristics of certain products may deteriorate as a result of compliance with environmental norms—examples of deterioration in automotive performance and the quality of paints and pigments may be cited—forcing consumption shifts within the affected product groups or between them. Lastly, there is a possible income-effect, with reduced consumption of affected and unaffected products as a result of significant EC-induced increases in product costs.

In the capital-goods sector, certain types of equipment may become obsolete due to their environmental characteristics. Shifts in the generation of electric power from fossil fuels to nuclear energy will have this effect, as will new "clean" ways of generating electricity which dispense with the heat cycle altogether. If public policy fosters the increased use of mass transit to replace the private automobile, we can expect demand and trade pattern to shift to other types of vehicles and transport equipment: a shift in trade flows from consumer durables into substitute capital goods.

Similar developments can be expected in the consumer nondurables sector. Demand alterations have already affected the detergent industry and, although trade in the final product is fairly limited relative to demand, trade in intermediate inputs is substantial. The packaging materials industry will also be affected as minimum-biodegradability standards are applied to products that are deemed damaging to the environment as solid wastes. More speculative are prospective shifts in demand for food products in response to concern with agricultural pollution and toxic residues in the food chain. Trade in fisheries products is the most notable example thus far, with certain types of meat and vegetable products potentially affected in the future.

It is difficult to gauge the extent to which individuals will shift their preferences in response to environmental damage entailed in the manufacture of consumer goods. Much depends on media coverage and emotionalism, and to a certain extent the effects may be short term in character; they will diminish as the environmental damage is alleviated or slips from the public consciousness.[31] Trade flows in certain products will be severely affected, but this phenomenon will be intermittent and without a consistent pattern. The one area where a permanent demand shift has affected trade involves furs, skins, and other products from animals in danger of extinction (e.g., crocodile leather, seal skins, ivory, leopard skins, whale meat, etc.), as well as certain types of woods (e.g., redwood) subject to an extremely long growth cycle. These products have traditionally occupied an important but diminishing role in international trade, and can be expected to decline to insignificance in the intermediate term—with possible subsequent resurgence in specific products amenable to conservation and "controlled harvesting" practices.

Perhaps the most important sectors in international trade potentially affected by demand-substitution are raw materials and fuels. The sulphur content of fuels has already produced dramatic shifts, and these can be expected to intensify. The sulphur content of coal and crude oil is important in determining trade flows because it varies significantly by source, rendering certain sources preferred over others. Where it is too high, desulfurization must be performed before it is acceptable for use as a fuel in stationary heat and power applications, and this influences competitiveness. Trade in natural gas, an inherently clean fuel, can be expected to grow rapidly, particularly in Europe. And where pipelines are not a feasible mode of transport between origin and destination, trade in liquified natural gas (LNG) can be expected to develop rapidly. For the same reason, trade in nuclear fuels may also grow substantially in the longer run. Although the emerging global fuel shortage will overshadow some of the environmental effects, they will nevertheless influence trade patterns in the intermediate term.

There is also likely to be some shift in demand for raw material inputs from synthetics to natural products, particularly where they are close substitutes and where the production of synthetics involves substantial environmental-control costs.[32] Some examples are substitution of natural rubber for synthetic rubber, and wood and leather for plastics. This may succeed in raising prices of certain raw materials and export receipts of countries producing them. It may also increase the elasticity of demand for the products in question thereby reducing their price volatility, although the problem of supply elasticity remains.

In general, the greater the EC cost component of a particular goods, the greater is the likelihood that less-pollutive products will replace it both in international trade flows and in the general configuration of demand patterns. The extent, of course, depends on the relevant cross-price elasticities of demand. The importance of such substitution for trade patterns can only be gauged once national environmental standards are known and have been translated into unit-cost estimates.

4. Trade-Policy Vectors

If indeed environmental controls relating to products and processes significantly influence international competitiveness and trade flows, then certain implications for commercial policy must be considered. First, how important are the cost-effects of EC norms in relation to tariffs and nontariff distortions of trade? If, for example, a given product is already subject to quantitative import controls, then tightened national environmental standards will have little or no impact on domestic producers' competitive viability in the home market. If high effected tariffs or other levies already severely restrict imports, the additional effective protection afforded by foreign EC standards, or the loss of effective protection in the case of domestic environmental measures, may be marginal.[33]

There is little available information as yet on the effective protective implications of environmental control. It is clear that in certain sectors the impact will not be very significant while in others it will be important—particularly primary metals, pulp and paper, and chemicals. The relative effects will clearly be greater within regional free-trade areas, and if future multilateral trade negotiations successfully culminate in major reductions in tariffs and nontariff barriers on manufactured products on a global basis.

Second, there is already some pressure building to establish countervailing duties or other special charges to offset competitive advantages of foreign suppliers operating under less stringent environmental standards. If differences in norms are the result of international variations in environmental assimilative capacity or social preference patterns—in the absence of transboundary effects—there is no a priori justification for such measures. EAC can be treated as a supply factor similar to a depletable but potentially regenerative natural resource, which enters into the determination of comparative advantage just like any other factor of production. And domestic demand for that factor enters into its pricing, as revealed in the domestic EC standards adopted by the society in question. To countervail competitive advantages attributable to environmental measures is thus no more justified than similar protection designed to offset differences in capital or labor costs.

These arguments will not, however, head off periodic EC-induced demands for protection, particularly where domestic environmental measures are wholly or partly implemented by means of punitive taxation or rigorous enforcement of standards.[34] One may even envisage the general imposition of countervailing duties based on the ad valorem equivalent (AVE) of domestic EC charges applied to all products where this issue is deemed troublesome, whether or not the imported goods were in fact produced under similar conditions of environmental stringency. Such charges would not be inconsistent with existing trade rules (Article III.1 of the GATT), which are concerned only with the principle that imported goods should be taxed no more heavily than domestically-produced goods.[35] They would also require rebate of the charge on exports, in order to avoid penalizing home produced goods in other countries applying a similar system. The scope for implicit protection in any such arrangements is obvious.

This type of scheme is very similar to the application of border taxes and the "destination principle" of adjustment for international differences in indirect business taxation, currently in widespread use. It would demand a complete schedule of A.V.E. compensatory EC adjustments paralleling the national tariff schedules for affected products. The incidence of these charges would vary widely among different kinds of goods, and would eliminate all EC incentives for the international reallocation of production.

It would also be exceedingly complex and difficult to administer in an equitable manner. For example, a domestic firm which succeeds in reducing the incidence of EC costs falling on its products as a result of existing norms would benefit substantially in the face of a continuation of equalization charges on competitive imports and rebates on its exports. Furthermore, elaborate investigative machinery would be required to set compensatory rates, including appeals procedures for the affected industries. Changes in these rates might require significant policy responses on the part of foreign governments. The system would also have to be adopted by all of the major competitor countries applying EC measures in order to avoid inequities, and hence its establishment would be complex indeed.

Aside from the industries most directly affected by pollution-abatement standards, the cost-incidence of countervailing import changes would be felt in a wide variety of user-industries as well. As a practical matter, therefore, compensatory surcharges and rebates would take the form of rough approximations or flat rates covering a variety of different manufacturing activities, and would involve the danger of serious overcompensation or undercompensation with respect to specific industries and products.

The problem becomes even more complex when this kind of system is used in conjunction with punitive pollution taxes and pollution abatement measures applied by domestic industry result in a reduction in the tax incidence. Logically, any import surcharges and export rebates should then be reduced along with the degree of conformity with EC standards and the concomitant reduction of associated punitive taxes. In the international environment this would place at a relative disadvantage precisely those suppliers progressing with environmental control but work in favor of laggards or those producing under less rigorous standards.[36] Retention of EC equalization duties and export rebates under such conditions would be environmentally undesirable clearly inconsistent with existing GATT rules.

Compensatory commercial policy arrangements of this nature can easily evolve into de facto nontariff distortions of international trade and lead to falsification of international competitiveness, e.g., if the surcharge/rebate is deliberately increased beyond justified levels to favor domestic industry. Moreover, there is sufficient room for misinterpretation on the part of trading partners, particularly by those favoring other solutions to the international competitive aspects of environmental control and those less concerned with the entire issue. The result is a danger of retaliation.

If the "polluter pays" concept is universally adopted, or at least adopted among all of the industrial countries, it should not be difficult to avoid the development of general commercial policy measures imposed for environmental reasons. Any pressure for compensatory protection will be roughly in proportion to prevailing differences in EC standards, but will be highly industry specific and product specific. If, however, significant supplier-countries do not subscribe to the "polluter pays" principle, or if there are major derogations from it in countries that do—e.g., via extensive subsidization—then offsetting import levies of quantative restrictions can be expected in the affected importing countries in the name of "fair" competition justification. Such restrictions would, like existing antidumping and countervailing measures, be aimed only at offending suppliers and would persist until a determination has been made that the problem has been rectified.[37]

5. Patterns of Industrial Location

If international differences in environmental standards and their enforcement are likely to affect patterns of international trade, they are equally likely to influence patterns of international investment. Given interregional and international differences in environmental assimilative capacity and/or collective preferences as reflected in EC norms, decisions affecting the location or relocation of industrial facilities will and should be influenced accordingly. Options available to the individual firm thus hinge on (a) the importance of EC as a cost element, (b) the existence of differences in EC standards, (c) differences in labor availability and quality, public services, transport costs and proximity to markets, and (d) the nature of the firm's own logistical network, the character of its product, and its rate of growth in required productive capacity.

There is as yet very little evidence that would indicate the possible future impact of EC induced international shifts in industrial location. There is, however, some evidence that this has indeed been occurring interregionally within industrial economies. In the United States, for example, a number of political jurisdictions have begun to discourage industrial location and new investment, following an implicit cost-benefit assessment that the negative environmental consequences of such invest substantially outweigh the attendant static and dynamic economic gains.[38] Particularly affected are the pollution intensive facilities such as steel mills, copper smelting plants, open-pit mines, chemical plants, refineries, and related transportation facilities. Also affected are public sector investments such as power plants, highways, and airports.

It is tempting to generalize that regions adopting antidevelopment policies for environmental reasons tend to be characterized by relatively high incomes and historical development patterns, as would be expected of areas adopting such a position in the growth-vs.-environment tradeoff. The political balance in other regions of the United States, particularly in the South, appears to be quite different and represents a fundamentally different evaluation of the alternatives. The result may be a major increase in the importance of environmental considerations in decisions regarding industrial location and interregional capital flows, and a shift in economic development and commercial trends within the nation as a whole. And we would expect environmental pressures to promote a gradual shift of pollution-intensive forms of economic activity from higher-income to lower-income regions domestically and from higher-income to lower-income countries internationally, with the range of activities affected gradually widening over time. This will have notable implications for the development process, patterns of international trade, and commercial policy.

Any such impact on the international economy will tend to be felt initially at an industry level and progressively spread to broader ranges of economic activity. Firms that find preferred sites excluded for environmental reasons have available alternatives which encompass both domestic and foreign locations, and there are bound to be certain international locational spillovers attributable to local or regional environmental control. As domestic environmental awareness and cost assessments increase in leading countries, these spillovers will tend to grow, with foreign locations appearing progressively more advantageous relative to domestic locations, and environmental considerations increasing in importance relative to other factors determining locational decisions. Since inter-country variations in ecological awareness are always likely to exceed inter-regional domestic variations, and since the imposition of homogeneous environmental control standards internationally is likely to lag well behind domestic harmonization, the scope for and extent of international locational spillovers will tend to be both significant and long-lived. There may indeed be instances where the export of pollution through capital investments abroad becomes national policy in certain economic sectors, to the benefit of both the capital-exporting and capital-importing countries. But the political sensitivity of this issue would ensure that any such policy will be applied with a great deal of circumspection.[39]

Not least important, trade flows will also be affected. Firms locating abroad for EC reasons may serve the home market and third markets from the new location, thereby raising home country imports and reducing exports of the products in question, although trade shifts in inputs may be in the opposite direction. Processing may be done closer to the sources of raw materials, particularly in developing countries, resulting in a rise in the average value of their exports. One would expect, for example, EC considerations to contribute to the development of refineries and petrochemical plants in petroleum-exporting countries, with high-value product rather than crude oil entering trade channels. Metallic ores, lumber, and certain chemicals may be similarly affected.

To the extent that some domestic suppliers remain as import competitors, abiding by strict EC norms, governmental reaction to such locational flight into "pollution havens" may be expected. This may take the form of highly differentiated import controls as between basic raw materials and successively higher levels of processing, and block some of the gains expected from locational shifts. At the same time, serious questions will be raised about the social responsibility of business flight to pollution havens, with regard to its impact on the domestic economy, the environment in recipient countries, and global environmental balance. Lastly, although less rigorus EC standards may initially have induced investment in a given host country, a point will eventually be reached when ecological balance will become a major concern there as well, and the same kinds of conflicts may arise as prompted the initial location decision. And these tensions may well be magnified at that point because the polluting firms are foreign-owned.

As noted earlier, virtually no information is available thus far on the sensitivity of industrial location decisions to international differences in EC norms. If emerging differences in standards in fact reflected differences in environmental assimilative capacity and social preferences—and if environmental impacts are indeed localized with minimal transboundary effects—then any resulting capital flows will tend to narrow the gap between marginal social costs and marginal social benefits on a global scale, and thereby serve the general welfare. But it is much too early to get an accurate picture of the variables involved in this calculus, or to make defensible forecasts—except that the impact will tend to be longer term in nature, often inseparable from other factors affecting international locational decisions.

6. New Products and Services

Environmental control may give rise to the development of a wide variety of goods and services (particularly technology) that are internationally traded. Products considered pollutants in their normal use will have to be altered in character to conform to new requirements. In the process, entirely new substitutes will involve or existing products will be modified using new components. For example, major U.S. imports in the form of rights to the Wankel rotary-combustion engine as well as platinum and other metals for catalytic converters can be traced directly to tightened EC regulations in the automobile industry, as can U.S. exports of aircraft-engine modifications to alleviate particulate emissions. Similarly, trade in new products and services will arise out of requirements to minimize the pollutive attributes of residuals, including a variety of chemicals, biodegradable and recyclable containers, and other products.

But there is even more potential for tradable innovation in the alleviation of pollutive processes, both in hardware and software. If we are correct that variations in environmental management among national states are largely manifestations of lead-lag relationships rather than long-term, enduring absolute differences, then the need for environmental control will eventually influence all national economies. This follows even if its incidence at any point in time may be quite different among individual countries—depending on its specific seriousness at the national and subnational level and on the accompanying political perceptions and public policy reactions. Lead-countries and affected firms will tend to be in the forefront of development of EC-sensitive production technology which, in turn, becomes highly exportable—through consulting services, licensing and other devices—to countries less advanced in this respect. Furthermore, certain types of EC hardware embodying this technology will evolve into competitive products on world markets. Examples include filters, wet scrubbers, electrostatic precipitators, waste recycling equipment, cooling towers, sewage treatment plants and components, measuring devices and instrumentation, etc.

Assuming that this proposition is correct, then countries leading in the EC effort will tend (on net) to emerge with a competitive advantage in international markets for the relevant product and services. The U.S. market for air pollution equipment alone is expected to grow from $150 million in 1970 to $600 million in 1980. Preliminary estimates gauge the size of the combined U.S.-European market in the mid-1970s at over $1 billion and growing at the rate of about 20 percent annually through the early 1980s. If this is correct, then the global market including Japan and the other industrial countries, as well as—eventually—the developing nations, could be very substantial indeed.[40]

Moreover, a demonstration-effect may develop whereby new and more efficient ways of coping with environmental problems emerge under pressure in the leading countries, causing lagging countries to adopt more vigorous standards and enforcement, and forcing their industries to conform using the technology and hardware developed abroad. A principal force in this process may be the multinational enterprise, which has the advantage of almost instantaneous intrafirm transfers of the appropriate technology. It simply applies capital and technology in the lagging countries to meet EC requirements that it has already met elsewhere, adapting the most advanced methods and efficient hardware available globally to the situation in question.

Much depends, however, on what the "product cycle" for environmental-control hardware looks like.[41] It is clear that required R&D efforts will be massive, and that much of the resultant manufacturing activity will be highly specialized and tailored to the relatively narrow requirements of specific jobs, both in terms of separate items and as components of major production facilities such as steel mills and petrochemical plants. But how rapidly can the built-in technology be transferred? And to what extent will "standard" products such as pumps, compressors, tanks, fine-mesh stainless steel and fabric filters, etc., be involved? There is considerable evidence available that points in one direction or the other, but no coherent pattern has emerged as yet. Consequently, it is premature to speculate on what the overall impact of this phenomenon on trade flows will be.

7. Recovery of Tradable Resources

One of the attributes of environmental control is that it usually involves removing something from the ecological system, and whatever is removed often has economic value, either as recovered or after further processing. Virtually all effluents are recoverable, including various kinds of stack emissions, municipal solid wastes, sewage, industrial scrap, even heat. Iron, steel, and certain nonferrous metals have long been reclaimed from various sources—particularly in times of national emergency—as have paper, rubber, glass, and other materials. As environmental standards are tightened, the range of reclaimed products widens to include sulphur (from stack emissions and desulferization plants) and other chemicals, building materials, metals not previously recovered, etc. Since they have to be taken out of the environment anyway under prevailing EC norms, they may take on the characteristics of a "free good."

Most of the kinds of materials presently reclaimed or for which recovery prospects are good enter the channels of international trade. Hence one would expect that materials recovery will have a significant impact on trade flows, as a positive by-product of environmental protection.

Projecting this impact is difficult because it depends on (a) demand changes, (b) supply of virgin materials, (c) EC standards and enforcement, (d) economics of materials-recovery, and (e) logistics of materials recovery. It is clear that demand for most recyclable materials, and materials for which recyclables are substitutes, will continue to grow, although its composition may change considerably in the longer run. It is also clear that depletion of natural resources will in the long-run raise costs of virgin raw materials—it will raise them in the short run as well if the long-term trends are anticipated in the market—and that the general trend will be a rise in price of most raw materials. This provides the incentive to recycle, which is bound to grow.

What is difficult to predict is future EC standards and their configuration across countries, as noted earlier. Once rigorous standards for effluent-removal have been applied, the effluent itself becomes a base-stock for materials recovery, and the question then turns on the economics and logistics of the recycling process. If raw material prices are low, there is little incentive to recycle and economic pressures may dictate disposal by landfill, incineration, or ocean dumping.[42] But if prices are high and rising, the issue becomes one of processing costs. In some cases it is simple: sulphur dioxide must be removed from stack emissions or from high-sulphur fuels, and elemental sulphur of high purity can be derived cheaply. In other cases it is difficult: the base-stock for materials recovery in municipal waste is of high intrinsic quality, but separation of its components is at present too high in cost to warrant major recovery projects.

Much depends on technology. Advances during the past decade indicate that large-scale materials recovery from municipal wastes, sewage, industrial atmosphere emissions and liquid discharges, may become economic in the next decade. If parallel advances are made collection and distribution systems, and if the economies of scale turn out to be favorable, then we can expect the impact of materials recovery on trade flows to be significant. It may not even be too far-fetched to predict the "mining" of past solid-waste dumps and landfills for the recyclable materials they contain, squandered by earlier generations because the economics were not conducive to reuse. Generally, countries with high levels of income and consumption will become important suppliers of recycled industrial raw materials. The United States already exports metal scrap, rags, and paper in volume, and one would expect such exports to expand and to encompass a much wider array of materials, depending on international demand and supply patterns. Industries processing recovered materials, including chemicals, building materials, fertilizers, and pharmaceuticals, can also be expected to gain in competitive advantage in countries that have large flows of recyclables, as will industries that depend on such processed or unprocessed materials in the production of manufactures and semi-manufactures.

Materials-recovery shows promise of restoring some degree of harmony in the use-reuse cycle on a global level, and dwindling stocks of natural resources will influence, through market pressures, the gradual movement toward ecological balance. Even in the energy sector, economic incineration of nonrecoverable organic materials may conserve natural fuels and thereby affect trade flows. But again, direction and magnitude of the possible impact of materials-recovery remains subject to a great deal of uncertainty.

8. Transport

One of the major determinants of international trade in certain products is the cost of transport. Generally, the lower the value of the traded product per unit size and/or weight, the greater the importance of transport costs per unit distance. For several types of traded goods, particularly fuels, ores and other basic raw materials, lumber, cereal grains and similar bulk commodities, transport costs assume major significance. And since the cost of transport is generally higher in international trade than in domestic trade, the foreign sector tends to be disproportionately sensitive to environmental control policies that affect the transportation industry.[43] This sensitivity is taking several forms:

a. *Marine safety requirements:* Apart from the general need for improved marine safety, a series of collisions involving tankships resulting in oil spills in the recent past have greatly increased pressures in this direction. Investment in anticollision hardware and improved crew training, together with tighter enforcement of existing regulations have and will raise shipping costs—both directly and as a result of delays attributable to more cautious traffic control, particularly in congested areas.

b. *Maximum size limitations:* Economics in bulk transport are achieved primarily by increasing vessel size. But the risk of environmental damage likewise grows with average vessel size, although not proportionately because of the reduced number of ship movements required to handle a given amount of cargo. Pressure is mounting to set limits on maximum vessel size and, unless countered by advances in the safety area, may raise transport costs significantly above what they otherwise would be.

c. *Liability:* Legal responsibility for accidental marine pollution is still being argued, but the trend is clearly toward increased liability for the shipowners, charterers, and shippers. This is raising marine insurance premiums and hence shipping costs. Full liability for environmental damage, however measured, could have a major impact.

d. *Operational changes:* Environmental concern is also affecting standard shipboard operating procedures. Examples include the flushing and cleansing of tanks at sea, sailing under ballast, disposal of shipboard sewage, and dumping of solid wastes. In each case the answer lies either in provision of on-board treatment plants or in performing the necessary operations in port. Both are expensive in terms of capital requirements, as well as port charges, average running times, and other variable costs, and will raise the cost of sea transport.

e. *Port restrictions:* Fear of environmental damage has closed several areas of development of ports, particularly for tankships, and most drastically on the U.S. East coast. This will require either suboptimal re-routing of supply flows or the development of offshore facilities at high cost, both of which will raise transport charges. At existing port facilities, stricter antipollution requirements in cargo handling procedures will have a similar effect.

f. *Restrictions on transmission lines:* The Alaska pipeline controversy is only the most visible of a growing array of actions against the environmental consequence of this form of transport. The disruption of domestic energy supply logistics will spill over onto the trade sector and lead to an increase in imports, a decrease in exports, or both.

g. *Emissions regulations:* There are relatively few air-pollution problems arising from marine and air transport. Particulate emissions from gas-turbine exhaust have already been mentioned, applying both to marine and aircraft propulsion units, and can be remedied fairly easily. Emission from steam-turbine and diesel vessels do not seem to be a serious problem and evidently can be alleviated without significant impact on shipping costs.

It is doubtful that any cost implications of environmental control for international transport will have a major impact on physical trade volumes in the near term, particularly in the critical area of fuels, because they represent a relatively small component of final price and may be submerged by continuing demand growth in the face of steadily more apparent supply limitations. But they will raise the landed value of traded products, which includes transport costs, and may occasionally disrupt normal flows of trade.

9. Transboundary Pollution

Apart from international economic issues raised by differences among nations in their approaches to environmental management, there is the question of direct environmental spillovers in the form of transboundary pollution. There are at least three sources of transboundary pollution: (a) differences in standards between geographically contiguous national states, with the degree of environmental despoilation acceptable to one and not acceptable to the other; (b) impact of pollution within national states on global common-property resources, including the oceans and the atmosphere; and (c) use by national states of certain means of alleviating pollution—such as river systems—which in turn impact on other nations. It is also useful to view transboundary pollution in terms of impact: (a) unidirectional transboundary environmental spillovers do not appreciably degrade the environment of the polluting country, e.g., the upstream-downstream problem; and (b) bidirectional transboundary pollution does impact significantly on the nation that is the source of the problem.[44]

Transboundary environmental issues take on regional and global dimensions, and must, out of necessity, be tackled at the intergovernmental level. Problems arising out of differences in national standards principally affect groups of countries occupying the same airshed and bordering on the same bodies of water. Serious issues have arisen in the case of the Great Lakes of North America, the Baltic and Mediterranean Seas, etc., as well as the Western European airshed.[45] These are almost entirely cases of bidirectional transboundary pollution, and the problem promises to get substantially worse in the intermediate term because of an absence of negotiating machinery or enforceable codes of behavior—even though bidirectionality gives each country an incentive to alleviate the problem. As in the U.S.-Canada case, solutions are indeed possible, partly because only two countries are involved. Institutions for multicountry negotiations are lacking, or, as in the case of OECD, relatively ineffective due to a diffusion of interests. Regional EC authorities have not made much headway, particularly in terms of obtaining supranational enforcement powers.

At the global level, solutions become even more difficult to achieve because of the much broader spectrum of interests involved and the wider ranges of concerns over the world ecosystem. Efforts have been made—as in the 1972 United Nations Conference on the Human Environment—to resolve the problem by mutual agreement on environmental liability: each nation is in principle liable for the damage its actions cause to the environment of others. The two critical issues that remain to be resolved are the definition of "damage" and the enforcement of "liability." The pattern of past United Nations successes and failures in formulating and enforcing meaningful resolutions on a variety of other issues does not augur well for its role in the resolution of transboundary environmental problems.[46]

If agreements are reached on transboundary EC issues arising from differences in national norms, the economic impact could be substantial. Widespread shifts in farming methods can be expected, for example, to prevent runoffs carrying fertilizers, pesticides and fungicides, and agricultural practices in this area would become more uniform. Industrial location may shift from areas where the possibility of transboundary pollution provided easy access to cheap disposal of wastes and effluents, to areas that seem suitable from a location-logistic viewpoint once the environmental inducement has been removed. While the net shift in location of industries may be costly in terms of structural readjustment and higher environmental related costs, it may actually approximate more closely the optimal location pattern in the absence of environmental considerations.

A special problem arises in the case of unidirectional environmental despoilation, where the polluting nation does not feel the impact of its actions and hence has no explicit incentive to mend its ways. Typical is the multipurpose use of a river system by several nations for transport, potable water, sewage and other waste-disposal, power, and perhaps irrigation. What one nation does may be geared entirely to its own problems and priorities, without due regard to what happens to the opposite or downstream country. The latter must accept what it gets, work with it as best it can given its own political and economic policy configurations, and influence the system accordingly. There is no explicit incentive to eliminate pollution; indeed there is a bias to maximize it because it is essentially costless for the political collectivity in question. Over time, this situation has greatly influenced patterns of industrial development among the advanced countries—patterns that threaten to be repeated in developing countries.

The solution is to raise the incremental costs of unidirectional transboundary pollution so that they exceed the incremental benefits to the offending country. This can be done by imposing bilateral or multilateral sanctions, or by changing the offender's perceptions of his own actions and their effects. Both are difficult but not impossible to achieve, depending on how the necessary political and economic leverage is distributed. More positive results can be attained by redefining the political collectivity to encompass all affected states and impose a coherent control system that minimizes the benefits of exploiting relative to the costs of maintaining the resource for the participants as a group. Experience with subnational collectivities in the United States—states, counties, special districts, and municipalities—shows that even this solution is extremely difficult to achieve without strong and binding central authority.

The outlook, then, is for slow progress in the areas of transboundary pollution, interspersed with periodic international conflicts as symptoms get recognized or exceed the existing level of tolerance and international political reaction develops. Principal industries affected will continue to be agriculture, electric power, iron and steel, nonferrous metals, chemicals, petroleum and particular kinds of manufacturing activity. Many can expect to benefit competitively from the expected policy lags in this area. But reactions, because they do take on international political dimensions, may be uncommonly harsh and entail substantial adjustment costs.

10. Depletable Resource Stocks

Much attention has been given to the "crisis" attributable to a constant stock of natural resources in the face of rapidly growing demand. This issue is often tied to the environmental questions because natural resource recovery itself frequently involves serious environmental disruption, because certain natural resources (climate, water supply, space) are part of the environment as normally defined, and because the same kinds of aggregate forces, such as population expansion and economic growth, have similar long-range implications for both the environment and the adequacy of natural resource supplies. The issue, and some of the remedies suggested to deal with it, have important implications for the future of the international economy.

Of greatest intermediate-range importance is the "energy crisis" with the outlook being for short-term, sometimes severe dislocations of supply and demand, and with an overriding, longer-term rise in global energy prices. In the very long run, however, the problem may become irrelevant with the development of energy sources not based on depletable natural resources.

Countries that previously had a balanced energy economy, as the United States and U.S.S.R., shift in the intermediate term to becoming major exporters or importers, or both. Countries that were large importers become less dependent on foreign supplies as local sources of the same fuel or substitutes are discovered and developed. Countries that were large exporters shift their strategy from maximum trade volumes at prevailing prices to restricting development and export, husbanding reserves, and exploiting their new-found leverage in the international marketplace. International commercial and financial relations will be affected in a variety of ways.

First, fuel-producing countries such as the United States previously geared to self-sufficiency, will become increasingly dependent on imports, and trade restrictions applied to fuels will gradually become redundant. Incentives for domestic exploration may be maintained or increased, but this will only slow the steady rise of energy imports. For the United States, these include crude oil, petroleum products and petrochemical feedstocks, liquified natural gas, liquified petroleum gas, natural gas via pipelines, and electric power. U.S. coal exports may be maintained or increase in the intermediate term, but decline over the long term as domestic prices rise and new users for coal are developed to the stage of economic viability. Incremental domestic production of fuels will be insufficient to meet incremental demand but the shortage will be narrowed as prices rise, by shale oil recovery, secondary recovery techniques, and the development of nuclear, fuel-cell, and other advanced sources of power.

Second, new fuel exporters will emerge as rising prices and shifting national energy policies stimulate exploration and recovery. The list that already includes the U.S.S.R., Nigeria and Indonesia, will doubtless grow in the future. These countries are chronically short of foreign exchange and the present value of export receipts is extremely high, causing them to opt for long-term supply contracts, liberal exploration rights, imported capital equipment including turn-key processing plants, and foreign technical-assistance arrangements. As they become mature energy exporters these policies will change, but not in the foreseeable future.

Third, the major volume suppliers of fuels to the world markets, including North Africa, Venezuela, Iran, and the Middle East have increased their bargaining power considerably, and have turned this into substantially higher crude oil prices. Supplier pressure on prices can be expected to continue, along with increasing caution regarding the volume of production and rates of depletion. There is a real question how a country that has one principal export commodity can maximize its long-term welfare when the supply elements underlying those exports have a finite life and are nonrenewable. One can predict that supplier cartels such as the Organization of Petroleum Exporting Countries (OPEC) will draw closer together and become more binding on the participants. Fuel exporting countries will also continue to press for increasing national participation in ownership, management, and control of production and transport facilities, and to renew demands for an increased share of export receipts.

One can also predict that efforts will be made to increase the value-added of exports based on crude oil and natural gas. Hence it will hardly be surprising—particularly in the light of the relatively lax EC standards likely to exist—to find refineries and petrochemical plants, as well as gas liquification plants, being built at the principal OPEC terminals. The major oil firms may be encouraged to participate, or the plants may be state-owned and built with technical assistance from abroad. This will signal a major change in the logistics of the fuel industry, with the stream of crude dividing into streams of product at the export terminals rather than at the import terminals or intermediate points, as has traditionally been the case.

Finally, it is not expected that pressures of this type originating at the supply end will be received passively in the major markets, particularly in the major fuel-deficit countries of Western Europe and Japan. Hence there is an expected tendency, already in evidence, for national governments to involve themselves individually and collectively directly in negotiations with the exporters, with the oil firms themselves playing an increasingly passive role in the critical phases of discussions. There is also the tendency to tie the principal energy suppliers to the industrial markets by trade agreements and other devices in the search for security in sources of fossil fuels.

The foregoing trends will characterize world energy markets in the foreseeable future, perhaps until the end of the century. Demand growth is fairly predictable, and supply estimates for traditional fuels are also reasonably good—albeit with greater margins for error. What is highly uncertain is the development of substitutes—immediately in the nuclear field but later in more exotic energy forms—and hence the uncertainty regarding the price and income elasticity of demand for oil, coal, and natural gas. Experience with nuclear power sources seems to indicate that the growth of on-line capacity will be gradual, slower than initial projections—partly for environmental reasons. But this does not preclude major breakthroughs in the 1980s or 1990s which would signal the start of a new ball game in the international energy market.

Natural resource-exporting countries will tend to be subject to the same kinds of market factors, but the pattern will be much more diffuse. Each type of mineral will exhibit a unique scarcity pattern, depending on discoveries of new supplies, demand growth, availability of viable substitutes, etc. In most cases, uncertainty about the direction and magnitude of market trends is much greater than in the case of fuels. Hence it is difficult to project what shifts in trade flows or changes in world prices will occur. It is even more difficult to project what will be the policy responses of the mineral exporting countries' governments in their efforts to maximize the contribution of available natural resources to national economic growth. They will demand increasing national control over mining and other recovery operations, as well as internal processing to attain higher value-added in exports.[47]

Another point that needs to be mentioned, about which very little is known as yet, is the exploitation of the sea-bed, both for fuels and other minerals. Undersea resources may drastically alter available supplies of certain raw materials and introduce an entirely new factor into world markets, and this needs to be drawn into any projections as a caveat. There is also the question of who "owns" these resources and how they are to be extracted. This is predominantly a legal issue with strong economic and political overtones, with which the United Nations is currently occupying itself.[48] Hopefully there will be a definitive and enforceable resolution of this problem well before technical advances make raw material extraction in volume from the seabed commercially feasible. In any case, the long-range implications for international economic relations are significant indeed.

11. Special Problems Relating to the Developing Countries

The developing nations of the world, encompassing two-thirds of its population, are faced with problems—overpopulation, hunger and malnutrition, unemployment and underemployment, illiteracy, rural-urban balance and chronic poverty—many of which can only be solved by economic growth in the conventional sense. This means absorbing larger proportions of the labor force in productive employment and raising efficiency in the use of scarce productive resources.

In this context, the reactions of political leaders in developing countries to pressures for environmental protection is predictable: within the social welfare function that faces them, ecological questions generally assume a subordinate role. Under present conditions, they simply cannot afford to forego maximum possible economic growth and generally must reject out of hand anything which may interfere materially with this objective. They cannot concern themselves with the fine points of industrial location, water pollution, or despoilation of the land, and a certain degree of environmental degradation is accepted as a necessary cost of the otherwise efficient achievement of their primary objectives. To them, ecological balance is often a luxury at this stage of their development, although it is generally recognized that excessive postponement of concern with this issue may give rise to major problems at a later stage.[49]

Second, the effects of environmental pollution are frequently less marked in developing countries because their environmental assimilative capacity may be quite high. Hot, dry climates tend to minimize the impact of certain effluents of production processes. High rainfall levels reduce the impact on air quality of some types of emissions. Low population densities reduce the effects of other types of pollution, and large undeveloped tracts of land render marginal encroachment by industry of minor significance. And the people themselves may operate under entirely different conceptions of the quality of life; they are concerned more with elementary survival, nutritional adequacy, and health than the environmental side-effects of the means of achieving these very fundamental goals.

On the basis of such dramatic differences in environmental assimilative capacity and social priorities, one would expect environmental control policies in the developing countries to differ fundamentally from those applied in the more advanced economies. This could manifest itself in different EC standards and timetables. With the marginal social benefit of pollution-intensive industries exceeding their marginal social cost in the developing countries, one would expect them to welcome investment in these sectors, even at some cost to the environment.[50] One would also expect them to have a relatively durable competitive advantage in the international markets for certain pollution-intensive product groups.

This may prove to be generally beneficial by promoting a convergence of marginal social benefits and costs on a global scale. The advanced countries benefit by having available products through imports from developing areas without the pollution-causing industrial processes, while at the same time much of the income generated in the developing countries will engender increased exports from the advanced economies. The developing countries benefit through: (a) increased employment, productivity and incomes; (b) increased capital inflows and capital formation; (c) improved social and economic overhead facilities; (d) enhanced educational and training levels of the work force; (e) increased and sustained exports and capacity to import, as well as (f) standard developmental linkages relating to supplier industries, the services sector, etc. Gradual transfers to the developing countries of certain types of pollution-intensive manufacturing activities should therefore benefit the international economy as a whole.[51] At the same time, such trends might be counteracted by pressures in advanced nations in cases of significant environmental spillovers, e.g., oceanic pollution or more general pollution of the atmosphere.

Commercial-policy offsets might also be employed under such circumstances. Goods produced in developing countries under high-pollution conditions may run into significant trade barriers when exported to the industrial markets and compete with products supplied under much more stringent environmental controls. This may occur whether or not conscious decisions are made to escape the latter by locating pollution-intensive activities in the developing countries. Moreover, certain commercial-policy reactions of this nature may affect suppliers located within developing economics in a disproportionate manner.

On the trade side, developing countries may be affected in several other ways as well:

a. There may be import restrictions in the advanced countries on goods produced with the aid of certain pesticides and the chemicals.

b. Certain traditional exports of developing countries which foster pollution may be restricted; there is already some evidence, for example, of geographical shifts in oil imports into the industrial countries as a result of the aforementioned restrictions on sulphur-dioxide emissions and on the permissible sulphur content of fuels. In many instances compliance with standards governing international trade in products considered to be environmentally damaging, may be extremely difficult for developing countries, particularly when these standards themselves are extremely vague.

c. Since many synthetic materials are produced in a manner highly damaging to the environment, the unit cost of synthetics tends to be rather sensitive to pollution control standards. This may well favor natural substitutes for the affected synthetics, particularly in the areas of fertilizers, food products, detergents, and oils and fats, all of which are major exports of the developing countries. Both from a cost and preference standpoint, there may thus be a partial offset to the long-term tendency in the substitution of synthetics for natural products, which may be of some benefit to suppliers operating in developing countries.

d. The problem of solid waste disposal in the advanced countries, as well as the generation of useful by-products from pollution control activities, may work to the detriment of suppliers of raw materials in the developing countries: recycling and the extensive use of secondary raw materials. This effect, however, will make itself felt very gradually over a long period of time.

e. Developing countries may benefit directly from environment control programs established in the advanced nations of the world by preserving their own resource bases. While certain of their own more immediate environmental needs—such as the separation of storm and sanitary sewers—might prove extremely expensive, ecological problems such as the disposal of solid wastes remain far in the future for most developing countries. The internal market for such wastes may be expected to absorb them for the foreseeable future. And producers in the developing countries may have the additional advantage of lower costs of pollution control attending new production facilities as opposed to the retrofitting of older plants in the industrial countries.

On the basis of differences in EAC and societal preferences regarding the environment between developed and developing countries, it might not be inappropriate to project that, on net, the EC issue may help rather than hinder the LDCs' position in the international economy. This may be a transitional phenomenon but it may in the interim assist them toward sustained and orderly export-led growth and the eventual achievement of economic balance. Indeed, stringent environmental control in the developed countries may favor both export promotion and import substitution in the developing economies by increasing the relative competitiveness of their exports and simultaneously reducing the relative competitiveness of their imports.

Nevertheless, the developing countries have several distinct concerns on the environmental front, some imagined and some real. They are worried that preoccupation with environmental management in the industrial countries will divert financial and real resources from needed economic assistance for development.[52] They are concerned that the developed countries will try to pressure them into adopting and enforcing environmental norms entirely inappropriate to their societies, including adverse project-appraisal in bilateral, multilateral, and international organization aid and lending programs because high levels of environmental safeguards are not being met.[53] They feel that they can adapt production facilities to their own environmental conditions, but fear that misdirected altruism and paternalism in the developed world will impede beneficial "capital exports with pollution."[54]

At the same time, the developing countries are hoping for special assistance in meeting some of the economic and social problems arising out of their ultimate need for environmental management. This includes aid for restructuring their national economies to meet environmental standards set elsewhere: If the industrial countries have ruined their own environment and want to enforce common standards, then they should pay for at least part of the maintenance of these standards in the LDCs, where the environment is still relatively undamaged.[55] They are hoping for special treatment, including postponement of remedial EC action, for any common standards and approaches to the problem agreed upon at the international level. This might be accompanied by an early warning, impact-cushioning form of technical assistance and prior consultations on new departures in environmental policy.

12. The Larger Issue:
Population and Growth

Finally there is the nagging question whether all of this is really relevant. If recent projections of the environmental consequences of continued historical growth trends (including resource depletion) are anywhere near the mark, the kinds of problems discussed in this chapter are close to irrelevant. Instead of being major issues of concern, they simply become minor symptoms of a problem that calls into question the very prospect of human survival. Demands on the life-support cababilities of the globe, caused by more people using more resources without adequately reintroducing those resources into the system, will eventually force severe limits on growth—and the only question is at what level of living that essentially stationary state will occur.

Projections of this type, based on dynamic growth models with essentially static constraints, inevitably conclude that growth must stop; that we can get more out of the limited capacity for growth that is left by drastically rearranging our priorities in virtually all areas of human endeavor. It is easy to dismiss such projections on the basis of obvious flaws in the assumptions and the dismal failure of such forecasts in the past. But this would be imprudent. Such studies do point out that bottlenecks will in fact develop, some earlier than others and some more serious and abrupt than others. They also indicate that if ultimate doom is to be prevented (or at least delayed) then the restoration of balance in the use and re-use of natural and common-property resources must be given top priority. If governments take this seriously, as they should, then some of the implications of environmental control for the international economy discussed here become very much more pronounced.[56] Lastly, they indicate that there are limits to everything within a given time-frame, and as those limits are approached the real cost of further growth becomes successively greater.

It is doubtful that economic growth will be purposely and seriously throttled for the sake of the global ecosystem. After all, growth is both a cause of and a cure for environmental despoilation, and the political feasibility of enforced growth limits is another question entirely.[57] But the limits will indeed make themselves felt as environmental damage becomes increasingly apparent and resources are directed to its restoration and control, and growth in conventional terms will be slower than it would be otherwise. Both demand and supply patterns will shift and the international commercial and financial implications of this shift is what this paper is all about.

There is one direct link between the normative policy prescriptions of growth/environment models and their actual implementation by national governments. This is the matter of population control, already being applied or considered in most nations. Whereas global population planning is well beyond reach at present, control at the national level will grow steadily stimulated periodically by threats of international displacement of people and problems of migration and localized internal symptoms of overcrowding.[58] This will affect growth, and it will also affect the international economy, since both demand for and supply of traded goods and services are in part a function of population.

The Present State of Theory
and Policy

In discussing the various ways in which environmental management may have a bearing on the future of the international economic order, we have attempted to incorporate as many of the theoretical issues and alternative policy scenarios as are apparent and plausible. The basic question is what weights should be attached to each in terms of its influence on the world economy in the future decades. Here the underlying problem of uncertainty is compounded; the fact that we know little about *how* the individual factors will affect the system makes assessments of their absolute and relative significance doubly difficult.

A theoretical underpinning of environmental economics is the question of externalities: the impact of economic activities—consumption or production—by one entity on those of others.[59] In standard general equilibrium systems, such interdependence always exists via the indirect linkage of relative prices and factor returns. But externalities produce a direct link via production and utility functions. Externalities are generally recognized as a major reason for the apparent difference between "net private product" and "net social product," and in a policy context for the rejection of perfect competition as a universal norm in the search for maximum social welfare.[60] Externalities can be internalized via the market mechanism, either wholly or partially, if a price is placed on the spillover. A new market for current waste-products will succeed in its internalization, and so will a charge levied on "bad" spillovers if the common-property resources involved were previously unpriced. The problem is that the market functions only imperfectly and that policy measures must be applied on behalf of the political collectivity in order to jog the system closer to some kind of societal optimum.[61]

Environmental externalities appear to develop rapidly as an economy grows, with substantial impact on society at large, as a problem " . . . not so much as between firms or industries, but as between, on the one hand, the producers and/or the users of spillover-creating goods and, on the other, the public at large."[62] As a result, any collective measures to deal with environmental spillovers has serious implications for both the distribution of welfare and for the applicable welfare criterion itself. This is because movement toward whatever welfare criterion has been selected to incorporate quality of the environment involves costs which do not fall equally on members of the collectivity. These so-called "transaction costs" include the cost of reaching an agreement among the affected parties and identifying who they are, the cost of maintaining and revising the agreed-upon standards, and the capital and continuing costs of implementing those standards.[63]

Specific social hypotheses that have arisen out of the issue of environmental spillovers include the following: (a) Environmental "bads" are inherently regressive in that environmental damage is associated with economic activities of higher-income groups in society and impacts disproportionately on lower-income groups. (b) EC trends may cause enterprises to intensify the environment spillovers in order to reap greater rewards from whatever remedial actions may be undertaken. (c) There is a difference between "welfare" and "ethical" symmetries in environmental spillovers and their control. Pollution benefits one group and harms another, but so does abstinence from pollution; and yet ethical guidelines can be devised which can indeed justify environmental controls.

(d) Much depends on the marginal social utility of additional real income relative to the marginal social disutility of accompanying environmental despoilation. Unless the functions can be shifted, this determines the rate at which per-capita real income growth will need to be constrained or even revised.[64] (e) The fact that certain kinds of environmental spillovers may have intergenerational consequences redefines the collectivity whose welfare needs to be maximized—with one group not having any voice in the relevant decisions. Consequently the tradeoff built into current policy may not reflect losses inflicted on posterity, and hence do not represent internalization of environmental externalities in the time dimension. (f) The time element in the development of new products and processes does not necessarily coincide with the time element in assessment of their long-term environmental consequences. This raises the probability of catastrophe and calls for extreme caution.[65]

Direct environmental spillovers are of concern principally in the area of transboundary pollution, and the real question is whether the foregoing conceptual points are valid in this context—in a world of politically sovereign national states. If they are, there is still the very real question whether they mean very much in the absence of supranational institutions or other vehicles for expressing and defending the interests of the whole. Altruism and exhortation may not be enough, and serious international conflicts may well arise in the future.

Policy developments in this area have been limited, partly because the required transnational forums have not existed. Some progress has been made in bilateral negotiations—as between the United States and Canada and between Germany and Switzerland—where bidirectional transboundary pollution has affected national interests. Far less progress has been made on a multilateral level, as in the OECD and EEC, in part because of the problem of mutuality of interests—with some countries concerned with a particular transboundary issue and others not—and because the requisite degree of supranational concern does not yet exist. At the global level it is expected that an appropriate agency will eventually coordinate all environmental affairs of the United Nations related to transboundary issues. But this will take time, and the potential effectiveness of any such agency remains an open question. One can expect that most progress in the intermediate term will be made on an ad hoc basis through interregional negotiations of countries directly concerned with individual instances of transboundary environmental despoilation. In addition, the EEC may obtain a certain degree of supranational authority in this field, but very little progress appears to have been made so far.[66]

Disregarding for a moment the transboundary issue, the implications of environmental control for the international economic order are basically traceable to differences among national states in attaching the problem of negative environmental spillovers within their own borders. These differences may be analyzed in terms of standards, timing, enforcement, and implementation.

With respect to standards it is clear that there will emerge differences in EC policies among national states based on differences in preference patterns at existing and foreseeable stages of development. If EC preferences are indeed sensitive to the level of income, then one can expect standards to diverge or converge in accordance with international differences in per capita income levels. If environmental quality is income-elastic they are more likely to converge than if they are income inelastic. The question is how wide the differences will be. The evidence thus far is insufficient to make even a preliminary determination. Certain countries such as the United States, Sweden, and Japan have begun to articulate national environmental policies which at least indicate serious governmental concern and provide reasonable grounds for projecting what standards may be in 1976 or 1980. Other countries, some with long-standing and rigorous EC norms at the regional and local level, do not seem to have adopted the issue as a matter of high societal priority. That is, they have not even reached the point where EC is a serious domestic political issue, a condition that probably represents a prerequisite to national planning for environmental management.

The issue of timing underlies the same kinds of uncertainties, and differs widely between nations. In the United States much of the enabling legislation was passed in the late 1960s, calling for far-reaching environmental reforms during the last third of the century. Establishment of an appropriate executive body in the form of the Environmental Protection Agency—which has taken its mandate seriously—together with vigorous use of the judicial system, have indicated quite clearly that an implicit and sometimes explicit timetable exists and will indeed be adhered to. Environment in the United States is a matter of national priority, backed by meaningful political support, that has been thoroughly debated and will be actively pursued in the coming decades.

Again, the question of timing abroad is much more uncertain, even among the industrial countries. Few national plans have been outlined at all, much less their phasing-in. In some cases, environmental management will be advanced in an ad hoc manner dealing with individual crises as they arise—often vigorously and expitiously—but without the purposefulness that would permit defensible projections of what conditions will be like five or ten years out. In others, a coherent national environmental plan will sooner or later emerge. As in the case of environmental standards, the status of policy in the area of timing is equally vague and equally diffuse.[67]

The issue of enforcement policy also seems to vary widely among nations and even interregionally within nations. As noted earlier, competitive pressures promote lax enforcement because it is not only the impacted firm or industry that is involved but also its suppliers, the services sector, its employees, the entire local or regional economy. Consequently, enforcement must be put into the hands of agencies not directly associated with the principal target of the EC measures themselves. The closer is this kind of association, the greater will be the pressures for pro forma or nonexistent enforcement. The greater its variance among countries, the greater the danger of trade distortions arising from this source. Because of its nature, there is virtually no systematic information on enforcement performance except by way of anecdotes, and no coherent trends that can be discerned.[68] On the other hand, enforcement of standards affecting polluting products (e.g., automobiles) has been pursued vigorously where the underlying standards have been promulgated.

Somewhat greater progress has been made on the question of implementation, particularly with the agreement on "polluter pays" as a general operating principle within the OECD group of countries in 1971. This agreement has yet to be turned into national policy among the participating countries, however, and preliminary evidence indicates that there will be considerable slippage. In the United States for example, accelerated depreciation has already been granted for EC capital equipment as has the issuance of tax exempt revenue bonds by subnational governmental units for the purpose of financing EC hardware for firms within their political jurisdictions. Both represent implicit subsidies, and must be considered as such together with government tax-financed R&D and the use by business of public EC facilities to a greater extent than financial contributions would warrant. On the other hand, punitive taxation is also used in the U.S., particularly in water pollution control, and is contemplated in the air pollution field in such forms as the proposed Sulphur tax.

Examples such as these indicate significant deviations of environmental policy from the pure "polluter pays" principle in the United States, and it would be reasonable to expect such deviations to develop in other countries as well—perhaps to an even greater extent, through direct subsidies to industry. Again, however, not enough is known about EC implementation abroad, or the direction of thinking in this area to make even preliminary judgments.

A special problem relates to the planning for environmental control in the Socialist countries of Eastern Europe and Asia (SCEEA). The principles underlying trade between centrally planned and market-oriented economies has not been well developed. The theory is the same, but use of that theory to predict the direction, product-composition, volume, or terms of East-West or intra-SCEEA trade leaves a great deal to be desired. The rules of the game are different, and we do not always understand them. The rules also change periodically, so that such behavioral constructs as can be developed tend to be unreliable. The evidence is that several of the SCEEA members are pursuing environmental goals as energetically as the more advanced developed market-economy countries (DMECs) and indeed implementation in a centrally-planned economy may be considerably easier.[69] But the implications for SCEEA-DMEC economic relations are virtually impossible to determine given the present state of knowledge of the way those relations are determined.

To summarize, the theory of externalities in welfare economics, as applied to the environmental issue, is well advanced and appears to be progressing rapidly.[70] Application of that theory to the international context via transboundary problems involves essentially an extension of that theory to the context of environmental spillovers between politically sovereign national states. Useful conceptual insights may in future be provided by law and political science, particularly in resolving conflicts arising out of this issue. The second section of this chapter surveyed the state of theory in the area of environmental control and its bearing on international economic and financial relations. It is evident that considerable research still needs to be done.

Research Priorities

It should be evident by now what some of the principal research needs are that would permit defensible assessments of the magnitude and direction of environmental effects on the future of the international economic order. Two critical areas of research fall outside the area of expertise of investigators likely to be concerned with this question, yet represent very fundamental inputs into any economic studies that might be undertaken.

First is the need for further basic and applied research into the causes and cures of environmental despoilation. This includes narrowing down the precise sources of damage to the environment and what immediate, long-term, and interregional effects on the human environment are. We began this chapter with an admonition of caution underlying the whole environment issue due to fundamental uncertainties in this regard. Reducing these uncertainties through research in the relevant physical and life sciences will make a major contribution to evaluating their economic implications. In the meantime we will have to live with them, and with the often bitter controversies to which they give rise. One way to deal with them is by means of alternative assumptions and employing sensitivity analysis, but this is not very satisfactory. In any event, the economic researcher needs to bear in mind that the presence of uncertainty may have perverse effects on the system, including irrationality and emotionalism on the one hand and extreme caution on the other. Both increase the hazards of economic research in this field.

Second is the need for investigation of political responses to environmental issues. Even if all of the consequences of environmental despoilation are known, and especially if they are not, reactions by political collectivities are likely to differ. The question is how and why they differ, and what kinds of factors affect the collective decisions that must be made and when they are made. The need here is for comparative research in the social and behavioral sciences focused on this problem, with a view to providing even preliminary indications about what policies nations are likely to adopt in the area of environment and how soon. Until such research has revealed the social equations underlying environmental management, reliance must be placed on a revealed preferences in this field—revealed by actions already taken and policy positions that seem to be evolving.

It seems reasonable to catalog the major areas of potentially fruitful research on the international economics of environment in the same sequence as the substantive issues where raised in the second section of this paper.

1. Environmental Policy Configurations. The most critical immediate need is a comprehensive inventory on national environmental management policies currently in effect and, to the extent possible, planned for the future in all countries (c), developed and developing, centrally-planned and market-oriented. Such an inventory should be classified by a standard list of pollutants (p), including air, water, thermal, radiation, noise, etc., applied to both stationary and mobile sources. The result would be a cxp matrix, updated regularly with many of the entries blank but permitting a scan-analysis of who is doing what, where. Presumably, the greatest density of entries would apply to the industrial countries.

A second major research need, based on the first, is a defensible set of estimates of the cost of pollution control, by product and by industry. Such cost estimates should contain capital costs, operating costs, R&D, depreciation and other applicable charges per dollar of final product and, using input-output analyses, also the EC costs of intermediate and raw-material inputs. Preliminary attempts to obtain such data are not as reliable as they should be, and much work needs to be done in this area. Estimates such as these would permit determination of which products bear heavy EC-loadings and which do not, and hence which products and industries may be affected by international differences in environmental management approaches.

Third, again contingent upon the foregoing, is a comparison of environmental control costs with the impact of trade barriers, such as tariffs and quotas, in an effective-protection framework of analysis.

Using appropriate demand and substitution elasticity estimates, further research could indicate the anticipated EC-induced shifts in trade flows and their impact on national economies. Other research might assess the impact of EC-enforcement differences on international prices—e.g., via subsidies, etc.,—and trade flows in individual products or product groups.

In the near term, a comprehensive approach of this type may not be possible, and it may be fruitful to perform a series of global industry-studies focused on sectors that are highly pollution-intensive in the first instance. Environmental control measures affecting a specific industry could be superimposed on a broadbased study analyzing supply economics, major markets, industrial structure and trade. One such study of the pulp and paper industry has been performed in OECD, and more superficial analyses of eleven industries' competitive responses to U.S. EC measures have been published recently under the auspices of the Council for Environmental Quality, the Council of Economic Advisers and the Department of Commerce—both mentioned earlier.[71]

2. Question of Economic Structure and Aggregate Impact. Apart from their impact on international trade in individual products, there are more aggregative issues involved as well. First, to what extent will environmental management pursued by different countries, at different speeds, in different ways, affect such economic variables on GNP, industrial production, the level of prices, employment, and the balance of payments? One study along these lines was subject to severe methodological and data limitations, but provided useful conceptual insights.[72] Another, using a national econometric model for the United States, employed better inputs of environmental data and more sophisticated methodology, but assumed that the United States alone pursues its EC goals while major competitor countries do not.[73] This is being remedied, at this writing, by similar econometric studies for several large trading nations to be combined with U.S. study into a multilateral net-impact analysis.

Aggregate econometric approaches promise to be very useful in the future, provided improved EC data become available, particularly for drawing balance of payments, foreign exchange, and long-term competitive implications. World trade models may also be of use, as will "project link" tying together national and regional econometric models into a system whereby simultaneous assessments can be made of responses to shifts in the salient parameters.

The problem also needs to be looked at from the supply side, in terms of environmental effects on comparative advantage. Environmental assimilative capacity (EAC) needs to be defined and measured and built into estimates of international competitiveness. We know that EC will divert resources away from production of tradeable goods and services. Precisely how will this affect the trade sector? Is EC inherently X-factor intensive, and what does this imply for countries that are respectively X-factor scarce or X-factor abundant?

In the form of goods and services, pollution is internationally-traded as a component of the production cost of these tradeables. If it is feasible to determine accurately the overall EC-loading of each tradeable product of each major supplier, it would be possible to assess whether a given country's imports are more pollution intensive than its exports and what this implies for the overall impact of environmental management on that country's trade. Such studies would also shed light on whether, in general, environmental management will in the end reinforce or countervail the basis of a country's competitive advantage in the international economy.

3. Trade in Polluting Products. Research in this area again depends on what EC standards are set in each country and how they are enforced, both with respect to residuals and products that pollute in their normal use. First, what will be the cost of bringing products up to standard, and how much of this cost is passed on to the final buyer in the short run and long run? How does this affect demand for the product in question, for substitutes, and for other products via the income effect? Are there systematic differences in pollution characteristics between imported and import-competing products, and to what extent will this affect trade flows? What are the economics of supply of the affected products, and how will this affect servicing of markets characterized by different environmental standards?

Certain studies along these lines are already underway, in particular an intensive OECD analysis of the problem as it affects the automobile industry scheduled for completion in late 1973. But substantial additional research is required on a product-by-product basis, identifying environmental attributes—including possible long-term effects—national standards and their implementation, resultant trade restrictions, and supply logistics. Since a basic problem is incompatibility of standards between nations, emphasis should be placed on an analysis of these incompatibilities, their trade implications, and possible ways of proceeding toward their harmonization. Particular attention needs to be placed on whether uniform standards are achievable or even desirable, and what this means for trade distortions over the long-run.

Additional research is needed on the extent to which EC norms bearing on products are applied in a discriminatory manner as between foreign and domestic goods, and how this may lead to a proliferation of non-tariff distortions of trade. To the extent that such standards affect demand patterns, how does this affect imports and exports of consumer durable and nondurable goods, capital equipment, intermediates, fuels, and raw materials? What new industries may emerge as a result of new opportunities arising from this source, and how does this affect the growth patterns of the countries involved. Conversely, what industries may be severely impacted in terms of their export performance and development path?

4. Trade Policy Vectors. A great deal of research has already been done on the difficult problem of nontariff barriers to trade. As stated above, significant additional NTBs may arise from enforcement of EC norms applied to polluting products. Their ostensible goal will be to force imports to conform to domestic standards. But the scope for measures intentionally applied for protectionist reasons is considerable. The question is what types of NTBs may be applied, what products may be particularly affected, and what their potential distortive effects on access to international markets are.

But potentially more serious are prospects for compensatory levies on imports produced abroad under EC standards less stringent than those applied at home. We have stated that such changes are unwarranted where cost differences are attributable to differences in EAC or environmental preferences, but may be justified by international differences in ways of implementing EC norms, particularly by means of explicit and implicit subsidies. Research needs to be done on how serious pressures for compensatory protection will be, what tradable products will be particularly affected, and what form countervailing measures might take.

If, for example, they are patterned after the "destination principle" of compensation for international differences in indirect business taxes, it may be possible to draw on some of the extensive literature in that field. In particular, one result deriving from research in this area should be operational guidelines for "fair" competition in the application of administering EC measures that may affect international competition and devising equitable compensatory trade-policy devices if this should fail.

5. Patterns of Industrial Location. Perhaps less is known about the locational effects of international differences in environmental standards than almost any other aspect of the subject. Will EC differences between nations be sufficient to force a relocation of production? If so, what industries will be affected and how will they relocate? How will this affect development and employment patterns, trade flows, and international payments? What commercial policy reactions might be applied in response to capital flight induced by pollution controls? What are the possible sources of conflict between the firm, the home country, and the host country in the case of EC-induced shifts in industrial location?

Again, most progress can probably be made through industry studies, because this is the level at which the various factors affecting plant location operate. Since industry has moved in response to differential EC policies in the United States, perhaps this example can be used to infer what might happen at the international level in the future. Measures of the sensitivity of industries to EC policies in their locational decisions are of critical importance. The hypothesis that the EC pressures will lead to a shift in industries from high- to low-income regions and countries needs to be tested: Does the political balance really tend to promote location of pollution-intensive plants in the poorer countries? Is there really a trend toward exporting pollution-intensive industries in some of the more advanced industrial countries?

6. New Products and Services. There is a basic question whether a massive and rapidly growing international market for EC hardware and software is a myth or a reality. How does the demand for EC equipment and technology react to tightening environmental standards? Will the same approaches to specific environmental goals be used everywhere, or will significant differences emerge? What is the R&D content of EC equipment, and does this indeed confer a material international competitive advantage on suppliers located in countries leading in environmental management? To what extent will this result in increased tangible exports, licensing, or other transactions that may represent a useful offset to lead-countries that otherwise tend to suffer competitive disadvantages in international markets? How long are the environmental leads and lags, since this determines in large measure the timing of any anticipated EC exports?

Other questions also need extensive investigation. One example is the operation of a demonstration-effect in environmental management among political jurisdictions. Another is the product-cycle of EC hardware and its adaptability to foreign production. In the area of polluting products, what shifts can be expected—either as a result of environmental controls or due to rising prices of pollution-intensive products—in the demand for goods and services? Which areas will be most heavily involved, and how will this affect pattern of international trade?

7. Recovery of Tradable Resources. There remains great uncertainty about the prospects for trade in recycled materials. What materials will be recovered as a result of tightened EC norms, and in what volumes? How much further processing is required to render them salable on national and international markets? How will they compare in quality and price with virgin materials? Where will the recovered materials originate, and where are the main centers of potential demand? Since recycled materials compete with virgin materials, how will this affect raw-materials prices and exports of the major supplier countries? Finally, how will trends in raw-materials prices develop and, in turn, how does this affect the incentive to recycle?

Empirical analysis in this area, as in the case of EC hardware, is difficult because standard trade statistics do not provide sufficient detail to permit differentiation between the products in question and other goods unrelated to environmental control. A basic need therefore is a reliable source of data indicating whether recycled materials are involved, and whether individual products or product groups are intended for EC purposes.

8. Transport. Research needs in this area are relatively straightforward. First, the capital and operating costs of environmental protection need to be identified and measured, including the risk of accidental discharges reflected in insurance costs and the real cost of shipping delays. These have to be related to the c.i.f. price of the affected products, in order to gauge their potential bearing on trade flows. Entire research studies can be performed on curtailment or elimination of transport facilities such as pipelines and bulk terminals on the international flow of energy supplies and other materials, particularly in terms of disrupting normal trade patterns and contributing to periodic shortages and crises under conditions of rapidly growing demand. Finally, the economies of alternative modes of transport need to be analyzed, both in terms of their own environmental attributes and as subsitutes for transportation methods already known to be environmentally damaging.

9. Transboundary Pollution. The basic question is to what extent transboundary environmental spillovers are economically damaging. The first need is a clear delineation of what the transboundary pollution impact zones are, and an assessment of whether the problem is sufficiently serious to warrant intergovernmental action. Second, there is the question of how environmental spillovers originating in one national state result in economic damage in other countries, and a need for defensible measures of the extent of this damage that can serve as a basis for the mutual search for acceptable solutions. A third question is what forms these solutions may take, and what their economic implications are, especially for the country that is the source of the problem. Assessments particularly need to be made of the need for relocation of industries and fundamental changes in their operating procedures, including the direct cost of environmental control.

On a broader scale, the question of oceanic and atmospheric pollution remains subject to extensive scientific and political uncertainty. Once the precise, long-term effects of individual contaminants on the biosphere have been identified and evaluated, rational solutions can be identified and the international machinery set up to implement them. Progress will probably be made on a piecemeal basis, considering individual contaminants such as mercury, cyanide, and DDT, and agreement sought on a relatively narrow base but progressively attacking additional contaminants as their impact becomes measurable and visible. The principal problem will be getting general agreement among disparate nations with widely differing social goals and political and economic systems, which vary equally widely in their subjective identification with the global ecosystem.

10. Depletable Resource Stocks. Considerable research has already been done in projecting the supply and demand for natural resources and energy sources. Most observers agree that the long-range energy picture is bright due to solar and nuclear power sources, but little information is available on the *timing* of these sources. In the meantime, there are probably sufficient fossil fuels available globally at rising prices to bridge the gap. But there are enough disharmonies in the distribution of fossil fuels between the major suppliers and the principal sources of demand that periodic energy crises will be unavoidable at least until the end of the century—disharmonies that will play an important role in shaping the future of the international economic order.

How will the direction and terms of international trade in fuels shift, and what will this mean for the economic structures and balances of payments of the affected countries? What are the optimum policy vectors for the energy-exporting countries, and how close to these optima will they in fact come? How will these policy responses influence trade and investment patterns, and economic relations between the affected countries? What of the role of the enterprise caught in the middle, with depleting resources and burgeoning demand bringing direct government-to-government confrontations? What do these developments imply for industries heavily dependent on energy supplies (e.g., aluminum) in terms of their international competitive viability? As nonfuel natural resources are depleted, how will this affect trade flows and the substitution of imports for one another in response to shifts in relative prices?

None of these questions have yet been answered. Their importance in international economic relations is proportional to the significance of fuels and raw materials in global trade flows, either directly or as contributory inputs, and investments in extactive industries in the international flow of capital, skilled manpower, management and technology.

11. Special Problems Relating to the Developing Countries. The bearing of the environmental issue on developing economies, and the research needs deriving therefrom, can largely be ascertained from the foregoing. In trade, transport, industrial location, recycled materials, demand-pattern shifts, national resources, and related issues there are always special implications arising out of the unique role played by the developing countries in the international economic system. Two research needs are basic. One is an assessment of the environmental priorities of the developing countries themselves. We know that certain EC problems in LDCs are well past the crisis stage, particularly separation of storm and sanitary sewers and uncontrolled urbanization. How much will it cost to alleviate these problems, and what are the external financing requirements to get the job done? To what extent will there be a diversion of economic resources internally to achieve these goals—as opposed to absorbing unemployed and underemployed resources—and what will this do to the developing countries' position in the international economy. A second research need concerns assessments of where the developing countries are going with respect to environmental management, once the crisis problems are alleviated. The hypothesis is that they will approach the issue gradually, with relatively low social priority, and that wide differences will emerge among them. The question is whether this hypothesis is correct, and how the various national EC programs will take shape over the next several decades.

A list of subtopics also bears investigation. Will environmental management as it advances in developed and developing societies accelerate or restrain the alleged secular deterioration of the LDCs' collective terms of trade? What will be the net terms of trade benefit arising out of price trends for fuels and raw materials? How will the criteria governing development finance absorb environmental considerations, and will this *on net* hinder or promote channeling external capital into projects evidencing a high marginal social value, as defined by the recipient country itself? Will the developing countries indeed benefit from the possible substitution of natural for synthetic materials, or is this largely a myth? What about the growing anxiety on pesticides and other potentially toxic residues in food products and its impact on productivity in topical agriculture and the marketability of its produce? Will the LDCs be forced to adopt the same environmental standards as are applied in the industrial nations, and what will this do to their growth and trade prospects? Will the competition from recycled material seriously impede LDC export volumes and prices, in comparison with what they otherwise would be?

These are but a small sample of the kinds of questions that need to be answered. There are ample indications that environment contains serious implications for the role of the developing nations in the world economic order. We know what some of them are. Wo do not know how they will ultimately affect the system. Again, basic inputs of environmental cause-and-effect and policy vectors are still missing for defensible empirical research, and filling these gaps in knowledge must be given first priority.

12. Population and Growth. It is difficult to separate research on the limits to global economic and population growth from that part of the system called the international economic order. Any growth constraints that are identified will clearly affect international economic transactions, while the latter may distribute more evenly demands made on the global ecosystem and hence promote the avoidance of serious bottlenecks.

Historically, it is certainly clear that international trade as well as flows of people, capital and technology has alleviated periodic environmental and other kinds of growth limits. The fundamental question is whether this can continue, and in what sectors it will be particularly effective. On the other hand, international commercial and productive-factor flows have also exacerbated regional growth limits in the past, and this is likely to continue and to intensify. The supply capabilities of the globe are limited, and redistribution of these capabilities via the international economic order can only partly alleviate this problem. The important issues are to what extent this can occur, and what kinds of variables will play a critical role.

A second question concerns the application of purposeful growth-limiting economic and social policies, particularly with respect to population. The necessity for such limits is not yet entirely clear, nor is their timing. Research on this question must go beyond dynamic econometric models, based on questionable assumptions and data-inputs of poor quality, within the context of fixed or relatively fixed resources. Forecasting technological change will be a major task, of fundamental importance for the outcome of such studies. This has never been very successful, and the question is whether improvements in its reliability are in prospect. However, it is a prerequisite for identification of future pressure-points and growth-limiting factors, and for assessing their implications for the international economy.

Notes

1. See James M. Buchanan, "Individual Choice in Voting and the Market," *Journal of Political Economy*, August 1954, and Anthony Downs, "An Economic Theory of Political Action in a Democracy," *Journal of Political Economy*, April 1957. For a different view see J. von Neumann and O. Morgenstern, *The Theory of Games and Economic Behavior* (Princeton, New Jersey: Princeton University Press, 1944).

2. For a comprehensive discussion of air and water pollution see W.L. Faith, *Air Pollution Control* (New York: John Wiley, 1959), and Allen V. Kneese and Blair T. Bower, *Managing Water Quality: Economics, Technology, Institutions* (Baltimore: Johns Hopkins Press, 1968).

3. For an excellent review of the issues, see Sir Solly Zuckerman, "Background Report on the Congress Theme" in *The Vienna Papers, Technology and Society: A Challenge to Private Enterprise*, XXIII Congress of the International Chamber of Commerce (Washington, D.C.: The United States Council of the ICC, 1971).

4. See Sam Peltzman and T. Nicholaus Tideman, "Local Versus National Pollution Control," Harvard University Discussion Paper No. 216, November 1971.

5. See J.E. Meade, "External Economies and Diseconomies in a Competitive Situation," *Economic Journal*, March 1952.

6. See Tax Foundation, *Pollution Control: Perspectives on the Government Role* (New York: Tax Foundation, Inc., 1971).

7. See Meade, op. cit., and also John McDonald, "How Social Responsibility Fits the Game of Business," *Fortune*, December 1970, pp. 104-106, 131-33.

8. See Zuhayr Mihdashi, *Business-Government Relations and Cooperation for Development: The Mineral-Metal Industries* (forthcoming).

9. For previous work in this field see: Charles Pearson and Wendy Takacs, "International Economic Implications of Environmental Control and Pollution Abatement Programs" in *United States International Economic Policy in an Interdependent World*, Compendium of Papers, Vol. I (Washington, D.C.: U.S. Government Printing Office, July 1971), pp. 777-90; General Agreement on Tariffs and Trade, *Industrial Pollution Control and International Trade* (Geneva: GATT, July 1971); UNCTAD, "The Implications of Environmental Measures for International Trade and Development," Research Division Memorandum No. 42, September 15, 1971 (mimeo); and papers by Allen V. Kneese, Harald B. Malmgren, and Ralph C. D'Arge in Allen V. Kneese, Sidney E. Rolfe and Joseph W. Harned (eds.) *Managing the Environment: International Economic Cooperation and Pollution Control* (New York: Frederick A. Praeger, 1971). Also Ingo Walter, "Environmental Control and the Patterns of International Trade and Investment: An Emerging Policy Issue," *Banca Nazionale del Lavoro Quarterly Review*, March 1972; Ralph C. D'Arge and Allen V. Kneese, "Environmental Quality and International Trade," *International Organization*, Spring 1972; and Ingo Walter, *Environmental Control and Consumer Protection*, Emerging Forces in Multinational Corporate Operations, Center for Multinational Studies Occasional Paper No. 2, (Washington, D.C.: CMS, April 1972).

10. R.H. Coase, "The Problem of Social Costs," *Journal of Law and Economics*, October 1960.

11. J. Agusto de Araujo Castro, "Environment and Development: The Case of the Less Developed Countries," *International Organization*, Spring 1972.

12. Robert Toulemon, "Pollution in an Enlarged EEC," *European Community*, July-August 1971.

13. C.R. Plott, "Externalities and Corrective Taxes," *Economica*, February 1966.

14. Gerard Eldin, "The Need for Intergovernmental Cooperation and Co-ordination Regarding the Environment," *OECD Observer*, February 1971.

15. Richard A. Carpenter, "Information for Decisions in Environmental Policy," *Research Management*, March 1971.

16. See Council on Environmental Quality, *Environmental Quality*, The Second Annual Report of the Council on Environmental Quality, August 1971 (Washington, D.C.: GPO, 1971).

17. See K. Turvey, "On Divergence Between Social Cost and Private Cost," *Economica*, August 1973; and S. Wellicz, "On External Diseconomies and the Government Assisted Invisible Hand," *Economica*, November 1964.

18. For several interesting case studies, see Council on Environmental Quality, Department of Commerce, and Environmental Protection Agency, *The Economic Impact of Pollution Control: A Summary of Recent Studies* (Washington, D.C.: GPO, March 1972).

19. Cf. CEQ, op. cit., and Sanford Rose, "The Economics of Environmental Quality," *Fortune*, February 1970, p. 178.

20. See S.P. Magee and W.F. Ford, "Environmental Pollution, The Terms of Trade and the Balance of Payments of the United States," *Kyklos*, Fasc. 1, 1972.

21. CEQ, op. cit.

22. See Kneese and D'Arge, op. cit.

23. See I. Walter, "Environmental Control and Patterns of International Trade and Investment," op. cit.

24. Cf. W.A. Leontief and A. Ford, "Air Pollution and Economic Structure: Empirical Results of Input-Output Calculations," Harvard University (*mimeo.*), 1970; R.G. Ridker, Economic Costs of Air Pollution (New York: Frederick A. Praeger, 1967), and Ingo Walter, "The Pollution Content of American Foreign Trade," New York University (*mimeo.*), 1972.

25. See I. Walter, "The Pollution of American Foreign Trade," loc. cit.

26. For some examples of present data availability see *Survey of Current Business* (September 1970, p. 18); *23rd Annual McGraw-Hill Survey of Business Plans for New Plant and Equipment*, cited in Hearings before the Sub-Committee on Air and Water Pollution, Committee on Public Works, U.S. Senate, 91st Congress, Second Session (pp. 390-91). See also The Conference Board Record, February 1970; CEQ, op. cit.; and Jean Brashares, "Cost Estimates for Environmental Improvement Program," Appendix B. in A.V. Kneese et al. op. cit., p. 17.

27. Cf. Dennis L. Meadows and Jorgen Randers, "Adding the Time Dimension to Environmental Policy," *International Organization*, Spring 1972; also J.W. Bishop and H.W. Hubbard, *Let the Seller Beware* (Washington, D.C.: Washington National Press, Inc., 1969).

28. David A. Aaker and George S. Day (eds.), *Consumerism: Search for the Consumer Interest*, (New York: Free Press, 1971).

29. See Ingo Walter, "Nontariff Barriers and the Free Trade Area Option," *Banca Nazionale del Lavoro Quarterly Review*, March 1969.

30. For an interesting study, see Erwin K. Scheuch, "Environmental Protection—and Protection from the Environment," *Monat*, No. 267, December 1970.

31. Cf. G.A. Jentz, "Federal Regulation of Advertising," *American Business Law Journal*, January 1968; also D. Cohen, "The Federal Trade Commission and the Regulation of Advertising," *Journal of Marketing*, January 1969.

32. See UNCTAD, op. cit., and "Environment and Development: The Founex Report," *International Conciliation*, January 1972.

33. See Ingo Walter, "Environmental Management and Effective Protection," New York University (*mimeo*.), 1972.

34. Peter Bohm, "Pollution: Taxation or Purification?" *Kyklos*, Fasc. 3, 1972.

35. General Agreement on Tariffs and Trade, *Articles and Selected Documents* (Geneva: GATT, 1969).

36. Peter Bohm, op. cit.

37. For an inventory of nontariff barriers to trade that might be applied in the name of environmental control, see Ingo Walter, "Environmental Control and Consumer Protection," loc. cit., p. 38ff. On NTBs in general see the following: R.E. Baldwin, *Nontariff Distortions of International Trade* (Washington, D.C.: Brookings, 1970); Gerard and Victoria Curzon, *Hidden Barriers to International Trade* (London: Trade Policy Research Centre, 1971); and Ingo Walter, "Nontariff Barriers and the Free Trade Area Option," *Banca Nazionale del Lavoro Quarterly Review*, March 1969; "United States Nontariff Measures and Trade Preferences for Latin America," *Inter-American Economic Affairs*, Spring 1970; "Nontariff Barriers and the Export Performance of Developing Countries," *American Economic Review*, Papers and Proceedings, May 1971; "The Pattern of Nontariff Obstacles to International Market Access," *Weltwirtschaftliches Archiv*, Bd. 108, Heft 1, 1972; "Nontariff Distortions and Trade Preferences for Developing Countries: Some Preliminary Evidence," *Economia Internazionale*, September 1972; and H.H. Glisman and A. Neu, "Towards New Agreements on International Trade Liberalization: Methods and Examples of Measuring Nontariff Trade Barriers," *Weltwirtschaftliches Archiv*, Bd. 107.

38. Some recent developments are reviewed in "Fellow Americans, Keep Out!" *Forbes*, June 15, 1971.

39. See James A. Lee, "Environmental Considerations in Development Finance," *International Organization*, Spring 1972.

40. Science and Technology Report, "Pollution Control Market to Grow Rapidly," *Commerce Today*, September 18, 1972.

41. See Raymond Vernon, "International Investment and International

Trade in the Product Cycle," *Quarterly Journal of Economics*, May 1966; and W. Gruber and D. Mehta and R. Vernon, "The R & D Factor in International Trade and International Investment by United States Industries," *Journal of Political Economy*, February 1967.

42. "A Study of Environmental Problems in Waste Management," in Economic Commission for Europe, *ECE Symposium on Problems Relating to Environment* (New York: United Nations, 1971).

43. Cf. "A Study of Environmental Conditions and Problems in the Sector of Transportation," in ECE, op. cit.

44. See R.C. D'Arge and A.V. Kneese, op. cit.

45. See "A Study of Environmental Conditions and Problems in a Country-side Region Attracting Mass Tourism: The Yugoslav Adriatic Coast," in ECE, op. cit.

46. Cf. Per Magnus Wijkman, "Second-Best Solution at Stockholm," *Intereconomics*, September 1972.

47. See Z. Mikdashi, op. cit.

48. Cf. "Study on Environmental Conditions and Problems of Energy Production" and "Nuclear Power and Its Relationship to the Environment," in ECE, op. cit.

49. Thomas L. Blair, "The Environmental Crisis in the Third World," *Intereconomics*, February 1972.

50. Mahbub Ul-Haq, "International Implications of the Environmental Concern," Paper Presented at the Columbia-United Nations Conference on Development and Environment, March 1972.

51. See UNCTAD, op. cit.

52. See "The Founex Report," loc. cit.

53. Cf. Michael L. Hoffman, "Development Finance and the Environment," *Finance and Development*, September 1970.

54. Shigeo Tsuru, "Aid, Investment and the Environment," Columbia University-United Nations Conference on Development and Environment, April 15, 1972.

55. See the Proceedings of the Third United Nations Conference on Trade and Development, Santiago, Chile, April 1972.

56. Cf. Nazli Choucri and James P. Bennett, "Population, Resources and Technology: Political Implications of the Environmental Crisis," *International Organization*, Spring, 1972.

57. For a useful discussion of the general issue, see Judd Polk, "Social Costs of Economic Growth," in *The Vienna Papers*, loc. cit., pp. 31-38.

58. See N. Choucri, op. cit.

59. J.M. Buchanan and W.C. Stubblebine, "Externality," *Economica*, November 1962.

60. E.J. Mishan, "The Postwar Literature on Externalities: An Interpretive Essay," *Journal of Economic Literature*, March 1971.

61. R.V. Ayres and A.V. Kneese, "Production, Consumption and Externalities," *American Economic Review*, June 1969.

62. E.J. Mishan, op. cit.

63. E.J. Mishan, "Welfare Criteria for External Effects," *American Economic Review*, September 1961.

64. E.J. Mishan, "The Relationship Between Joint Products, Collective Goods, and External Effects," *Journal of Political Economy*, May 1969.

65. See also W.J. Baumol, "External Economies and Second-Order Optimality Conditions," *American Economic Review*, June 1964; and T. Scitovsky, "Two Concepts of External Economies," *Journal of Political Economy*, April 1964.

66. See Gerard Eldin, "The Need for Intergovernmental Cooperation and Coordination Regarding the Environment," *OECD Observer*, February 1971.

67. Cf. Harald B. Malmgren, "Environmental Management and the International Economy," in Allen V. Kneese et al. (eds.), op. cit.

68. See J.A. de Larderel and A-M Boutin, "How do European (and American) Companies Really Manage Pollution?" *European Business*, Winter 1972.

69. See "A Study of Environmental Conditions and Problems in the Industrial Region of Upper Silesia," in ECE, op. cit.

70. See also OECD, *Problems of Environmental Economics* (Paris: OECD, 1972); K.E. Boulding, et al., *Economics of Pollution* (New York: New York University Press, 1971), J.C. Hite, et al., *The Economics of Environmental Quality* (Washington, D.C.: American Enterprise Institute, September 1972); and W.J. Baumol, "Environmental Protection at Minimum Cost," *American Journal of Economics and Sociology*, October 1971.

71. CEQ, op. cit.

72. R.C. D'Arge and A.V. Kneese, op. cit.

73. CEQ, op. cit.

Index

About the Author

C. Fred Bergsten is currently a Senior Fellow at the Brookings Institution. From January 1969 until May 1971, he was Assistant for International Economic Affairs on the Senior Staff of the National Security Council. He remains a consultant to several government agencies. Dr. Bergsten was a Visiting Fellow at the Council on Foreign Relations in 1968 and again in 1971. From 1963 to 1967, he was in the Office of International Monetary Affairs at the Department of State. He has published several books and numerous articles on a wide range of international economic issues. He received the masters and Ph.D. degrees from the Fletcher School of Law and Diplomacy.